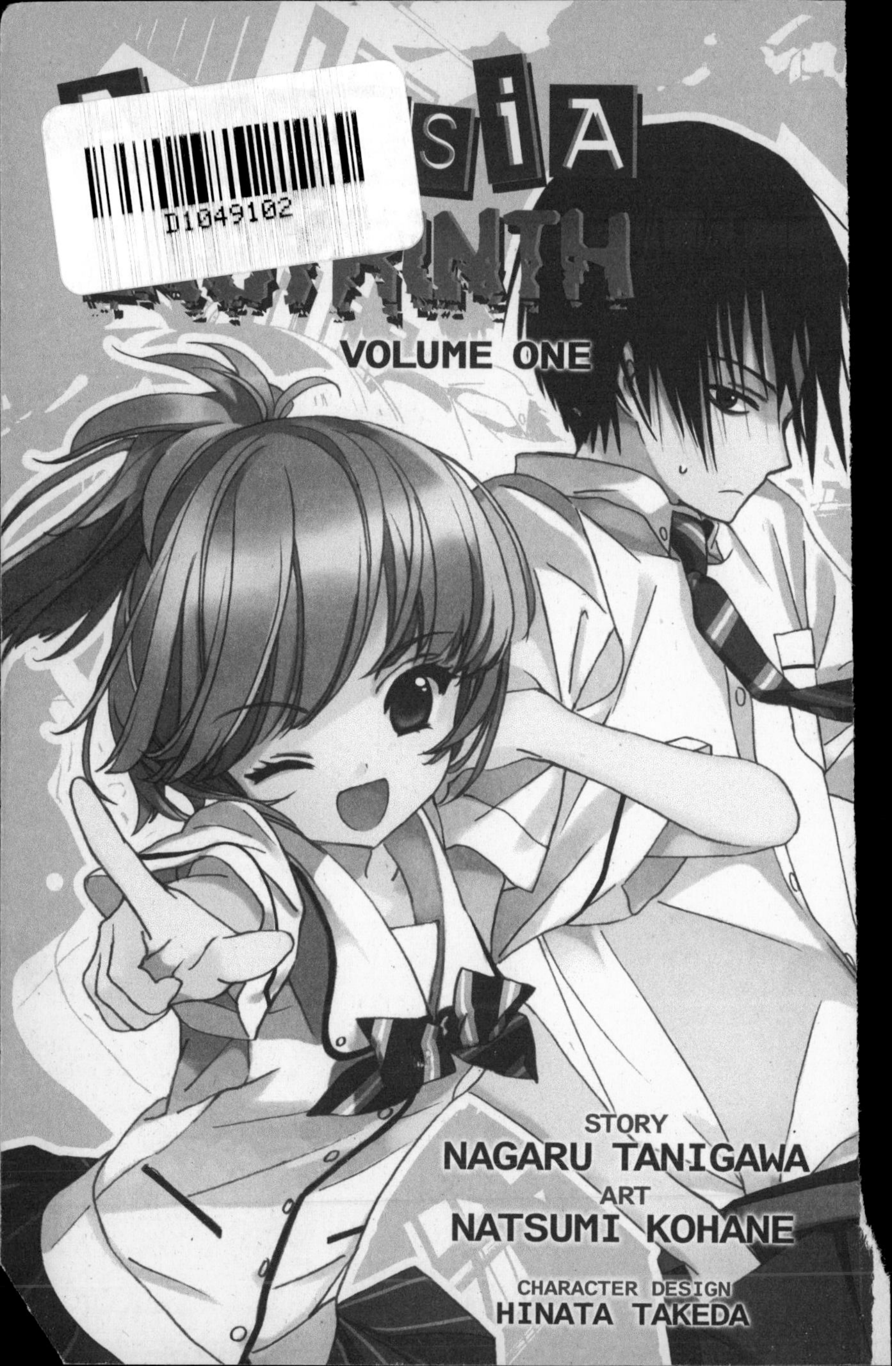
SiA
NTH
VOLUME ONE
STORY
NAGARU TANIGAWA
ART
NATSUMI KOHANE
CHARACTER DESIGN
HINATA TAKEDA

AMNESiA
LABYRINTH VOL. 1

story by **Nagaru Tanigawa**   art by **Natsumi Kohane**

STAFF CREDITS

translation	**Nan Rymer**
adaptation	**Shannon Fay**
lettering & layout	**Nicky Lim**
cover design	**Nicky Lim**
copy editor	**Shanti Whitesides**
editor	**Adam Arnold**
publisher	**Jason DeAngelis**
	Seven Seas Entertainment

AMNESIA LABYRINTH VOL. 1
© 2009 Nagaru Tanigawa
© 2009 Kohane Nasumi
First published in 2009 by Media Works Inc., Tokyo, Japan.
English translation rights arranged with ASCII MEDIA WORKS.

Visit us online at www.gomanga.com.

ISBN: 978-1-934876-93-0

Printed in Canada

First Printing: February 2011

10 9 8 7 6 5 4 3 2 1

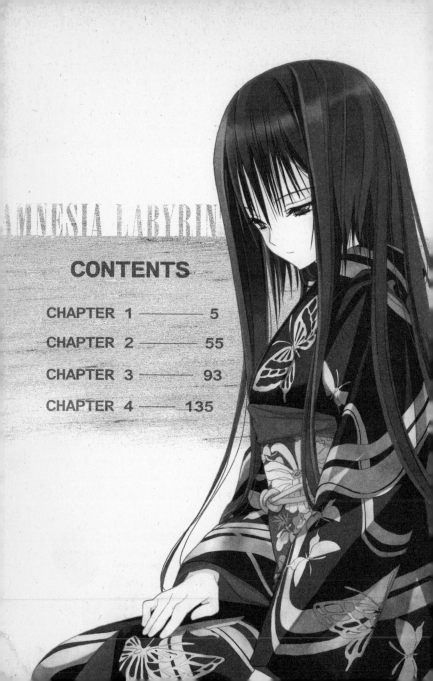

AMNESIA LABYRINTH

CONTENTS

AMNESIA
LABYRINTH

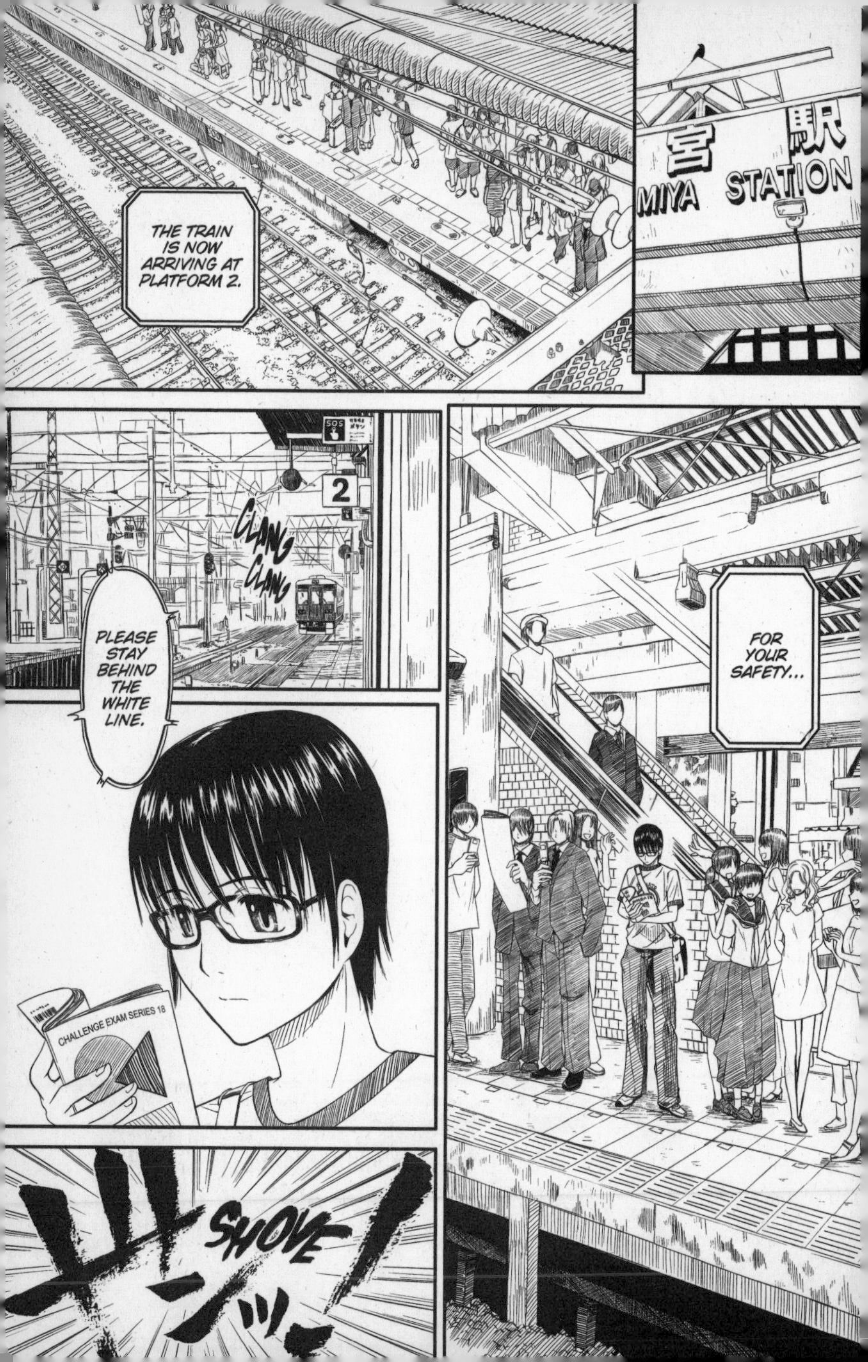
宮 駅
MIYA STATION
THE TRAIN IS NOW ARRIVING AT PLATFORM 2.
FOR YOUR SAFETY...
2
CLANG CLANG
PLEASE STAY BEHIND THE WHITE LINE.
CHALLENGE EXAM SERIES 18
SHOVE

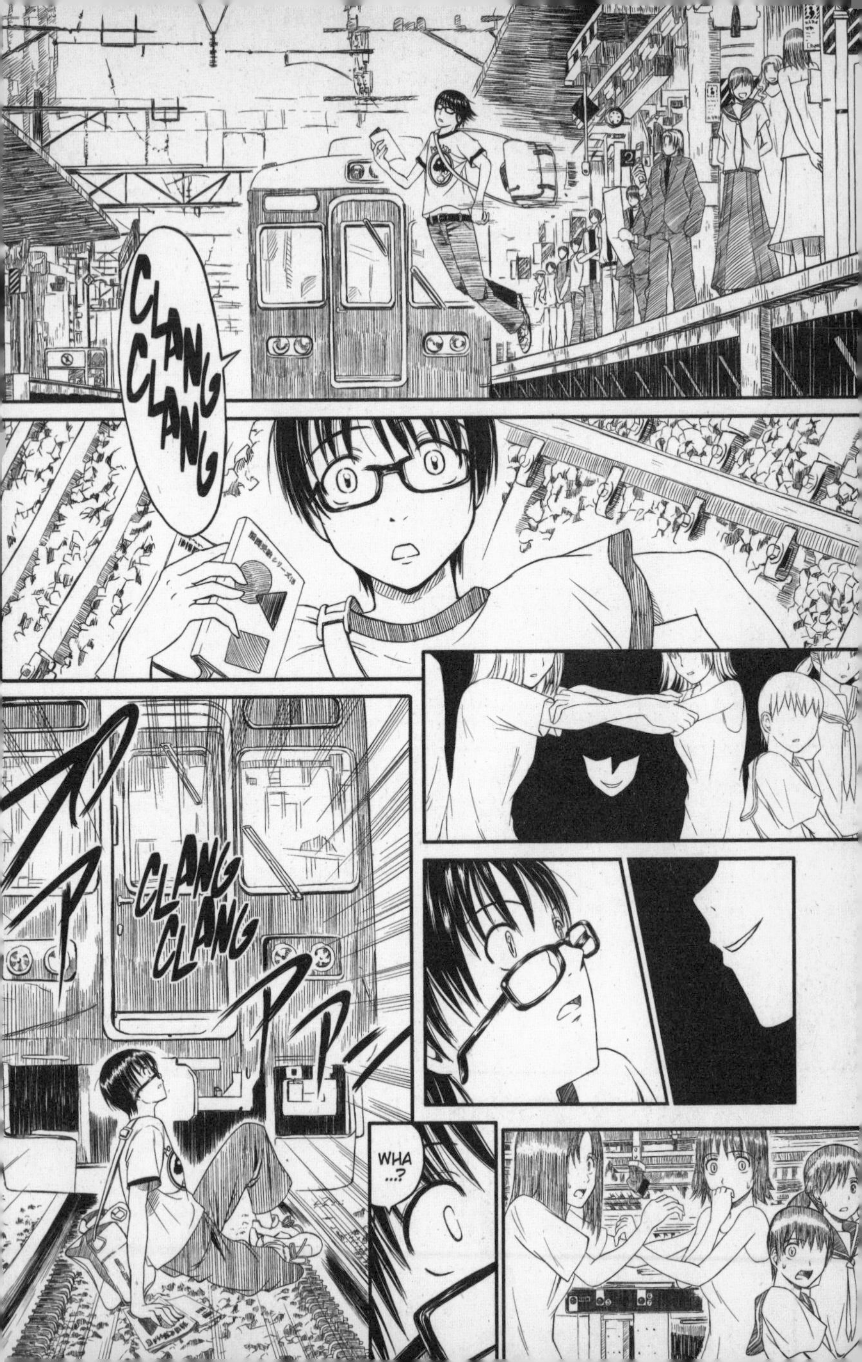
CLANG CLANG
CLANG CLANG
WHA ...?

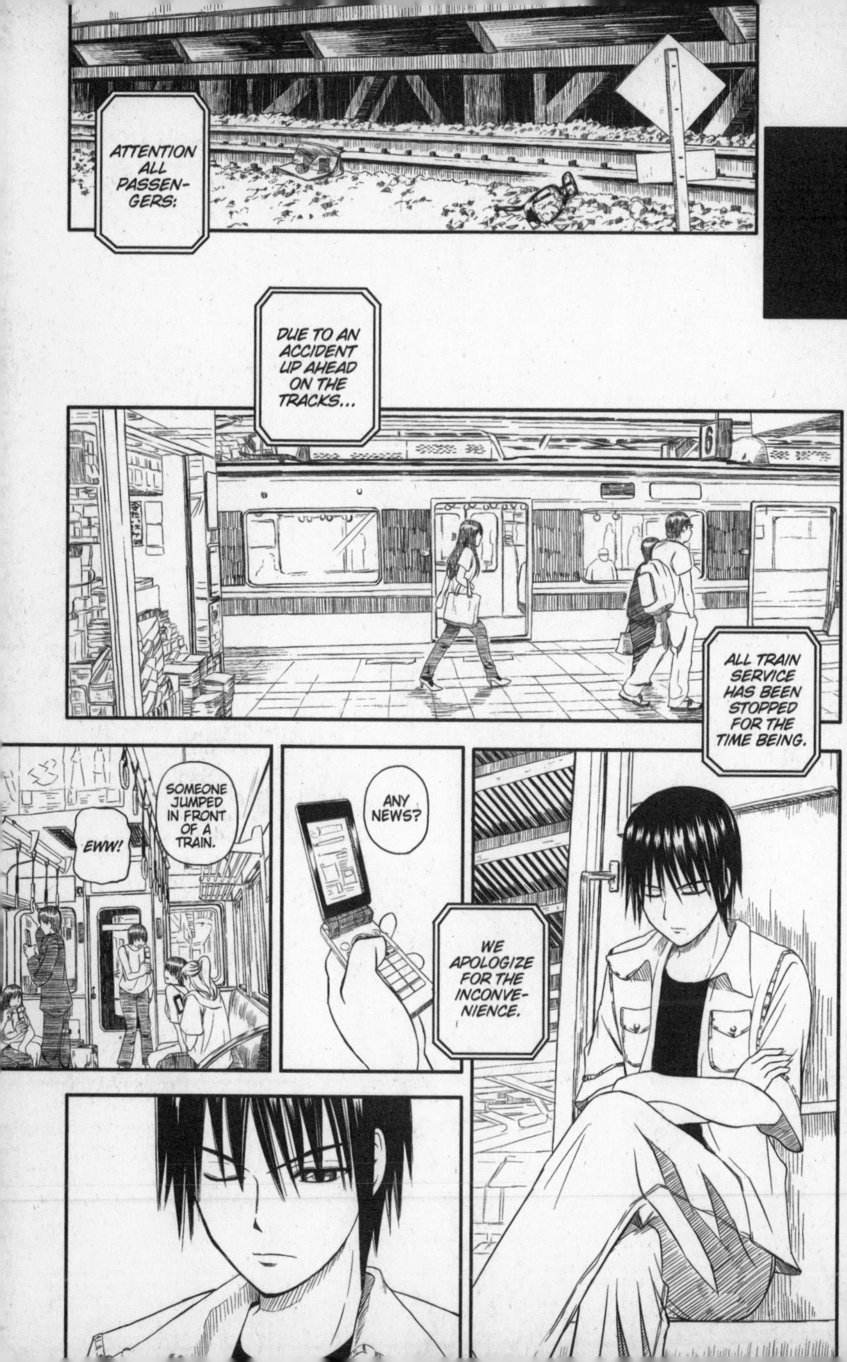
ATTENTION ALL PASSEN-GERS:
DUE TO AN ACCIDENT UP AHEAD ON THE TRACKS...
ALL TRAIN SERVICE HAS BEEN STOPPED FOR THE TIME BEING.
WE APOLOGIZE FOR THE INCONVE-NIENCE.
ANY NEWS?
SOMEONE JUMPED IN FRONT OF A TRAIN.
EWW!

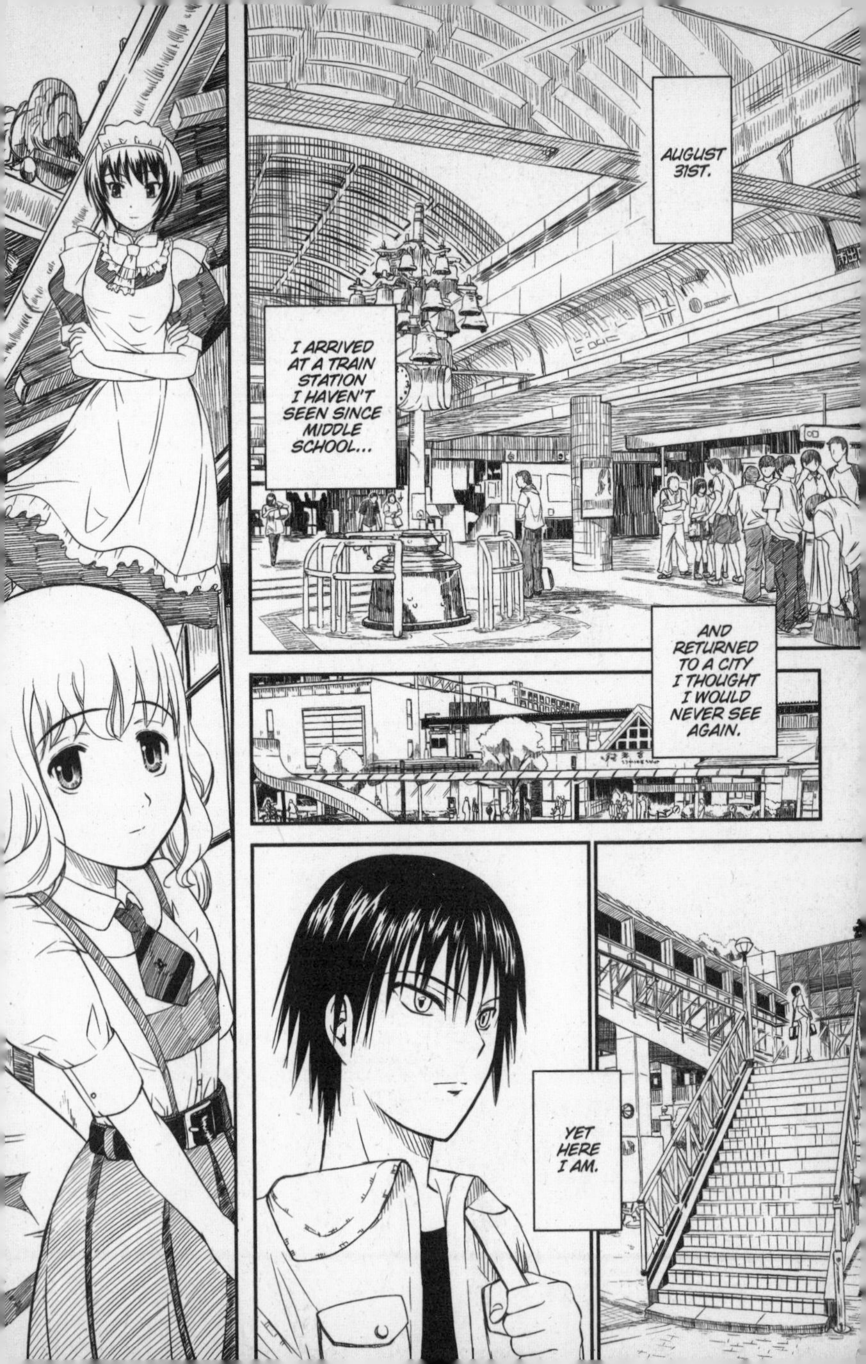
AUGUST 31ST.
I ARRIVED AT A TRAIN STATION I HAVEN'T SEEN SINCE MIDDLE SCHOOL...
AND RETURNED TO A CITY I THOUGHT I WOULD NEVER SEE AGAIN.
YET HERE I AM.

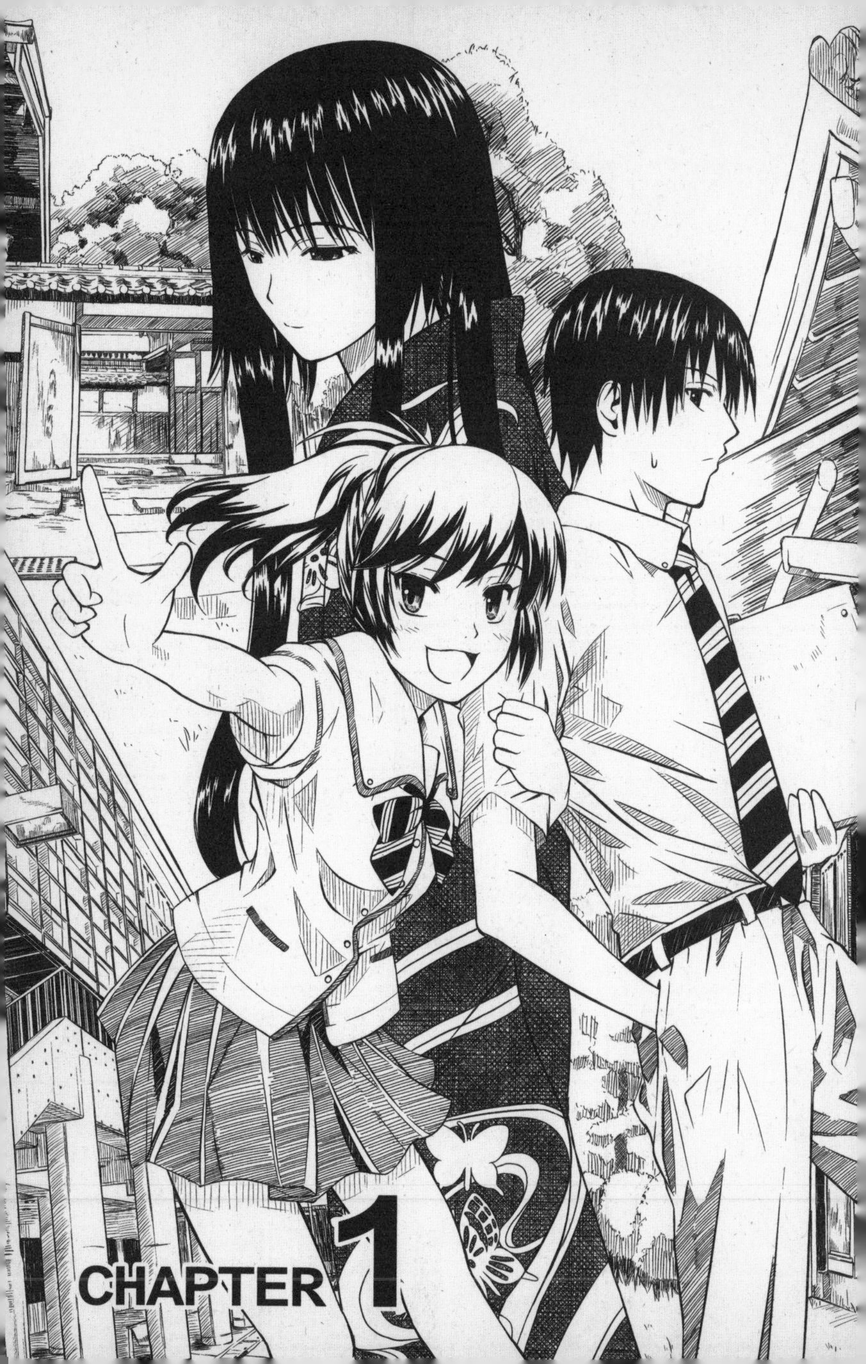
CHAPTER 1

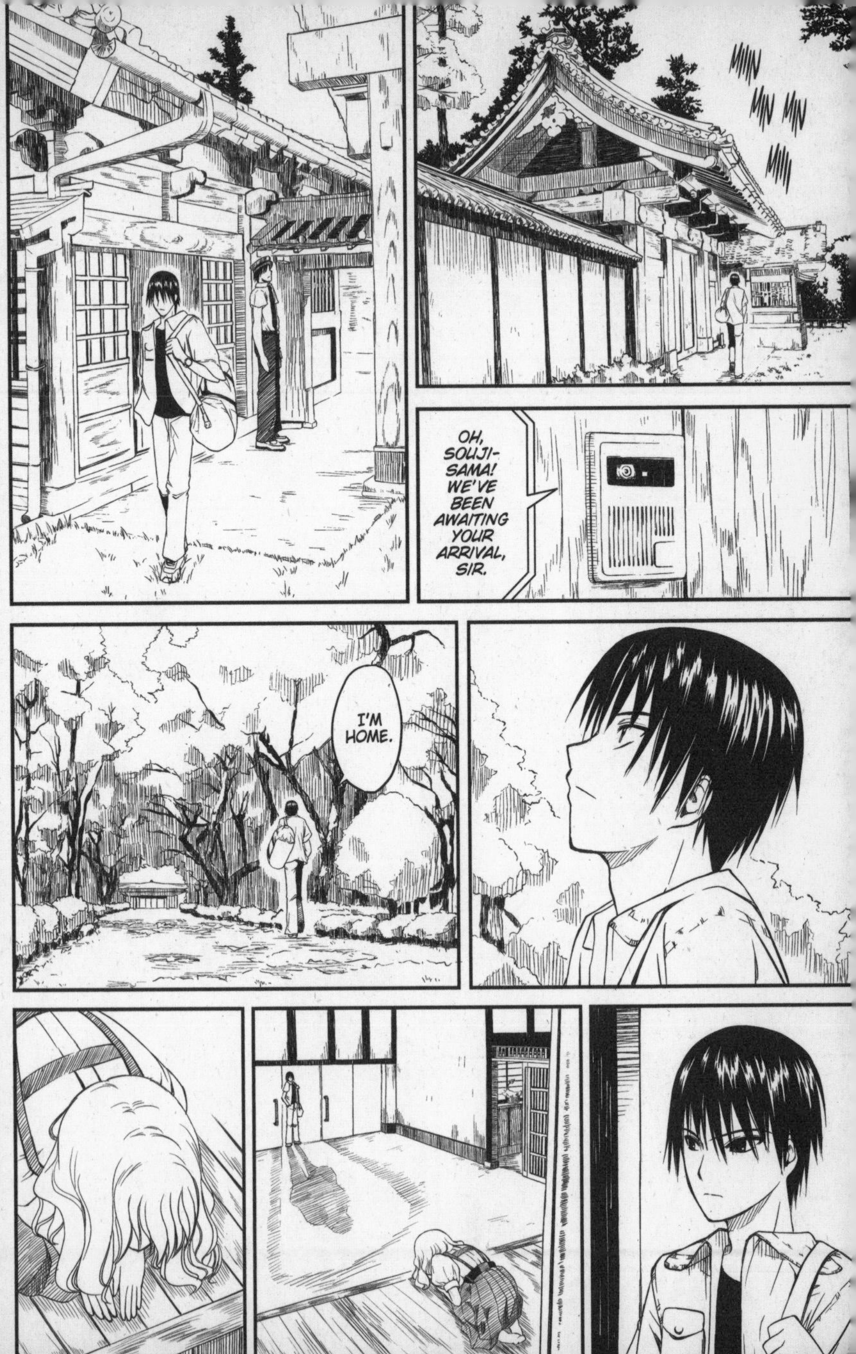
MIIN
MIN MIN
MIII
OH, SOUJI-SAMA! WE'VE BEEN AWAITING YOUR ARRIVAL, SIR.
I'M HOME.

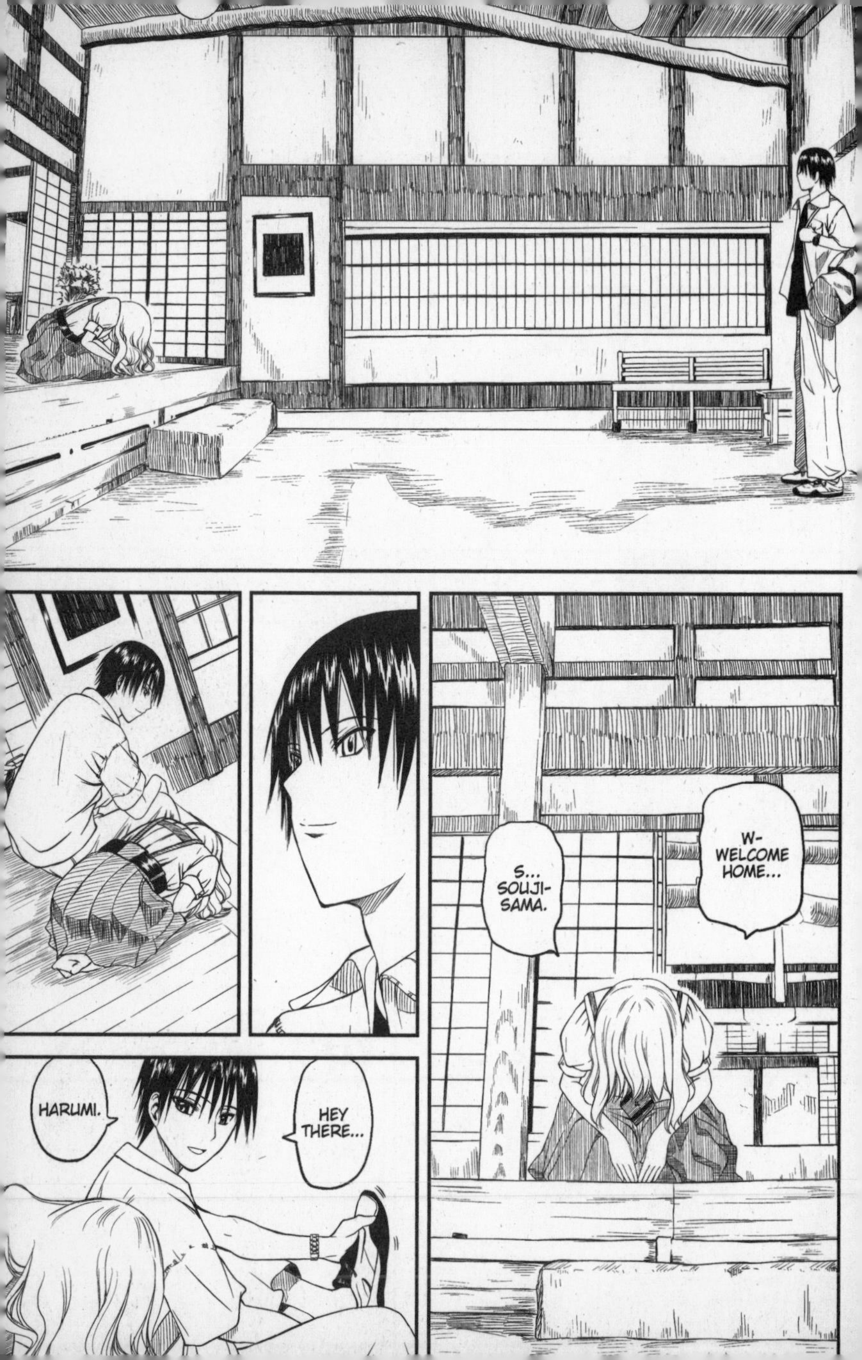
W- WELCOME HOME...
S... SOUJI-SAMA.
HEY THERE...
HARUMI.

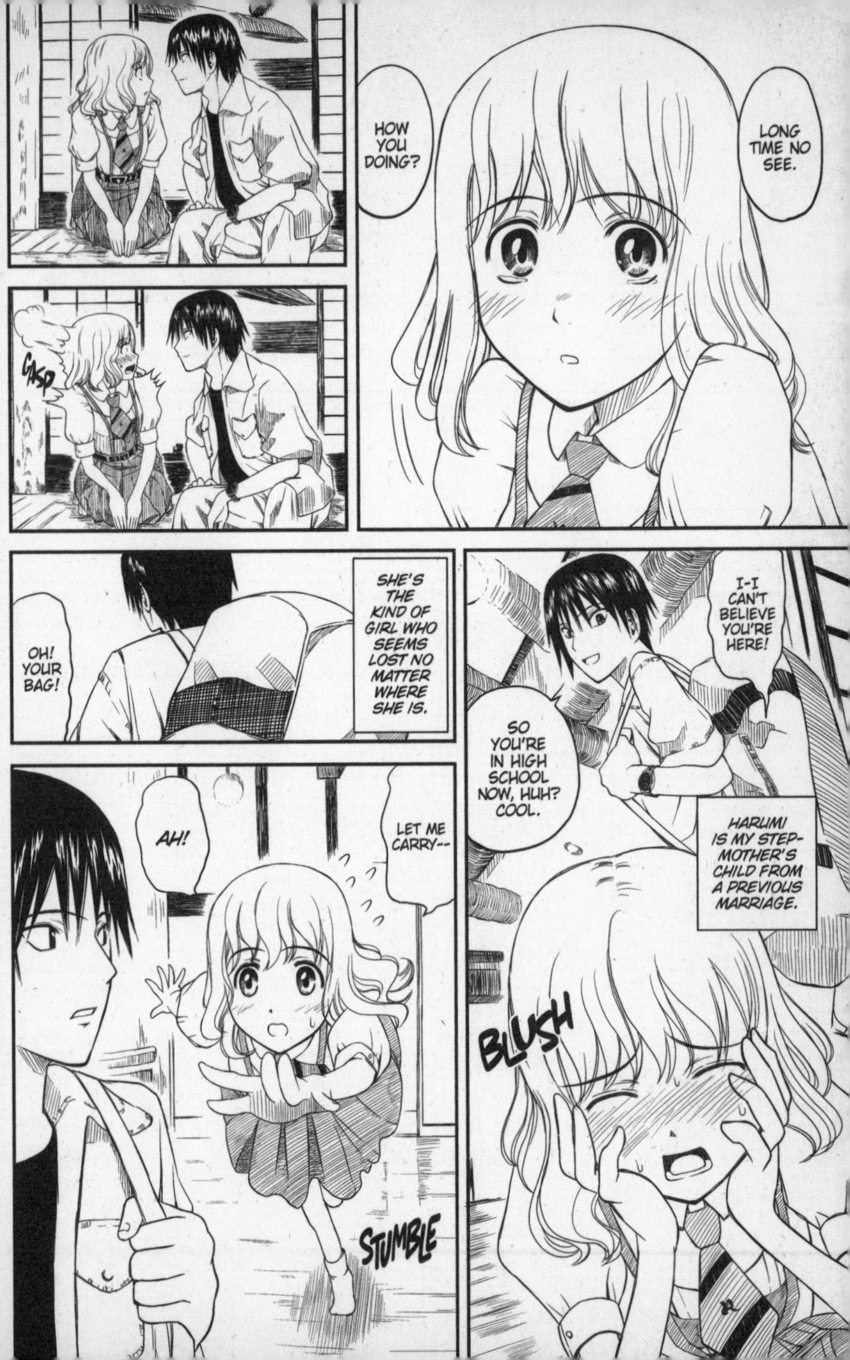
LONG TIME NO SEE.
HOW YOU DOING?
GASP
I-I CAN'T BELIEVE YOU'RE HERE!
SO YOU'RE IN HIGH SCHOOL NOW, HUH? COOL.
HARUMI IS MY STEP-MOTHER'S CHILD FROM A PREVIOUS MARRIAGE.
BLUSH
SHE'S THE KIND OF GIRL WHO SEEMS LOST NO MATTER WHERE SHE IS.
OH! YOUR BAG!
LET ME CARRY--
AH!
STUMBLE

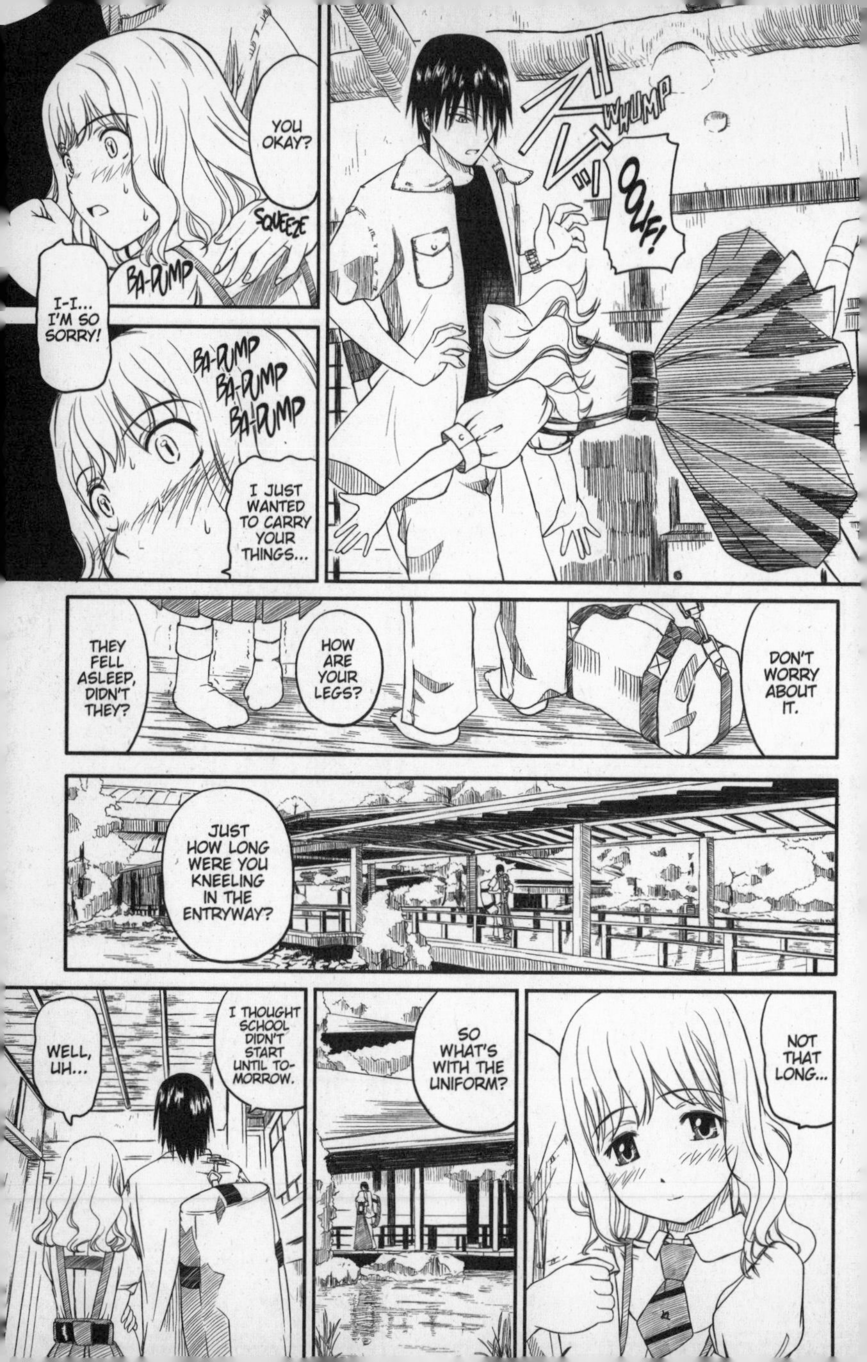
WHUMP
OOF!
YOU OKAY?
SQUEEZE
BA-DUMP
I-I... I'M SO SORRY!
BA-DUMP BA-DUMP BA-DUMP
I JUST WANTED TO CARRY YOUR THINGS...
DON'T WORRY ABOUT IT.
HOW ARE YOUR LEGS?
THEY FELL ASLEEP, DIDN'T THEY?
JUST HOW LONG WERE YOU KNEELING IN THE ENTRYWAY?
NOT THAT LONG...
SO WHAT'S WITH THE UNIFORM?
I THOUGHT SCHOOL DIDN'T START UNTIL TO-MORROW.
WELL, UH...

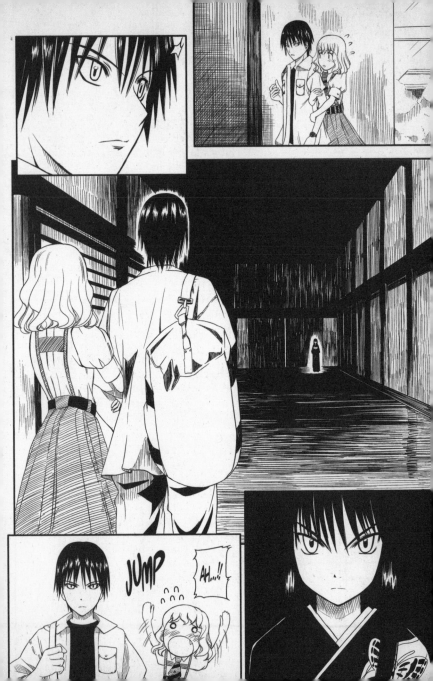

JUMP

AH....!!

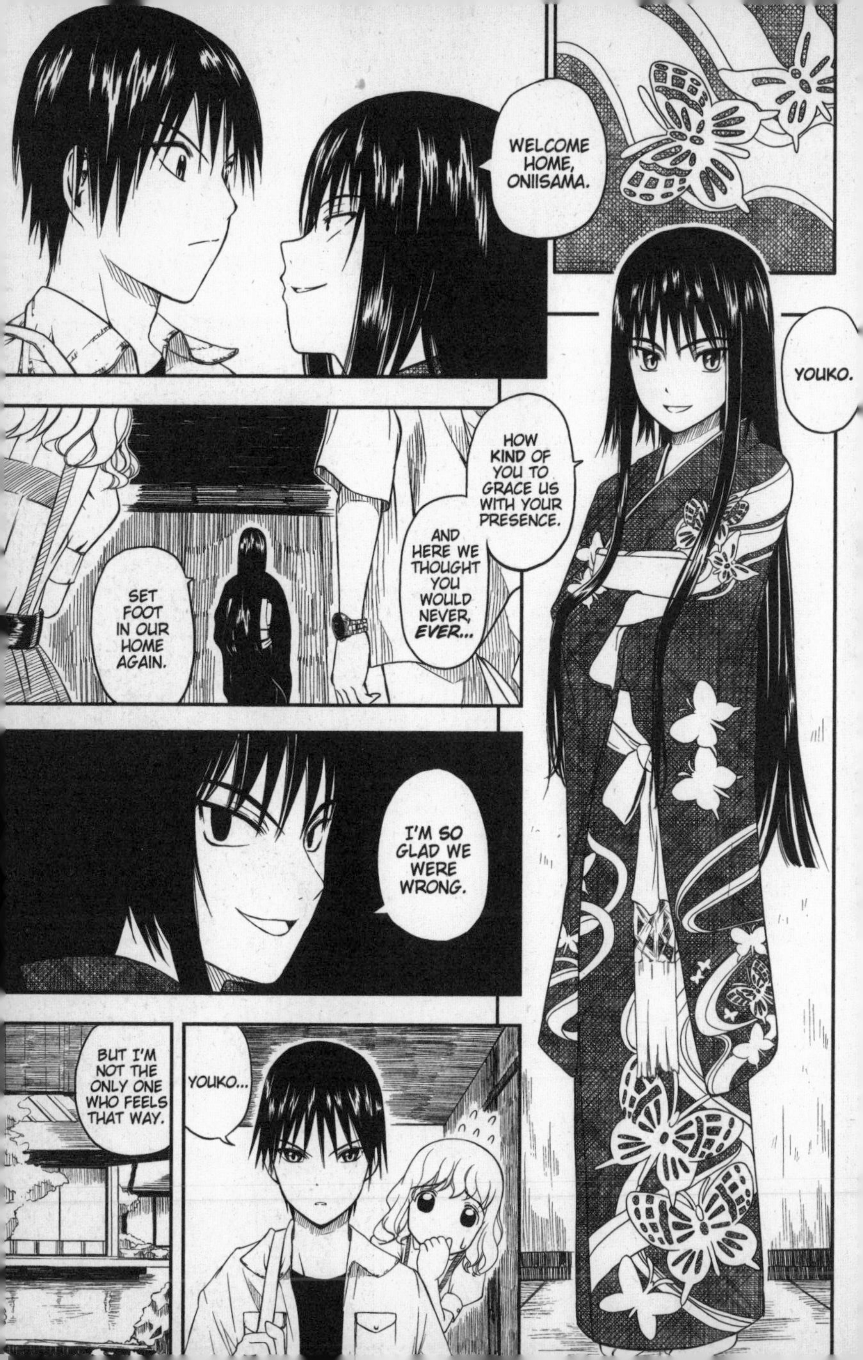
WELCOME HOME, ONIISAMA.
YOUKO.
HOW KIND OF YOU TO GRACE US WITH YOUR PRESENCE.
AND HERE WE THOUGHT YOU WOULD NEVER, *EVER...*
SET FOOT IN OUR HOME AGAIN.
I'M SO GLAD WE WERE WRONG.
YOUKO...
BUT I'M NOT THE ONLY ONE WHO FEELS THAT WAY.

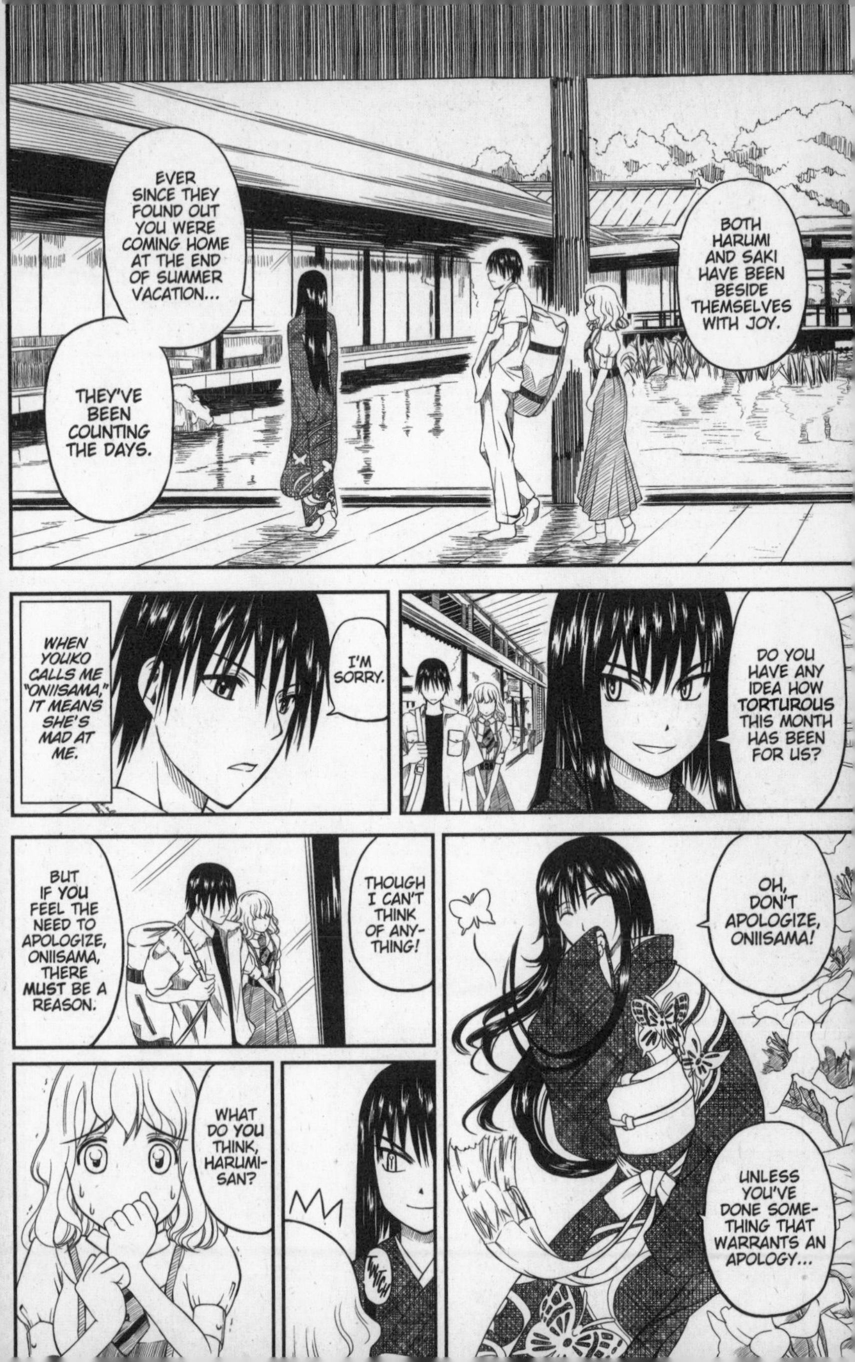
BOTH HARUMI AND SAKI HAVE BEEN BESIDE THEMSELVES WITH JOY.
EVER SINCE THEY FOUND OUT YOU WERE COMING HOME AT THE END OF SUMMER VACATION...
THEY'VE BEEN COUNTING THE DAYS.
DO YOU HAVE ANY IDEA HOW TORTUROUS THIS MONTH HAS BEEN FOR US?
I'M SORRY.
WHEN YOUKO CALLS ME "ONIISAMA," IT MEANS SHE'S MAD AT ME.
OH, DON'T APOLOGIZE, ONIISAMA!
UNLESS YOU'VE DONE SOME-THING THAT WARRANTS AN APOLOGY...
THOUGH I CAN'T THINK OF ANY-THING!
BUT IF YOU FEEL THE NEED TO APOLOGIZE, ONIISAMA, THERE MUST BE A REASON.
WHAT DO YOU THINK, HARUMI-SAN?
TWITCH

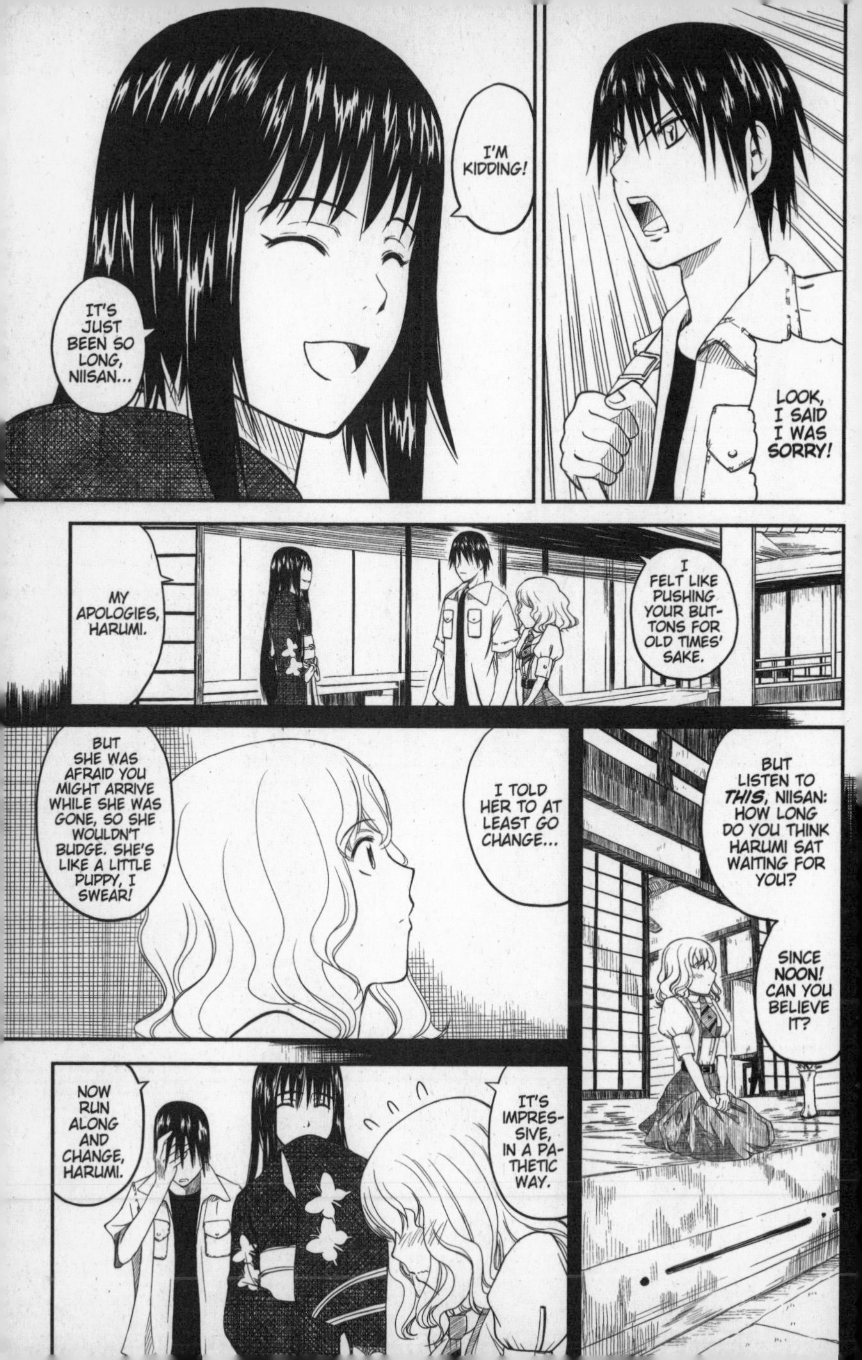
LOOK, I SAID I WAS SORRY!
I'M KIDDING!
IT'S JUST BEEN SO LONG, NIISAN...
I FELT LIKE PUSHING YOUR BUTTONS FOR OLD TIMES' SAKE.
MY APOLOGIES, HARUMI.
BUT LISTEN TO *THIS*, NIISAN: HOW LONG DO YOU THINK HARUMI SAT WAITING FOR YOU?
SINCE NOON! CAN YOU BELIEVE IT?
I TOLD HER TO AT LEAST GO CHANGE...
BUT SHE WAS AFRAID YOU MIGHT ARRIVE WHILE SHE WAS GONE, SO SHE WOULDN'T BUDGE. SHE'S LIKE A LITTLE PUPPY, I SWEAR!
IT'S IMPRESSIVE, IN A PATHETIC WAY.
NOW RUN ALONG AND CHANGE, HARUMI.

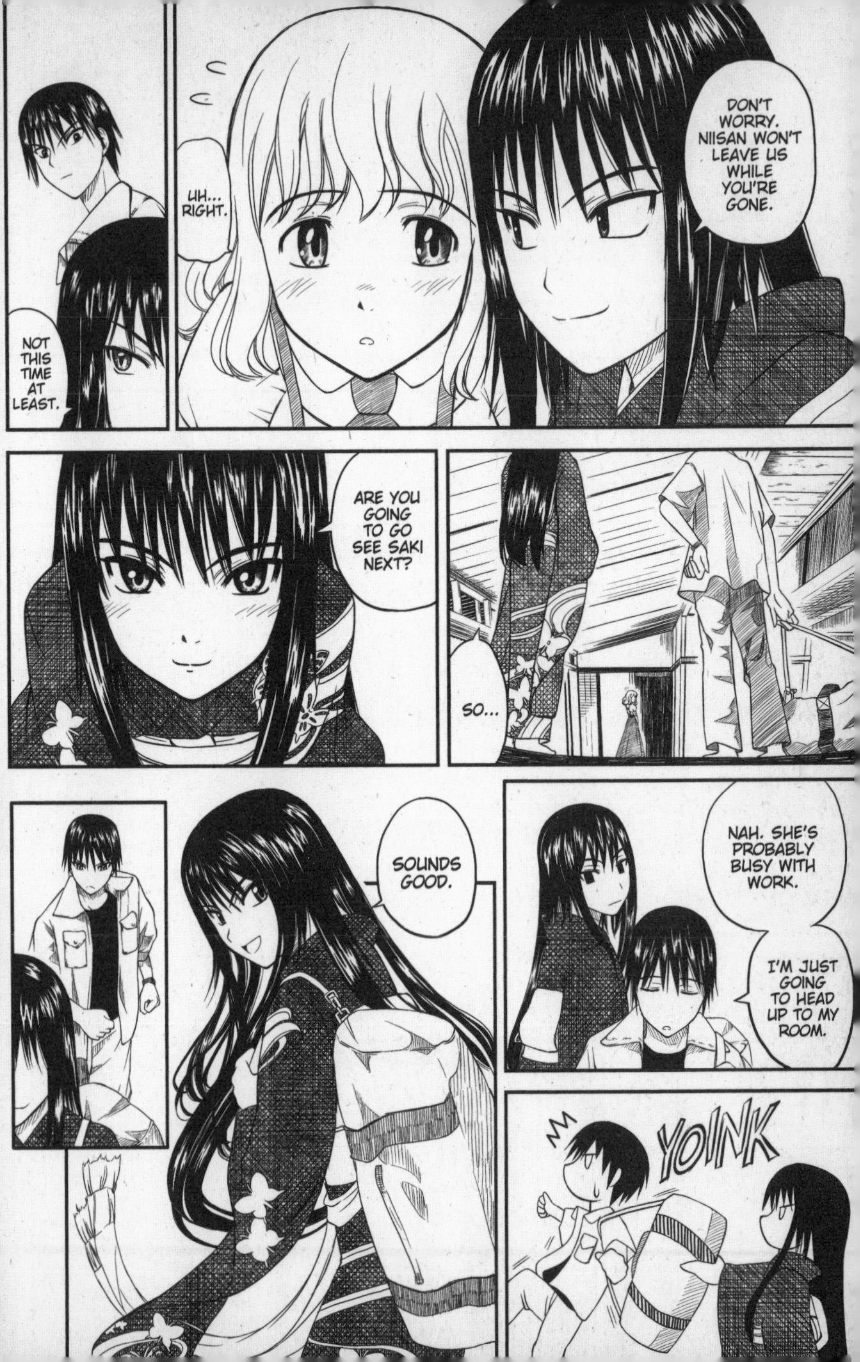
DON'T WORRY. NIISAN WON'T LEAVE US WHILE YOU'RE GONE.
UH... RIGHT.
NOT THIS TIME AT LEAST.
SO...
ARE YOU GOING TO GO SEE SAKI NEXT?
NAH. SHE'S PROBABLY BUSY WITH WORK.
I'M JUST GOING TO HEAD UP TO MY ROOM.
YOINK
SOUNDS GOOD.

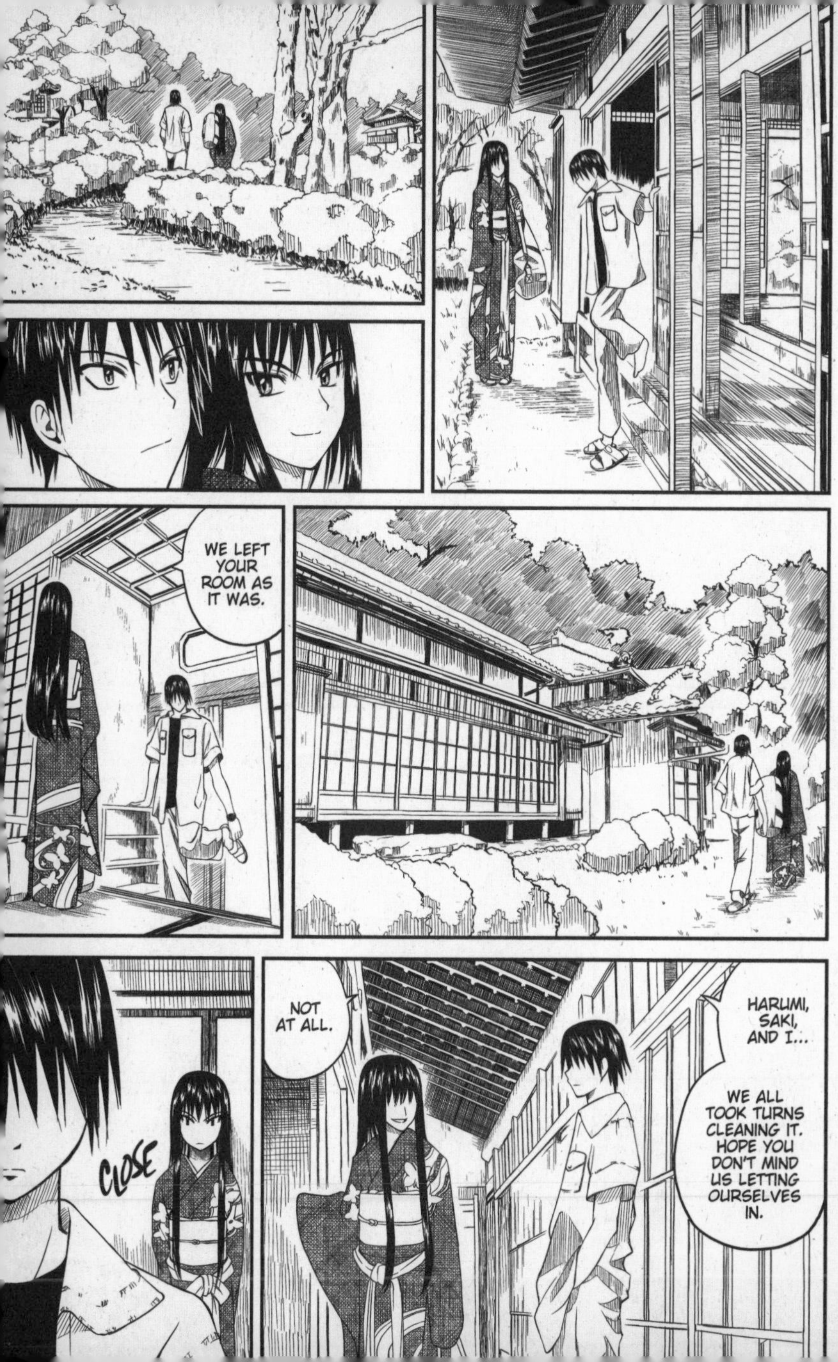
WE LEFT YOUR ROOM AS IT WAS.
HARUMI, SAKI, AND I...
WE ALL TOOK TURNS CLEANING IT. HOPE YOU DON'T MIND US LETTING OURSELVES IN.
NOT AT ALL.
CLOSE

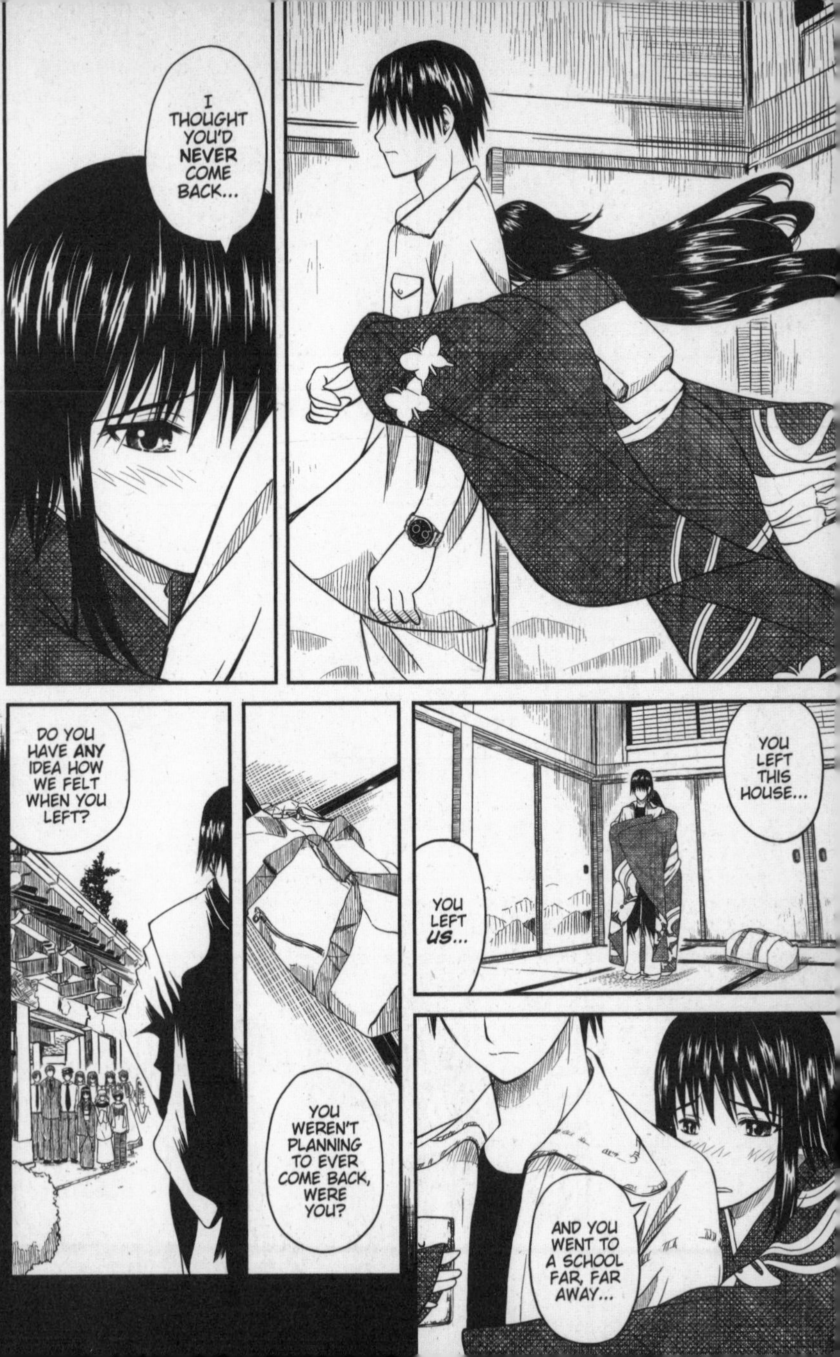
I THOUGHT YOU'D NEVER COME BACK...
YOU LEFT THIS HOUSE...
YOU LEFT *US*...
AND YOU WENT TO A SCHOOL FAR, FAR AWAY...
YOU WEREN'T PLANNING TO EVER COME BACK, WERE YOU?
DO YOU HAVE ANY IDEA HOW WE FELT WHEN YOU LEFT?

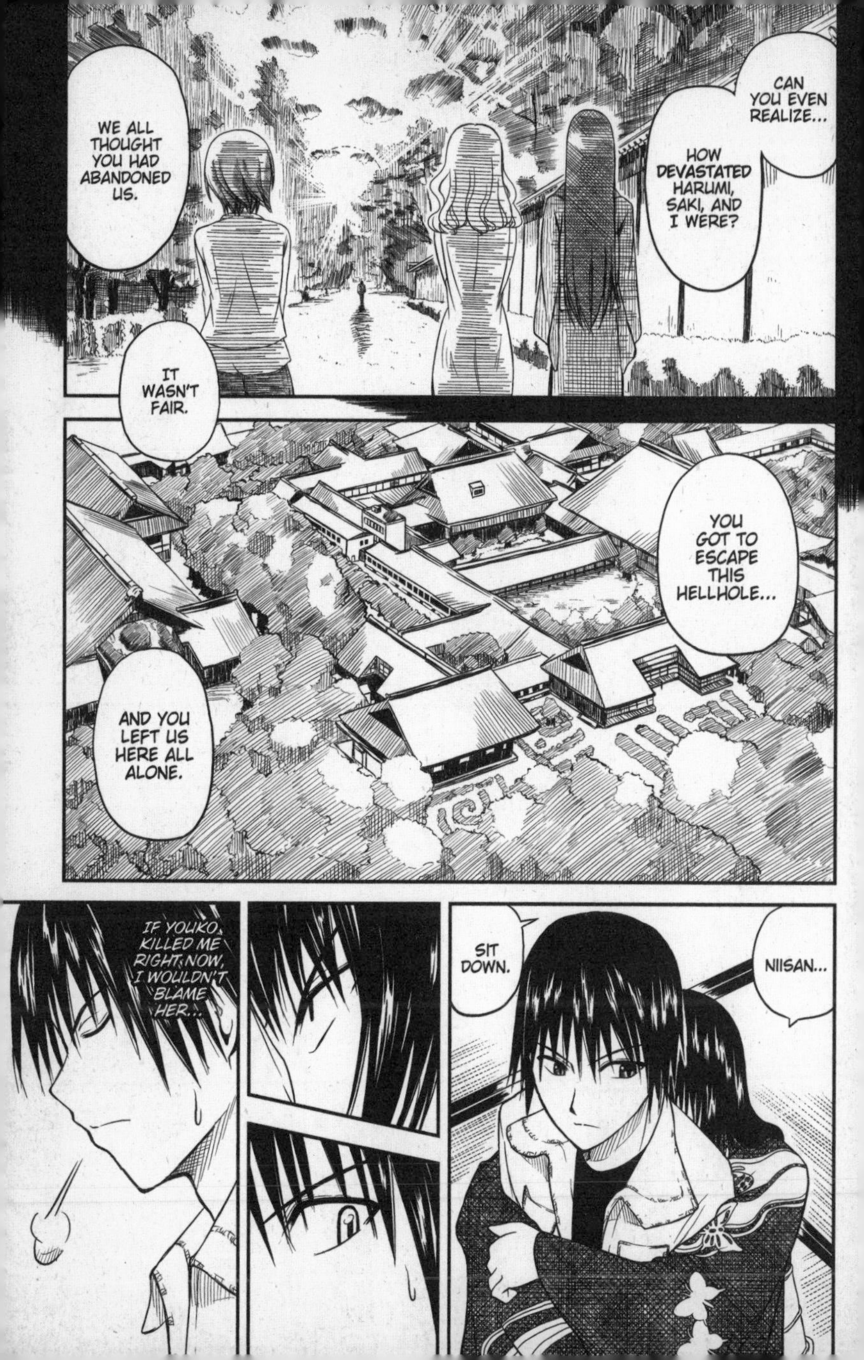
CAN YOU EVEN REALIZE...
HOW DEVASTATED HARUMI, SAKI, AND I WERE?
WE ALL THOUGHT YOU HAD ABANDONED US.
IT WASN'T FAIR.
YOU GOT TO ESCAPE THIS HELLHOLE...
AND YOU LEFT US HERE ALL ALONE.
NIISAN...
SIT DOWN.
IF YOUKO KILLED ME RIGHT NOW, I WOULDN'T BLAME HER...

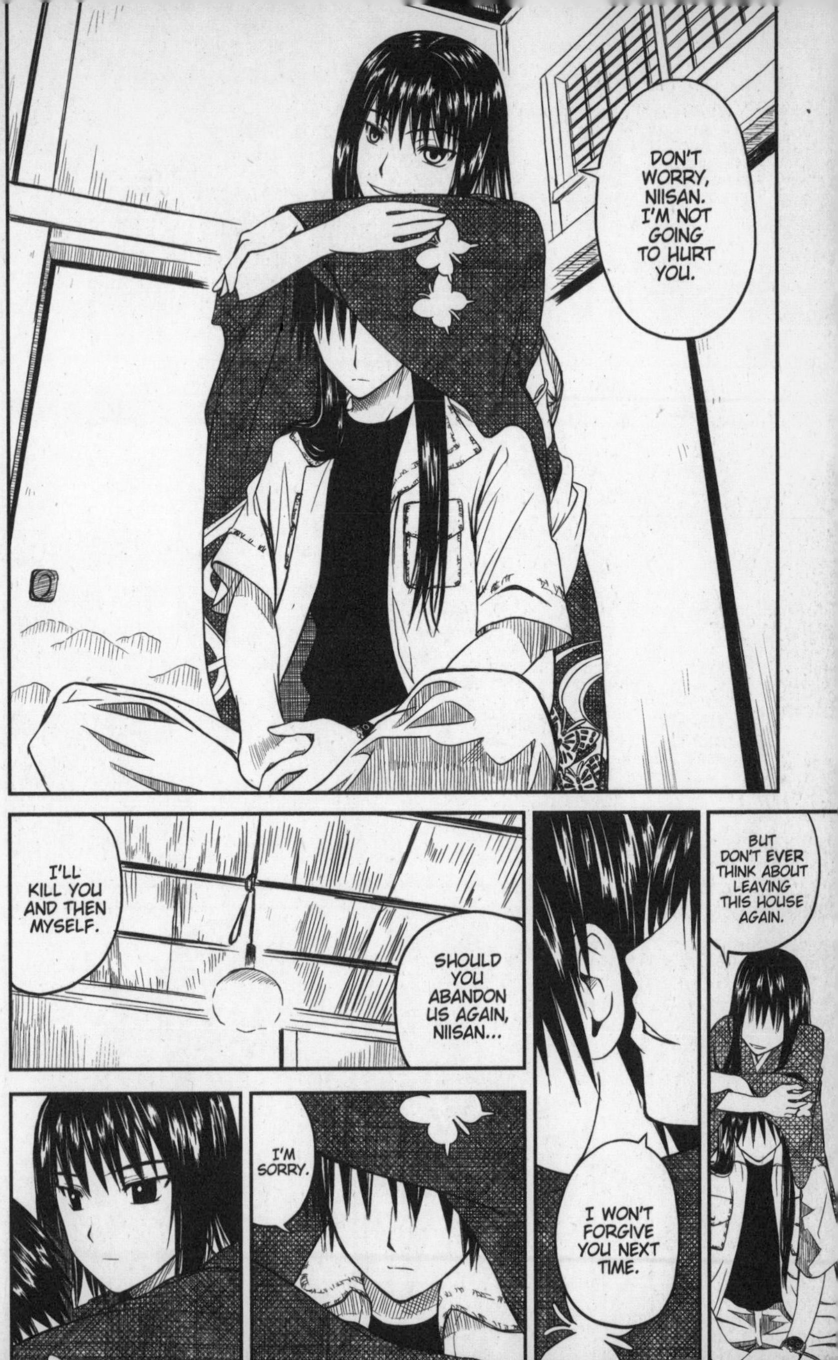
DON'T WORRY, NIISAN. I'M NOT GOING TO HURT YOU.
BUT DON'T EVER THINK ABOUT LEAVING THIS HOUSE AGAIN.
I WON'T FORGIVE YOU NEXT TIME.
SHOULD YOU ABANDON US AGAIN, NIISAN...
I'LL KILL YOU AND THEN MYSELF.
I'M SORRY.

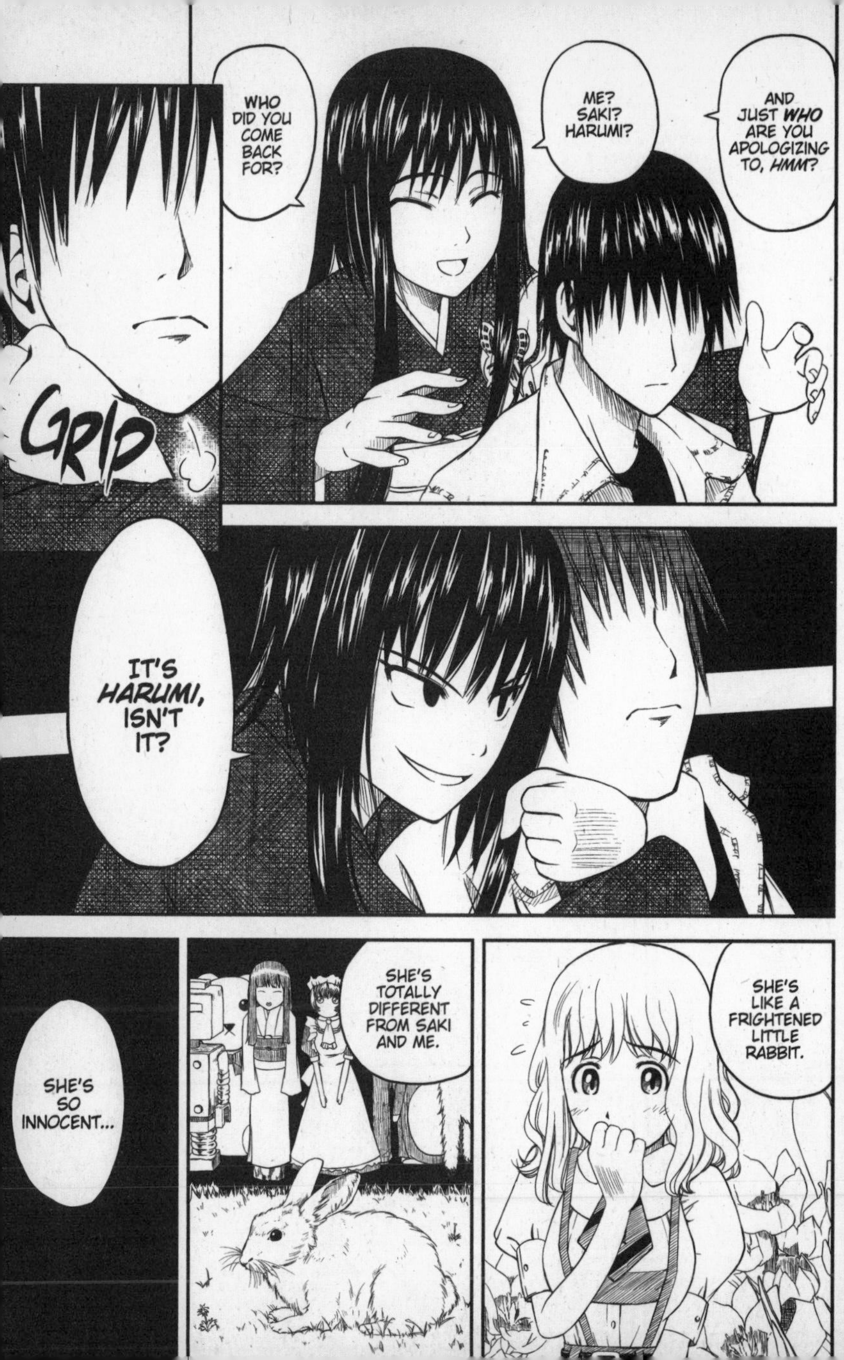
AND JUST WHO ARE YOU APOLOGIZING TO, HMM?
ME? SAKI? HARUMI?
WHO DID YOU COME BACK FOR?
GRIP
IT'S HARUMI, ISN'T IT?
SHE'S LIKE A FRIGHTENED LITTLE RABBIT.
SHE'S TOTALLY DIFFERENT FROM SAKI AND ME.
SHE'S SO INNOCENT...

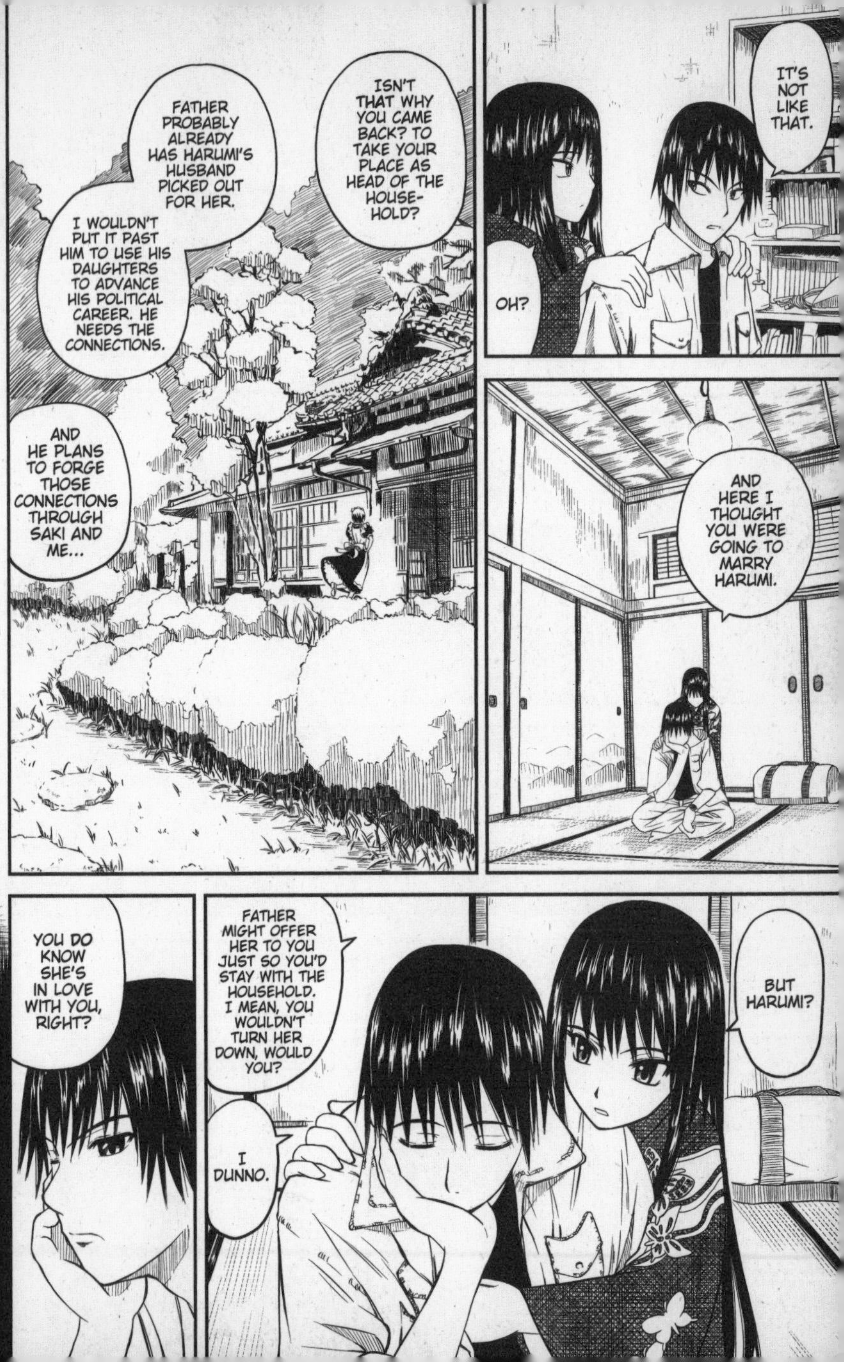
IT'S NOT LIKE THAT.
OH?
AND HERE I THOUGHT YOU WERE GOING TO MARRY HARUMI.
ISN'T THAT WHY YOU CAME BACK? TO TAKE YOUR PLACE AS HEAD OF THE HOUSE-HOLD?
FATHER PROBABLY ALREADY HAS HARUMI'S HUSBAND PICKED OUT FOR HER.
I WOULDN'T PUT IT PAST HIM TO USE HIS DAUGHTERS TO ADVANCE HIS POLITICAL CAREER. HE NEEDS THE CONNECTIONS.
AND HE PLANS TO FORGE THOSE CONNECTIONS THROUGH SAKI AND ME...
BUT HARUMI?
FATHER MIGHT OFFER HER TO YOU JUST SO YOU'D STAY WITH THE HOUSEHOLD. I MEAN, YOU WOULDN'T TURN HER DOWN, WOULD YOU?
I DUNNO.
YOU DO KNOW SHE'S IN LOVE WITH YOU, RIGHT?

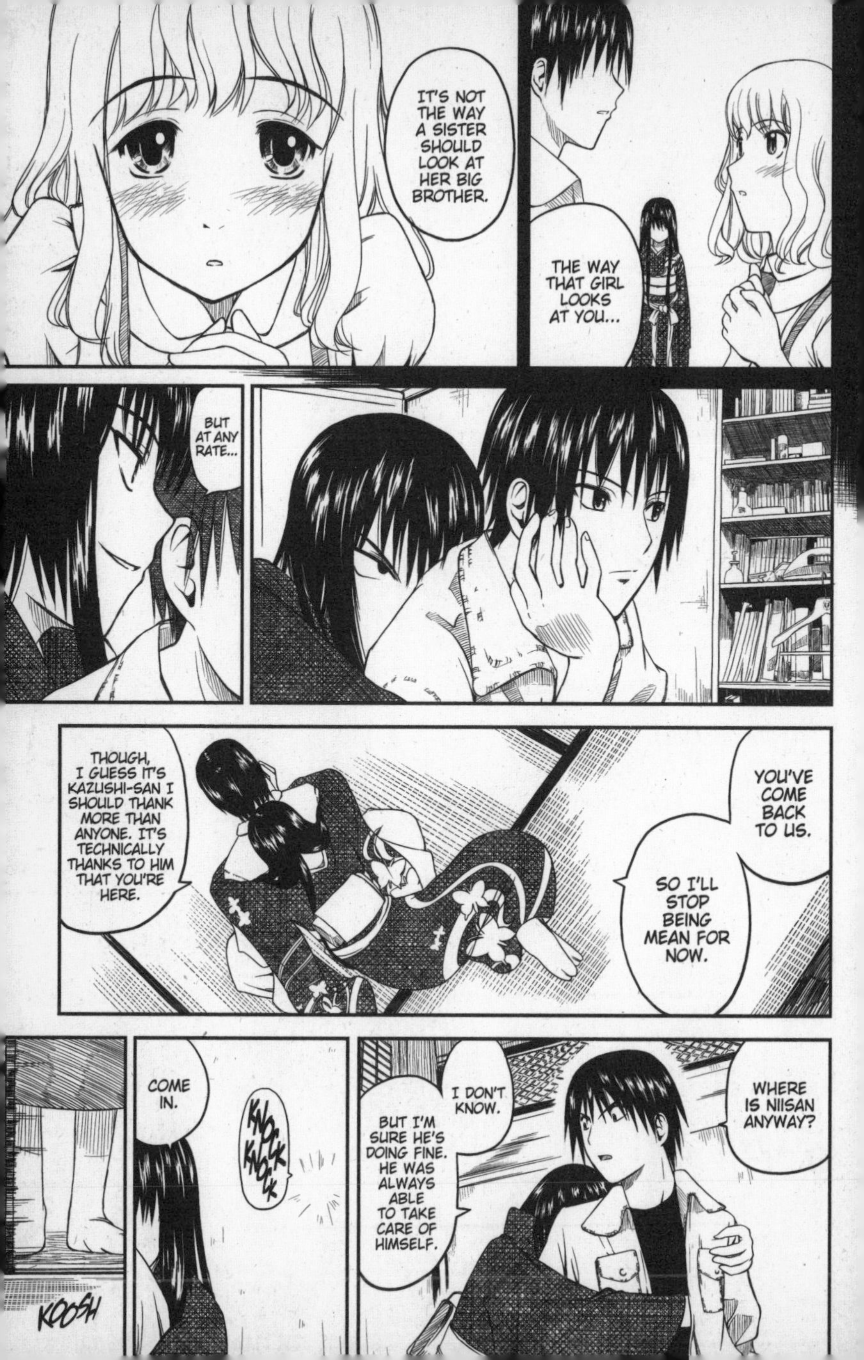
THE WAY THAT GIRL LOOKS AT YOU...
IT'S NOT THE WAY A SISTER SHOULD LOOK AT HER BIG BROTHER.
BUT AT ANY RATE...
YOU'VE COME BACK TO US.
SO I'LL STOP BEING MEAN FOR NOW.
THOUGH, I GUESS IT'S KAZUSHI-SAN I SHOULD THANK MORE THAN ANYONE. IT'S TECHNICALLY THANKS TO HIM THAT YOU'RE HERE.
WHERE IS NIISAN ANYWAY?
I DON'T KNOW.
BUT I'M SURE HE'S DOING FINE. HE WAS ALWAYS ABLE TO TAKE CARE OF HIMSELF.
KNOCK KNOCK
COME IN.
KOOSH

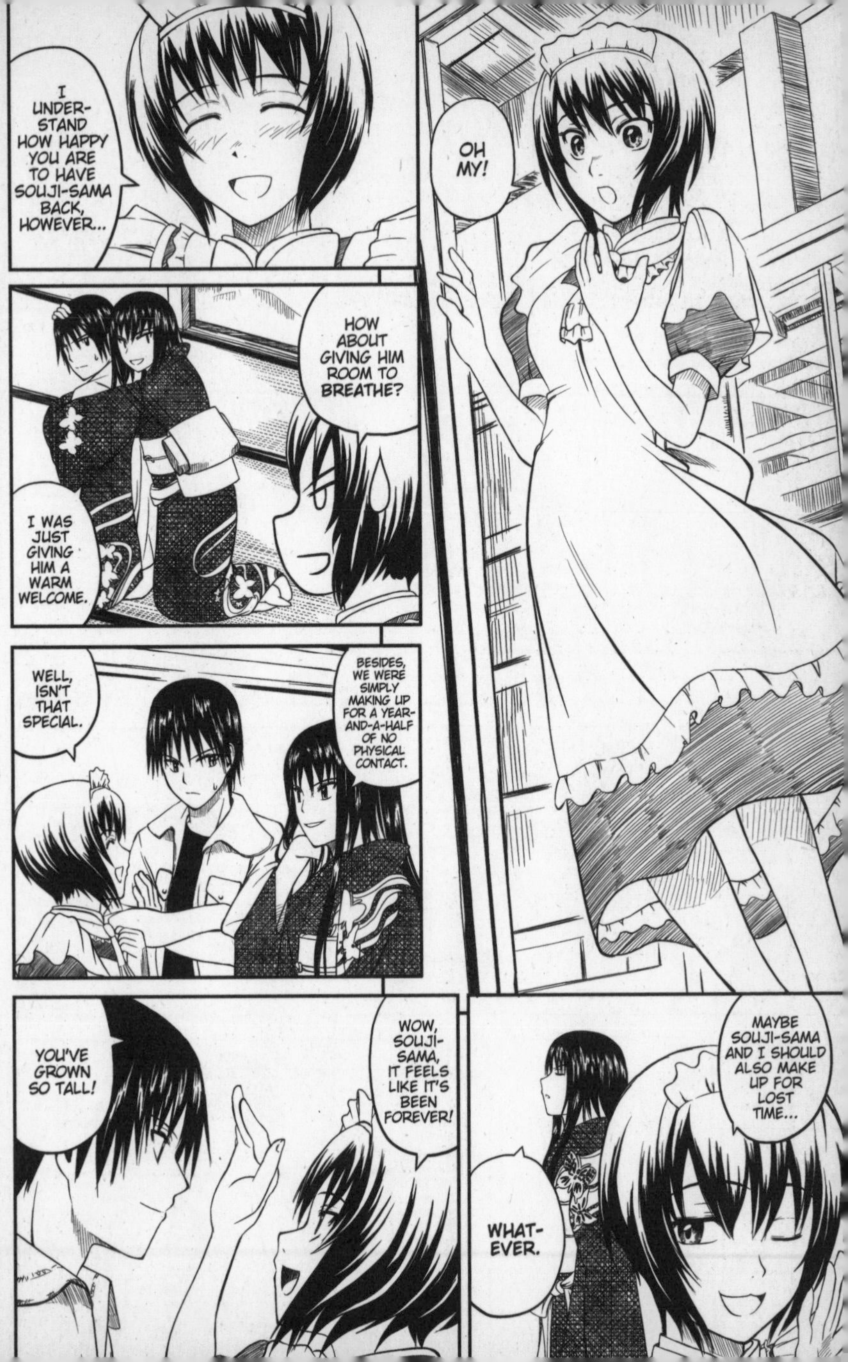
OH MY!
I UNDERSTAND HOW HAPPY YOU ARE TO HAVE SOUJI-SAMA BACK, HOWEVER...
HOW ABOUT GIVING HIM ROOM TO BREATHE?
I WAS JUST GIVING HIM A WARM WELCOME.
BESIDES, WE WERE SIMPLY MAKING UP FOR A YEAR-AND-A-HALF OF NO PHYSICAL CONTACT.
WELL, ISN'T THAT SPECIAL.
MAYBE SOUJI-SAMA AND I SHOULD ALSO MAKE UP FOR LOST TIME...
WHAT-EVER.
WOW, SOUJI-SAMA, IT FEELS LIKE IT'S BEEN FOREVER!
YOU'VE GROWN SO TALL!

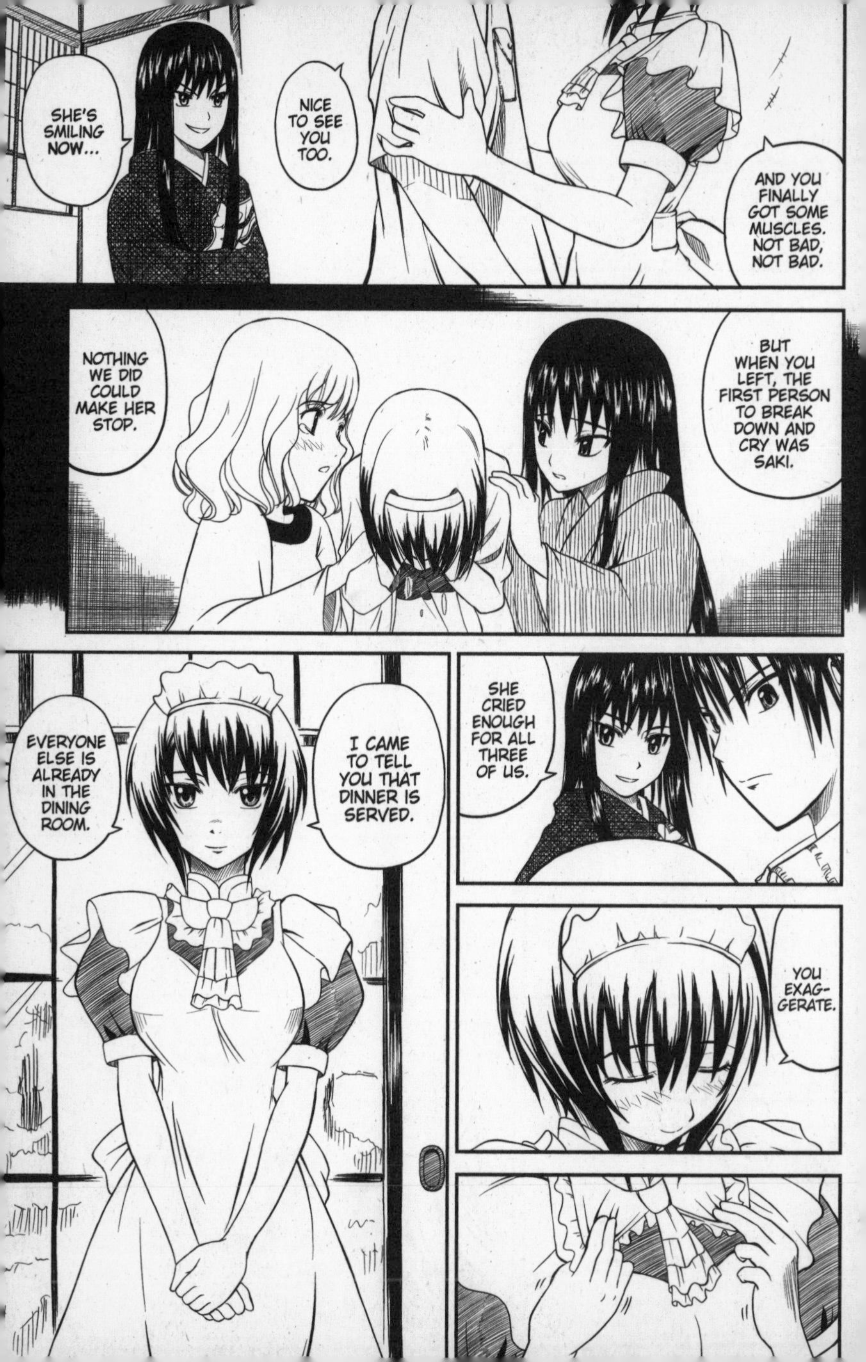
AND YOU FINALLY GOT SOME MUSCLES. NOT BAD, NOT BAD.
NICE TO SEE YOU TOO.
SHE'S SMILING NOW...
BUT WHEN YOU LEFT, THE FIRST PERSON TO BREAK DOWN AND CRY WAS SAKI.
NOTHING WE DID COULD MAKE HER STOP.
SHE CRIED ENOUGH FOR ALL THREE OF US.
YOU EXAG-GERATE.
I CAME TO TELL YOU THAT DINNER IS SERVED.
EVERYONE ELSE IS ALREADY IN THE DINING ROOM.

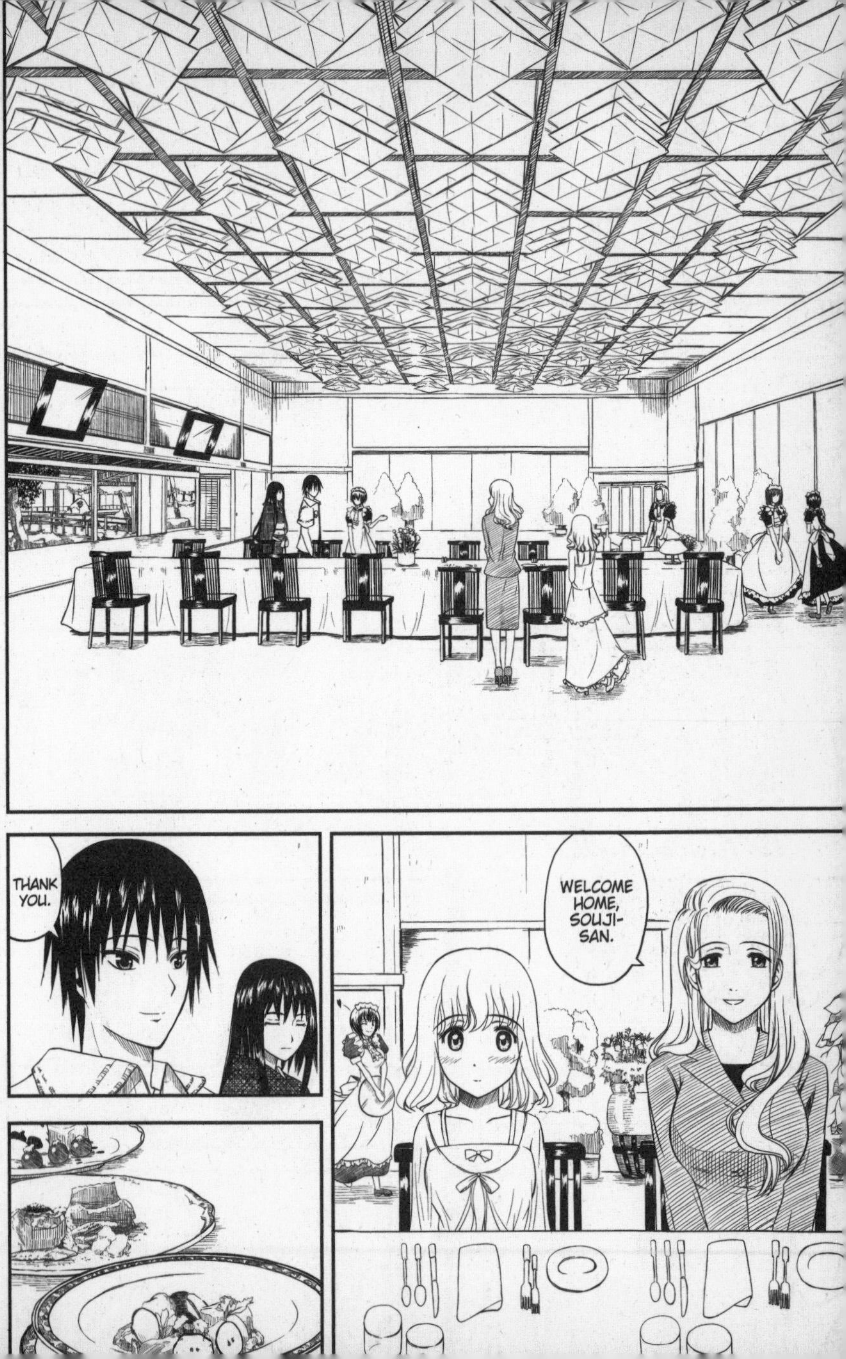
WELCOME HOME, SOUJI-SAN.
THANK YOU.

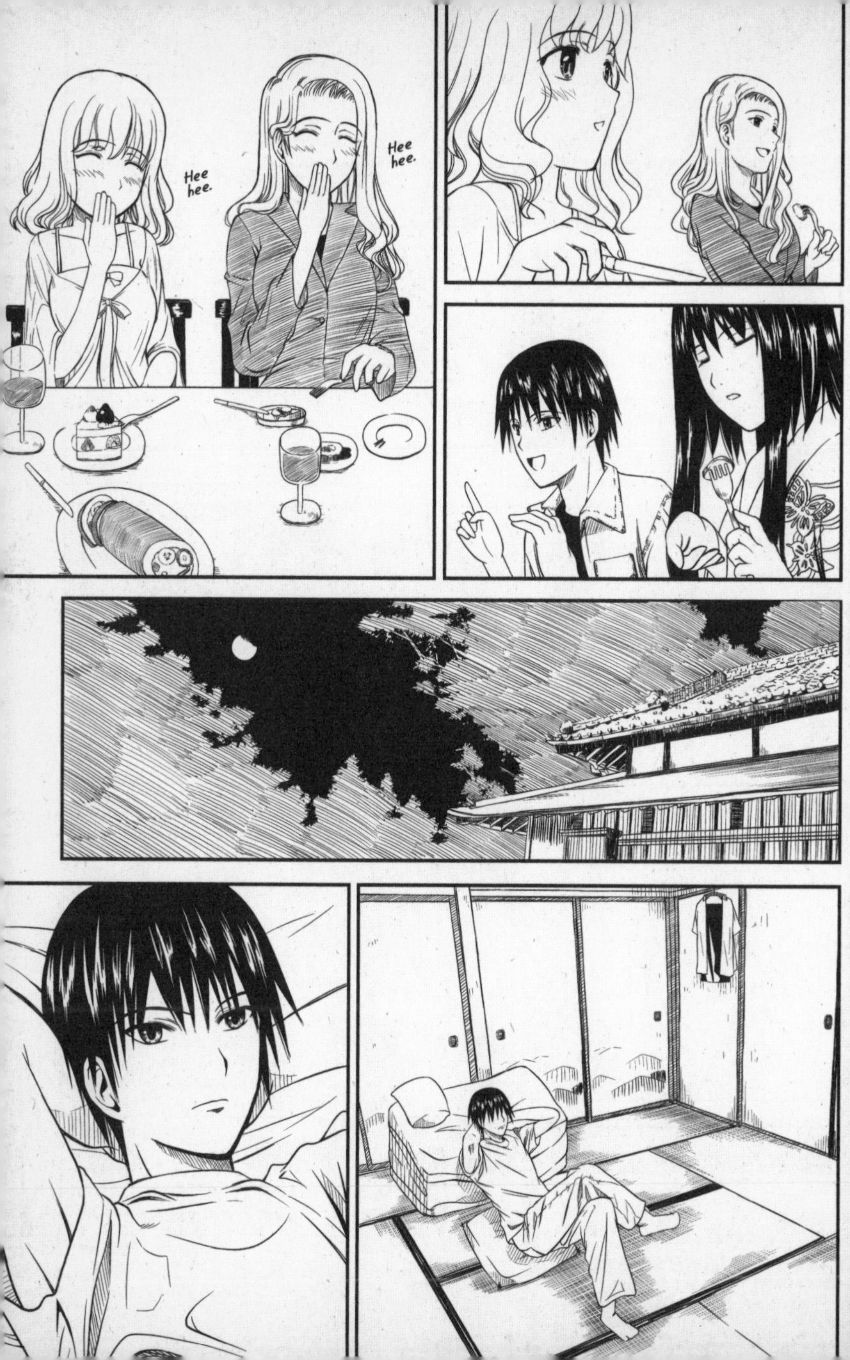
Hee hee.
Hee hee.

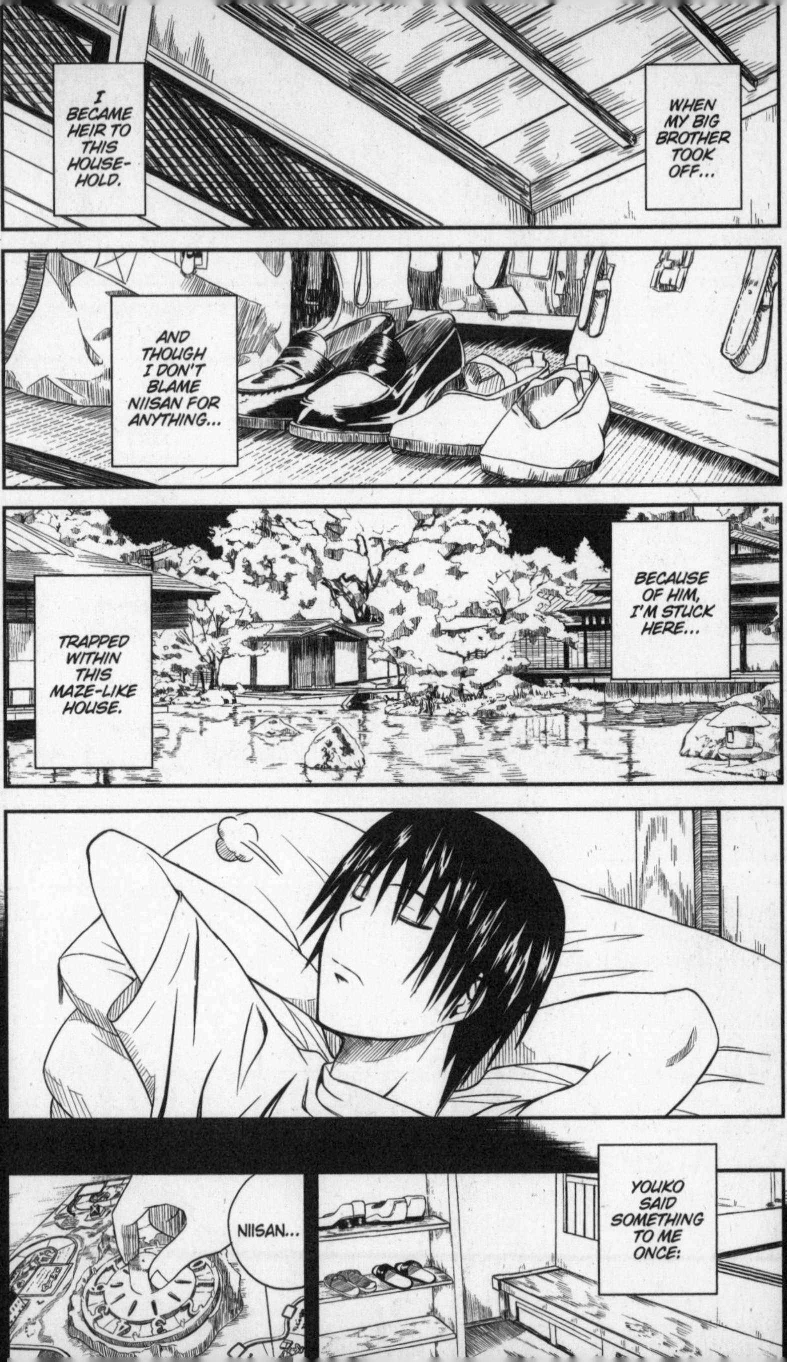
WHEN MY BIG BROTHER TOOK OFF...
I BECAME HEIR TO THIS HOUSE-HOLD.
AND THOUGH I DON'T BLAME NIISAN FOR ANYTHING...
BECAUSE OF HIM, I'M STUCK HERE...
TRAPPED WITHIN THIS MAZE-LIKE HOUSE.
YOUKO SAID SOMETHING TO ME ONCE:
NIISAN...

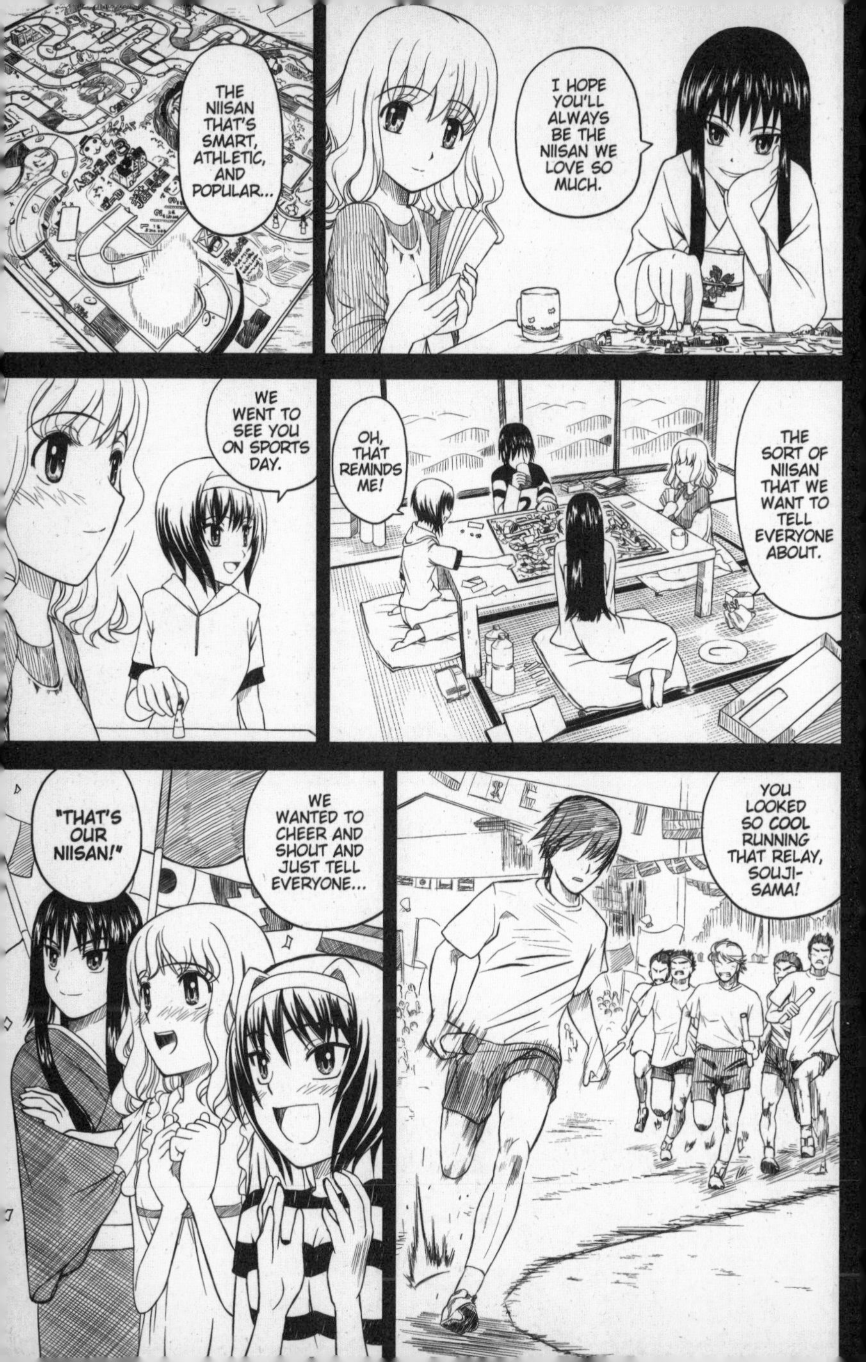
I HOPE YOU'LL ALWAYS BE THE NIISAN WE LOVE SO MUCH.
THE NIISAN THAT'S SMART, ATHLETIC, AND POPULAR...
THE SORT OF NIISAN THAT WE WANT TO TELL EVERYONE ABOUT.
OH, THAT REMINDS ME!
WE WENT TO SEE YOU ON SPORTS DAY.
YOU LOOKED SO COOL RUNNING THAT RELAY, SOUJI-SAMA!
WE WANTED TO CHEER AND SHOUT AND JUST TELL EVERYONE...
"THAT'S OUR NIISAN!"

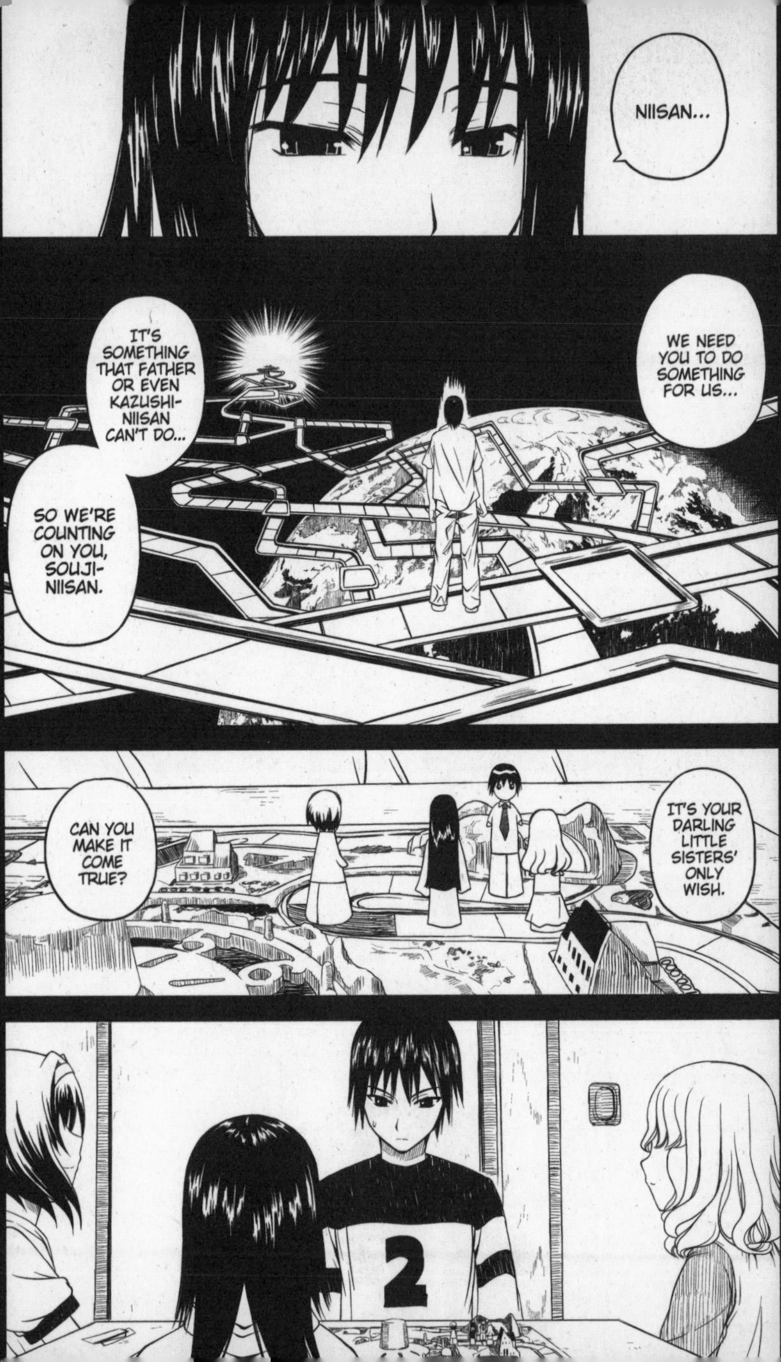
NIISAN...
WE NEED YOU TO DO SOMETHING FOR US...
IT'S SOMETHING THAT FATHER OR EVEN KAZUSHI-NIISAN CAN'T DO...
SO WE'RE COUNTING ON YOU, SOUJI-NIISAN.
IT'S YOUR DARLING LITTLE SISTERS' ONLY WISH.
CAN YOU MAKE IT COME TRUE?

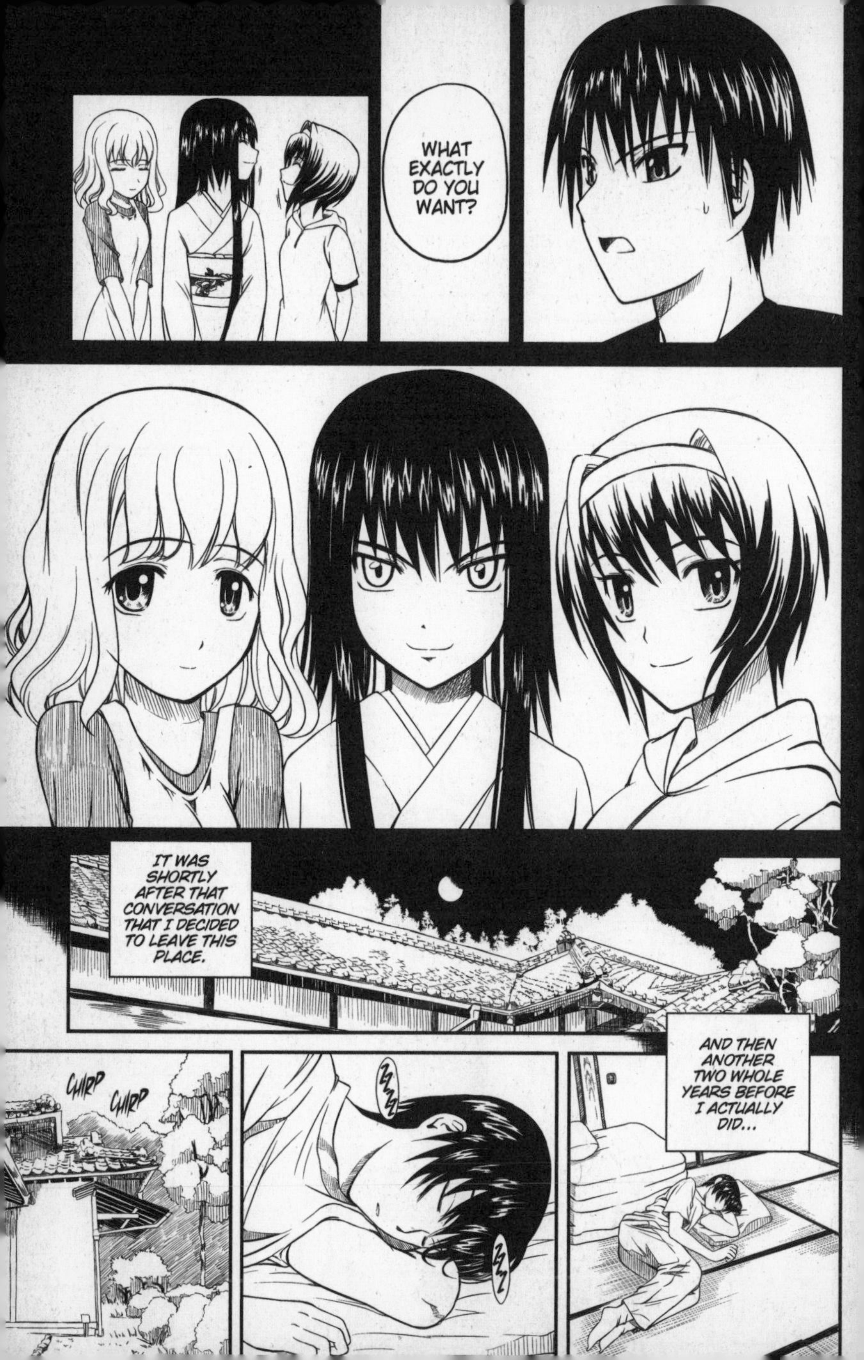
WHAT EXACTLY DO YOU WANT?
IT WAS SHORTLY AFTER THAT CONVERSATION THAT I DECIDED TO LEAVE THIS PLACE.
AND THEN ANOTHER TWO WHOLE YEARS BEFORE I ACTUALLY DID...
ZZZ
ZZZ
CHIRP
CHIRP

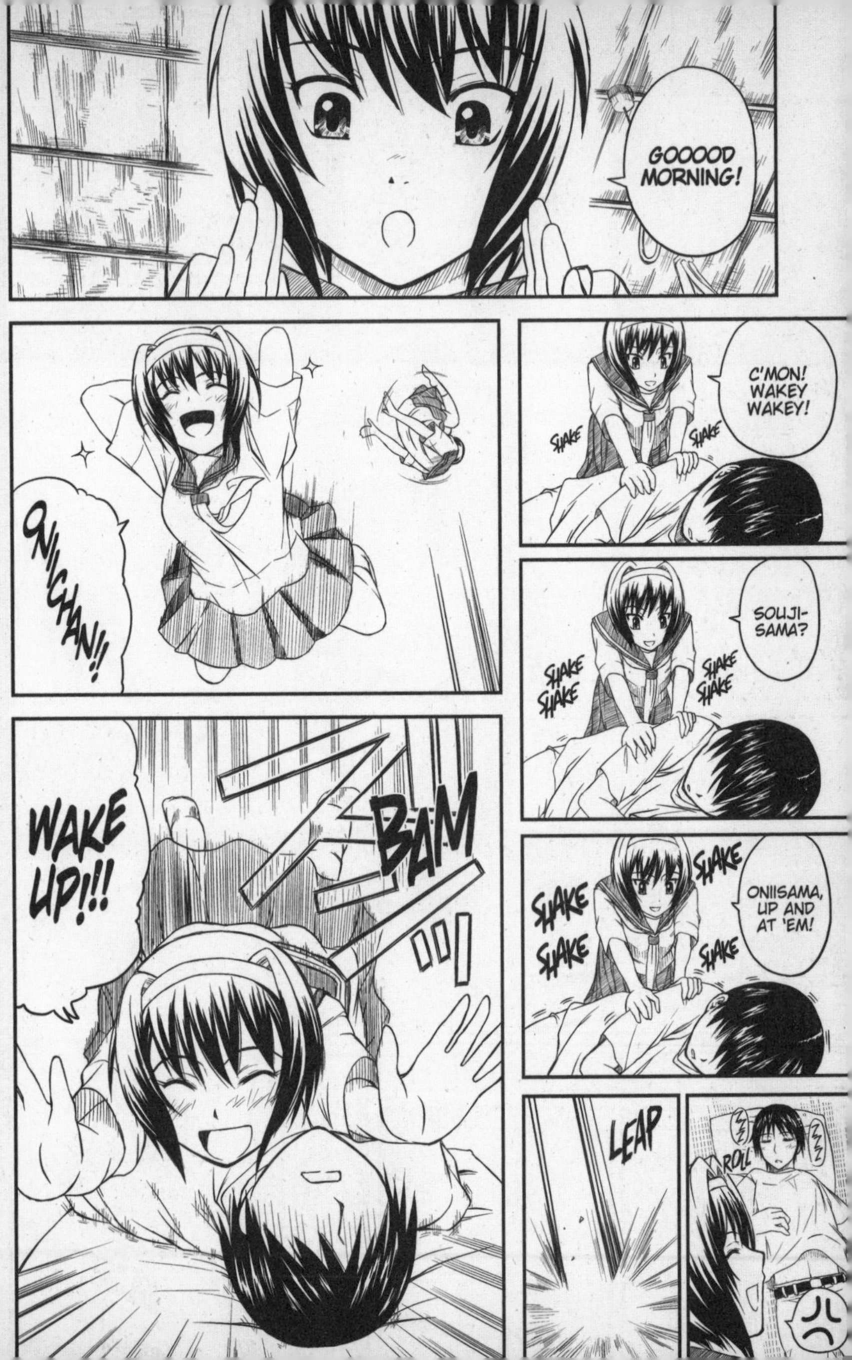
GOOOOD MORNING!
C'MON! WAKEY WAKEY!
SHAKE
SHAKE
SOUJI-SAMA?
SHAKE SHAKE
SHAKE SHAKE
ONIISAMA, UP AND AT 'EM!
SHAKE
SHAKE
SHAKE
SHAKE
ZZZ
ZZZ
ROLL
LEAP
ONIICHAN!!
WAKE UP!!!
BAM

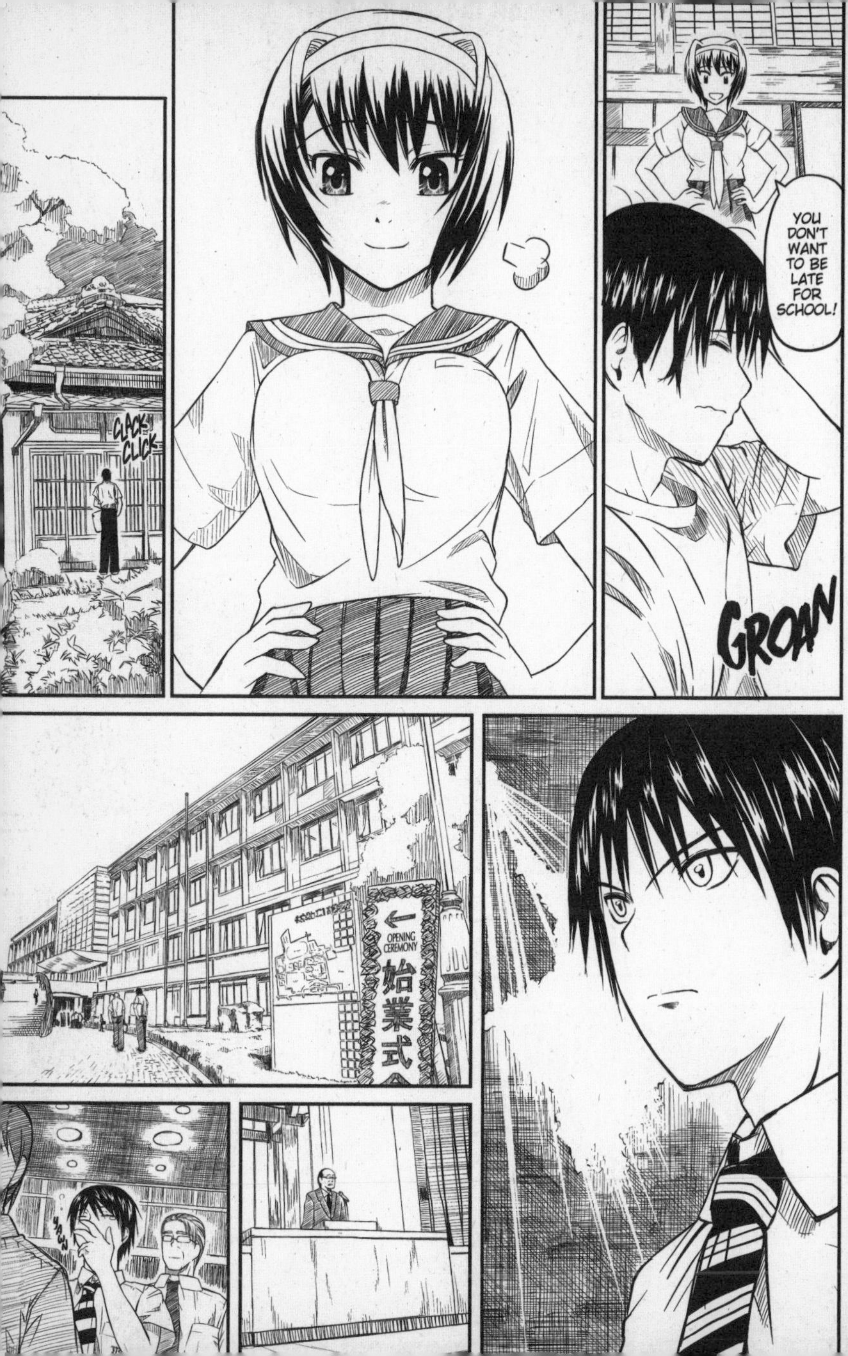
YOU DON'T WANT TO BE LATE FOR SCHOOL!
GROAN
CLACK CLICK
OPENING CEREMONY
始業式
YAWN

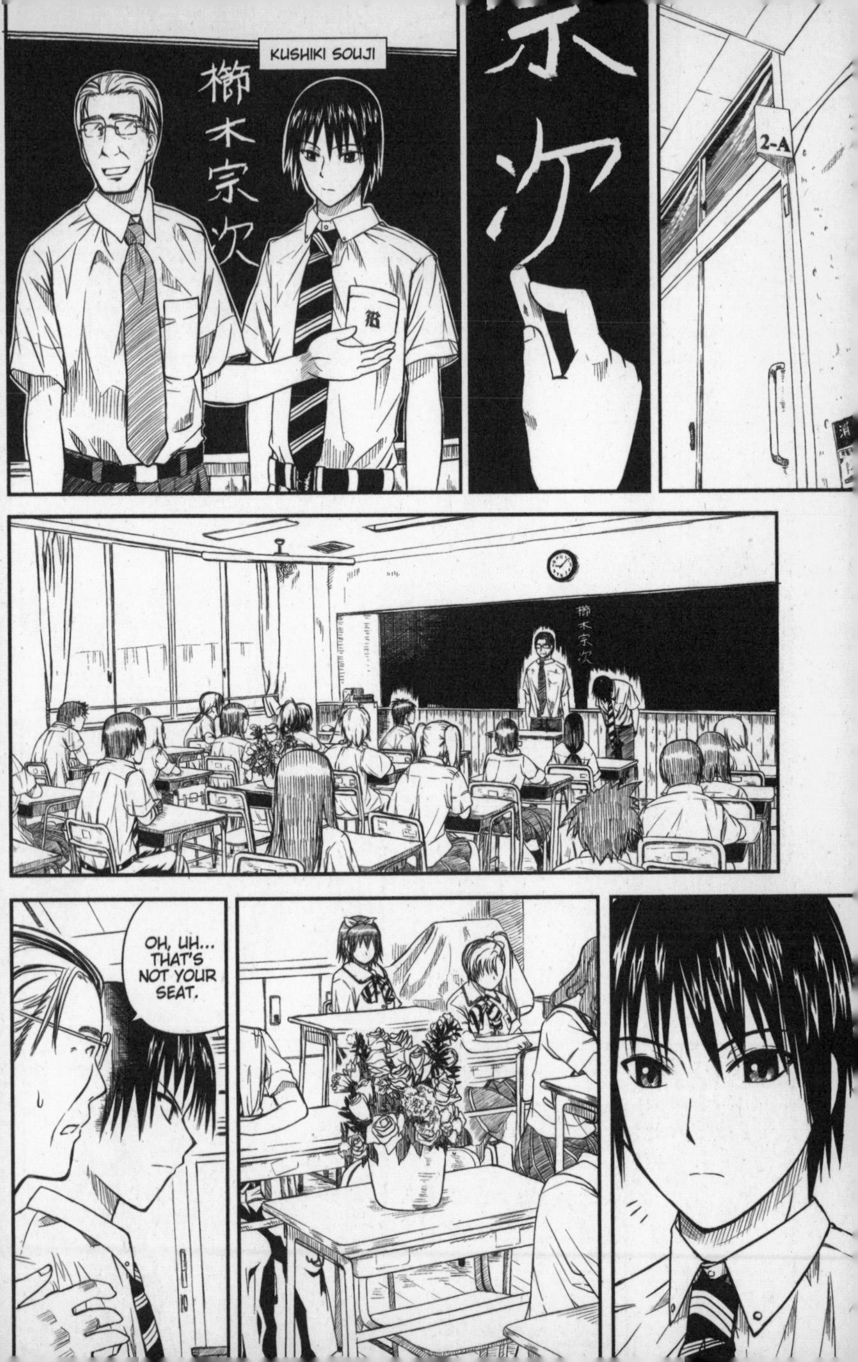
2-A
KUSHIKI SOUJI
櫛木宗次
櫛木宗次
OH, UH... THAT'S NOT YOUR SEAT.

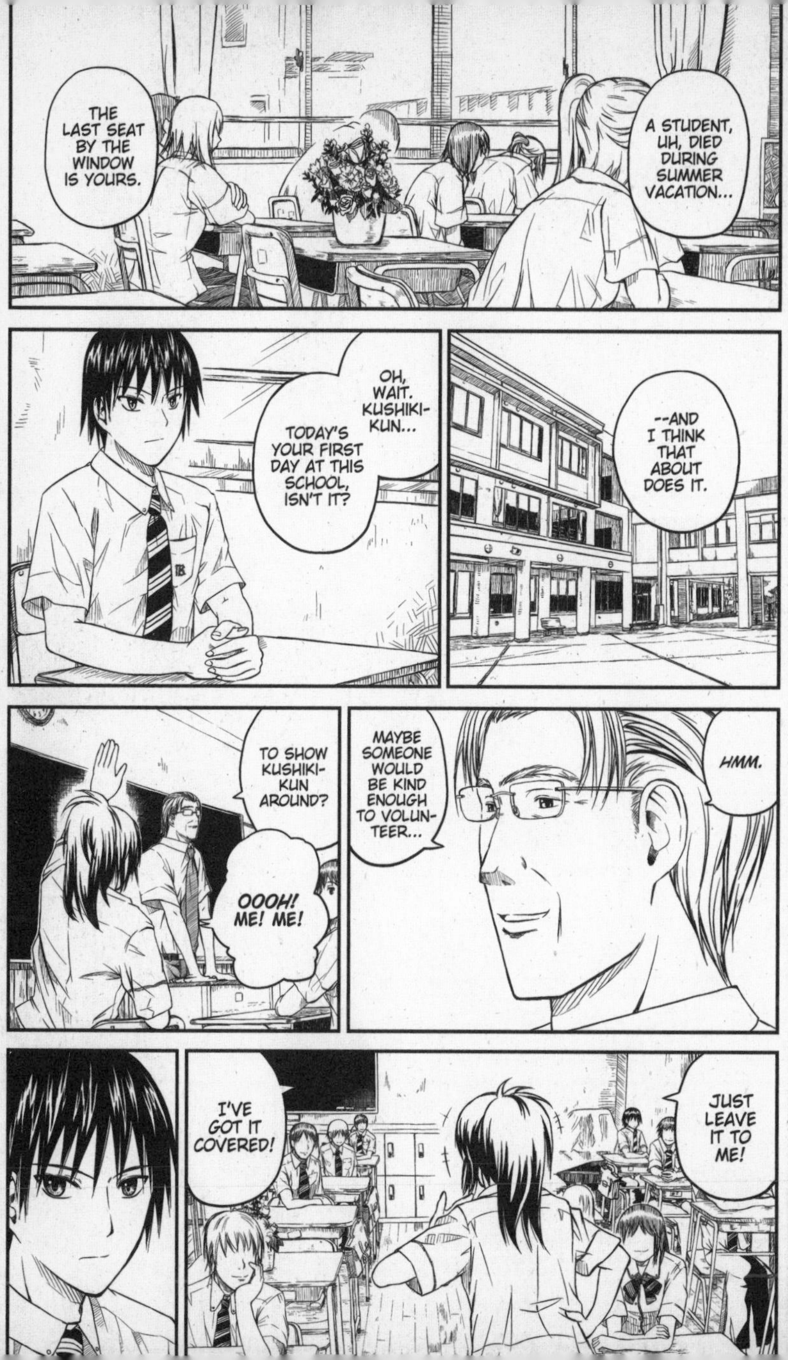
A STUDENT, UH, DIED DURING SUMMER VACATION...
THE LAST SEAT BY THE WINDOW IS YOURS.
--AND I THINK THAT ABOUT DOES IT.
OH, WAIT. KUSHIKI-KUN...
TODAY'S YOUR FIRST DAY AT THIS SCHOOL, ISN'T IT?
HMM.
MAYBE SOMEONE WOULD BE KIND ENOUGH TO VOLUNTEER...
TO SHOW KUSHIKI-KUN AROUND?
OOOH! ME! ME!
JUST LEAVE IT TO ME!
I'VE GOT IT COVERED!

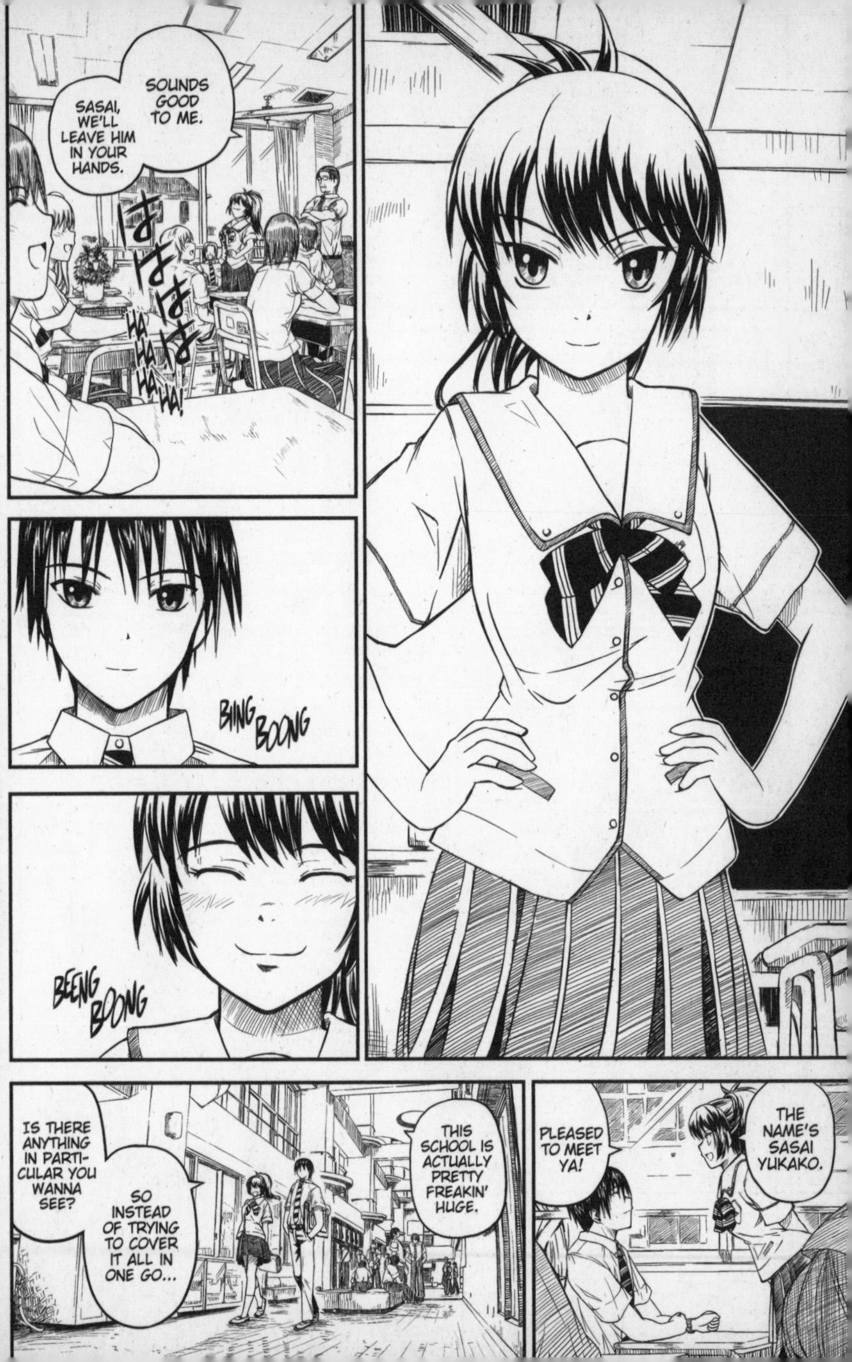
SOUNDS GOOD TO ME.
SASAI, WE'LL LEAVE HIM IN YOUR HANDS.
ははは
HA HA HA HA!
BING BOONG
BEENG BOONG
THE NAME'S SASAI YUKAKO.
PLEASED TO MEET YA!
THIS SCHOOL IS ACTUALLY PRETTY FREAKIN' HUGE.
SO INSTEAD OF TRYING TO COVER IT ALL IN ONE GO...
IS THERE ANYTHING IN PARTICULAR YOU WANNA SEE?

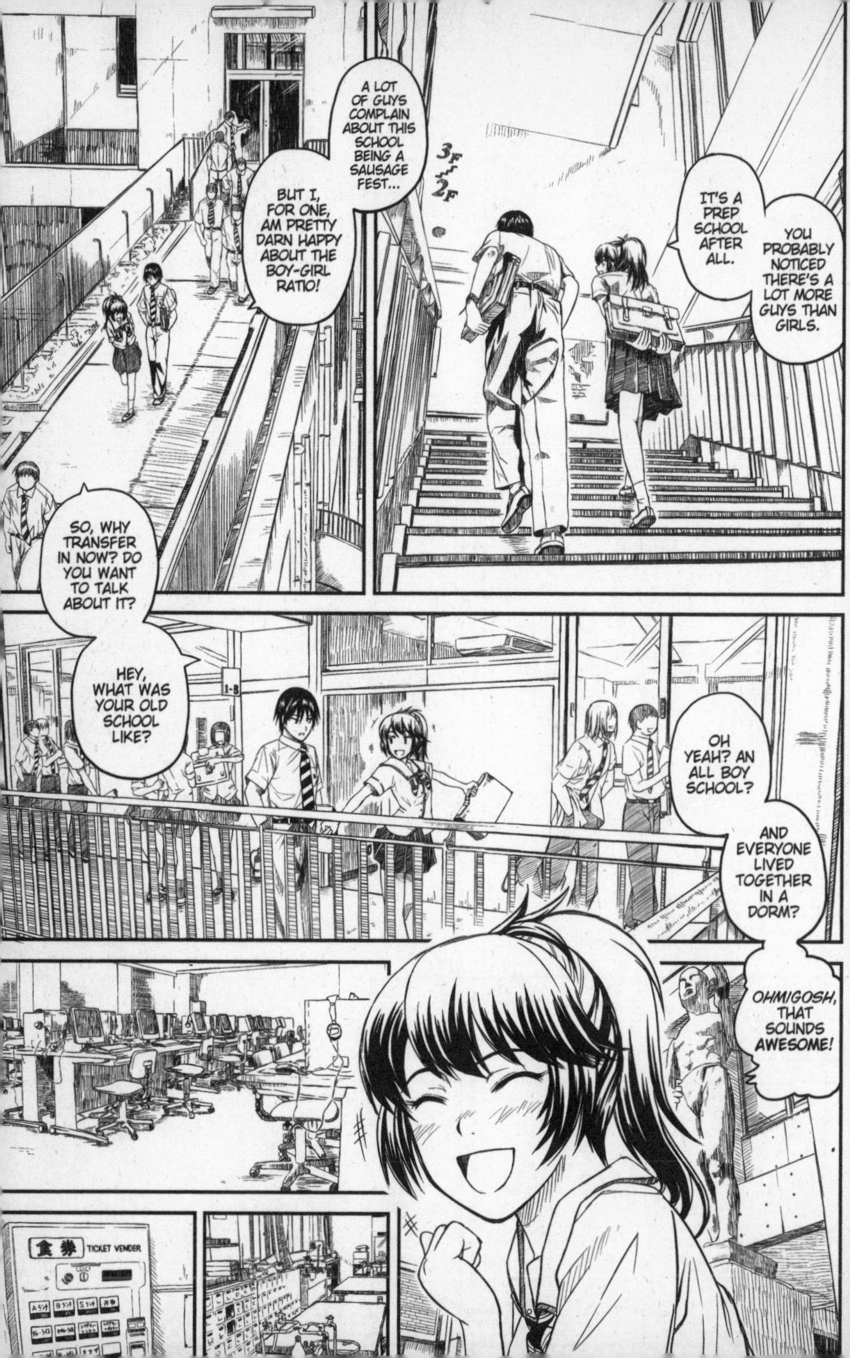
YOU PROBABLY NOTICED THERE'S A LOT MORE GUYS THAN GIRLS.
IT'S A PREP SCHOOL AFTER ALL.
3F
2F
A LOT OF GUYS COMPLAIN ABOUT THIS SCHOOL BEING A SAUSAGE FEST...
BUT I, FOR ONE, AM PRETTY DARN HAPPY ABOUT THE BOY-GIRL RATIO!
SO, WHY TRANSFER IN NOW? DO YOU WANT TO TALK ABOUT IT?
HEY, WHAT WAS YOUR OLD SCHOOL LIKE?
1-B
OH YEAH? AN ALL BOY SCHOOL?
AND EVERYONE LIVED TOGETHER IN A DORM?
OHMIGOSH, THAT SOUNDS AWESOME!
食券 TICKET VENDER

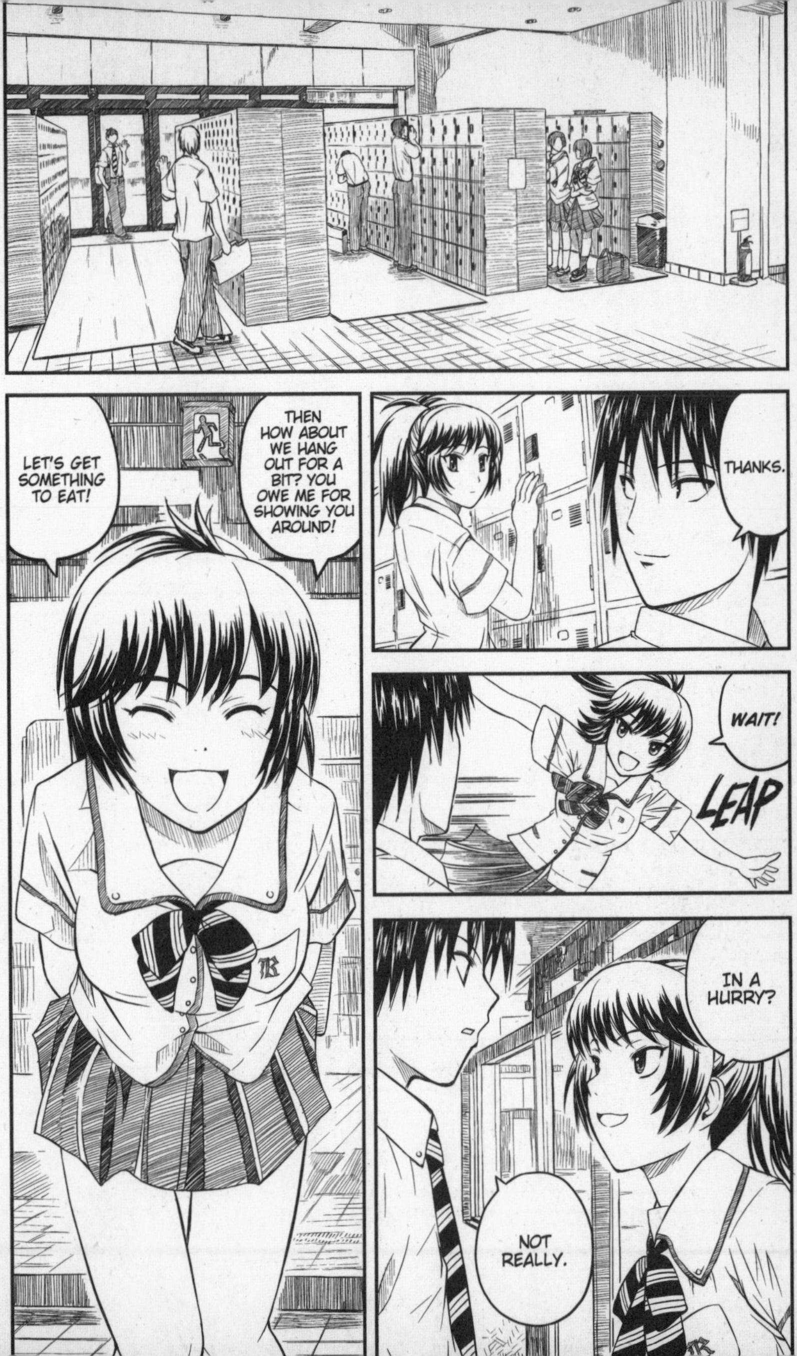
THANKS.
WAIT!
LEAP
IN A HURRY?
NOT REALLY.
THEN HOW ABOUT WE HANG OUT FOR A BIT? YOU OWE ME FOR SHOWING YOU AROUND!
LET'S GET SOMETHING TO EAT!

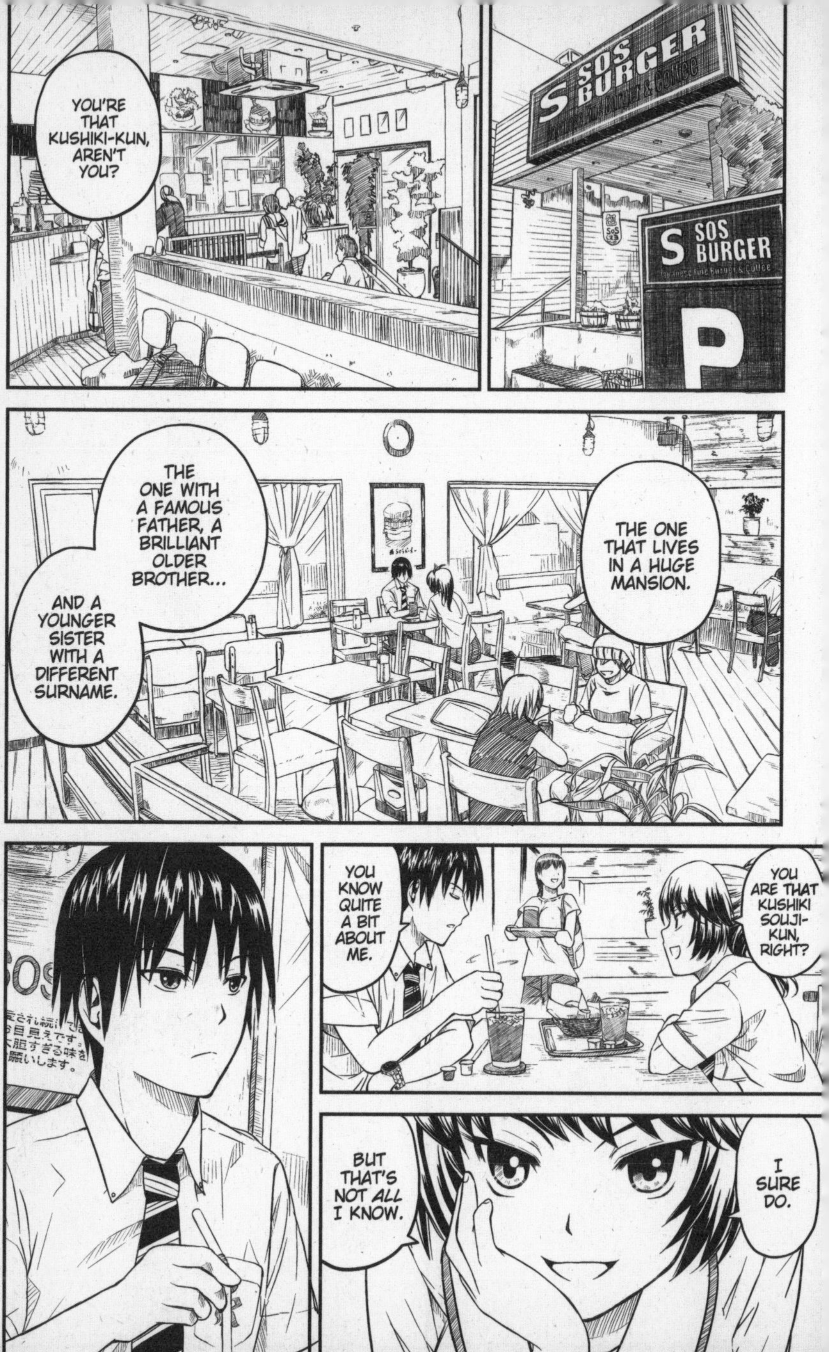
SOS BURGER
SOS BURGER
Japanese Fine Burger & Coffee
P
YOU'RE THAT KUSHIKI-KUN, AREN'T YOU?
THE ONE THAT LIVES IN A HUGE MANSION.
THE ONE WITH A FAMOUS FATHER, A BRILLIANT OLDER BROTHER...
AND A YOUNGER SISTER WITH A DIFFERENT SURNAME.
YOU ARE THAT KUSHIKI SOUJI-KUN, RIGHT?
YOU KNOW QUITE A BIT ABOUT ME.
I SURE DO.
BUT THAT'S NOT *ALL* I KNOW.

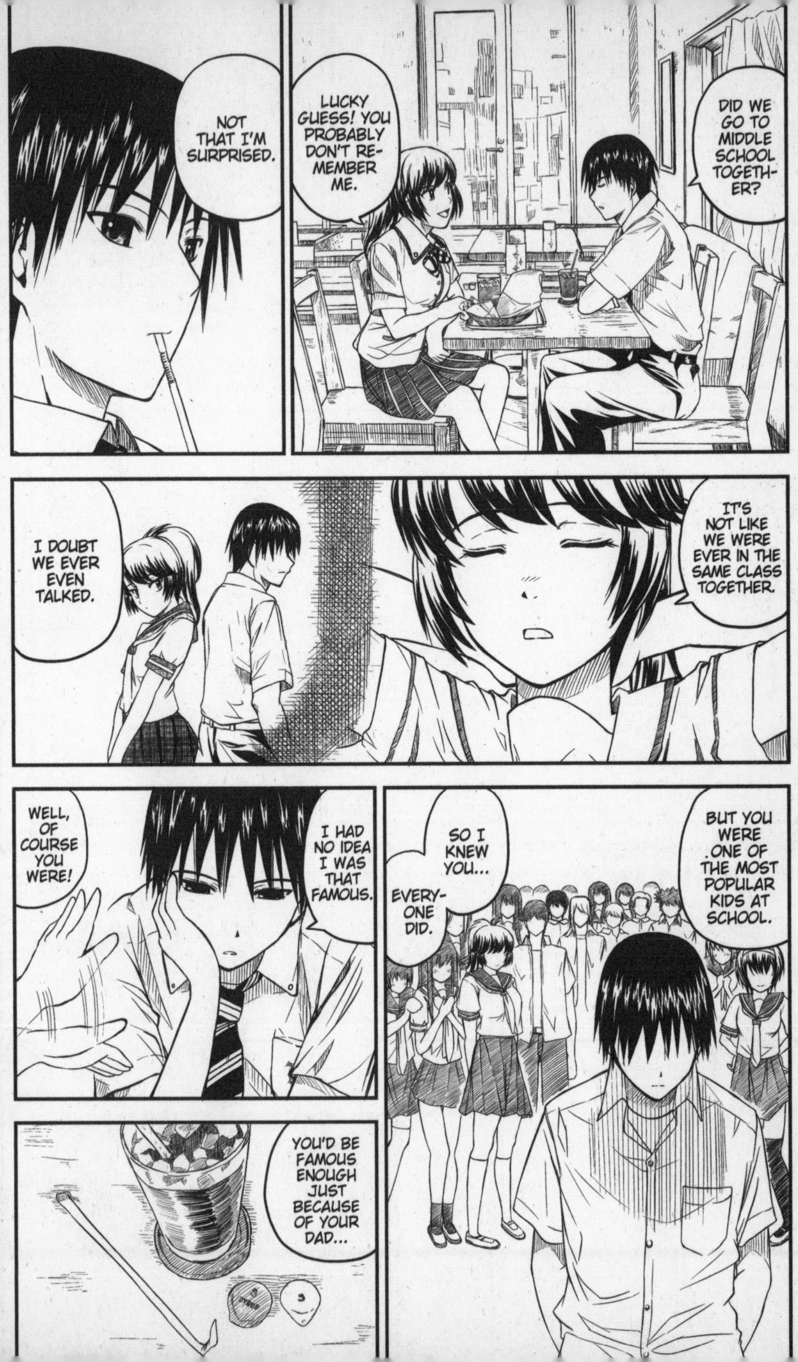
DID WE GO TO MIDDLE SCHOOL TOGETHER?
LUCKY GUESS! YOU PROBABLY DON'T REMEMBER ME.
NOT THAT I'M SURPRISED.
IT'S NOT LIKE WE WERE EVER IN THE SAME CLASS TOGETHER.
I DOUBT WE EVER EVEN TALKED.
BUT YOU WERE ONE OF THE MOST POPULAR KIDS AT SCHOOL.
SO I KNEW YOU...
EVERYONE DID.
I HAD NO IDEA I WAS THAT FAMOUS.
WELL, OF COURSE YOU WERE!
YOU'D BE FAMOUS ENOUGH JUST BECAUSE OF YOUR DAD...

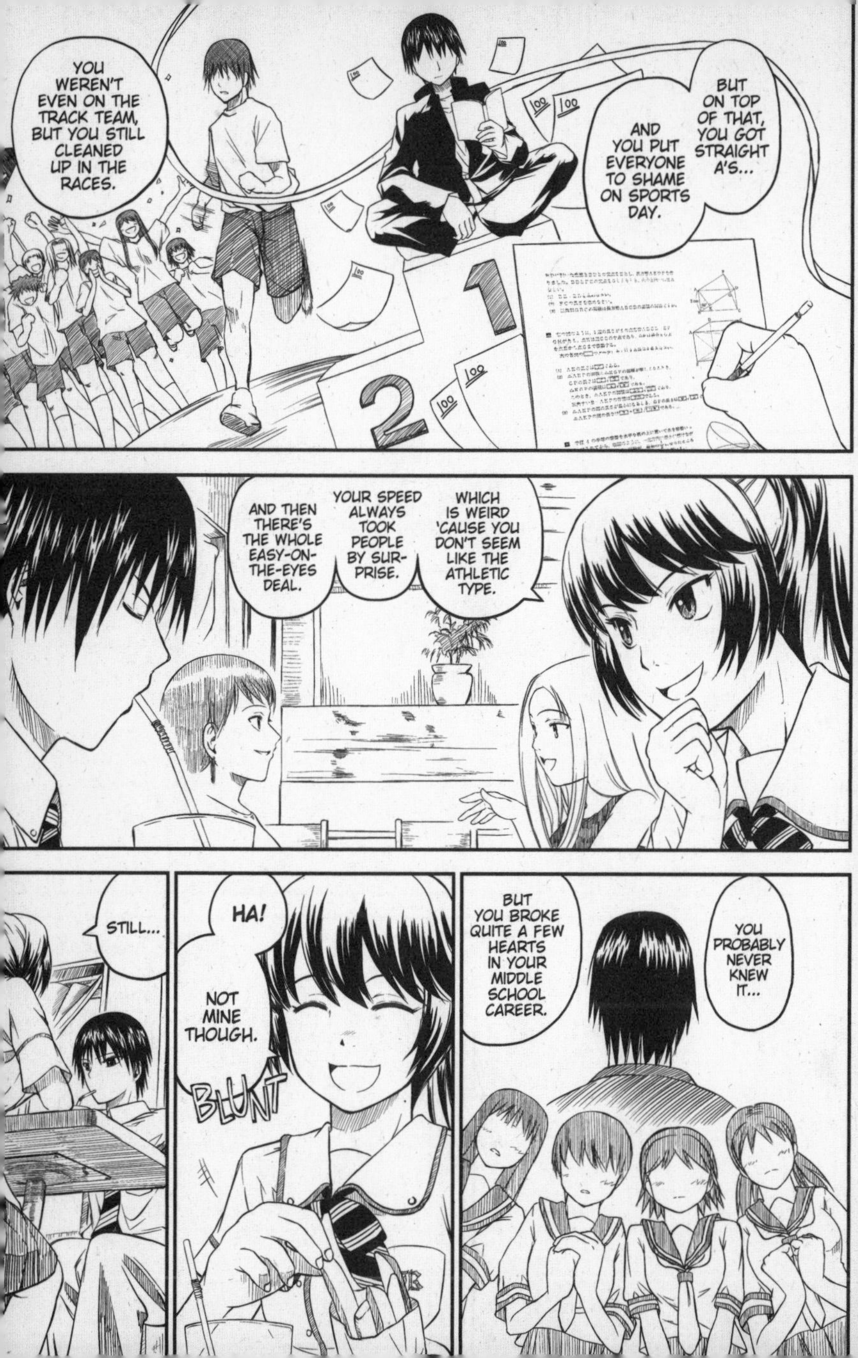
BUT ON TOP OF THAT, YOU GOT STRAIGHT A'S...
AND YOU PUT EVERYONE TO SHAME ON SPORTS DAY.
YOU WEREN'T EVEN ON THE TRACK TEAM, BUT YOU STILL CLEANED UP IN THE RACES.
WHICH IS WEIRD 'CAUSE YOU DON'T SEEM LIKE THE ATHLETIC TYPE.
YOUR SPEED ALWAYS TOOK PEOPLE BY SUR-PRISE.
AND THEN THERE'S THE WHOLE EASY-ON-THE-EYES DEAL.
YOU PROBABLY NEVER KNEW IT...
BUT YOU BROKE QUITE A FEW HEARTS IN YOUR MIDDLE SCHOOL CAREER.
HA!
NOT MINE THOUGH.
BLUNT
STILL...

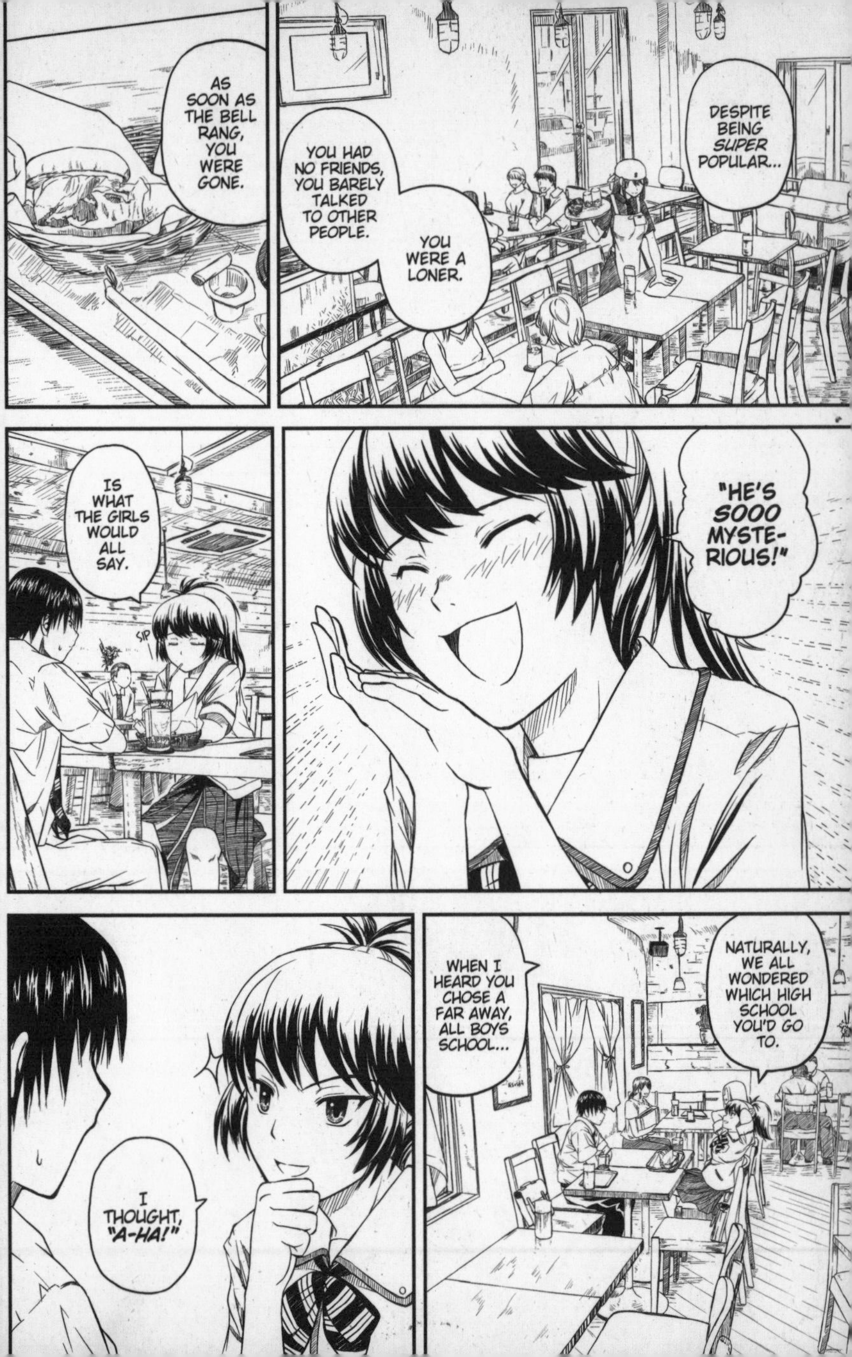
DESPITE BEING SUPER POPULAR...
YOU HAD NO FRIENDS, YOU BARELY TALKED TO OTHER PEOPLE.
YOU WERE A LONER.
AS SOON AS THE BELL RANG, YOU WERE GONE.
"HE'S SOOO MYSTERIOUS!"
IS WHAT THE GIRLS WOULD ALL SAY.
SIP
NATURALLY, WE ALL WONDERED WHICH HIGH SCHOOL YOU'D GO TO.
WHEN I HEARD YOU CHOSE A FAR AWAY, ALL BOYS SCHOOL...
I THOUGHT, "A-HA!"

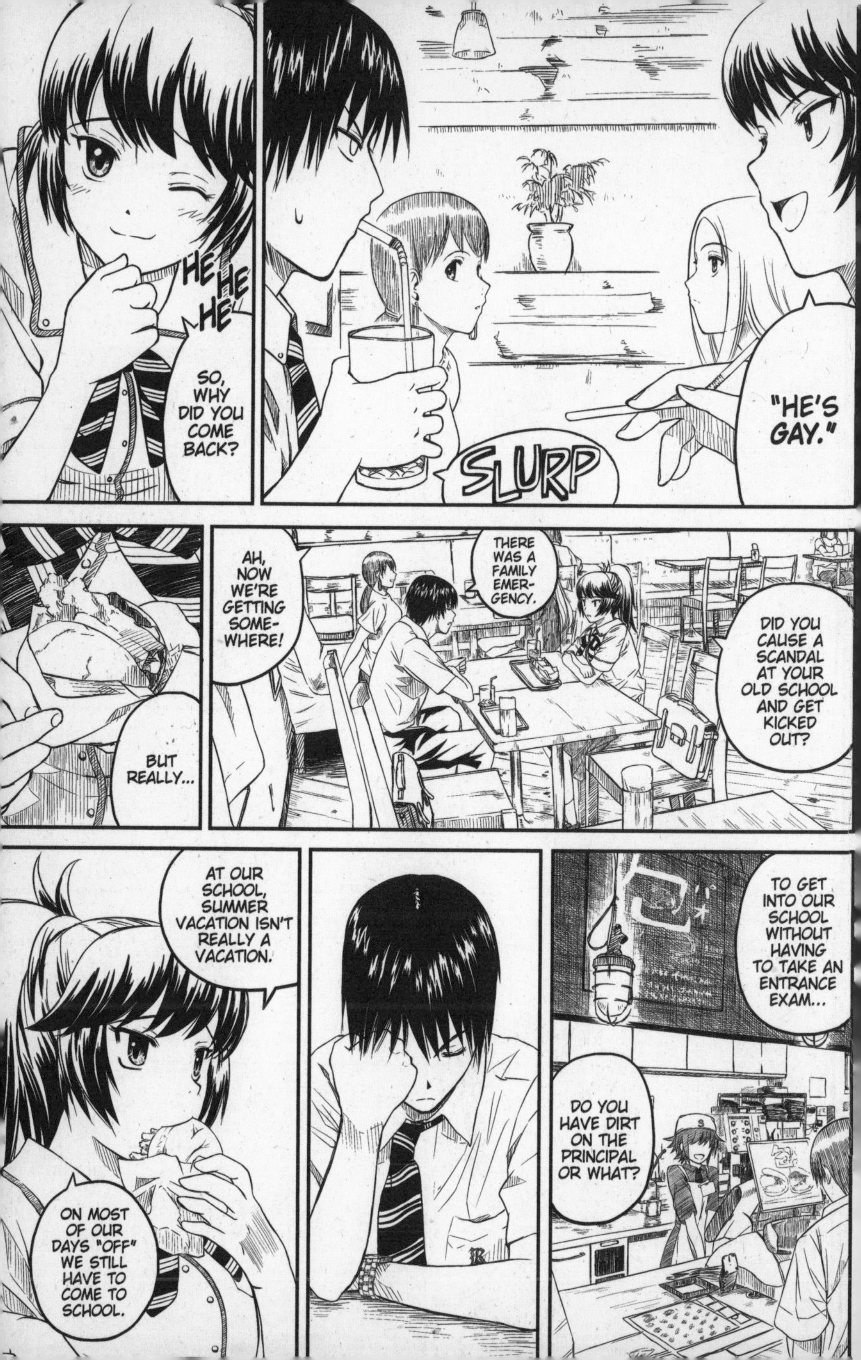
"HE'S GAY."
SLURP
HE HE HE
SO, WHY DID YOU COME BACK?
DID YOU CAUSE A SCANDAL AT YOUR OLD SCHOOL AND GET KICKED OUT?
THERE WAS A FAMILY EMERGENCY.
AH, NOW WE'RE GETTING SOME-WHERE!
BUT REALLY...
TO GET INTO OUR SCHOOL WITHOUT HAVING TO TAKE AN ENTRANCE EXAM...
DO YOU HAVE DIRT ON THE PRINCIPAL OR WHAT?
AT OUR SCHOOL, SUMMER VACATION ISN'T REALLY A VACATION.
ON MOST OF OUR DAYS "OFF" WE STILL HAVE TO COME TO SCHOOL.

YOU KNOW, PEOPLE ARE ALREADY TALKING ABOUT YOU.

THEY'RE AMONG THE TOP IN THE NATION.

YOUR GRADES...

AND I GET WHY.

成績優秀者

回北進テスト
月15日実施)

3科			
1位 115点		辰 怜	346
音町 一臣	360	内田 幸兵	333
		宮野 太志	308
2位 114点		佐藤 博上	351
入江 宏益	337	※宮坐 親子	346
※土田 音江	366	※石橋 礼羅	350
		※高部 砂芋	337
櫛木 宗次	370	石倉 勇基	329
		57位 112点	
※益田 乃々	339	水無瀬 一雄	304
		※鳥崎 万理	322
6位 112点		※熊田 二月	317
伊藤 尚	331	坂東 矢祖輔	29
矢口 敏郎	329	松岡 信彦	260
※葉丹 寿子	345	雨宮 清華	309
※外園 美樹	351	※若林 小太郎	3
※美里 オリザ	341	※亀本 由紀	310
古城		※森中 真央	319

THOSE MOCK EXAMS?

YOU KNOW HOW EXAM COMPANIES HAVE THOSE TESTS YOU TAKE AT SCHOOL...

WELL, YOUR OLD SCHOOL AND THIS ONE...

USE THE SAME COMPANY'S TEST.

AND AFTER A FEW WEEKS, WE GET THIS MASS LIST WITH THE RESULTS.

YOUR NAME IS ALWAYS PRETTY HIGH UP.

SO YEAH, I GUESS I CAN SEE WHY THE SCHOOL WAIVED THE EXAM FOR YOU.

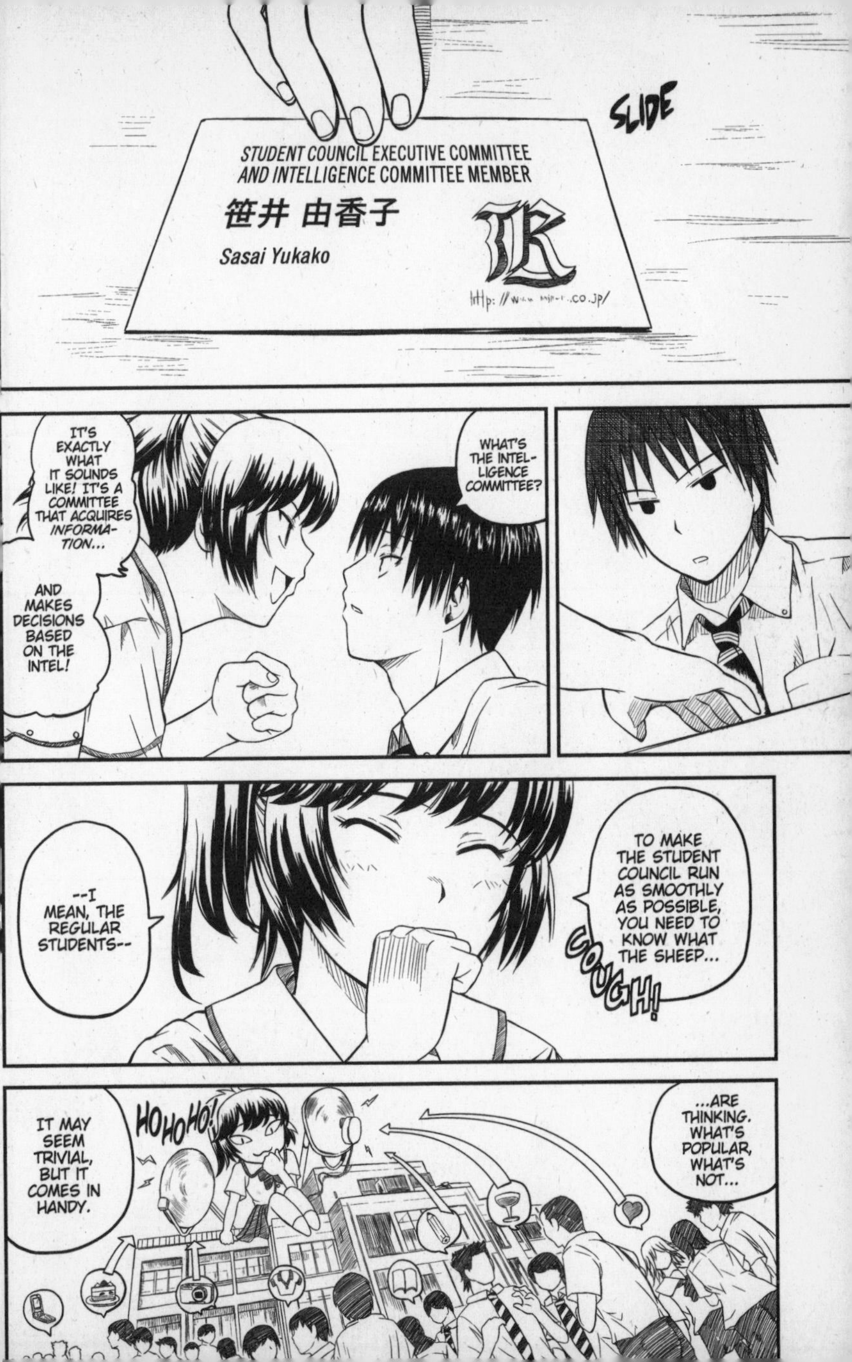
SLIDE
STUDENT COUNCIL EXECUTIVE COMMITTEE
AND INTELLIGENCE COMMITTEE MEMBER
笹井 由香子
Sasai Yukako
WHAT'S THE INTEL-LIGENCE COMMITTEE?
IT'S EXACTLY WHAT IT SOUNDS LIKE! IT'S A COMMITTEE THAT ACQUIRES *INFORMATION*...
AND MAKES DECISIONS BASED ON THE INTEL!
TO MAKE THE STUDENT COUNCIL RUN AS SMOOTHLY AS POSSIBLE, YOU NEED TO KNOW WHAT THE SHEEP...
COUGH!
--I MEAN, THE REGULAR STUDENTS--
...ARE THINKING. WHAT'S POPULAR, WHAT'S NOT...
HOHOHO!
IT MAY SEEM TRIVIAL, BUT IT COMES IN HANDY.

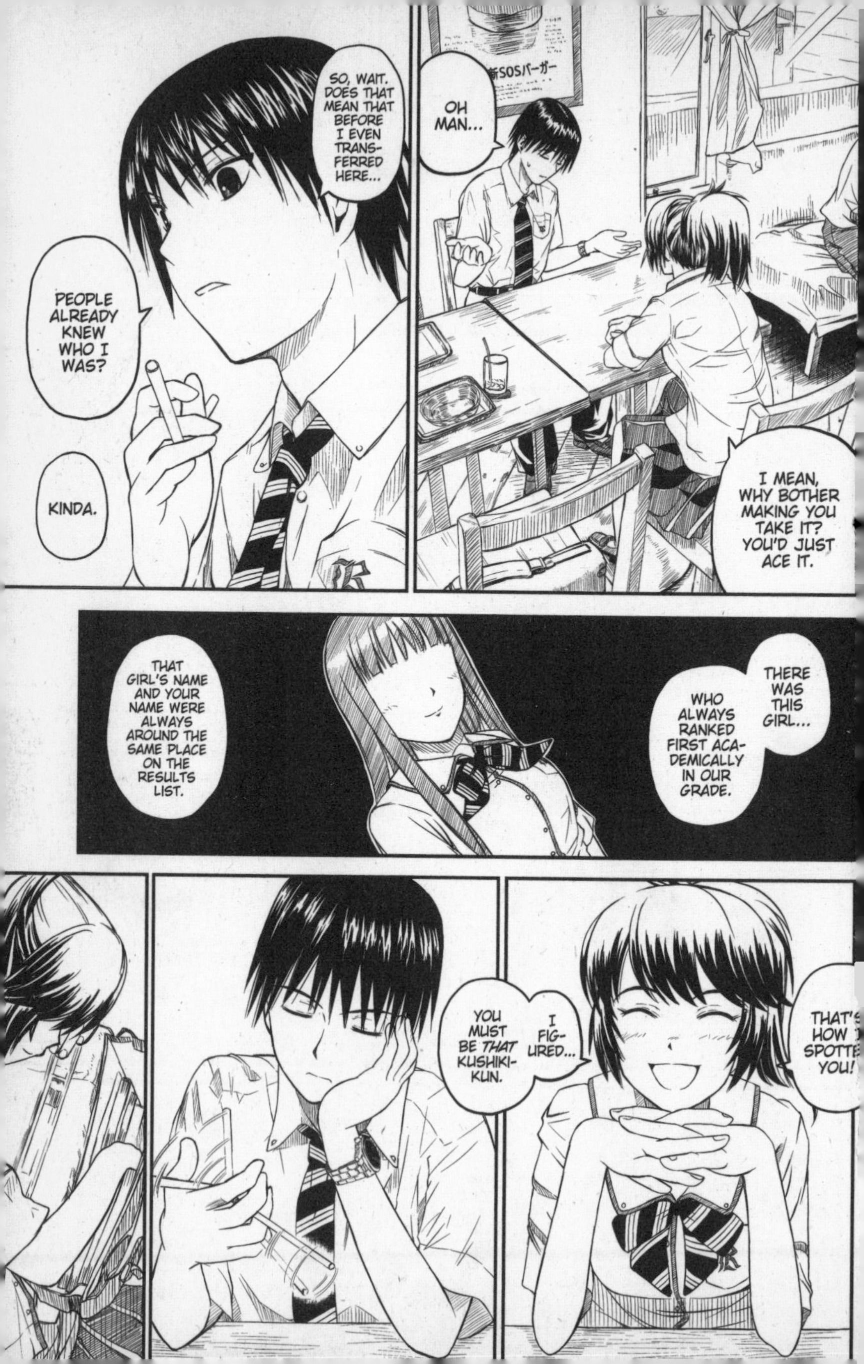

新SOSバーガー
OH MAN...
I MEAN, WHY BOTHER MAKING YOU TAKE IT? YOU'D JUST ACE IT.
SO, WAIT. DOES THAT MEAN THAT BEFORE I EVEN TRANS-FERRED HERE...
PEOPLE ALREADY KNEW WHO I WAS?
KINDA.
THERE WAS THIS GIRL...
WHO ALWAYS RANKED FIRST ACA-DEMICALLY IN OUR GRADE.
THAT GIRL'S NAME AND YOUR NAME WERE ALWAYS AROUND THE SAME PLACE ON THE RESULTS LIST.
THAT'S HOW I SPOTTE YOU!
I FIG-URED...
YOU MUST BE *THAT* KUSHIKI-KUN.

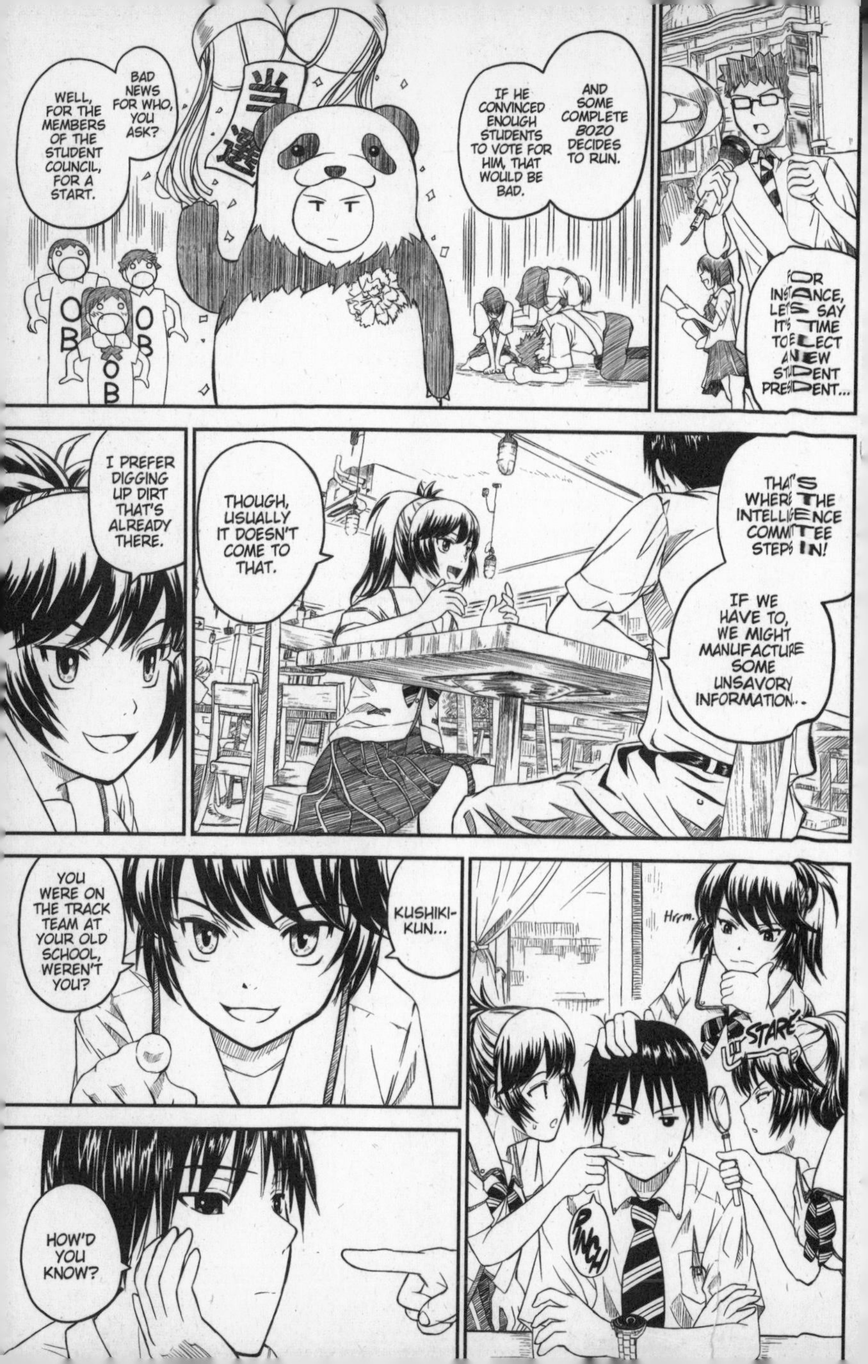
FOR INSTANCE, LET'S SAY IT'S TIME TO ELECT A NEW STUDENT PRESIDENT...
AND SOME COMPLETE BOZO DECIDES TO RUN.
IF HE CONVINCED ENOUGH STUDENTS TO VOTE FOR HIM, THAT WOULD BE BAD.
BAD NEWS FOR WHO, YOU ASK?
WELL, FOR THE MEMBERS OF THE STUDENT COUNCIL, FOR A START.
当選
OB
OB
OB
THAT'S WHERE THE INTELLIGENCE COMMITTEE STEPS IN!
IF WE HAVE TO, WE MIGHT MANUFACTURE SOME UNSAVORY INFORMATION...
THOUGH, USUALLY IT DOESN'T COME TO THAT.
I PREFER DIGGING UP DIRT THAT'S ALREADY THERE.
Hrrm.
STARE
PINCH
KUSHIKI-KUN...
YOU WERE ON THE TRACK TEAM AT YOUR OLD SCHOOL, WEREN'T YOU?
HOW'D YOU KNOW?

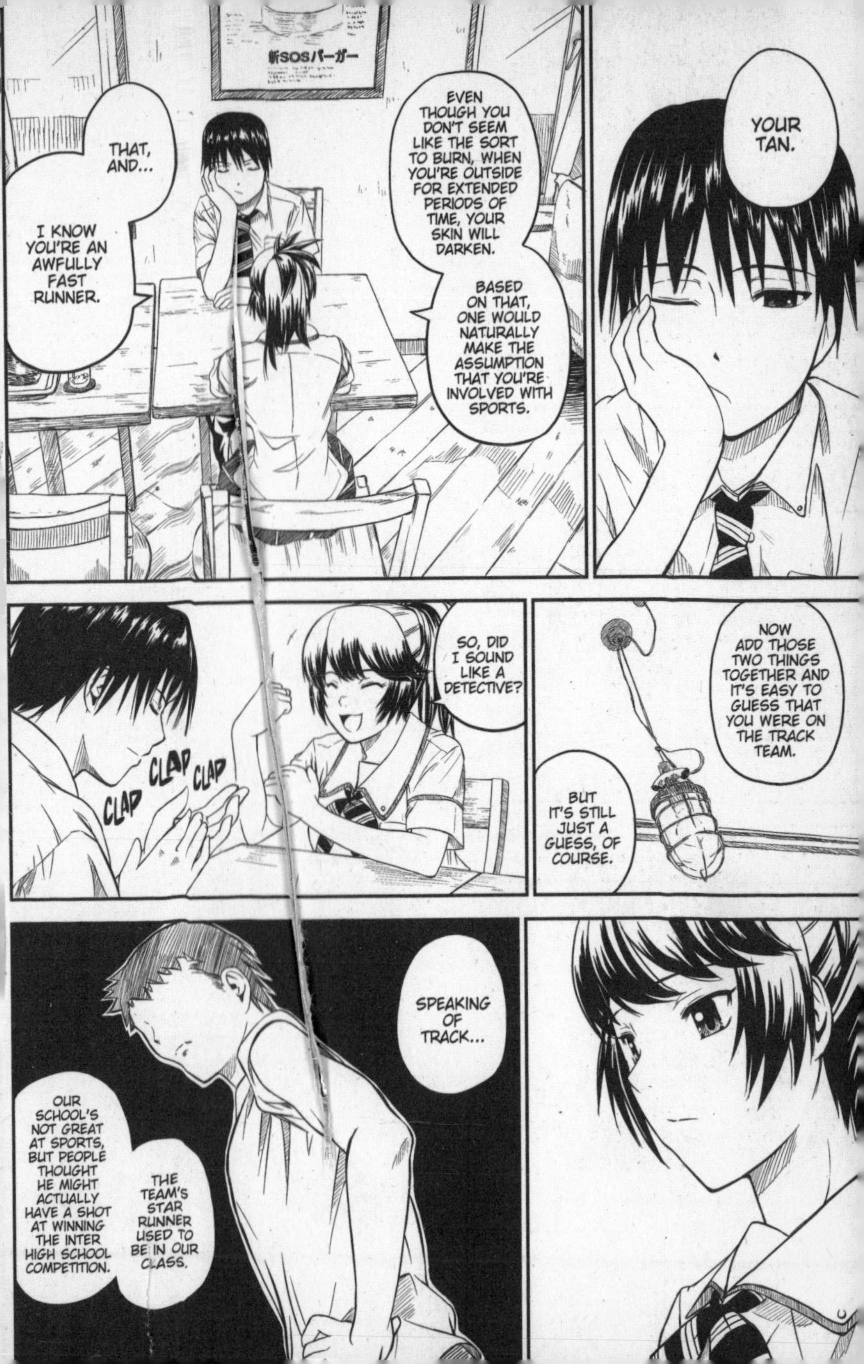
YOUR TAN.
新SOSバーガー
EVEN THOUGH YOU DON'T SEEM LIKE THE SORT TO BURN, WHEN YOU'RE OUTSIDE FOR EXTENDED PERIODS OF TIME, YOUR SKIN WILL DARKEN.
BASED ON THAT, ONE WOULD NATURALLY MAKE THE ASSUMPTION THAT YOU'RE INVOLVED WITH SPORTS.
THAT, AND...
I KNOW YOU'RE AN AWFULLY FAST RUNNER.
NOW ADD THOSE TWO THINGS TOGETHER AND IT'S EASY TO GUESS THAT YOU WERE ON THE TRACK TEAM.
BUT IT'S STILL JUST A GUESS, OF COURSE.
SO, DID I SOUND LIKE A DETECTIVE?
CLAP
CLAP
CLAP
SPEAKING OF TRACK...
THE TEAM'S STAR RUNNER USED TO BE IN OUR CLASS.
OUR SCHOOL'S NOT GREAT AT SPORTS, BUT PEOPLE THOUGHT HE MIGHT ACTUALLY HAVE A SHOT AT WINNING THE INTER HIGH SCHOOL COMPETITION.

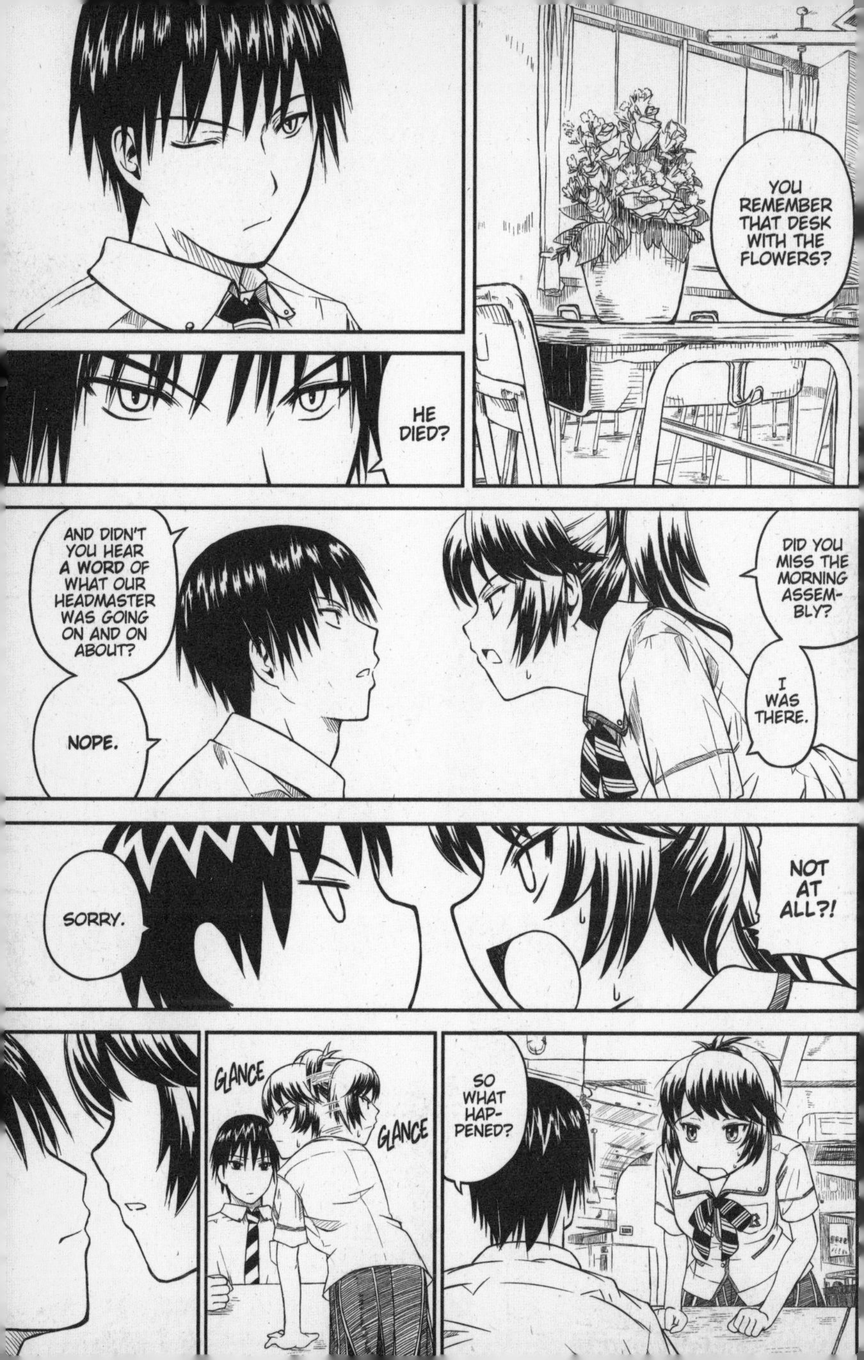
YOU REMEMBER THAT DESK WITH THE FLOWERS?
HE DIED?
DID YOU MISS THE MORNING ASSEM-BLY?
I WAS THERE.
AND DIDN'T YOU HEAR A WORD OF WHAT OUR HEADMASTER WAS GOING ON AND ON ABOUT?
NOPE.
NOT AT ALL?!
SORRY.
SO WHAT HAP-PENED?
GLANCE
GLANCE

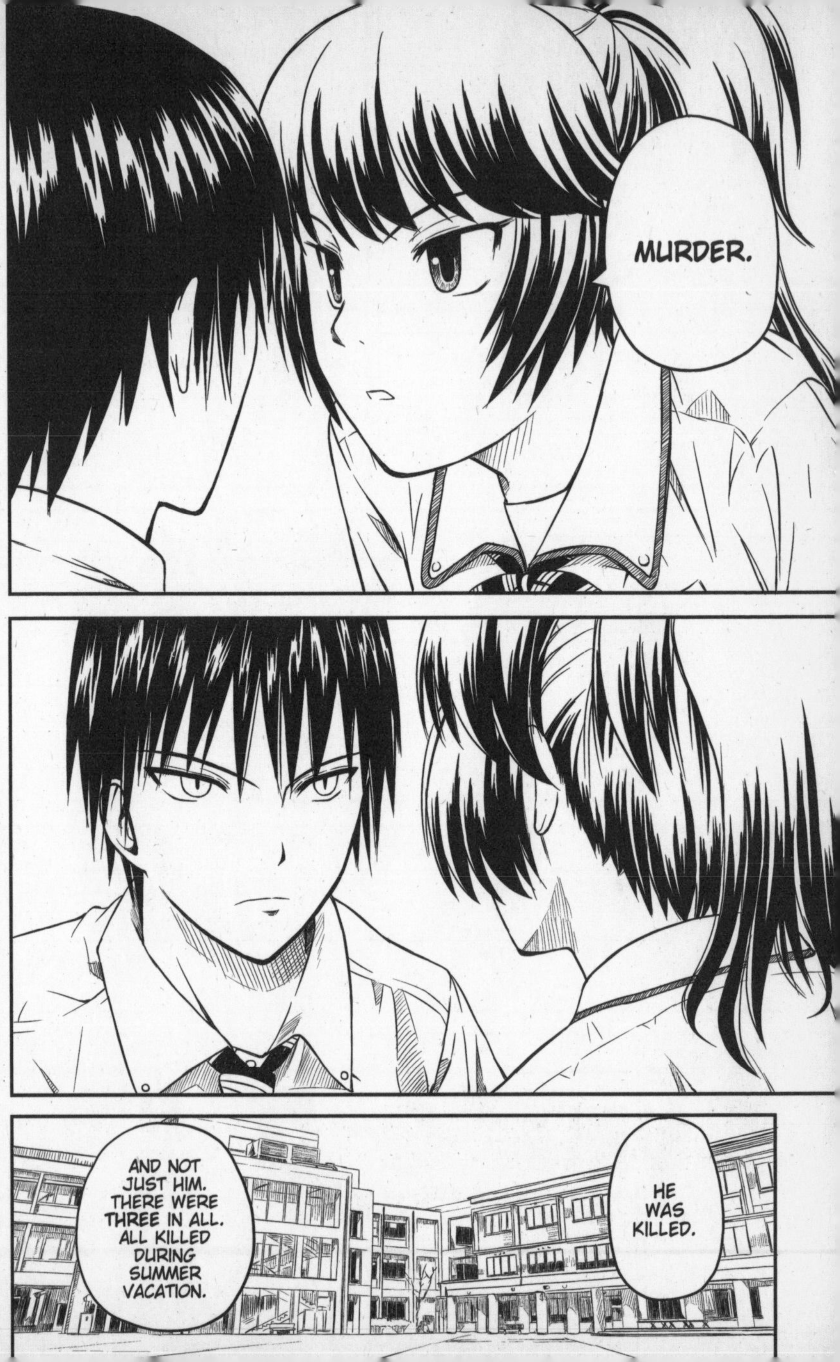
MURDER.
HE WAS KILLED.
AND NOT JUST HIM. THERE WERE THREE IN ALL. ALL KILLED DURING SUMMER VACATION.

AMNESIA
LABYRINTH

Amnesia Labyrinth CHARACTER FILE 1

KUSHIKI YOUKO

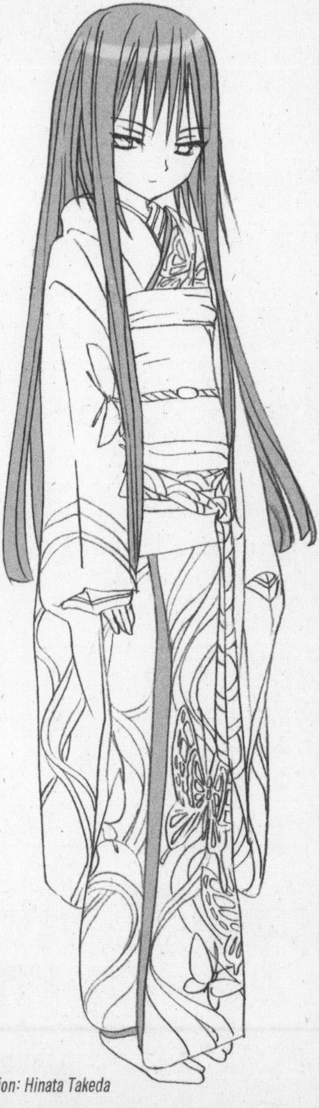

The oldest daughter of the Kushiki Household, she's also Souji's full-blood younger sister. The mysterious beauty of her faint smile hides her true emotions. She has feelings for Souji far beyond what is normal for a younger sister, and toys with him using affected speech and warped actions.

Illustration: Hinata Takeda

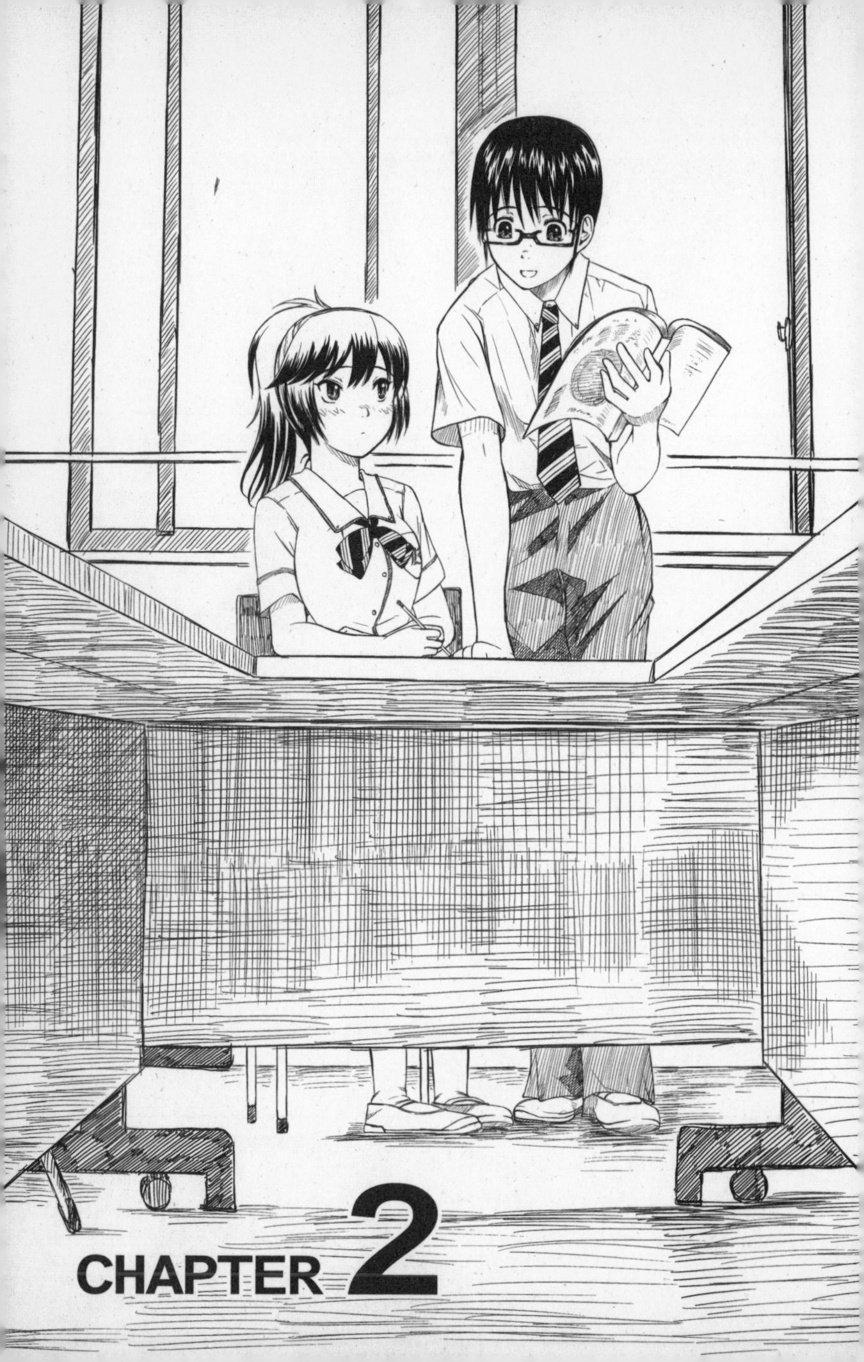
CHAPTER 2

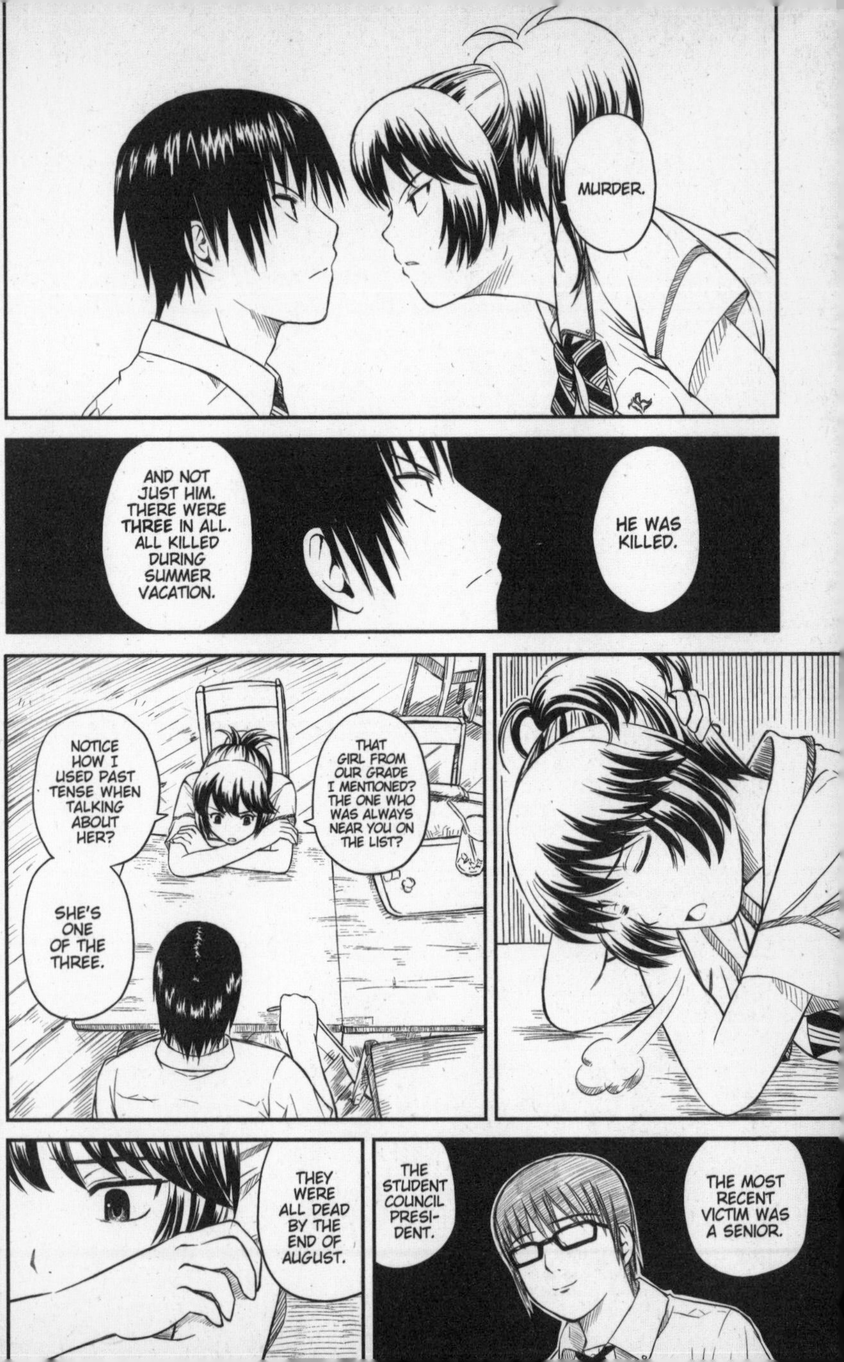
MURDER.
HE WAS KILLED.
AND NOT JUST HIM. THERE WERE THREE IN ALL. ALL KILLED DURING SUMMER VACATION.
THAT GIRL FROM OUR GRADE I MENTIONED? THE ONE WHO WAS ALWAYS NEAR YOU ON THE LIST?
NOTICE HOW I USED PAST TENSE WHEN TALKING ABOUT HER?
SHE'S ONE OF THE THREE.
THE MOST RECENT VICTIM WAS A SENIOR.
THE STUDENT COUNCIL PRESI-DENT.
THEY WERE ALL DEAD BY THE END OF AUGUST.

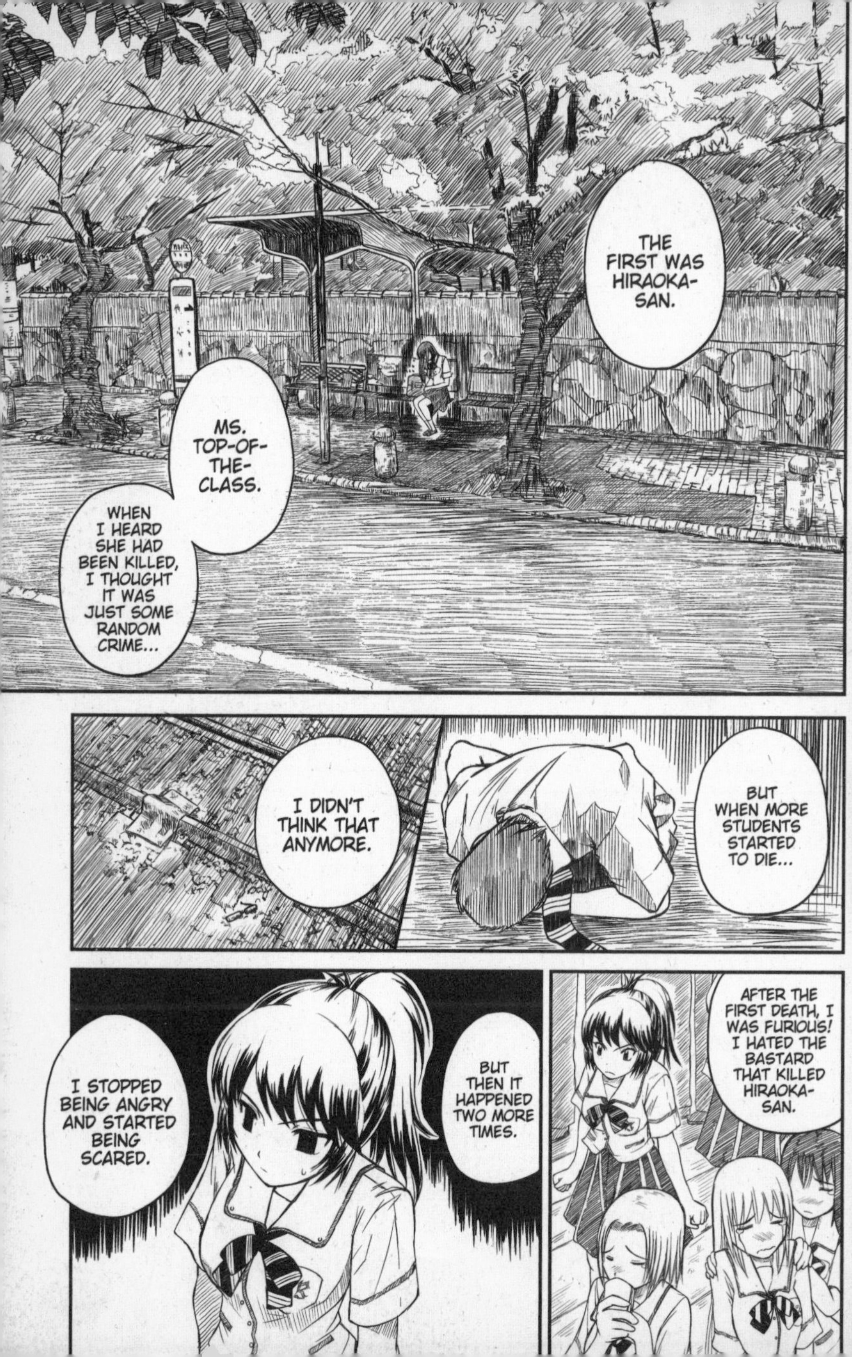
THE FIRST WAS HIRAOKA-SAN.
MS. TOP-OF-THE-CLASS.
WHEN I HEARD SHE HAD BEEN KILLED, I THOUGHT IT WAS JUST SOME RANDOM CRIME...
BUT WHEN MORE STUDENTS STARTED TO DIE...
I DIDN'T THINK THAT ANYMORE.
AFTER THE FIRST DEATH, I WAS FURIOUS! I HATED THE BASTARD THAT KILLED HIRAOKA-SAN.
BUT THEN IT HAPPENED TWO MORE TIMES.
I STOPPED BEING ANGRY AND STARTED BEING SCARED.

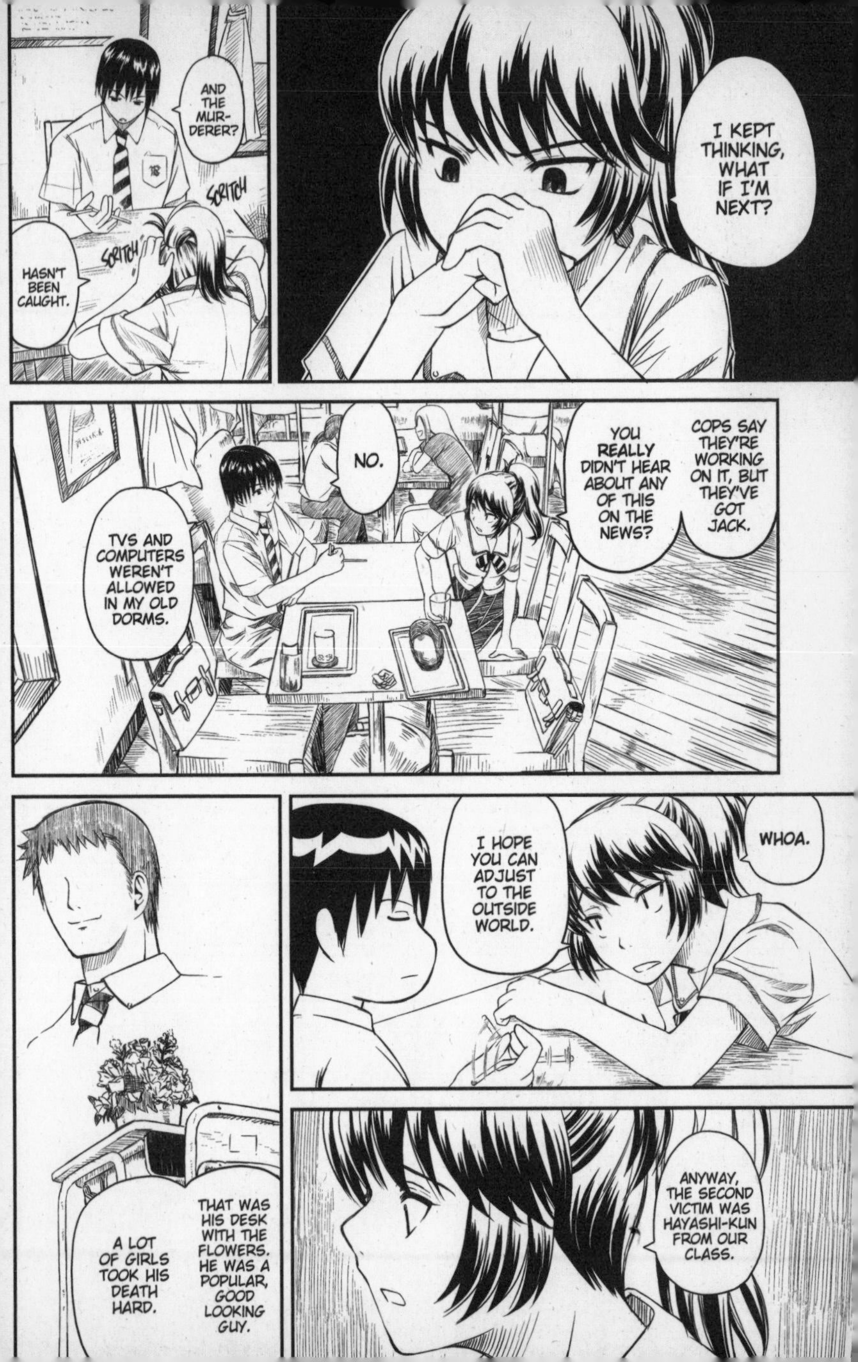
I KEPT THINKING, WHAT IF I'M NEXT?
AND THE MUR-DERER?
SCRITCH
SCRITCH
HASN'T BEEN CAUGHT.
COPS SAY THEY'RE WORKING ON IT, BUT THEY'VE GOT JACK.
YOU REALLY DIDN'T HEAR ABOUT ANY OF THIS ON THE NEWS?
NO.
TVS AND COMPUTERS WEREN'T ALLOWED IN MY OLD DORMS.
WHOA.
I HOPE YOU CAN ADJUST TO THE OUTSIDE WORLD.
ANYWAY, THE SECOND VICTIM WAS HAYASHI-KUN FROM OUR CLASS.
THAT WAS HIS DESK WITH THE FLOWERS. HE WAS A POPULAR, GOOD LOOKING GUY.
A LOT OF GIRLS TOOK HIS DEATH HARD.

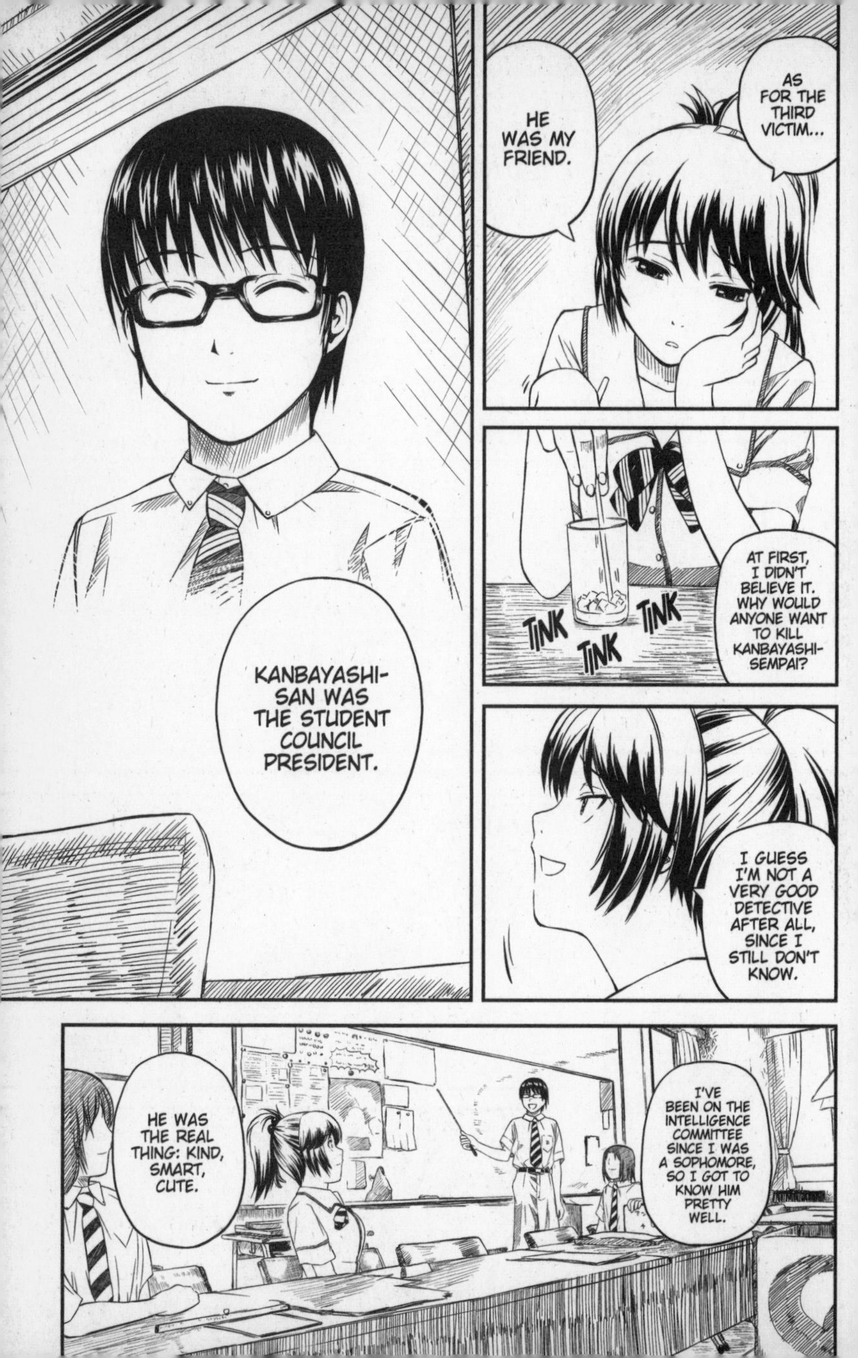
AS FOR THE THIRD VICTIM...
HE WAS MY FRIEND.
AT FIRST, I DIDN'T BELIEVE IT. WHY WOULD ANYONE WANT TO KILL KANBAYASHI-SEMPAI?
TINK
TINK
TINK
I GUESS I'M NOT A VERY GOOD DETECTIVE AFTER ALL, SINCE I STILL DON'T KNOW.
KANBAYASHI-SAN WAS THE STUDENT COUNCIL PRESIDENT.
I'VE BEEN ON THE INTELLIGENCE COMMITTEE SINCE I WAS A SOPHOMORE, SO I GOT TO KNOW HIM PRETTY WELL.
HE WAS THE REAL THING: KIND, SMART, CUTE.

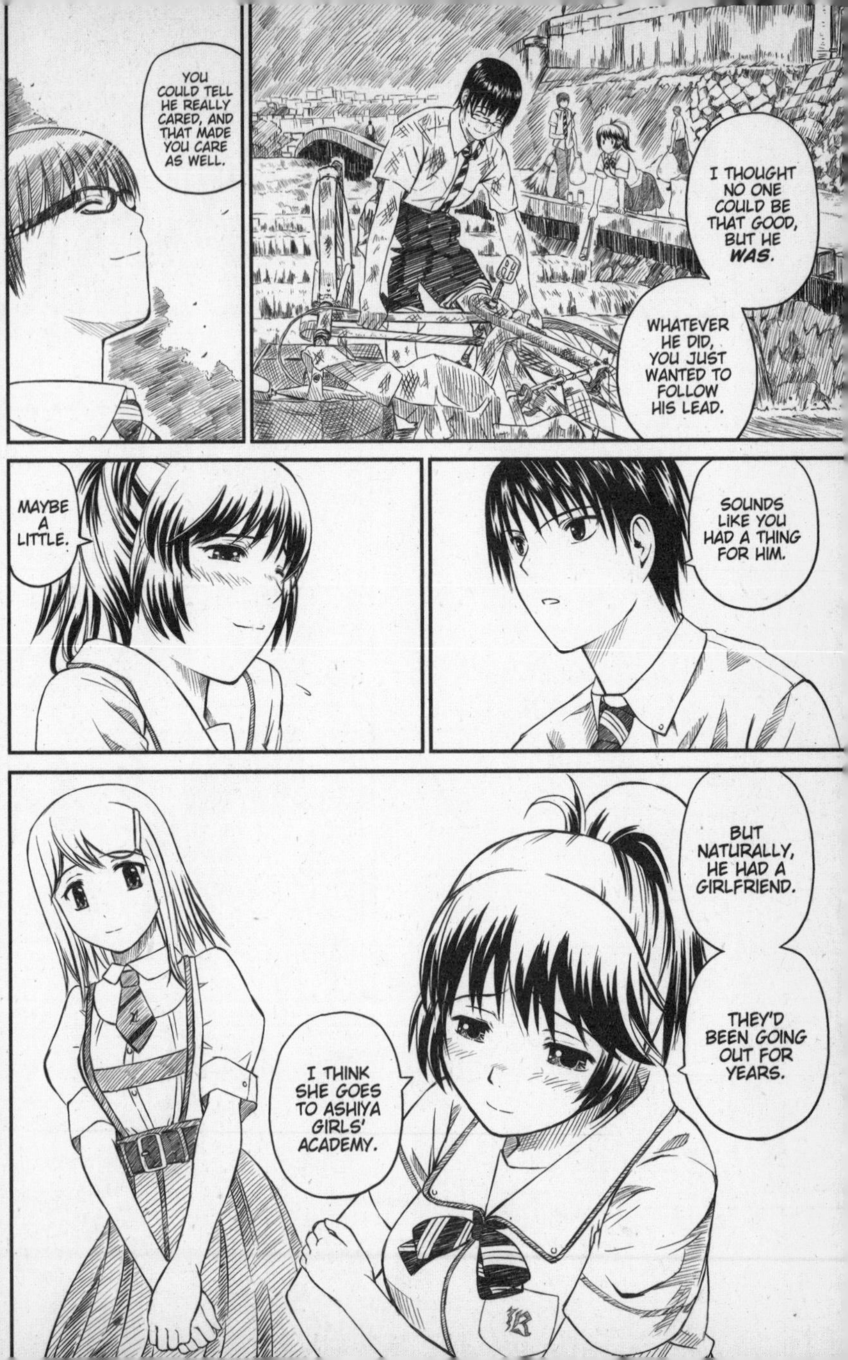
I THOUGHT NO ONE COULD BE THAT GOOD, BUT HE *WAS*.
WHATEVER HE DID, YOU JUST WANTED TO FOLLOW HIS LEAD.
YOU COULD TELL HE REALLY CARED, AND THAT MADE YOU CARE AS WELL.
SOUNDS LIKE YOU HAD A THING FOR HIM.
MAYBE A LITTLE.
BUT NATURALLY, HE HAD A GIRLFRIEND.
THEY'D BEEN GOING OUT FOR YEARS.
I THINK SHE GOES TO ASHIYA GIRLS' ACADEMY.

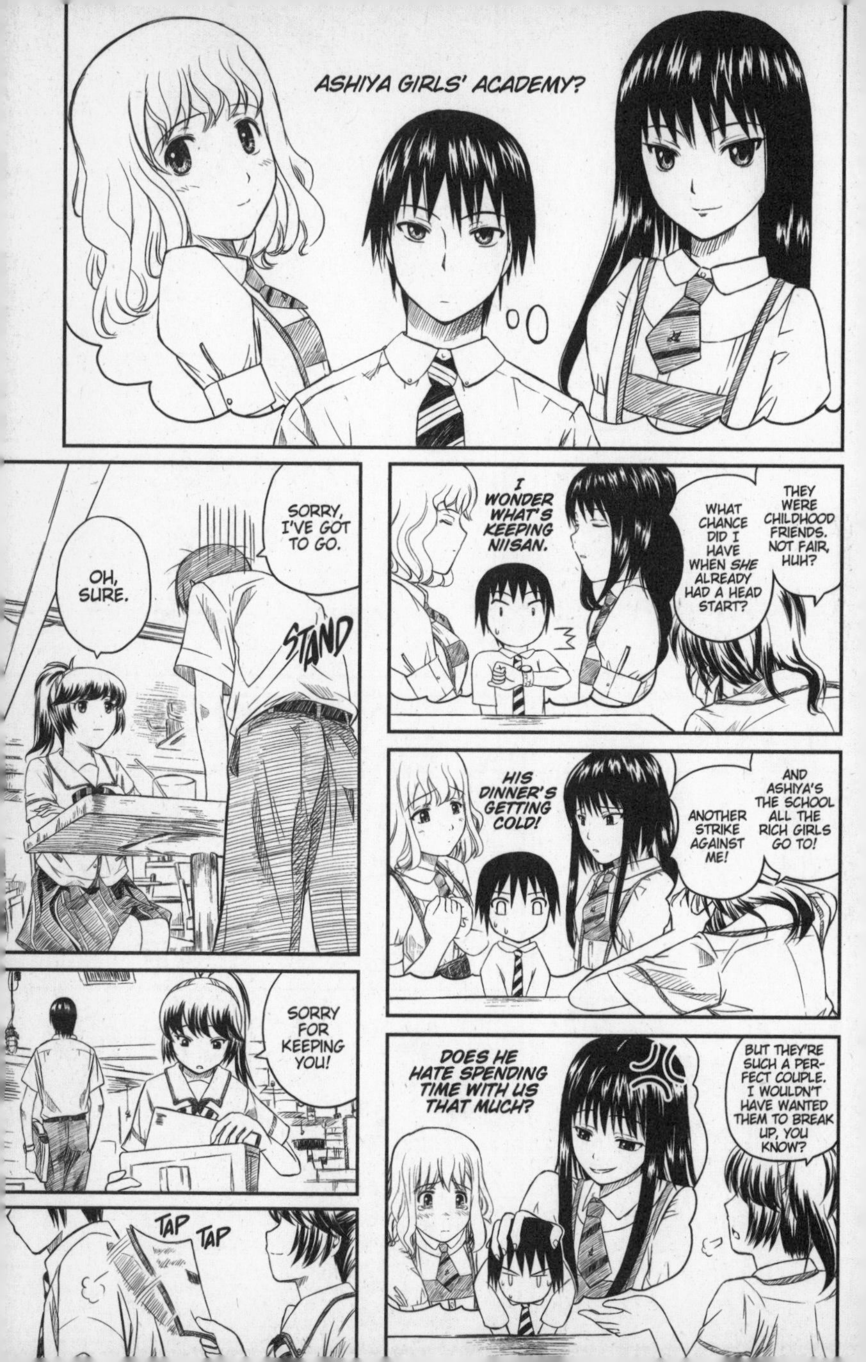
ASHIYA GIRLS' ACADEMY?
THEY WERE CHILDHOOD FRIENDS. NOT FAIR, HUH?
WHAT CHANCE DID I HAVE WHEN SHE ALREADY HAD A HEAD START?
I WONDER WHAT'S KEEPING NIISAN.
AND ASHIYA'S THE SCHOOL ALL THE RICH GIRLS GO TO!
ANOTHER STRIKE AGAINST ME!
HIS DINNER'S GETTING COLD!
BUT THEY'RE SUCH A PERFECT COUPLE. I WOULDN'T HAVE WANTED THEM TO BREAK UP, YOU KNOW?
DOES HE HATE SPENDING TIME WITH US THAT MUCH?
SORRY, I'VE GOT TO GO.
OH, SURE.
STAND
SORRY FOR KEEPING YOU!
TAP
TAP

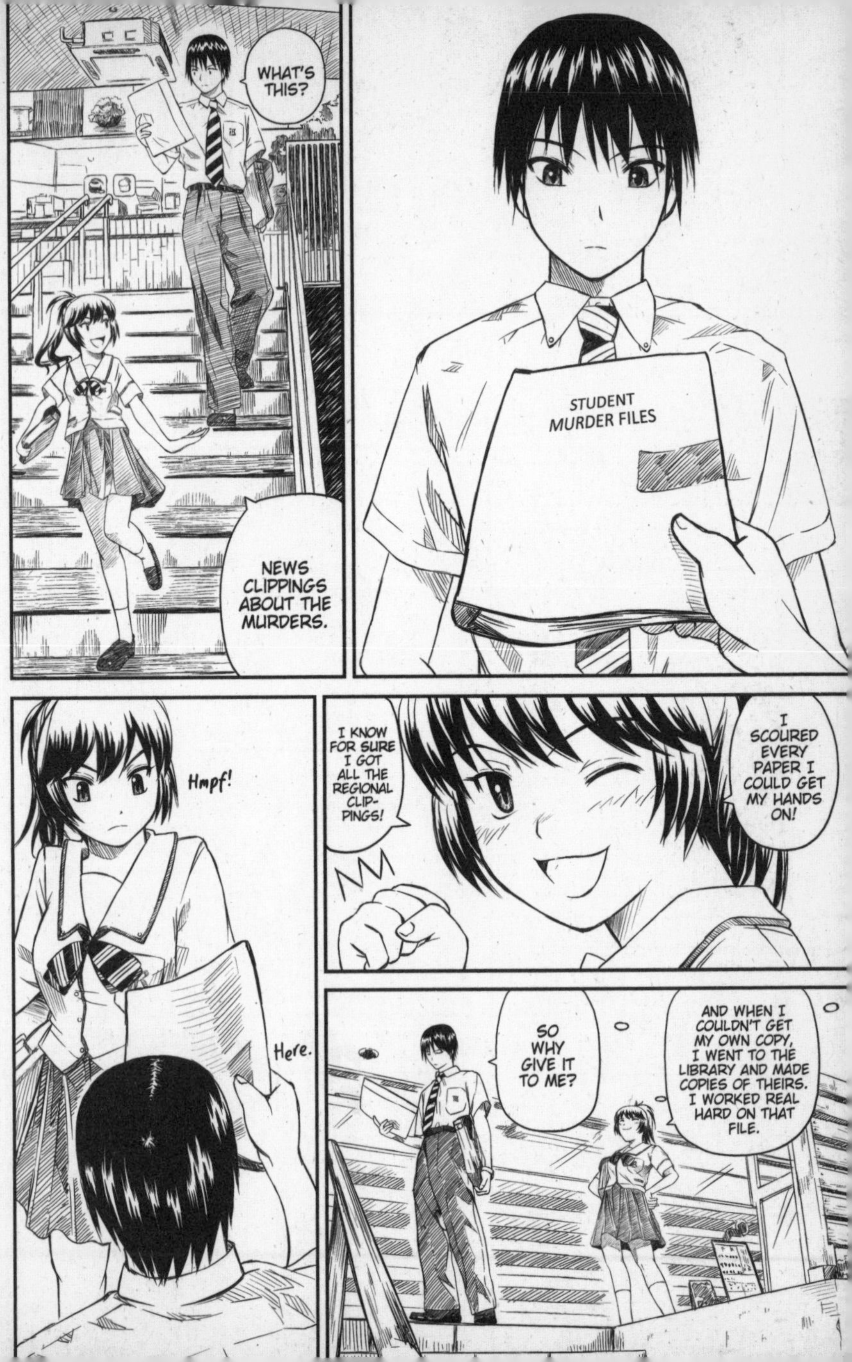
STUDENT MURDER FILES
WHAT'S THIS?
NEWS CLIPPINGS ABOUT THE MURDERS.
I SCOURED EVERY PAPER I COULD GET MY HANDS ON!
I KNOW FOR SURE I GOT ALL THE REGIONAL CLIP-PINGS!
AND WHEN I COULDN'T GET MY OWN COPY, I WENT TO THE LIBRARY AND MADE COPIES OF THEIRS. I WORKED REAL HARD ON THAT FILE.
SO WHY GIVE IT TO ME?
Hmpf!
Here.

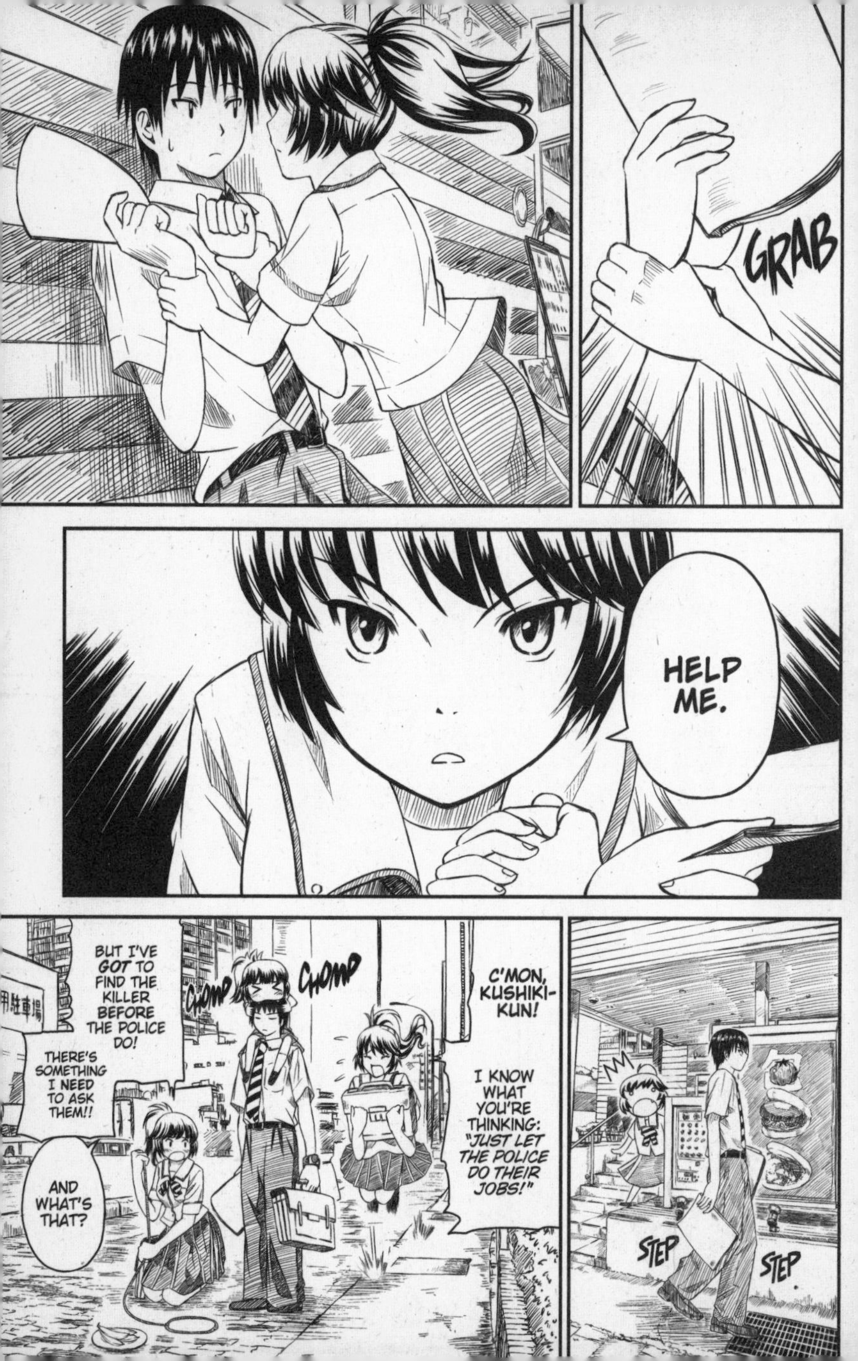
GRAB
HELP ME.
STEP
STEP
C'MON, KUSHIKI-KUN!
I KNOW WHAT YOU'RE THINKING: "JUST LET THE POLICE DO THEIR JOBS!"
CHOMP
CHOMP
BUT I'VE *GOT* TO FIND THE KILLER BEFORE THE POLICE DO!
THERE'S SOMETHING I NEED TO ASK THEM!!
AND WHAT'S THAT?

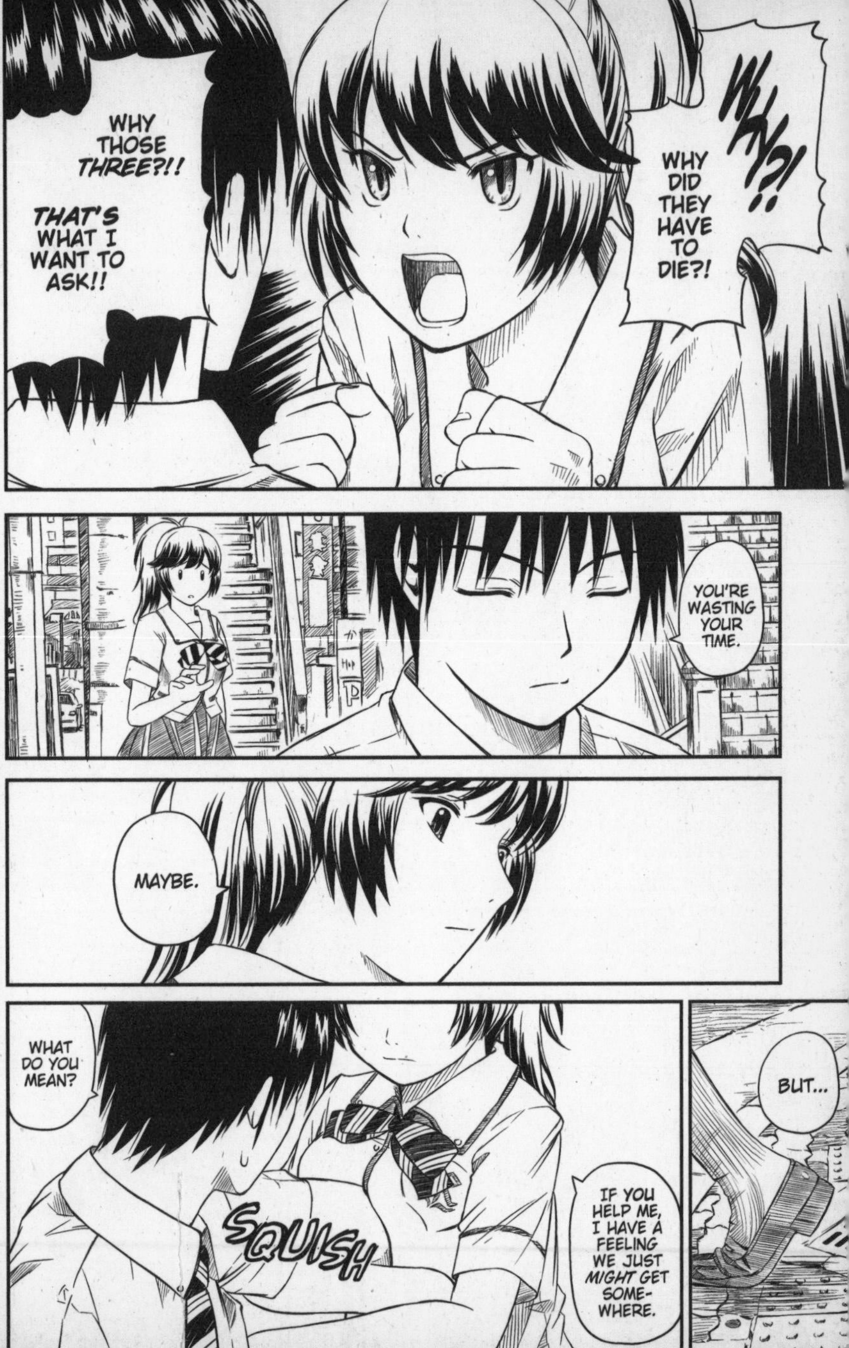
WHY?!!
WHY DID THEY HAVE TO DIE?!
WHY THOSE THREE?!!
THAT'S WHAT I WANT TO ASK!!
YOU'RE WASTING YOUR TIME.
MAYBE.
BUT...
WHAT DO YOU MEAN?
SQUISH
IF YOU HELP ME, I HAVE A FEELING WE JUST MIGHT GET SOME-WHERE.

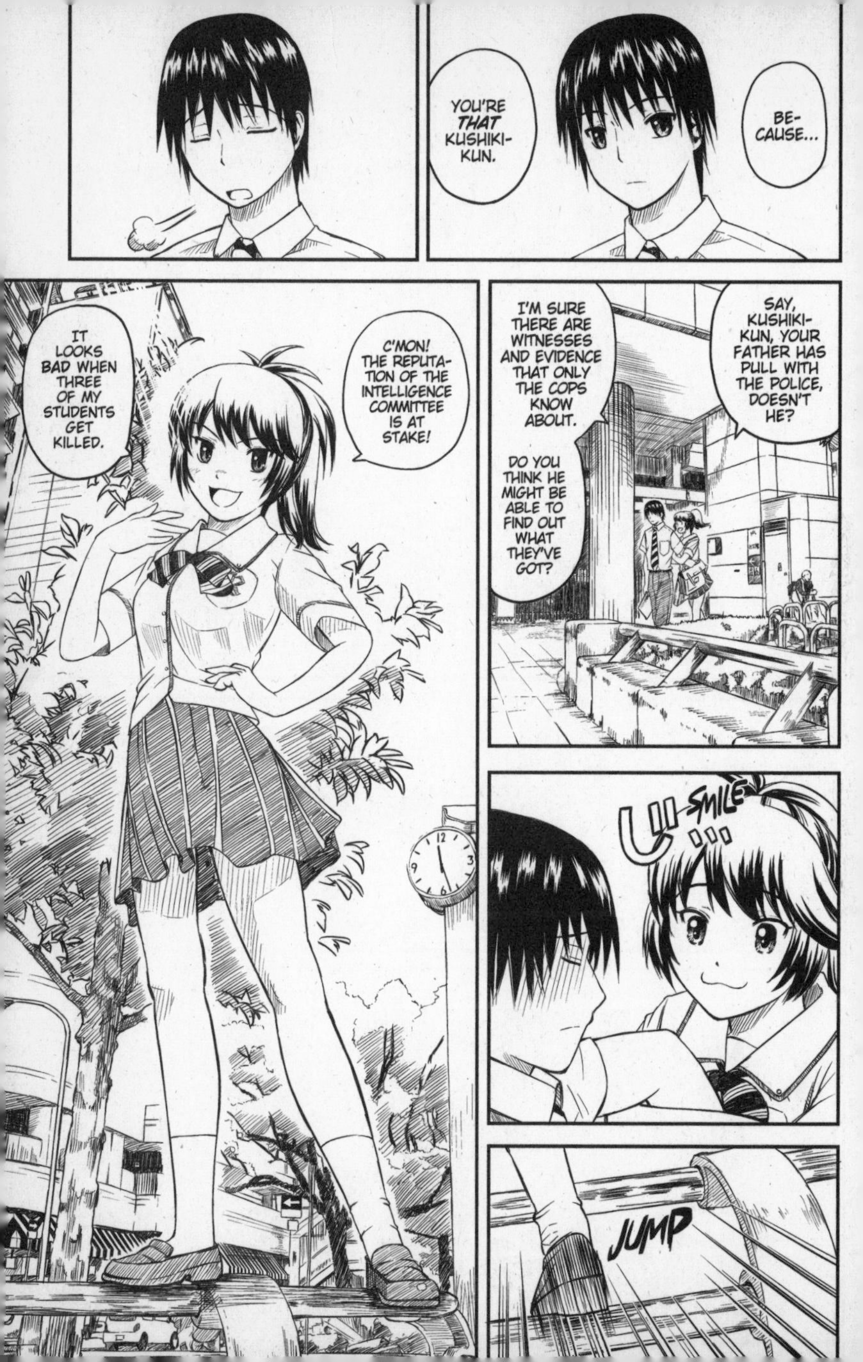

BE-CAUSE...
YOU'RE *THAT* KUSHIKI-KUN.
SAY, KUSHIKI-KUN, YOUR FATHER HAS PULL WITH THE POLICE, DOESN'T HE?
I'M SURE THERE ARE WITNESSES AND EVIDENCE THAT ONLY THE COPS KNOW ABOUT.
DO YOU THINK HE MIGHT BE ABLE TO FIND OUT WHAT THEY'VE GOT?
SMILE
...
JUMP
C'MON! THE REPUTATION OF THE INTELLIGENCE COMMITTEE IS AT STAKE!
IT LOOKS BAD WHEN THREE OF MY STUDENTS GET KILLED.

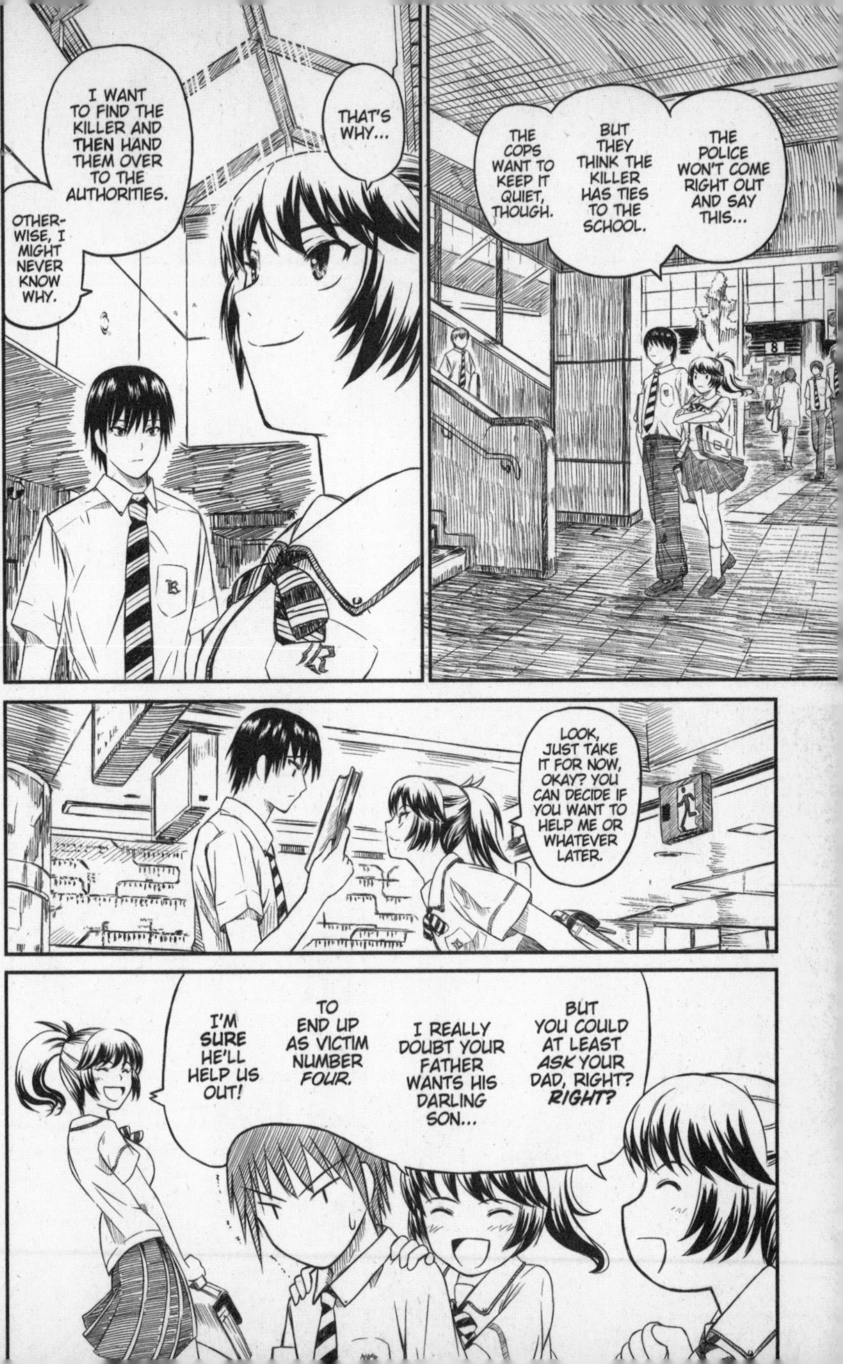
THE POLICE WON'T COME RIGHT OUT AND SAY THIS...
BUT THEY THINK THE KILLER HAS TIES TO THE SCHOOL.
THE COPS WANT TO KEEP IT QUIET, THOUGH.
THAT'S WHY...
I WANT TO FIND THE KILLER AND THEN HAND THEM OVER TO THE AUTHORITIES.
OTHER-WISE, I MIGHT NEVER KNOW WHY.
LOOK, JUST TAKE IT FOR NOW, OKAY? YOU CAN DECIDE IF YOU WANT TO HELP ME OR WHATEVER LATER.
BUT YOU COULD AT LEAST *ASK* YOUR DAD, RIGHT? ***RIGHT?***
I REALLY DOUBT YOUR FATHER WANTS HIS DARLING SON...
TO END UP AS VICTIM NUMBER *FOUR.*
I'M SURE HE'LL HELP US OUT!

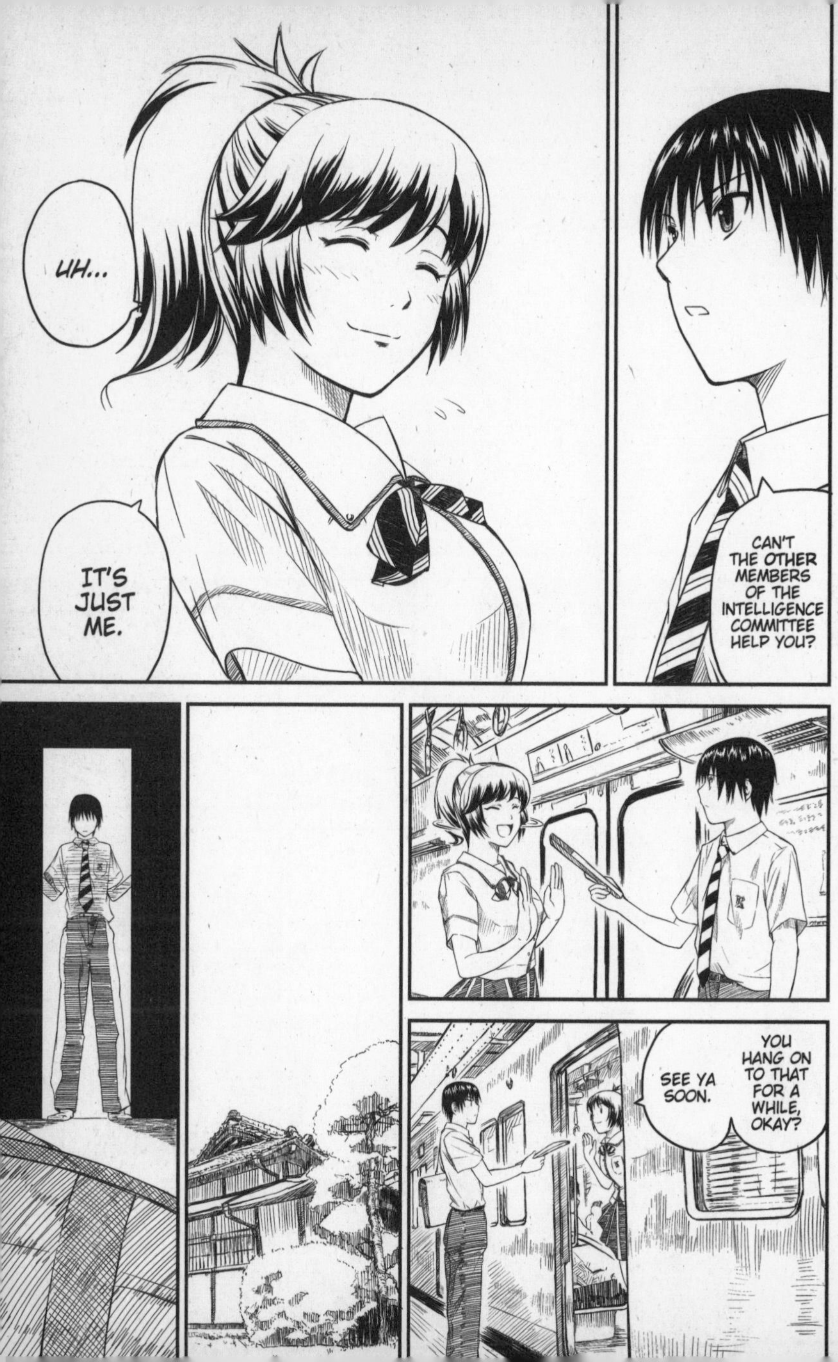
CAN'T THE OTHER MEMBERS OF THE INTELLIGENCE COMMITTEE HELP YOU?
UH...
IT'S JUST ME.
YOU HANG ON TO THAT FOR A WHILE, OKAY?
SEE YA SOON.

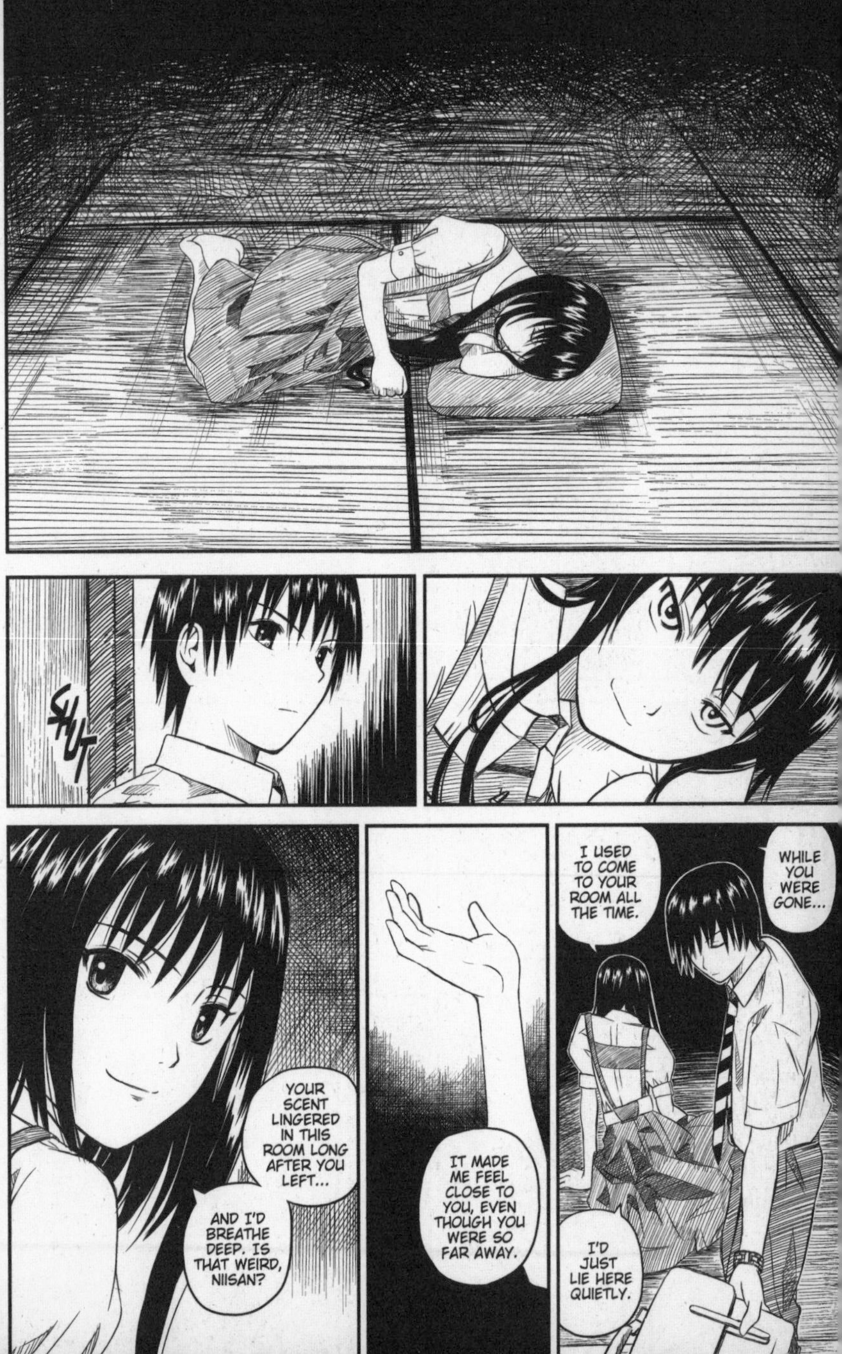
SHUT
WHILE YOU WERE GONE...
I USED TO COME TO YOUR ROOM ALL THE TIME.
I'D JUST LIE HERE QUIETLY.
IT MADE ME FEEL CLOSE TO YOU, EVEN THOUGH YOU WERE SO FAR AWAY.
YOUR SCENT LINGERED IN THIS ROOM LONG AFTER YOU LEFT...
AND I'D BREATHE DEEP. IS THAT WEIRD, NIISAN?

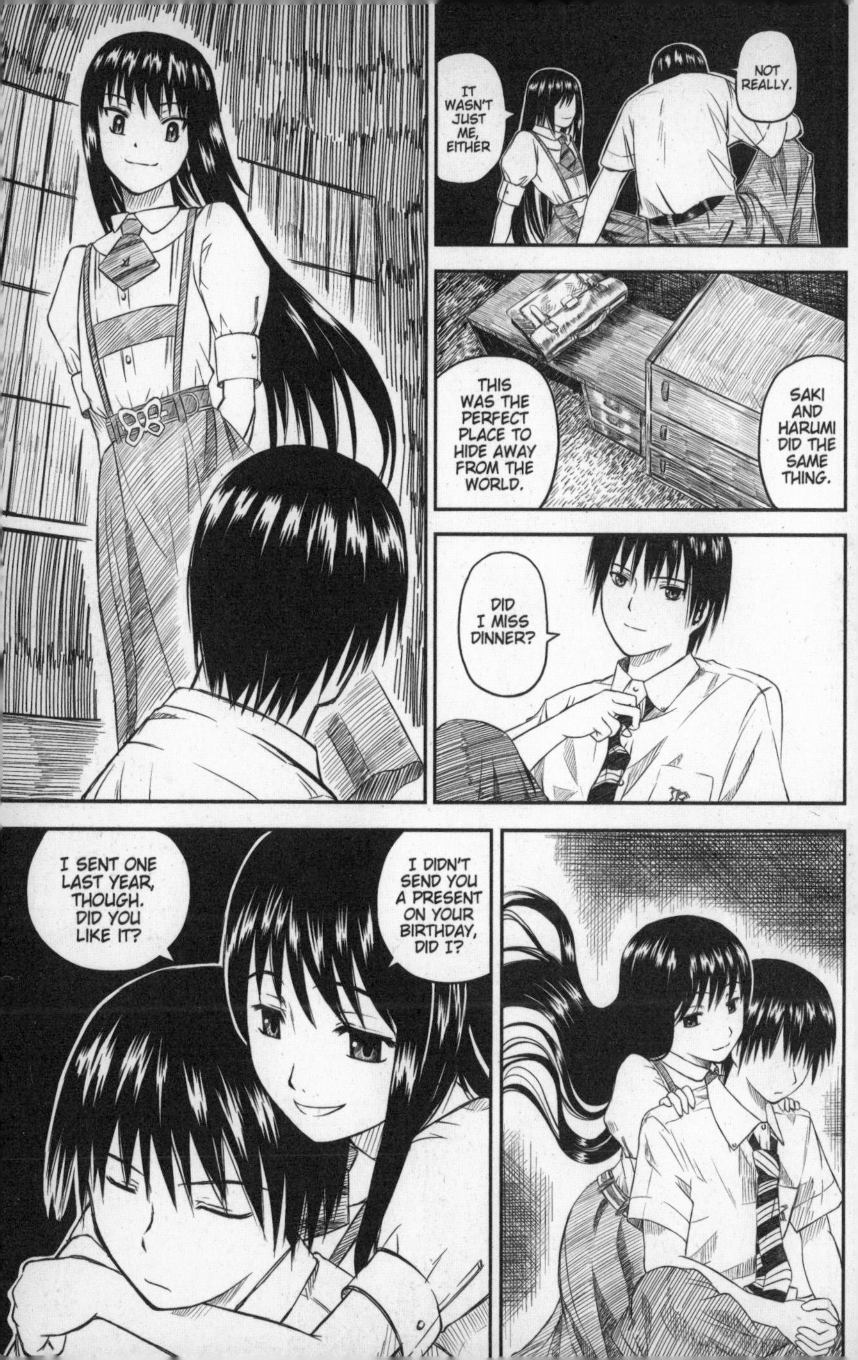
NOT REALLY.
IT WASN'T JUST ME, EITHER
SAKI AND HARUMI DID THE SAME THING.
THIS WAS THE PERFECT PLACE TO HIDE AWAY FROM THE WORLD.
DID I MISS DINNER?
I DIDN'T SEND YOU A PRESENT ON YOUR BIRTHDAY, DID I?
I SENT ONE LAST YEAR, THOUGH. DID YOU LIKE IT?

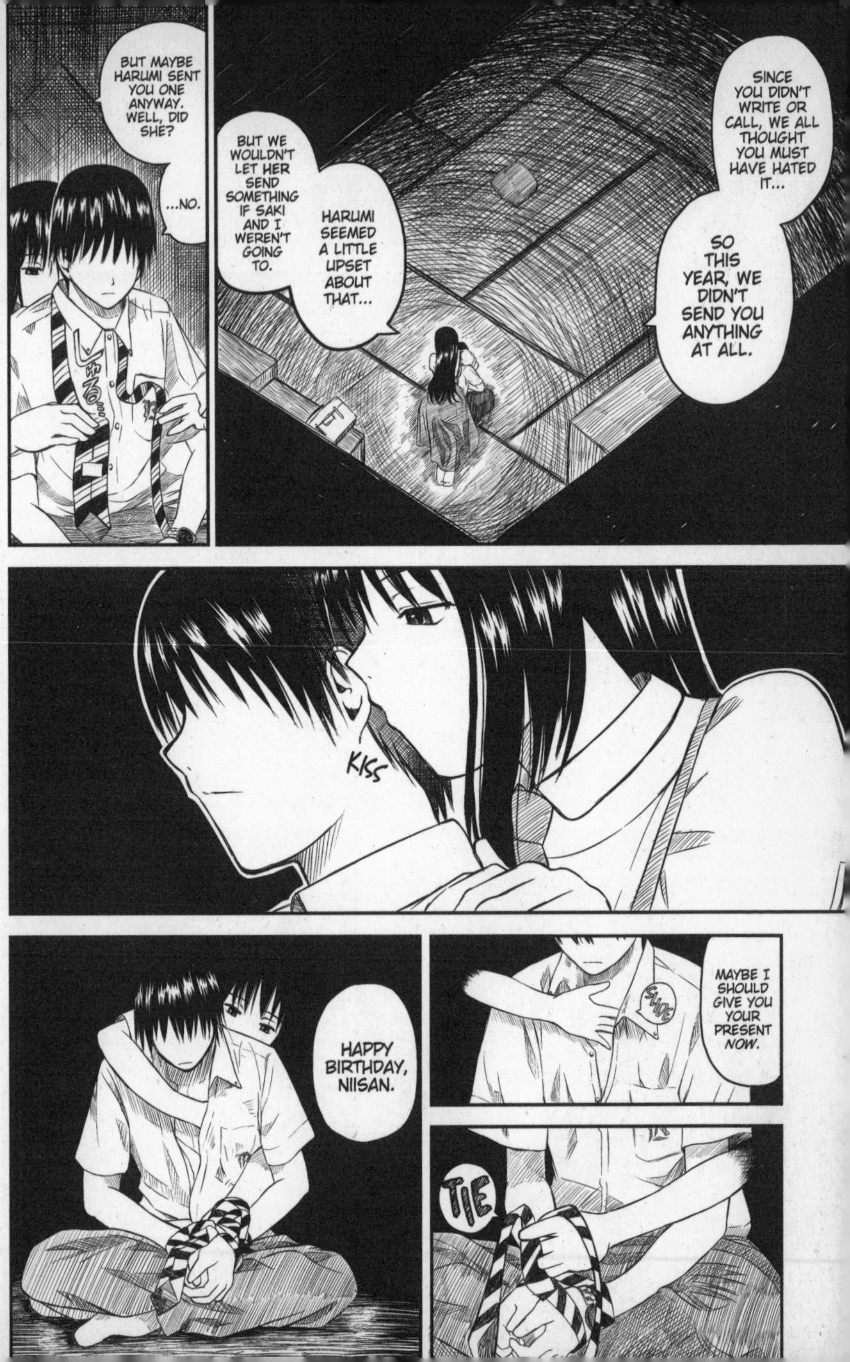
SINCE YOU DIDN'T WRITE OR CALL, WE ALL THOUGHT YOU MUST HAVE HATED IT...
SO THIS YEAR, WE DIDN'T SEND YOU ANYTHING AT ALL.
HARUMI SEEMED A LITTLE UPSET ABOUT THAT...
BUT WE WOULDN'T LET HER SEND SOMETHING IF SAKI AND I WEREN'T GOING TO.
BUT MAYBE HARUMI SENT YOU ONE ANYWAY. WELL, DID SHE?
...NO.
しゅる...
KISS
MAYBE I SHOULD GIVE YOUR YOUR PRESENT *NOW*.
SLIDE
TIE
HAPPY BIRTHDAY, NIISAN.

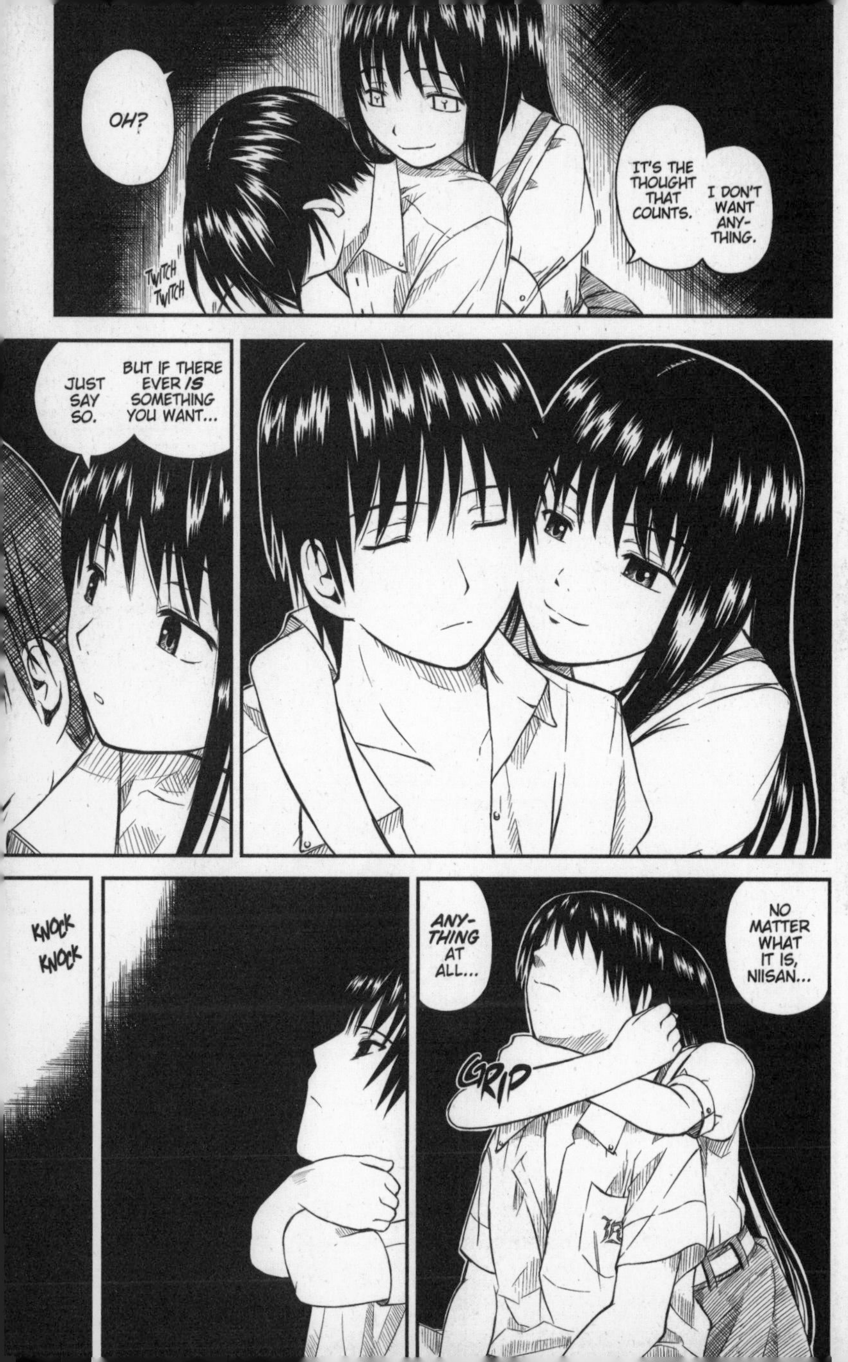
I DON'T WANT ANYTHING.
IT'S THE THOUGHT THAT COUNTS.
OH?
TWITCH TWITCH
BUT IF THERE EVER IS SOMETHING YOU WANT...
JUST SAY SO.
NO MATTER WHAT IT IS, NIISAN...
ANYTHING AT ALL...
GRIP
KNOCK KNOCK

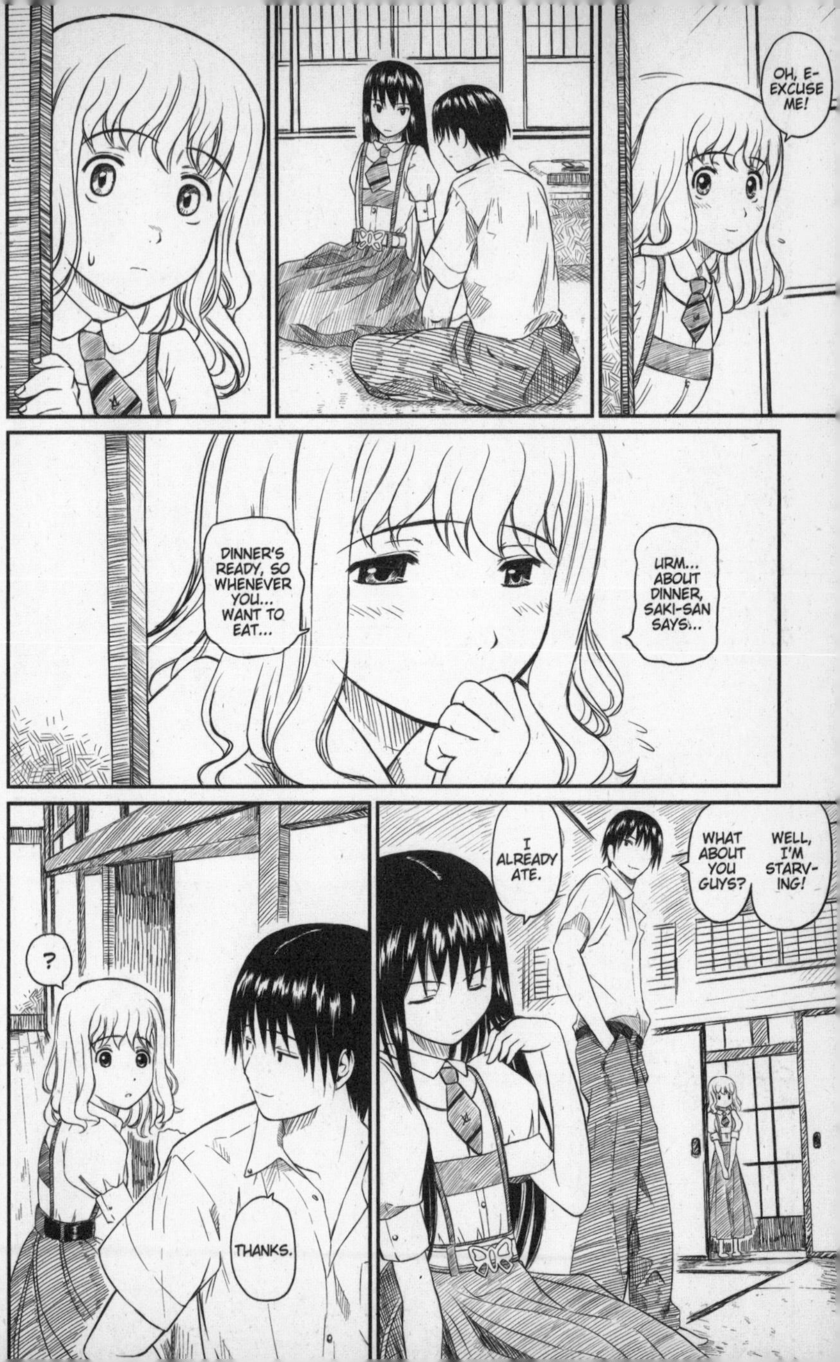
OH, E-EXCUSE ME!
URM... ABOUT DINNER, SAKI-SAN SAYS...
DINNER'S READY, SO WHENEVER YOU... WANT TO EAT...
WELL, I'M STARV-ING!
WHAT ABOUT YOU GUYS?
I ALREADY ATE.
?
THANKS.

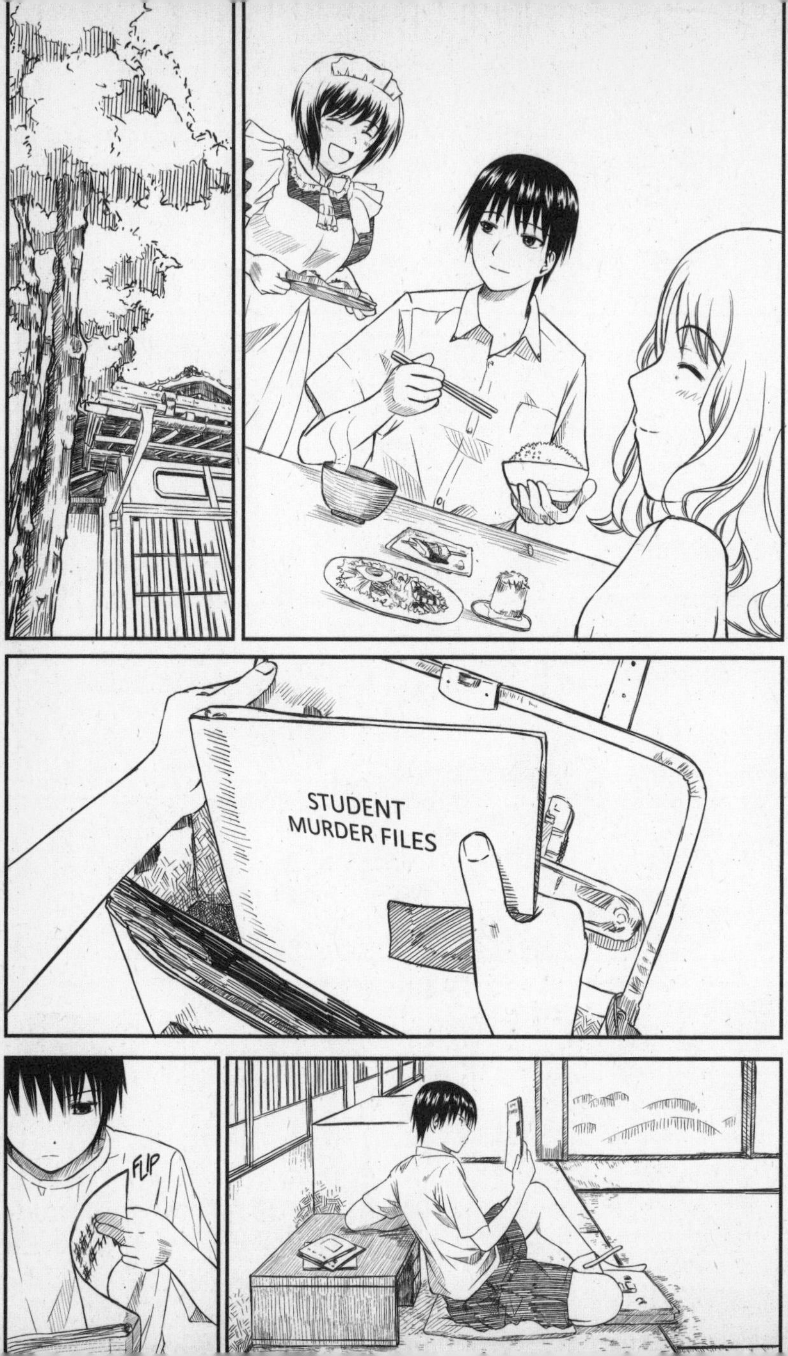
STUDENT
MURDER FILES
FLIP

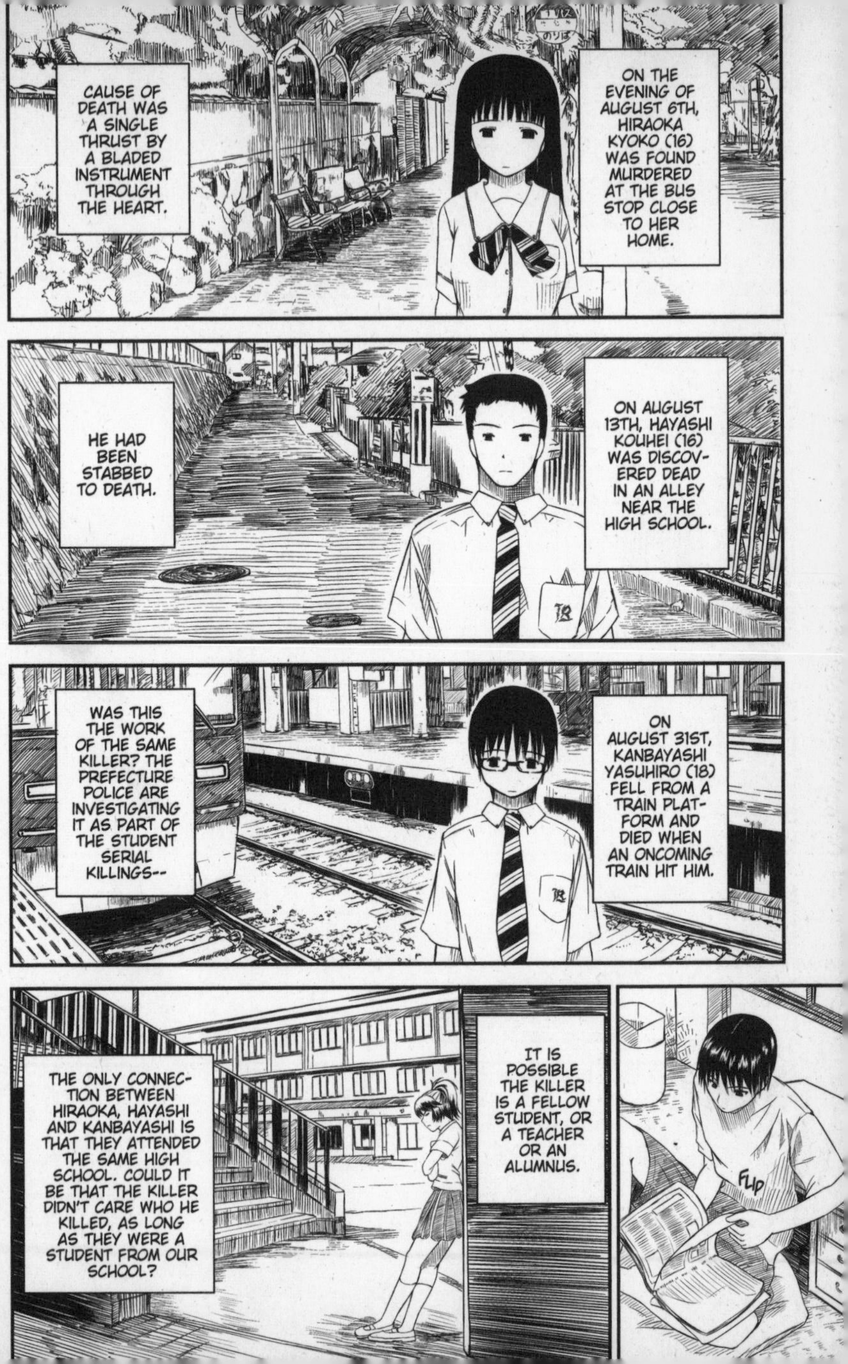
ON THE EVENING OF AUGUST 6TH, HIRAOKA KYOKO (16) WAS FOUND MURDERED AT THE BUS STOP CLOSE TO HER HOME.
CAUSE OF DEATH WAS A SINGLE THRUST BY A BLADED INSTRUMENT THROUGH THE HEART.
ON AUGUST 13TH, HAYASHI KOUHEI (16) WAS DISCOVERED DEAD IN AN ALLEY NEAR THE HIGH SCHOOL.
HE HAD BEEN STABBED TO DEATH.
ON AUGUST 31ST, KANBAYASHI YASUHIRO (18) FELL FROM A TRAIN PLATFORM AND DIED WHEN AN ONCOMING TRAIN HIT HIM.
WAS THIS THE WORK OF THE SAME KILLER? THE PREFECTURE POLICE ARE INVESTIGATING IT AS PART OF THE STUDENT SERIAL KILLINGS--
FLIP
IT IS POSSIBLE THE KILLER IS A FELLOW STUDENT, OR A TEACHER OR AN ALUMNUS.
THE ONLY CONNECTION BETWEEN HIRAOKA, HAYASHI AND KANBAYASHI IS THAT THEY ATTENDED THE SAME HIGH SCHOOL. COULD IT BE THAT THE KILLER DIDN'T CARE WHO HE KILLED, AS LONG AS THEY WERE A STUDENT FROM OUR SCHOOL?

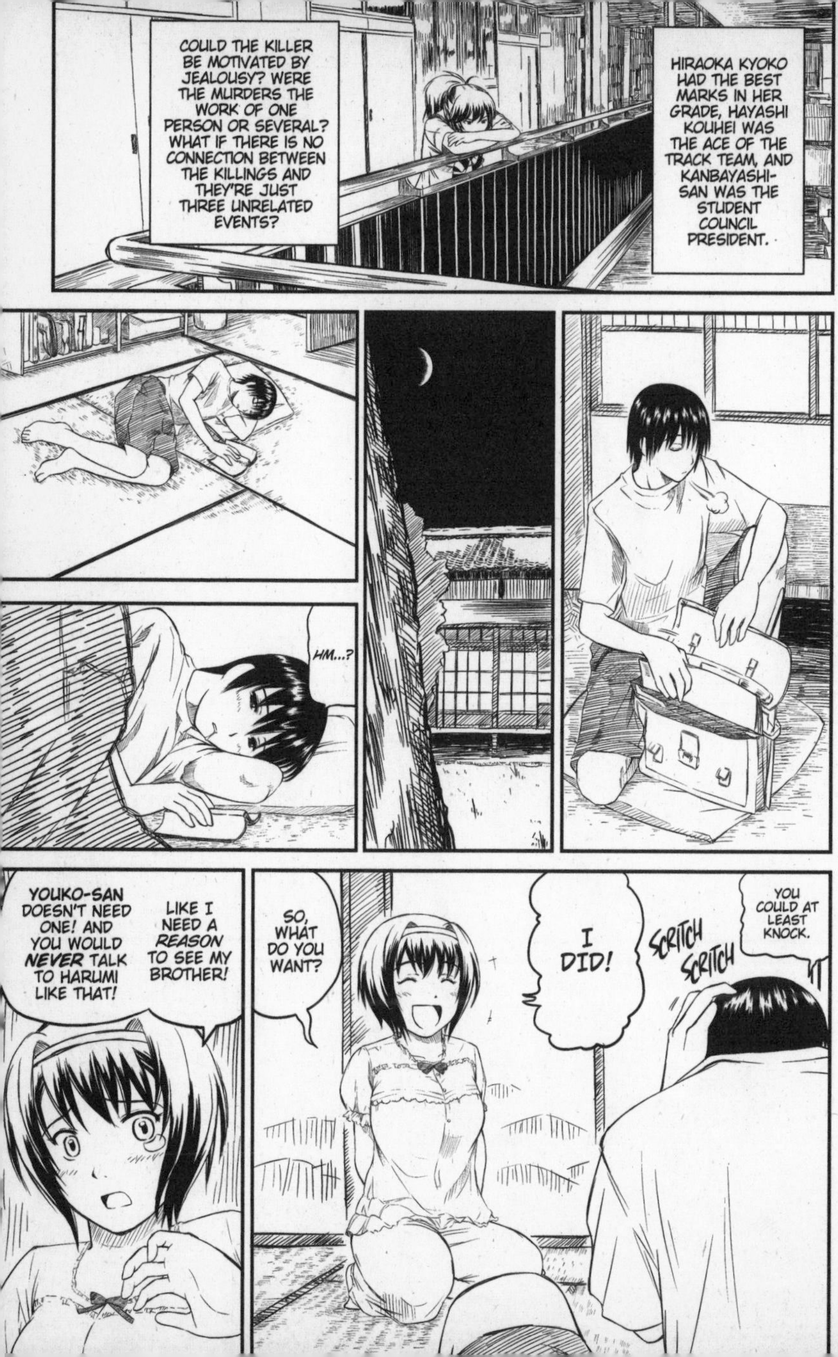
HIRAOKA KYOKO HAD THE BEST MARKS IN HER GRADE, HAYASHI KOUHEI WAS THE ACE OF THE TRACK TEAM, AND KANBAYASHI-SAN WAS THE STUDENT COUNCIL PRESIDENT.
COULD THE KILLER BE MOTIVATED BY JEALOUSY? WERE THE MURDERS THE WORK OF ONE PERSON OR SEVERAL? WHAT IF THERE IS NO CONNECTION BETWEEN THE KILLINGS AND THEY'RE JUST THREE UNRELATED EVENTS?
HM...?
YOU COULD AT LEAST KNOCK.
SCRITCH SCRITCH
I DID!
SO, WHAT DO YOU WANT?
LIKE I NEED A REASON TO SEE MY BROTHER!
YOUKO-SAN DOESN'T NEED ONE! AND YOU WOULD NEVER TALK TO HARUMI LIKE THAT!

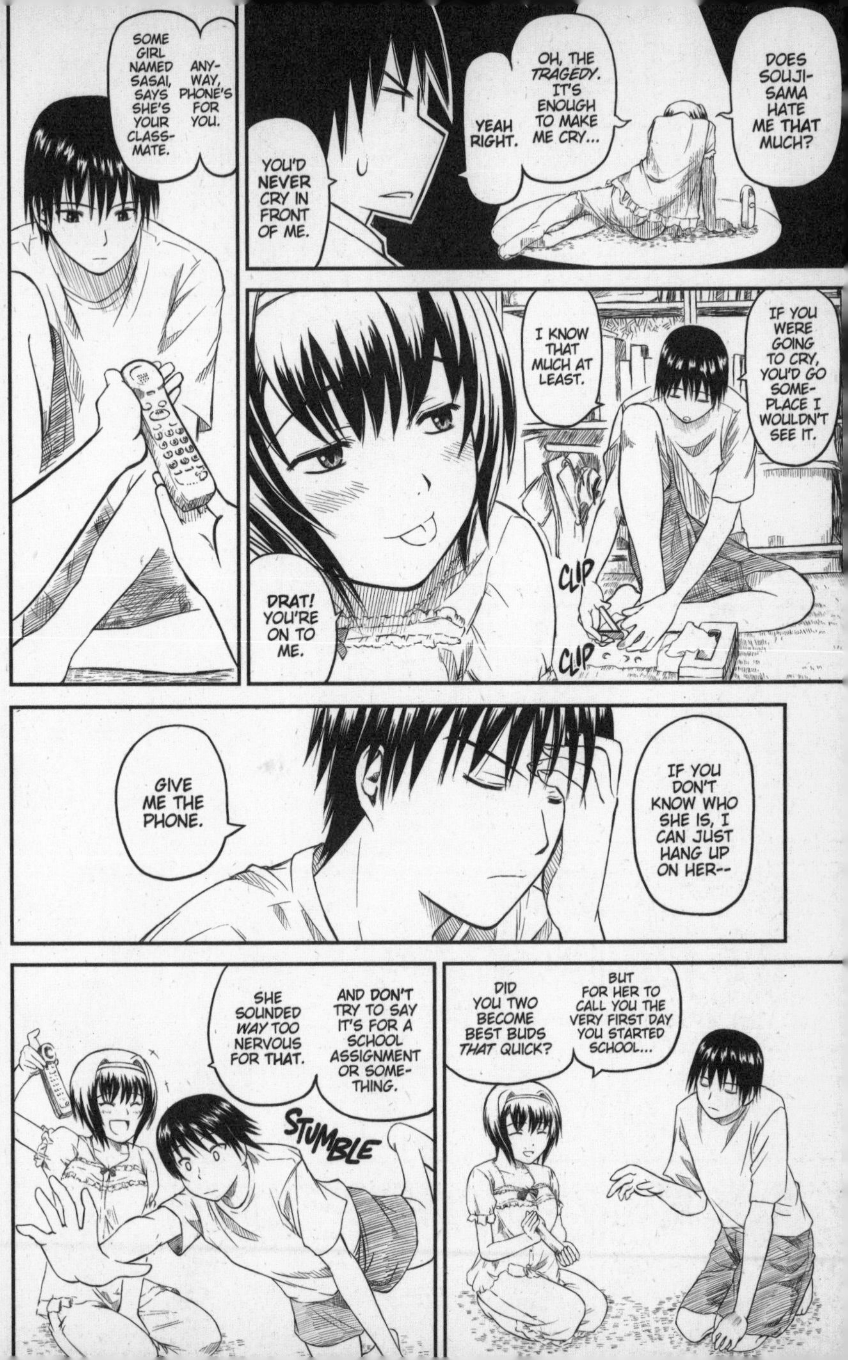
DOES SOUJI-SAMA HATE ME THAT MUCH?
OH, THE *TRAGEDY*. IT'S ENOUGH TO MAKE ME CRY...
YEAH RIGHT.
YOU'D NEVER CRY IN FRONT OF ME.
IF YOU WERE GOING TO CRY, YOU'D GO SOMEPLACE I WOULDN'T SEE IT.
I KNOW THAT MUCH AT LEAST.
CLIP
CLIP
DRAT! YOU'RE ON TO ME.
ANYWAY, PHONE'S FOR YOU.
SOME GIRL NAMED SASAI, SAYS SHE'S YOUR CLASSMATE.
IF YOU DON'T KNOW WHO SHE IS, I CAN JUST HANG UP ON HER--
GIVE ME THE PHONE.
BUT FOR HER TO CALL YOU THE VERY FIRST DAY YOU STARTED SCHOOL...
DID YOU TWO BECOME BEST BUDS *THAT* QUICK?
AND DON'T TRY TO SAY IT'S FOR A SCHOOL ASSIGNMENT OR SOMETHING.
SHE SOUNDED *WAY* TOO NERVOUS FOR THAT.
STUMBLE

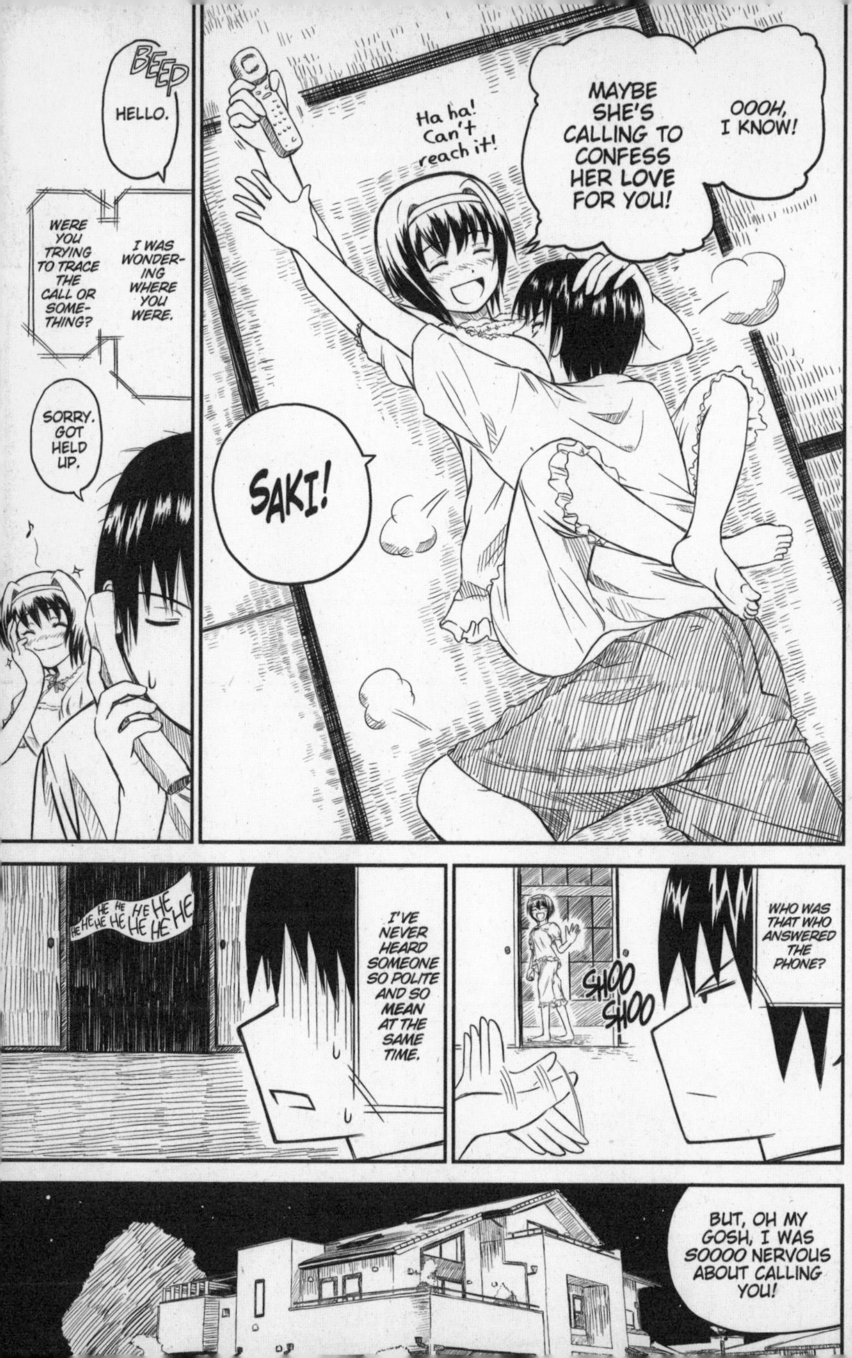
OOOH, I KNOW!
MAYBE SHE'S CALLING TO CONFESS HER LOVE FOR YOU!
Ha ha! Can't reach it!
SAKI!
BEEP
HELLO.
I WAS WONDERING WHERE YOU WERE.
WERE YOU TRYING TO TRACE THE CALL OR SOMETHING?
SORRY. GOT HELD UP.
WHO WAS THAT WHO ANSWERED THE PHONE?
SHOO SHOO
I'VE NEVER HEARD SOMEONE SO POLITE AND SO MEAN AT THE SAME TIME.
HE HE HE HE HE HE HE HE HE HE
BUT, OH MY GOSH, I WAS SOOOO NERVOUS ABOUT CALLING YOU!

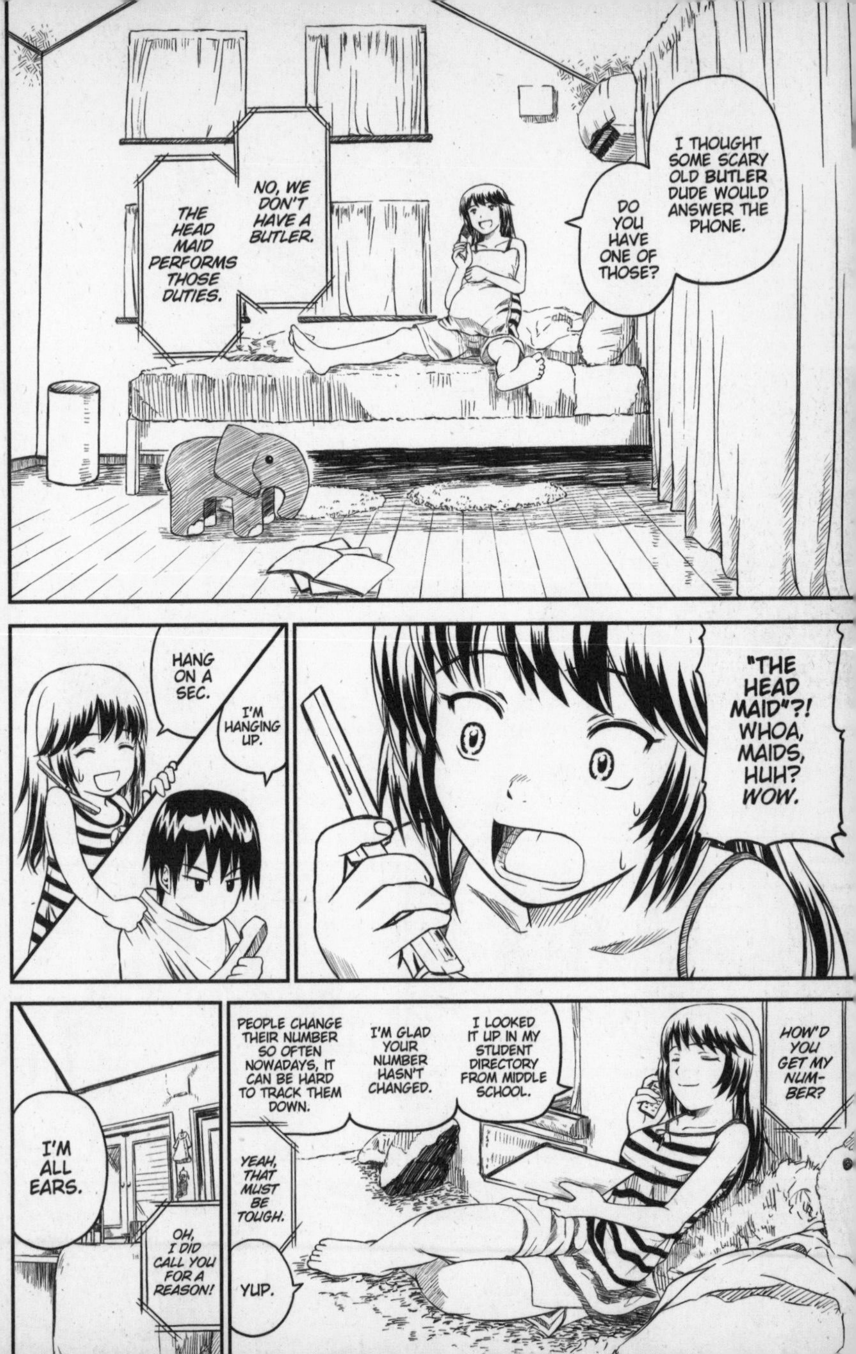
I THOUGHT SOME SCARY OLD BUTLER DUDE WOULD ANSWER THE PHONE.
DO YOU HAVE ONE OF THOSE?
NO, WE DON'T HAVE A BUTLER.
THE HEAD MAID PERFORMS THOSE DUTIES.
"THE HEAD MAID"?! WHOA, MAIDS, HUH? WOW.
HANG ON A SEC.
I'M HANGING UP.
HOW'D YOU GET MY NUM-BER?
I LOOKED IT UP IN MY STUDENT DIRECTORY FROM MIDDLE SCHOOL.
I'M GLAD YOUR NUMBER HASN'T CHANGED.
PEOPLE CHANGE THEIR NUMBER SO OFTEN NOWADAYS, IT CAN BE HARD TO TRACK THEM DOWN.
YEAH, THAT MUST BE TOUGH.
YUP.
OH, I DID CALL YOU FOR A REASON!
I'M ALL EARS.

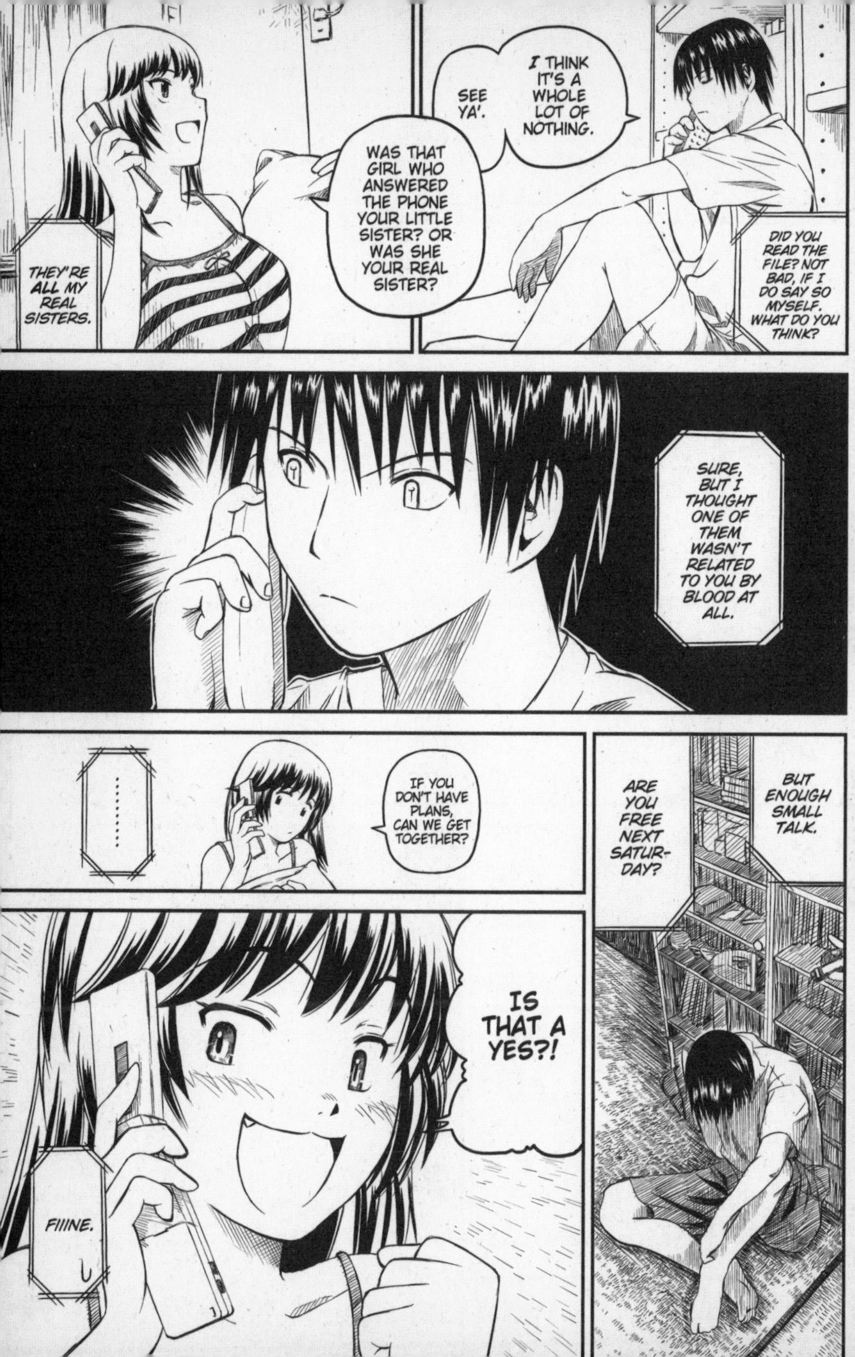
DID YOU READ THE FILE? NOT BAD, IF I DO SAY SO MYSELF. WHAT DO YOU THINK?
I THINK IT'S A WHOLE LOT OF NOTHING.
SEE YA'.
WAS THAT GIRL WHO ANSWERED THE PHONE YOUR LITTLE SISTER? OR WAS SHE YOUR REAL SISTER?
THEY'RE ALL MY REAL SISTERS.
SURE, BUT I THOUGHT ONE OF THEM WASN'T RELATED TO YOU BY BLOOD AT ALL.
BUT ENOUGH SMALL TALK.
ARE YOU FREE NEXT SATURDAY?
IF YOU DON'T HAVE PLANS, CAN WE GET TOGETHER?
......
IS THAT A YES?!
FIIINE.

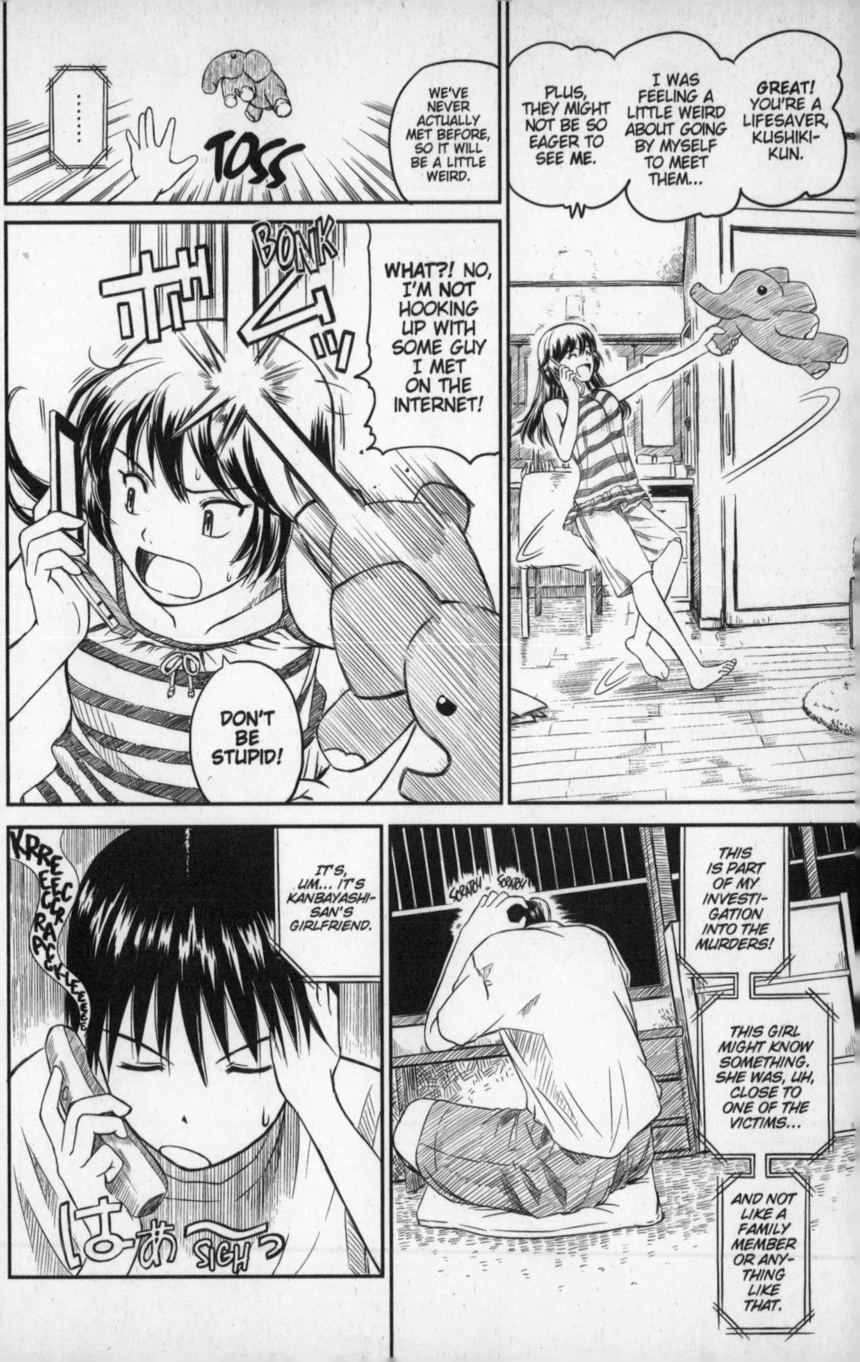
GREAT! YOU'RE A LIFESAVER, KUSHIKI-KUN.
I WAS FEELING A LITTLE WEIRD ABOUT GOING BY MYSELF TO MEET THEM...
PLUS, THEY MIGHT NOT BE SO EAGER TO SEE ME.
WE'VE NEVER ACTUALLY MET BEFORE, SO IT WILL BE A LITTLE WEIRD.
......
TOSS
BONK
WHAT?! NO, I'M NOT HOOKING UP WITH SOME GUY I MET ON THE INTERNET!
DON'T BE STUPID!
THIS IS PART OF MY INVESTIGATION INTO THE MURDERS!
SCRATCH SCRATCH
THIS GIRL MIGHT KNOW SOMETHING. SHE WAS, UH, CLOSE TO ONE OF THE VICTIMS...
AND NOT LIKE A FAMILY MEMBER OR ANYTHING LIKE THAT.
IT'S, UM... IT'S KANBAYASHI-SAN'S GIRLFRIEND.
KRREEECCRRAACCKLEEEEE
はあ~ SIGH

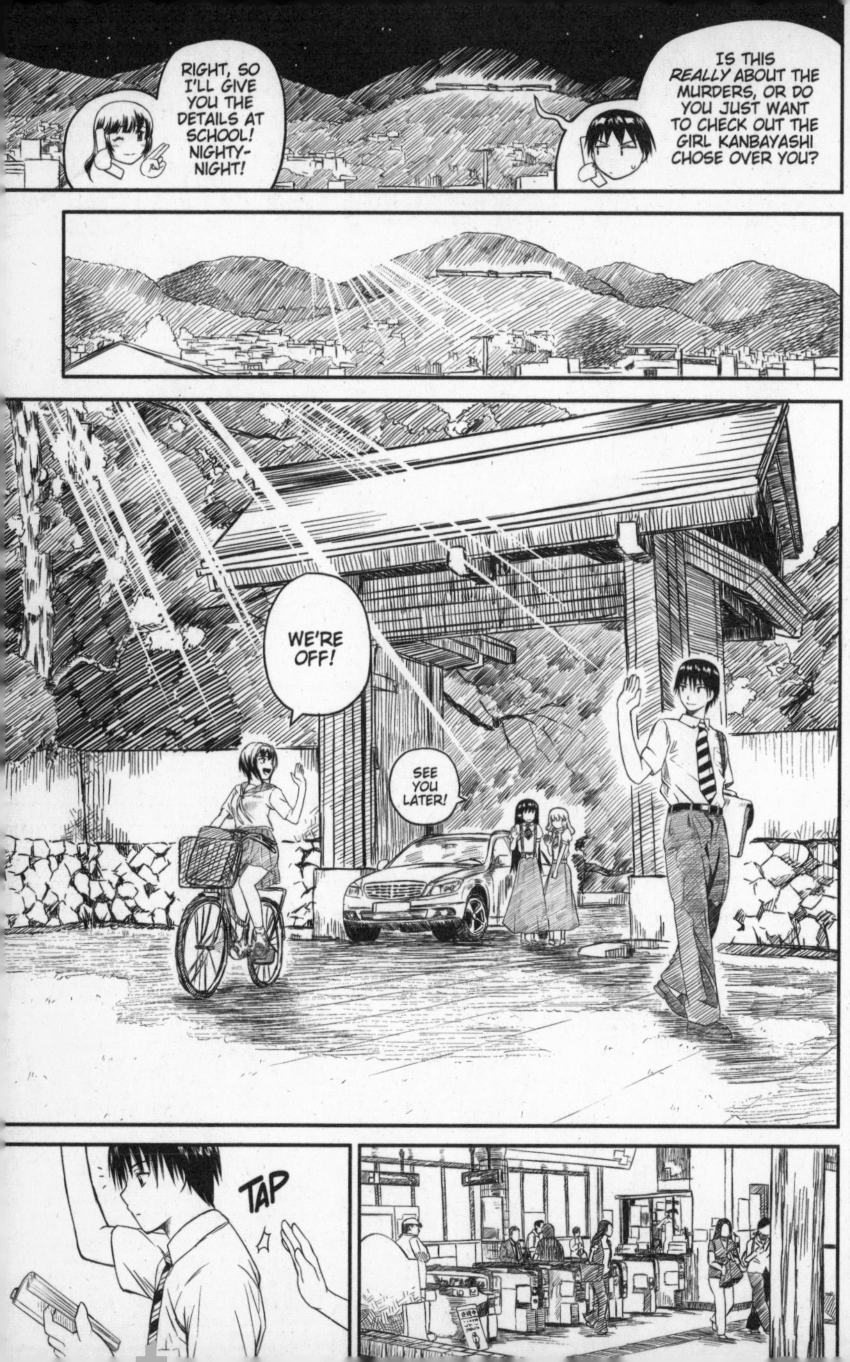
IS THIS *REALLY* ABOUT THE MURDERS, OR DO YOU JUST WANT TO CHECK OUT THE GIRL KANBAYASHI CHOSE OVER YOU?
RIGHT, SO I'LL GIVE YOU THE DETAILS AT SCHOOL! NIGHTY-NIGHT!
WE'RE OFF!
SEE YOU LATER!
TAP

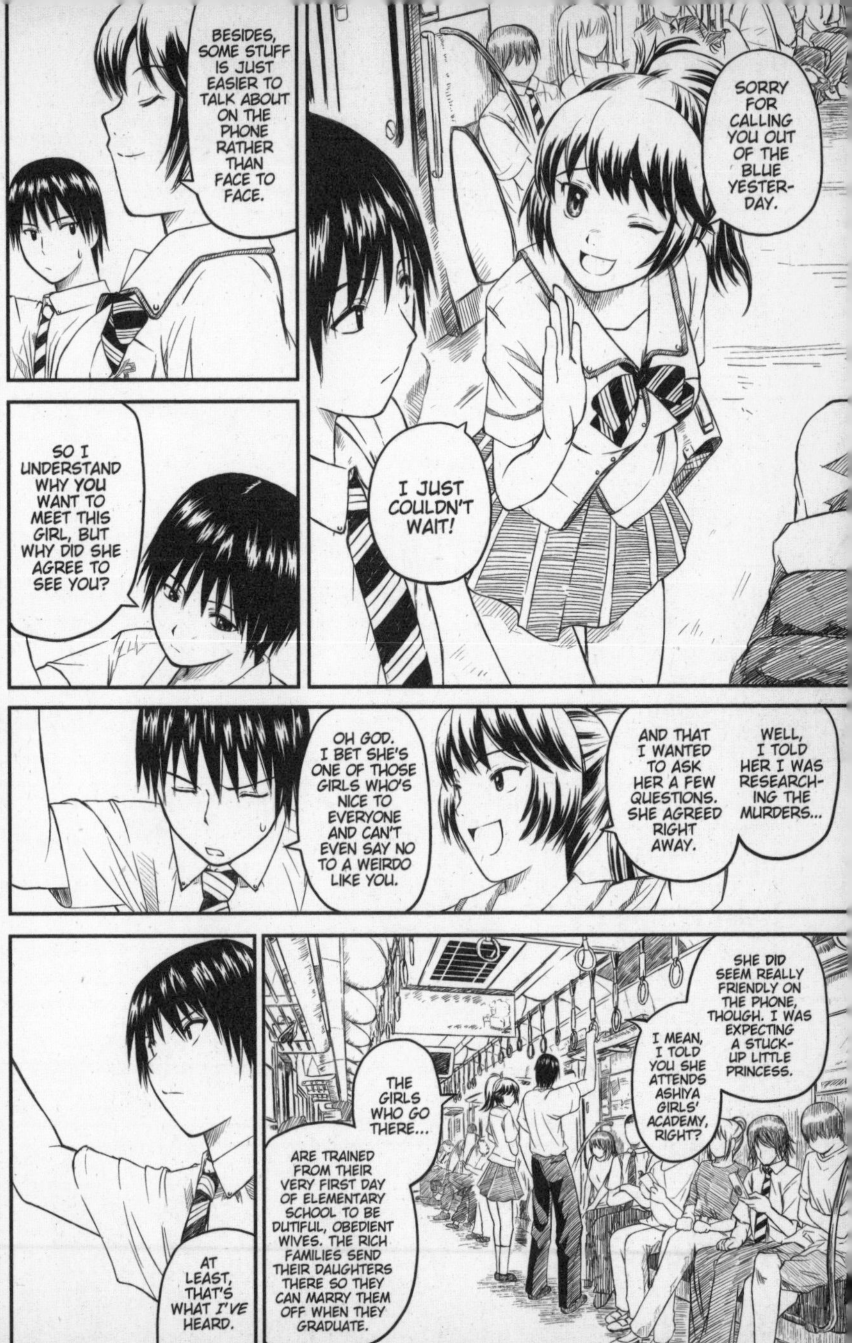
SORRY FOR CALLING YOU OUT OF THE BLUE YESTER-DAY.
I JUST COULDN'T WAIT!
BESIDES, SOME STUFF IS JUST EASIER TO TALK ABOUT ON THE PHONE RATHER THAN FACE TO FACE.
SO I UNDERSTAND WHY YOU WANT TO MEET THIS GIRL, BUT WHY DID SHE AGREE TO SEE YOU?
WELL, I TOLD HER I WAS RESEARCH-ING THE MURDERS...
AND THAT I WANTED TO ASK HER A FEW QUESTIONS. SHE AGREED RIGHT AWAY.
OH GOD. I BET SHE'S ONE OF THOSE GIRLS WHO'S NICE TO EVERYONE AND CAN'T EVEN SAY NO TO A WEIRDO LIKE YOU.
SHE DID SEEM REALLY FRIENDLY ON THE PHONE, THOUGH. I WAS EXPECTING A STUCK-UP LITTLE PRINCESS.
I MEAN, I TOLD YOU SHE ATTENDS ASHIYA GIRLS' ACADEMY, RIGHT?
THE GIRLS WHO GO THERE...
ARE TRAINED FROM THEIR VERY FIRST DAY OF ELEMENTARY SCHOOL TO BE DUTIFUL, OBEDIENT WIVES. THE RICH FAMILIES SEND THEIR DAUGHTERS THERE SO THEY CAN MARRY THEM OFF WHEN THEY GRADUATE.
AT LEAST, THAT'S WHAT *I'VE* HEARD.

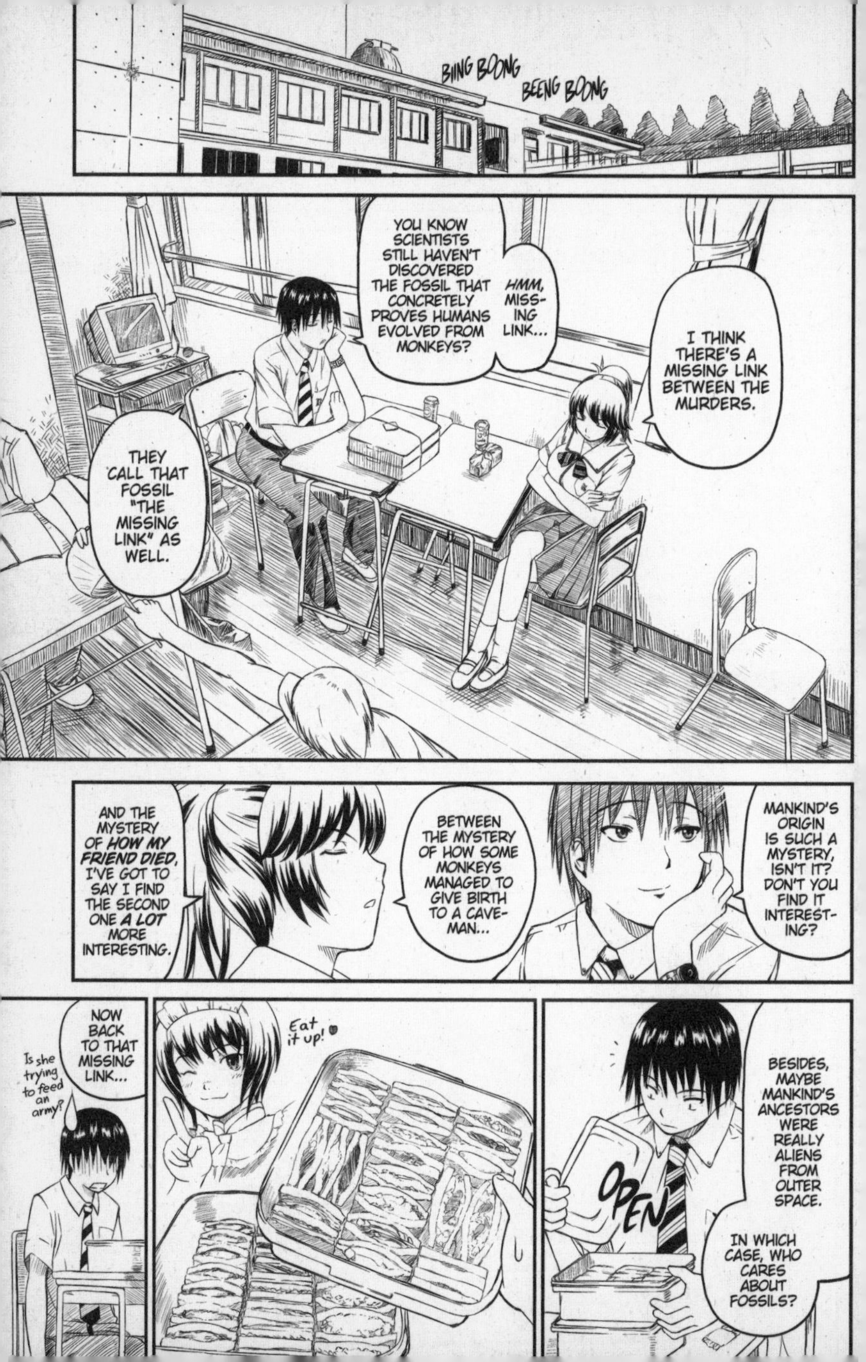
BIING BOONG
BEENG BOONG
I THINK THERE'S A MISSING LINK BETWEEN THE MURDERS.
HMM, MISSING-LINK...
YOU KNOW SCIENTISTS STILL HAVEN'T DISCOVERED THE FOSSIL THAT CONCRETELY PROVES HUMANS EVOLVED FROM MONKEYS?
THEY CALL THAT FOSSIL "THE MISSING LINK" AS WELL.
MANKIND'S ORIGIN IS SUCH A MYSTERY, ISN'T IT? DON'T YOU FIND IT INTERESTING?
BETWEEN THE MYSTERY OF HOW SOME MONKEYS MANAGED TO GIVE BIRTH TO A CAVEMAN...
AND THE MYSTERY OF *HOW MY FRIEND DIED*, I'VE GOT TO SAY I FIND THE SECOND ONE *A LOT* MORE INTERESTING.
BESIDES, MAYBE MANKIND'S ANCESTORS WERE REALLY ALIENS FROM OUTER SPACE.
IN WHICH CASE, WHO CARES ABOUT FOSSILS?
OPEN
Eat it up!
NOW BACK TO THAT MISSING LINK...
Is she trying to feed an army?

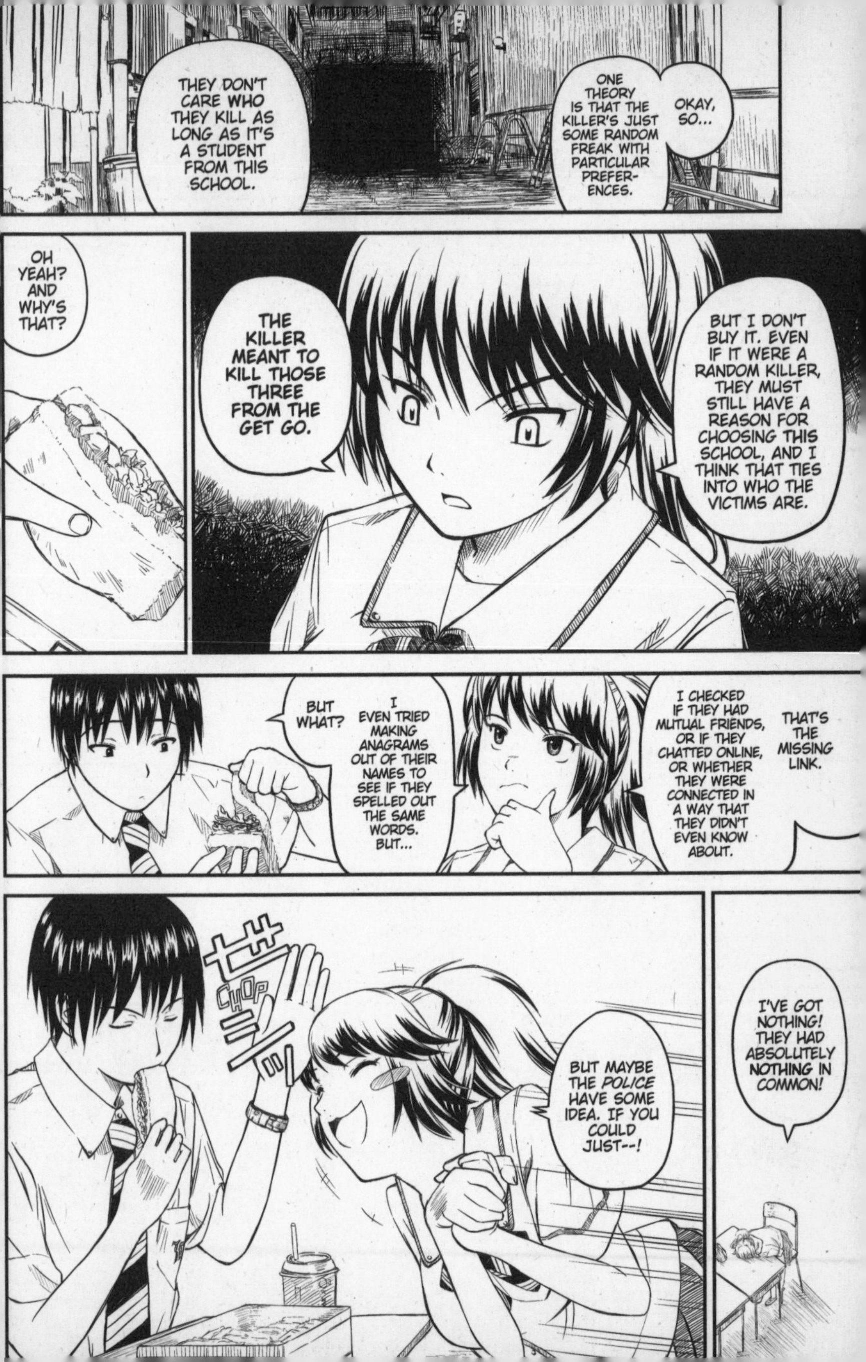
OKAY, SO...
ONE THEORY IS THAT THE KILLER'S JUST SOME RANDOM FREAK WITH PARTICULAR PREFER-ENCES.
THEY DON'T CARE WHO THEY KILL AS LONG AS IT'S A STUDENT FROM THIS SCHOOL.
BUT I DON'T BUY IT. EVEN IF IT WERE A RANDOM KILLER, THEY MUST STILL HAVE A REASON FOR CHOOSING THIS SCHOOL, AND I THINK THAT TIES INTO WHO THE VICTIMS ARE.
THE KILLER MEANT TO KILL THOSE THREE FROM THE GET GO.
OH YEAH? AND WHY'S THAT?
THAT'S THE MISSING LINK.
I CHECKED IF THEY HAD MUTUAL FRIENDS, OR IF THEY CHATTED ONLINE, OR WHETHER THEY WERE CONNECTED IN A WAY THAT THEY DIDN'T EVEN KNOW ABOUT.
I EVEN TRIED MAKING ANAGRAMS OUT OF THEIR NAMES TO SEE IF THEY SPELLED OUT THE SAME WORDS. BUT...
BUT WHAT?
I'VE GOT NOTHING! THEY HAD ABSOLUTELY NOTHING IN COMMON!
BUT MAYBE THE *POLICE* HAVE SOME IDEA. IF YOU COULD JUST--!
CHOP

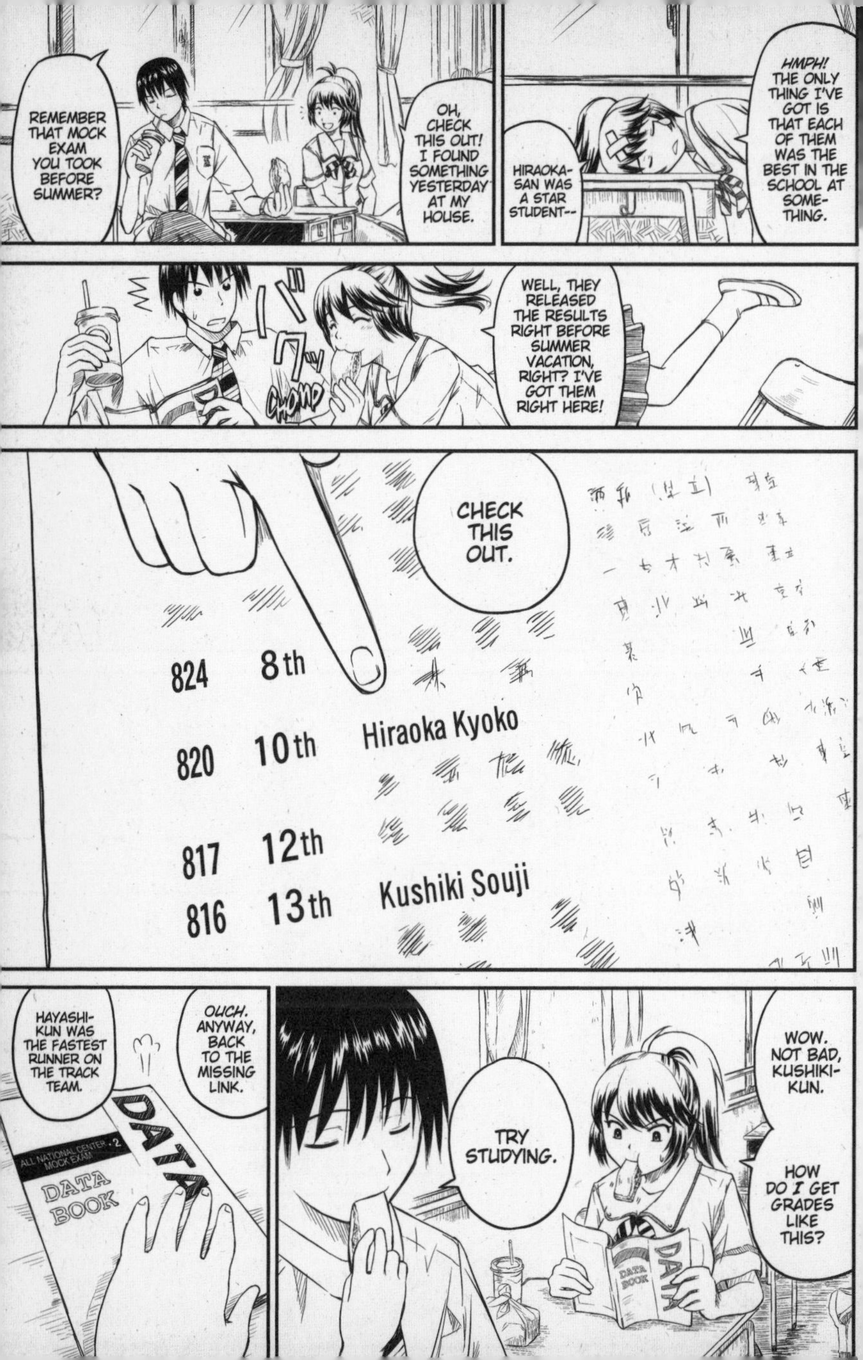
HMPH! THE ONLY THING I'VE GOT IS THAT EACH OF THEM WAS THE BEST IN THE SCHOOL AT SOME-THING.
HIRAOKA-SAN WAS A STAR STUDENT--
OH, CHECK THIS OUT! I FOUND SOMETHING YESTERDAY AT MY HOUSE.
REMEMBER THAT MOCK EXAM YOU TOOK BEFORE SUMMER?
WELL, THEY RELEASED THE RESULTS RIGHT BEFORE SUMMER VACATION, RIGHT? I'VE GOT THEM RIGHT HERE!
CHOMP
CHECK THIS OUT.
824 8th
820 10th Hiraoka Kyoko
817 12th
816 13th Kushiki Souji
WOW. NOT BAD, KUSHIKI-KUN.
HOW DO I GET GRADES LIKE THIS?
TRY STUDYING.
DATA
DATA BOOK
OUCH. ANYWAY, BACK TO THE MISSING LINK.
HAYASHI-KUN WAS THE FASTEST RUNNER ON THE TRACK TEAM.
ALL NATIONAL CENTER MOCK EXAM ·2
DATA
DATA BOOK

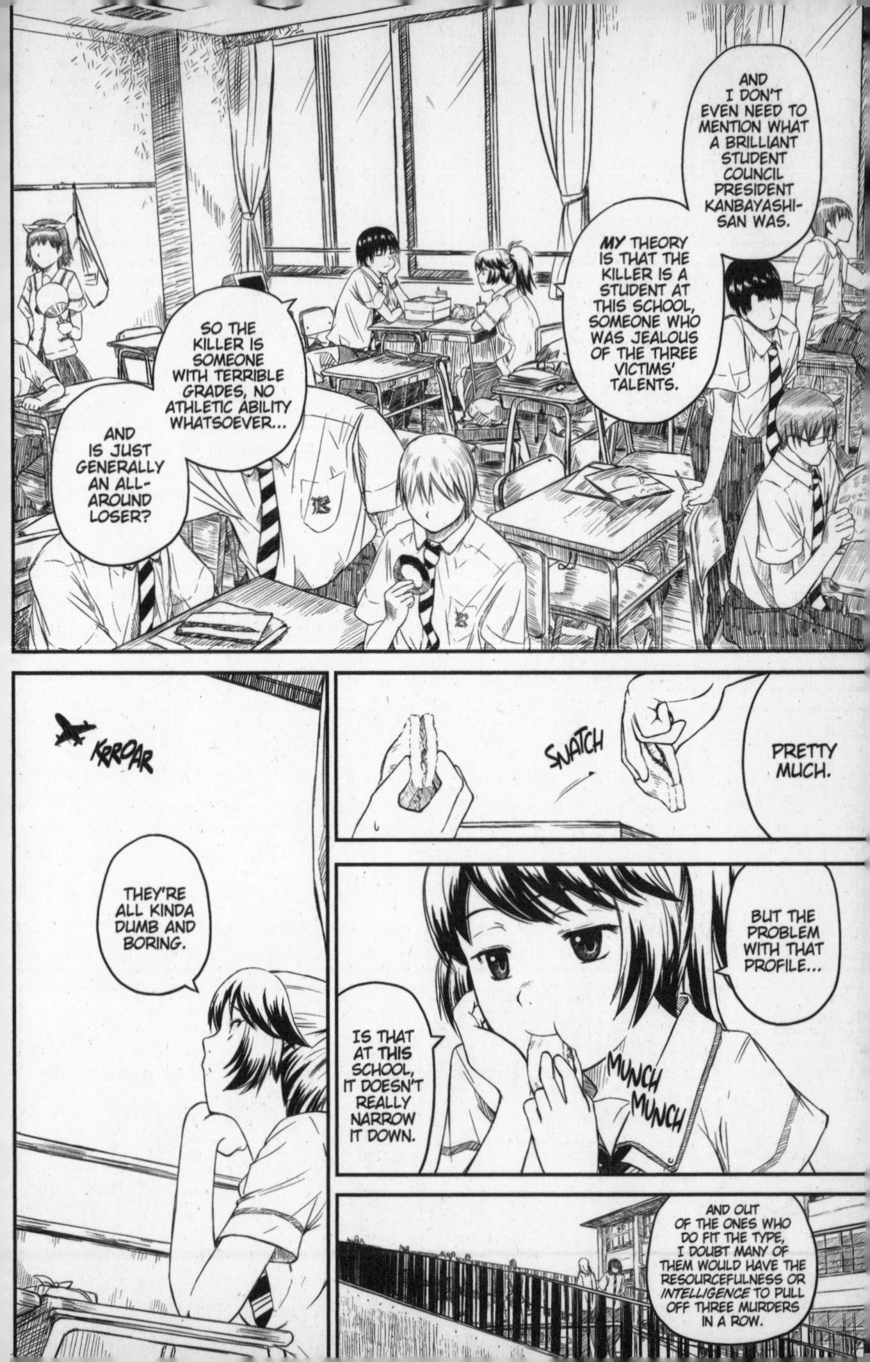
AND I DON'T EVEN NEED TO MENTION WHAT A BRILLIANT STUDENT COUNCIL PRESIDENT KANBAYASHI-SAN WAS.
MY THEORY IS THAT THE KILLER IS A STUDENT AT THIS SCHOOL, SOMEONE WHO WAS JEALOUS OF THE THREE VICTIMS' TALENTS.
SO THE KILLER IS SOMEONE WITH TERRIBLE GRADES, NO ATHLETIC ABILITY WHATSOEVER...
AND IS JUST GENERALLY AN ALL-AROUND LOSER?
PRETTY MUCH.
SNATCH
BUT THE PROBLEM WITH THAT PROFILE...
MUNCH MUNCH
IS THAT AT THIS SCHOOL, IT DOESN'T REALLY NARROW IT DOWN.
AND OUT OF THE ONES WHO DO FIT THE TYPE, I DOUBT MANY OF THEM WOULD HAVE THE RESOURCEFULNESS OR *INTELLIGENCE* TO PULL OFF THREE MURDERS IN A ROW.
KRROAR
THEY'RE ALL KINDA DUMB AND BORING.

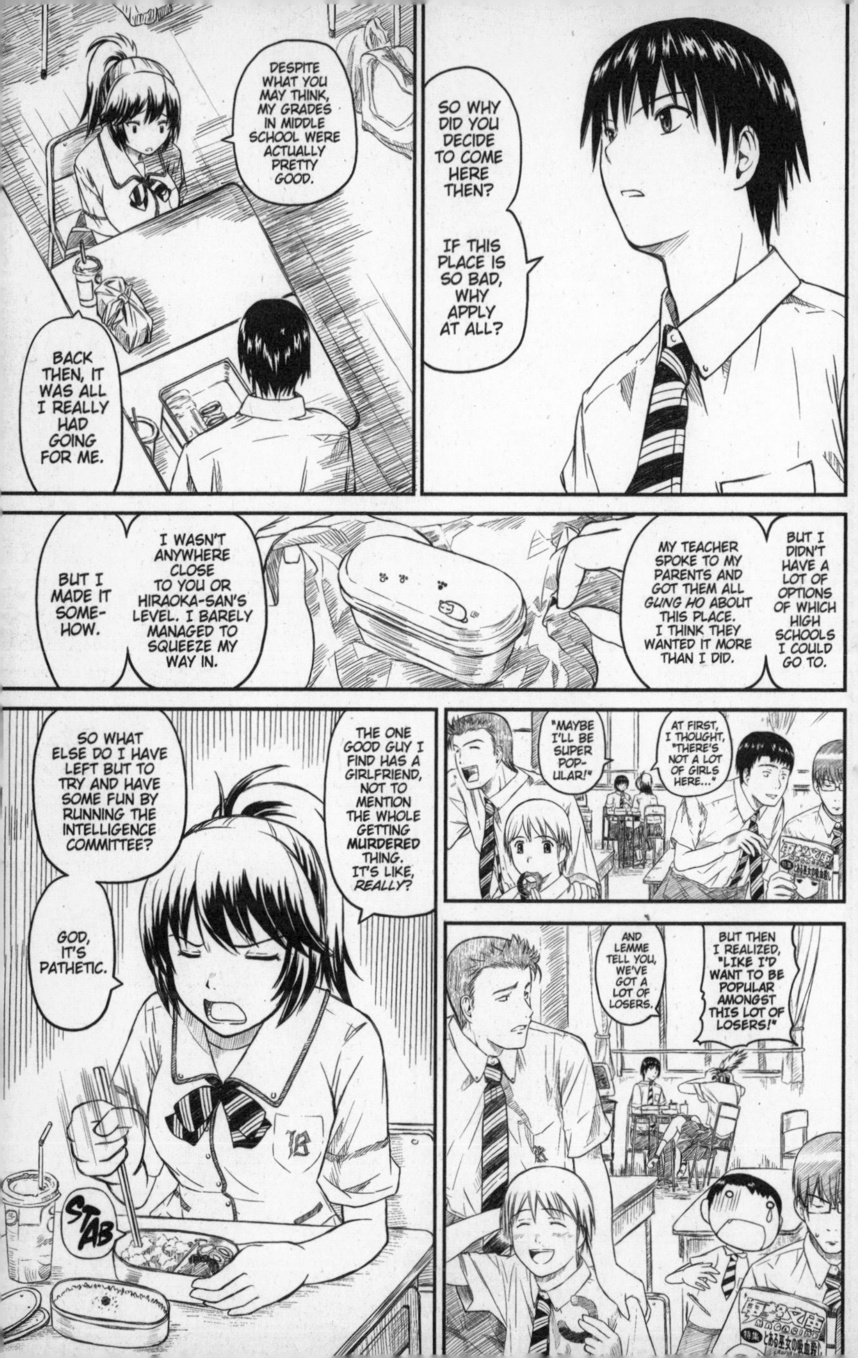
SO WHY DID YOU DECIDE TO COME HERE THEN?
IF THIS PLACE IS SO BAD, WHY APPLY AT ALL?
DESPITE WHAT YOU MAY THINK, MY GRADES IN MIDDLE SCHOOL WERE ACTUALLY PRETTY GOOD.
BACK THEN, IT WAS ALL I REALLY HAD GOING FOR ME.
BUT I DIDN'T HAVE A LOT OF OPTIONS OF WHICH HIGH SCHOOLS I COULD GO TO.
MY TEACHER SPOKE TO MY PARENTS AND GOT THEM ALL *GUNG HO* ABOUT THIS PLACE. I THINK THEY WANTED IT MORE THAN I DID.
I WASN'T ANYWHERE CLOSE TO YOU OR HIRAOKA-SAN'S LEVEL. I BARELY MANAGED TO SQUEEZE MY WAY IN.
BUT I MADE IT SOME-HOW.
AT FIRST, I THOUGHT, "THERE'S NOT A LOT OF GIRLS HERE..."
"MAYBE I'LL BE SUPER POP-ULAR!"
BUT THEN I REALIZED, "LIKE I'D WANT TO BE POPULAR AMONGST THIS LOT OF LOSERS!"
AND LEMME TELL YOU, WE'VE GOT A LOT OF LOSERS.
THE ONE GOOD GUY I FIND HAS A GIRLFRIEND, NOT TO MENTION THE WHOLE GETTING MURDERED THING. IT'S LIKE, *REALLY?*
SO WHAT ELSE DO I HAVE LEFT BUT TO TRY AND HAVE SOME FUN BY RUNNING THE INTELLIGENCE COMMITTEE?
GOD, IT'S PATHETIC.
STAB

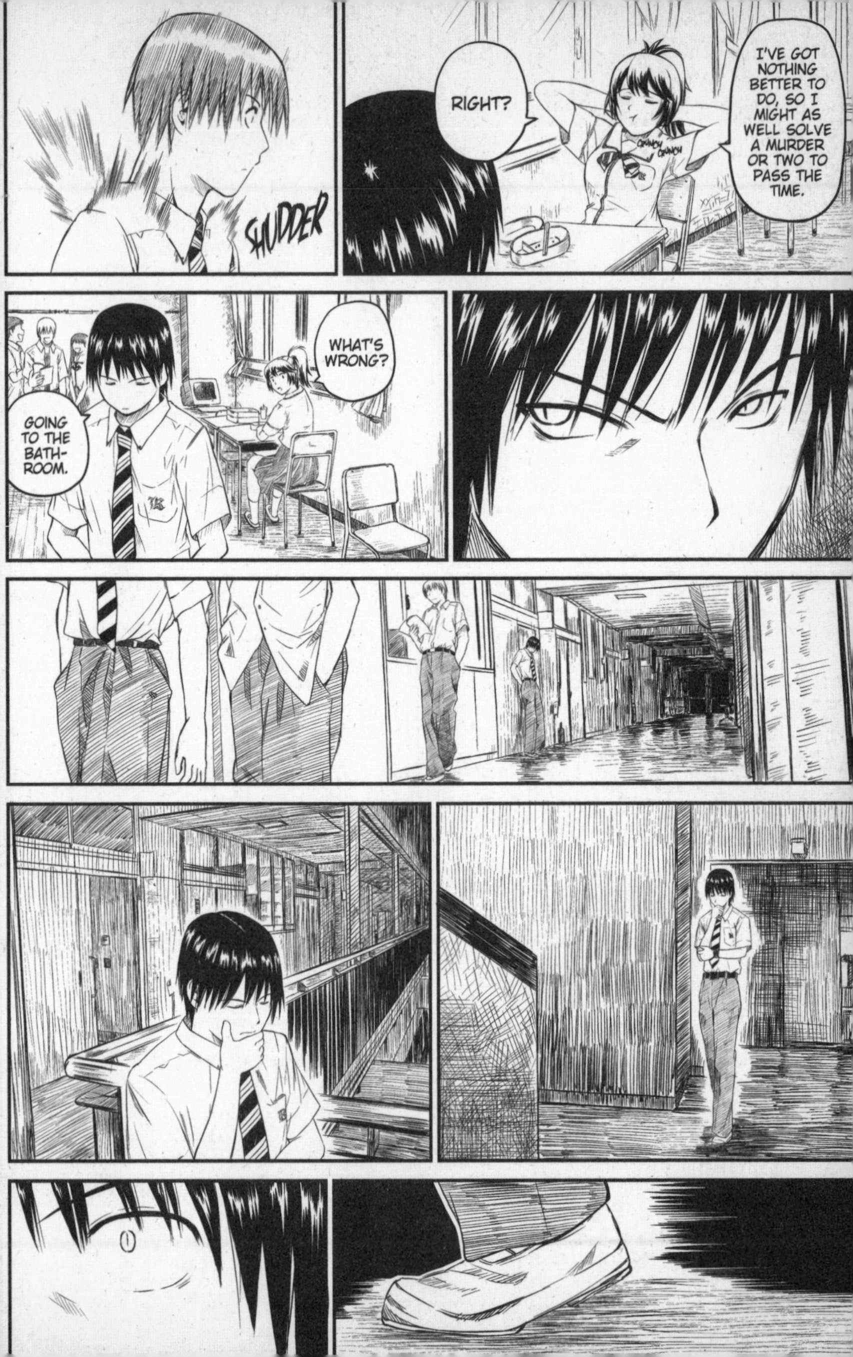
I'VE GOT NOTHING BETTER TO DO, SO I MIGHT AS WELL SOLVE A MURDER OR TWO TO PASS THE TIME.
CRUNCH CRUNCH
RIGHT?
SHUDDER
WHAT'S WRONG?
GOING TO THE BATH-ROOM.

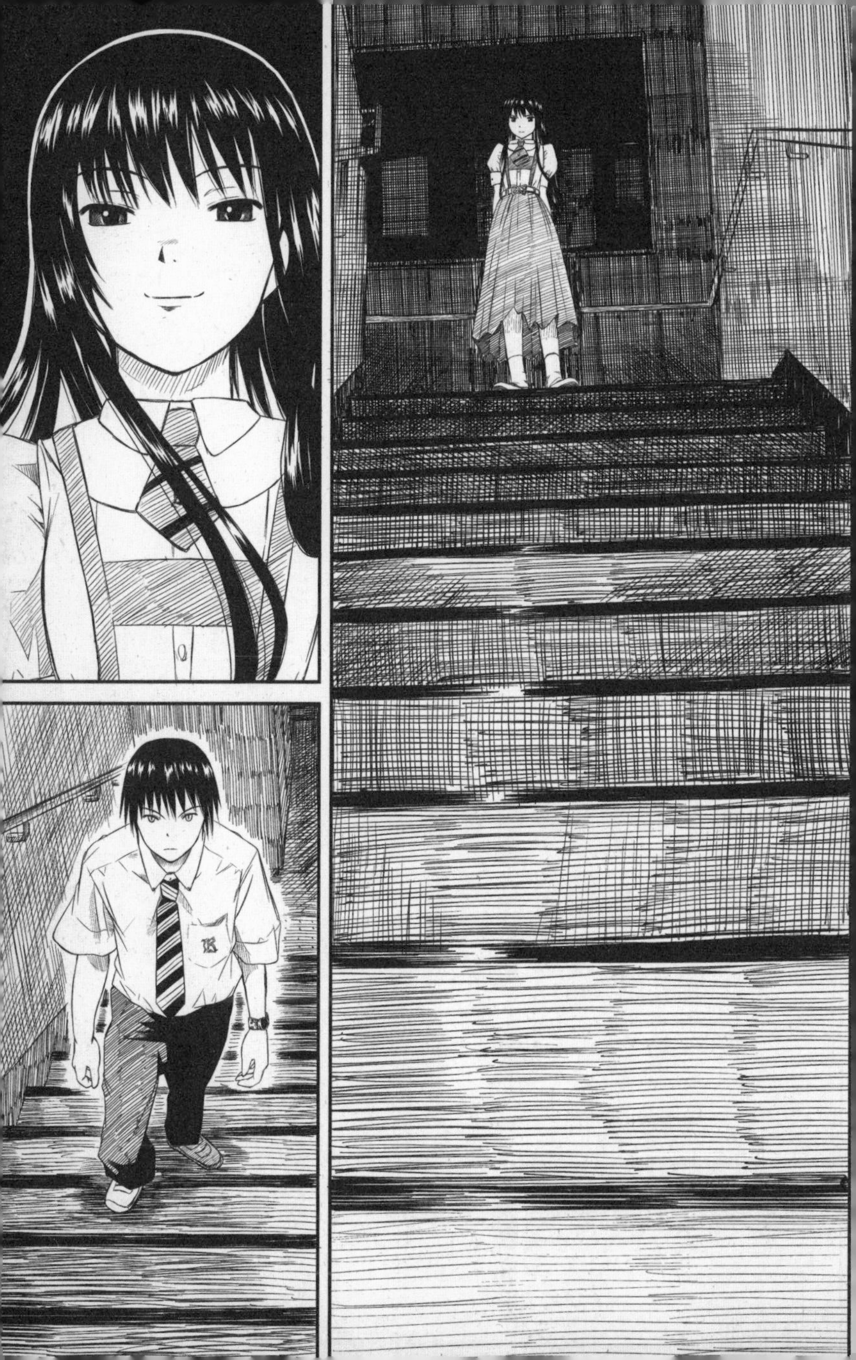

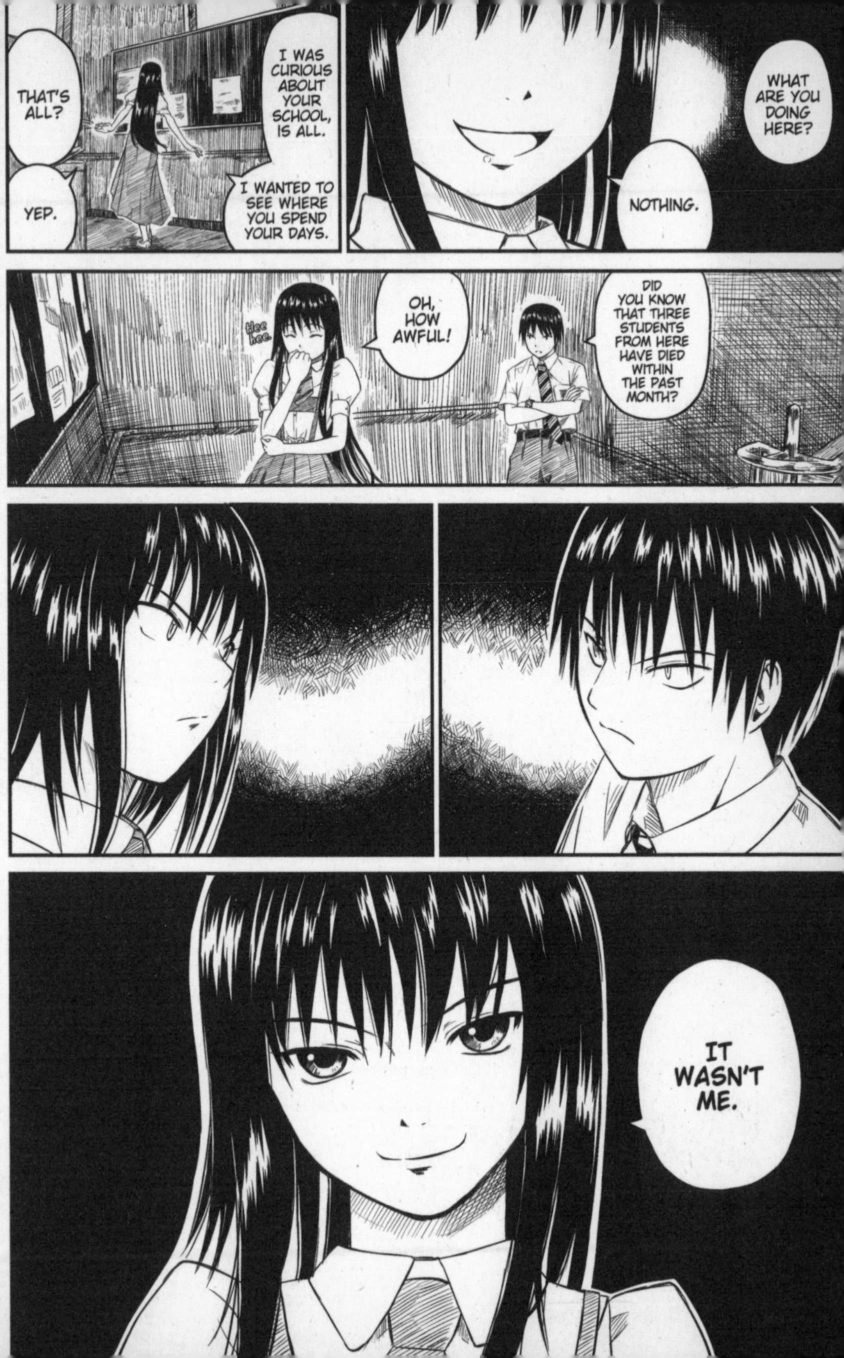
WHAT ARE YOU DOING HERE?
NOTHING.
I WAS CURIOUS ABOUT YOUR SCHOOL, IS ALL.
I WANTED TO SEE WHERE YOU SPEND YOUR DAYS.
THAT'S ALL?
YEP.
DID YOU KNOW THAT THREE STUDENTS FROM HERE HAVE DIED WITHIN THE PAST MONTH?
OH, HOW AWFUL!
Hee hee.
IT WASN'T ME.

AMNESIA LABYRINTH

Amnesia Labyrinth CHARACTER FILE 2

OGIWARA SAKI

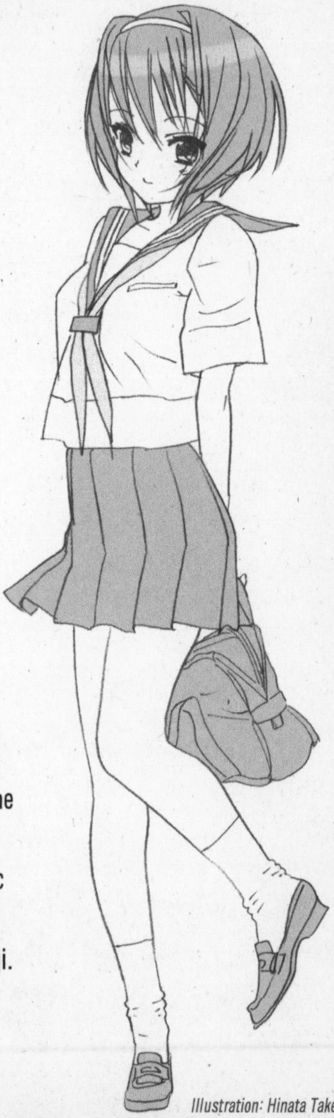

Souji's illegitimate younger sister. Like any normal girl she goes to school in the morning, but when she returns home, she works as a household maid by her own request. On the outside, she is energetic and cheerful, but much like Youko, she seems to be hiding something from Souji. And occasionally, a darker part of her nature surfaces.

Illustration: Hinata Takeda

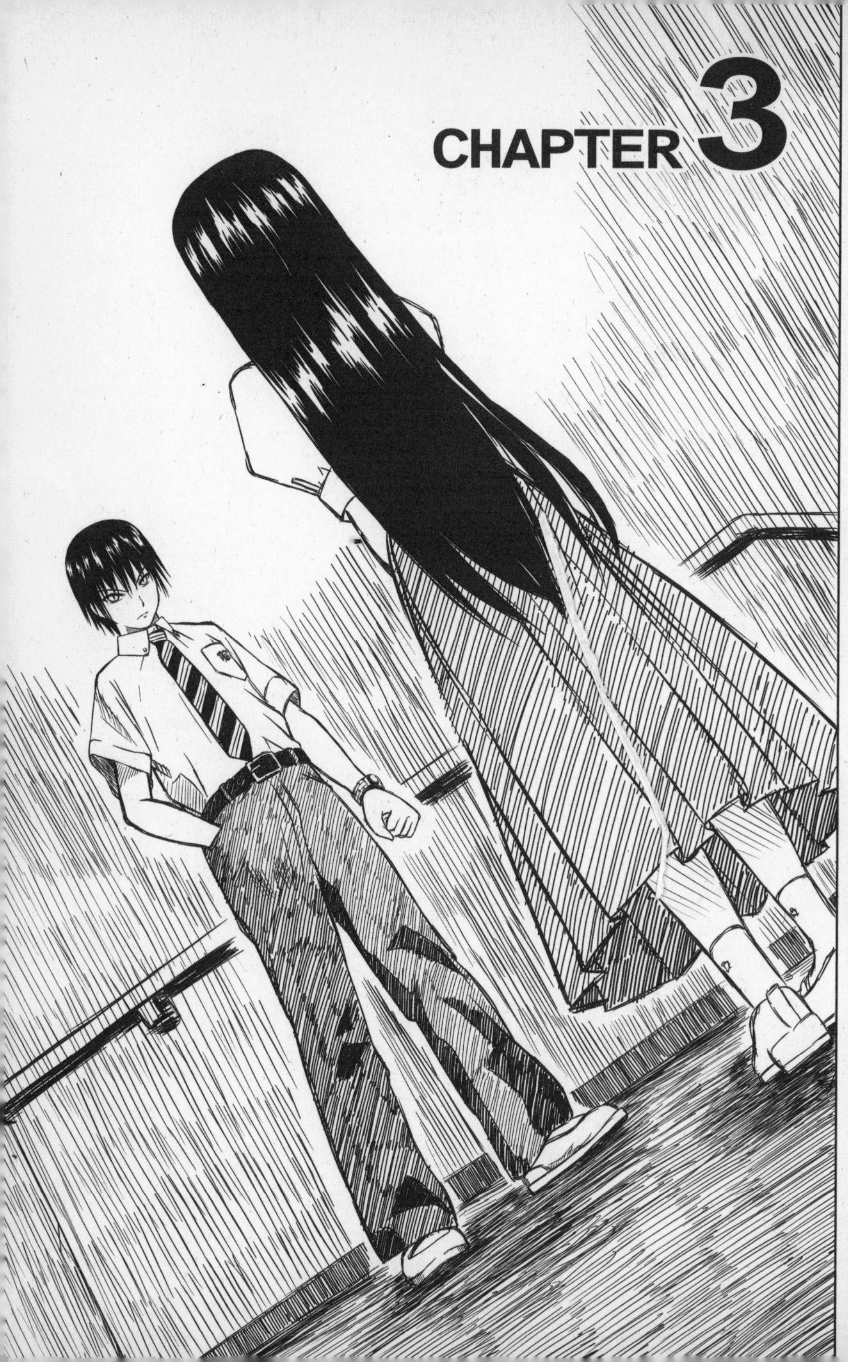
CHAPTER 3

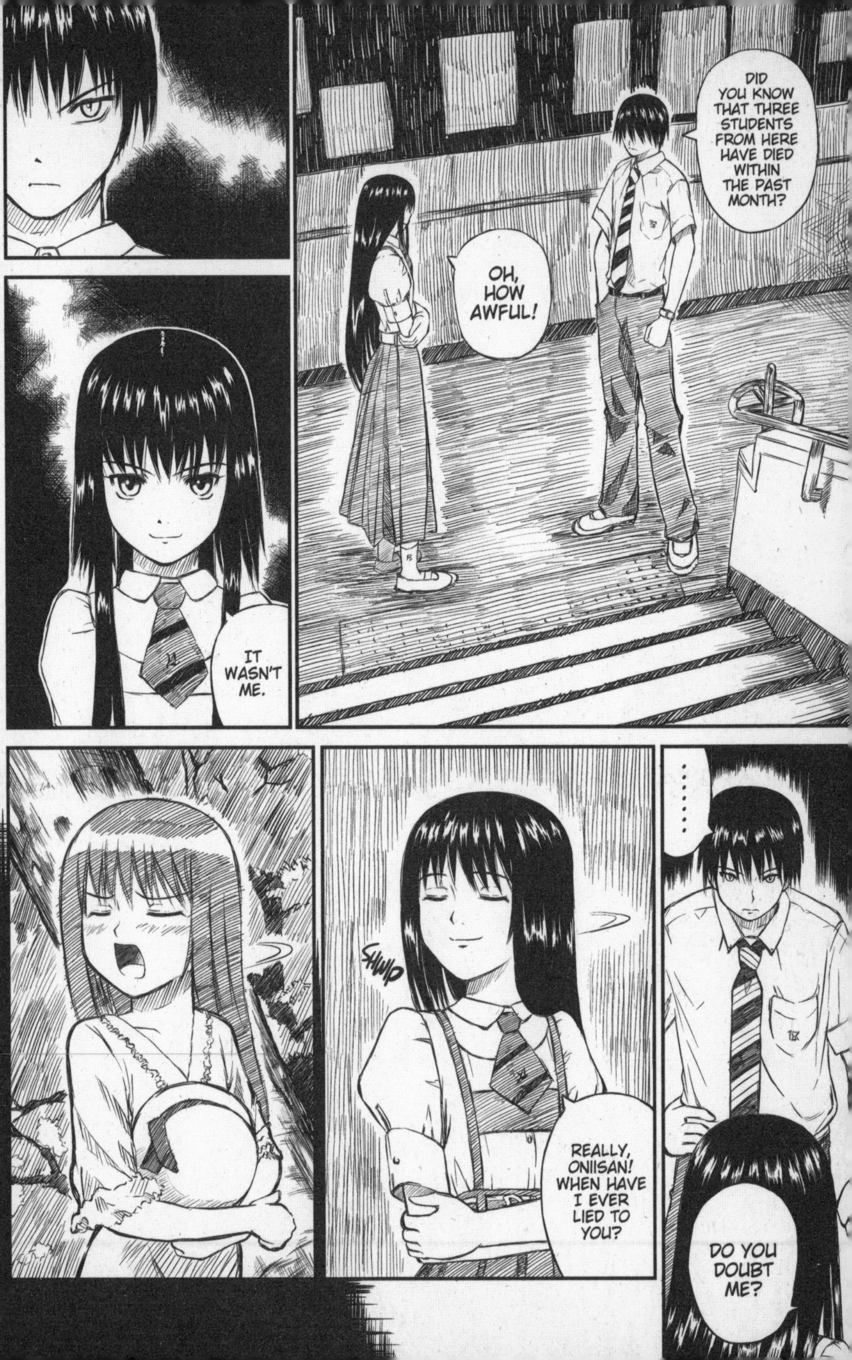
DID YOU KNOW THAT THREE STUDENTS FROM HERE HAVE DIED WITHIN THE PAST MONTH?
OH, HOW AWFUL!
IT WASN'T ME.
......
DO YOU DOUBT ME?
SHWIP
REALLY, ONIISAN! WHEN HAVE I EVER LIED TO YOU?

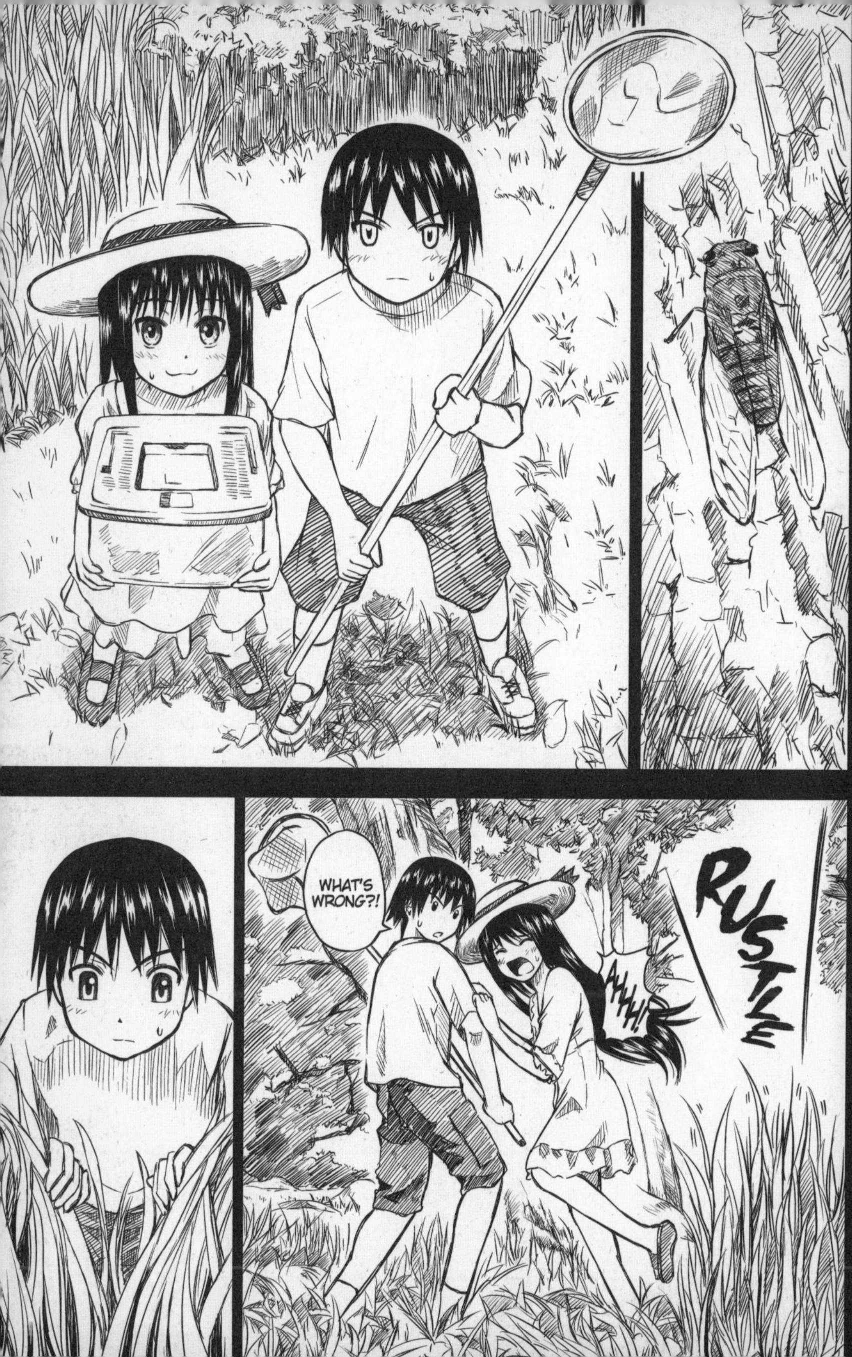
RUSTLE
AHHH!
WHAT'S WRONG?!

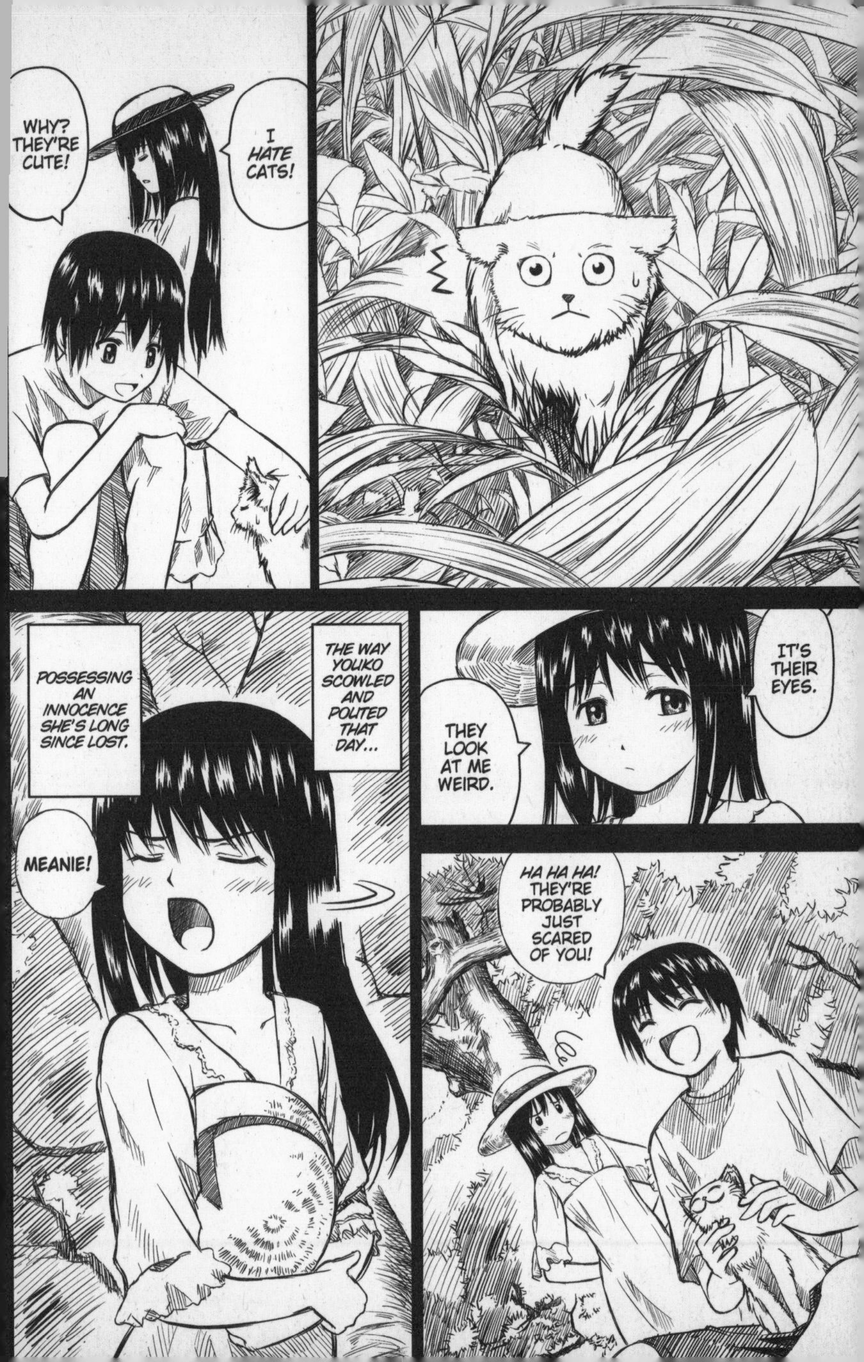
I HATE CATS!
WHY? THEY'RE CUTE!
IT'S THEIR EYES.
THEY LOOK AT ME WEIRD.
HA HA HA! THEY'RE PROBABLY JUST SCARED OF YOU!
THE WAY YOUKO SCOWLED AND POUTED THAT DAY...
POSSESSING AN INNOCENCE SHE'S LONG SINCE LOST.
MEANIE!

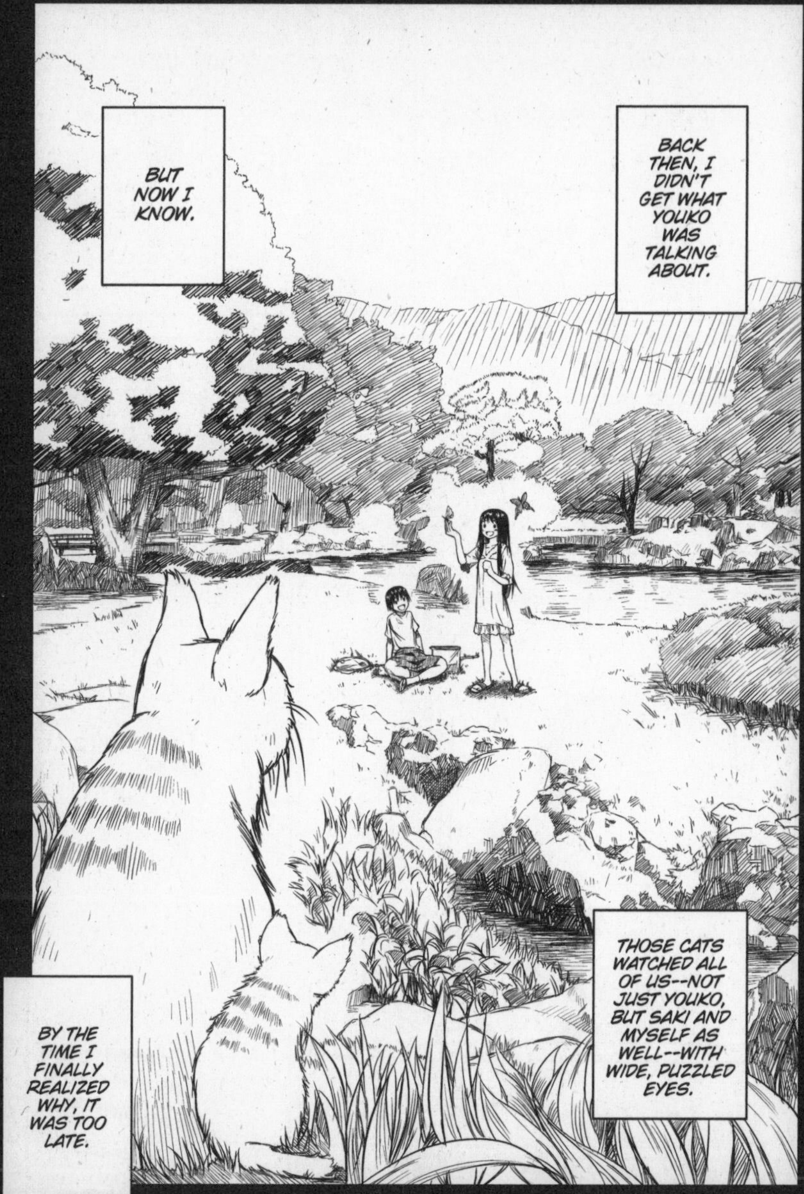
BACK THEN, I DIDN'T GET WHAT YOUKO WAS TALKING ABOUT.
BUT NOW I KNOW.
THOSE CATS WATCHED ALL OF US--NOT JUST YOUKO, BUT SAKI AND MYSELF AS WELL--WITH WIDE, PUZZLED EYES.
BY THE TIME I FINALLY REALIZED WHY, IT WAS TOO LATE.

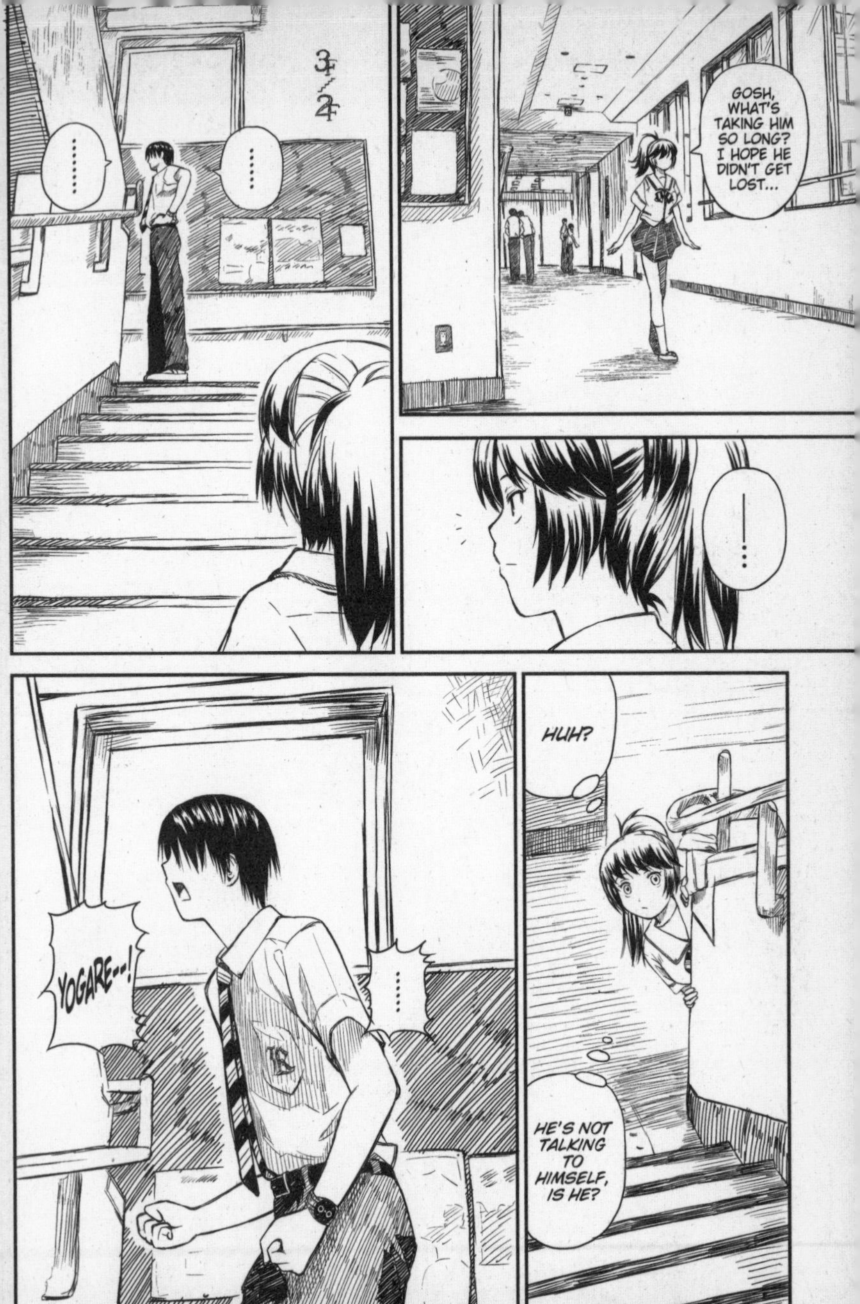
GOSH, WHAT'S TAKING HIM SO LONG? I HOPE HE DIDN'T GET LOST...
!...
......
......
HUH?
HE'S NOT TALKING TO HIMSELF, IS HE?
YOGARE--!
......

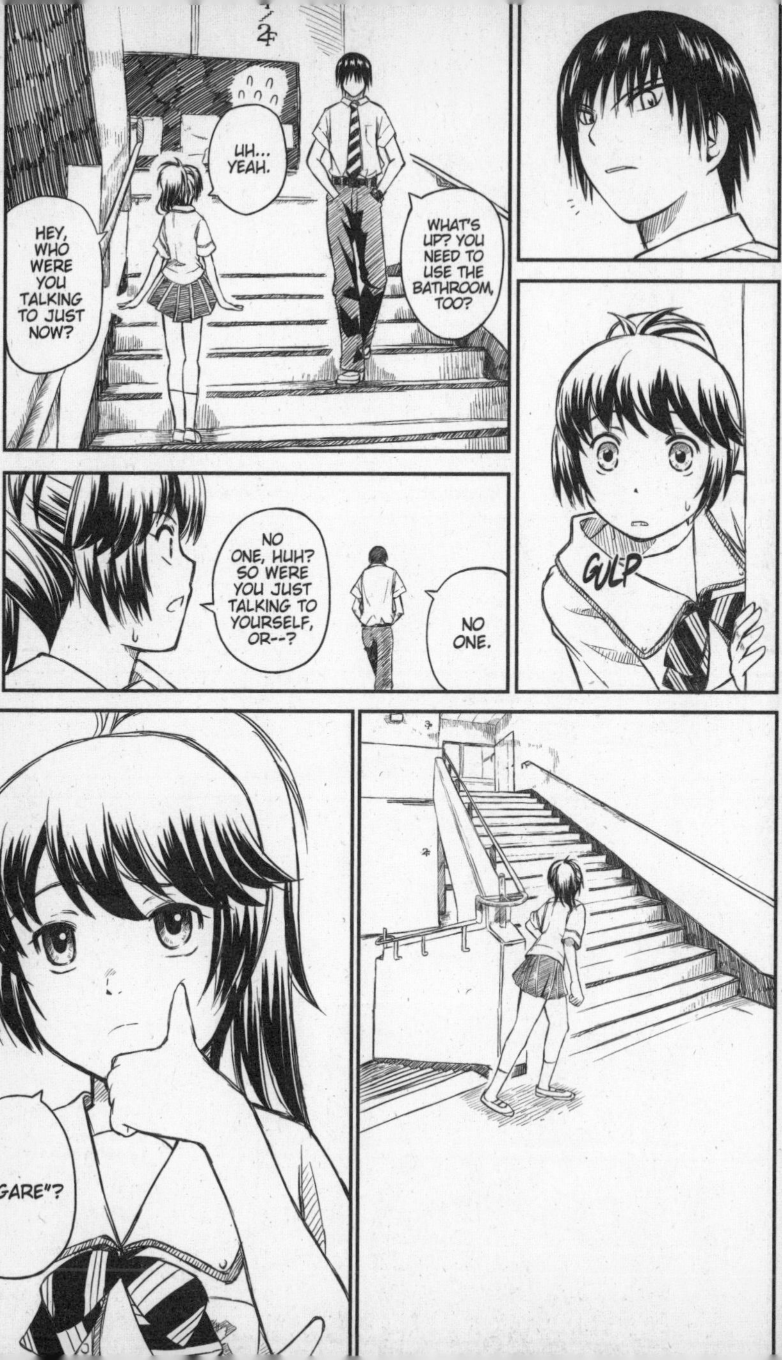
2F
WHAT'S UP? YOU NEED TO USE THE BATHROOM, TOO?
UH... YEAH.
HEY, WHO WERE YOU TALKING TO JUST NOW?
GULP
NO ONE.
NO ONE, HUH? SO WERE YOU JUST TALKING TO YOURSELF, OR--?
"YOGARE"?

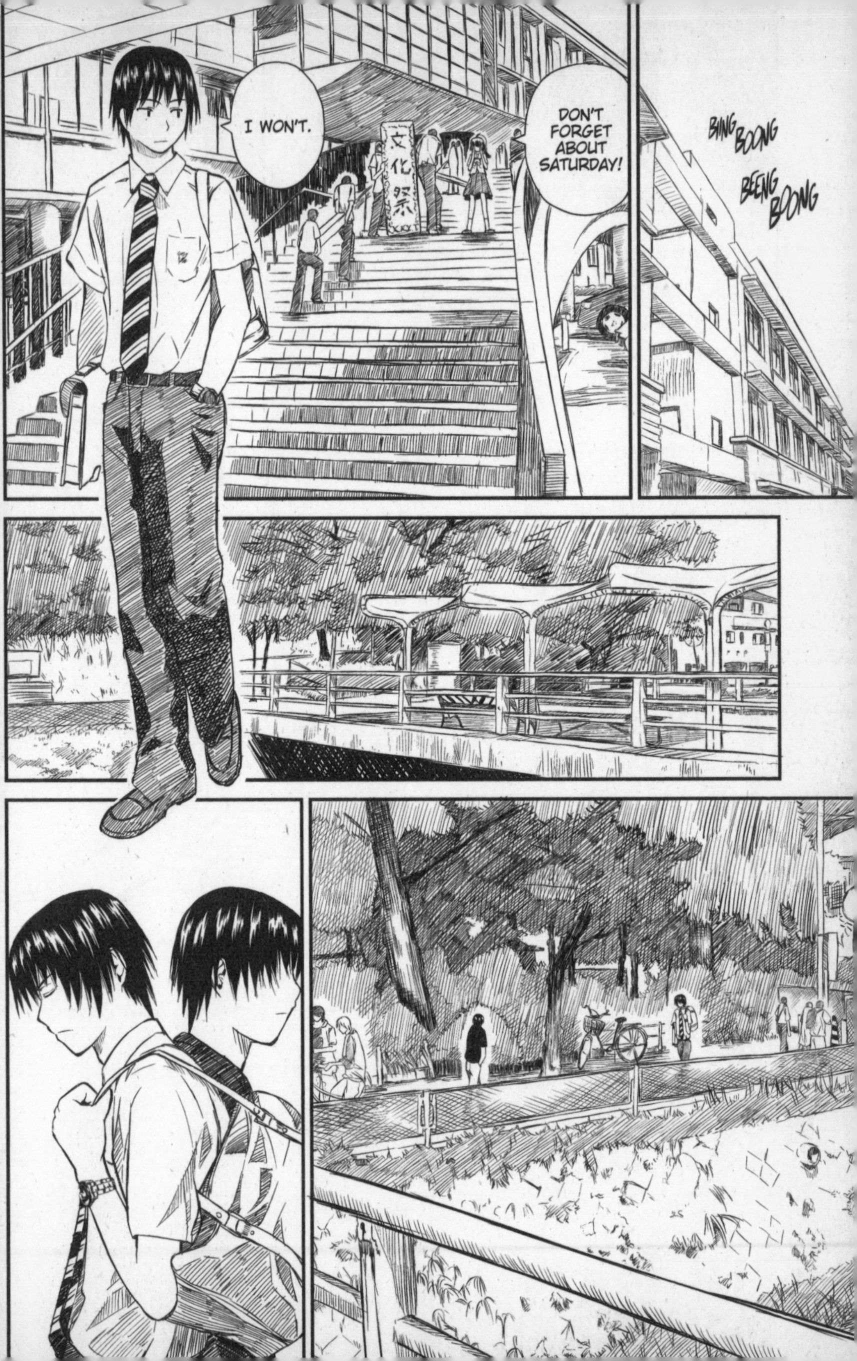
BING BOONG
BEENG BOONG
DON'T FORGET ABOUT SATURDAY!
I WON'T.
文化祭

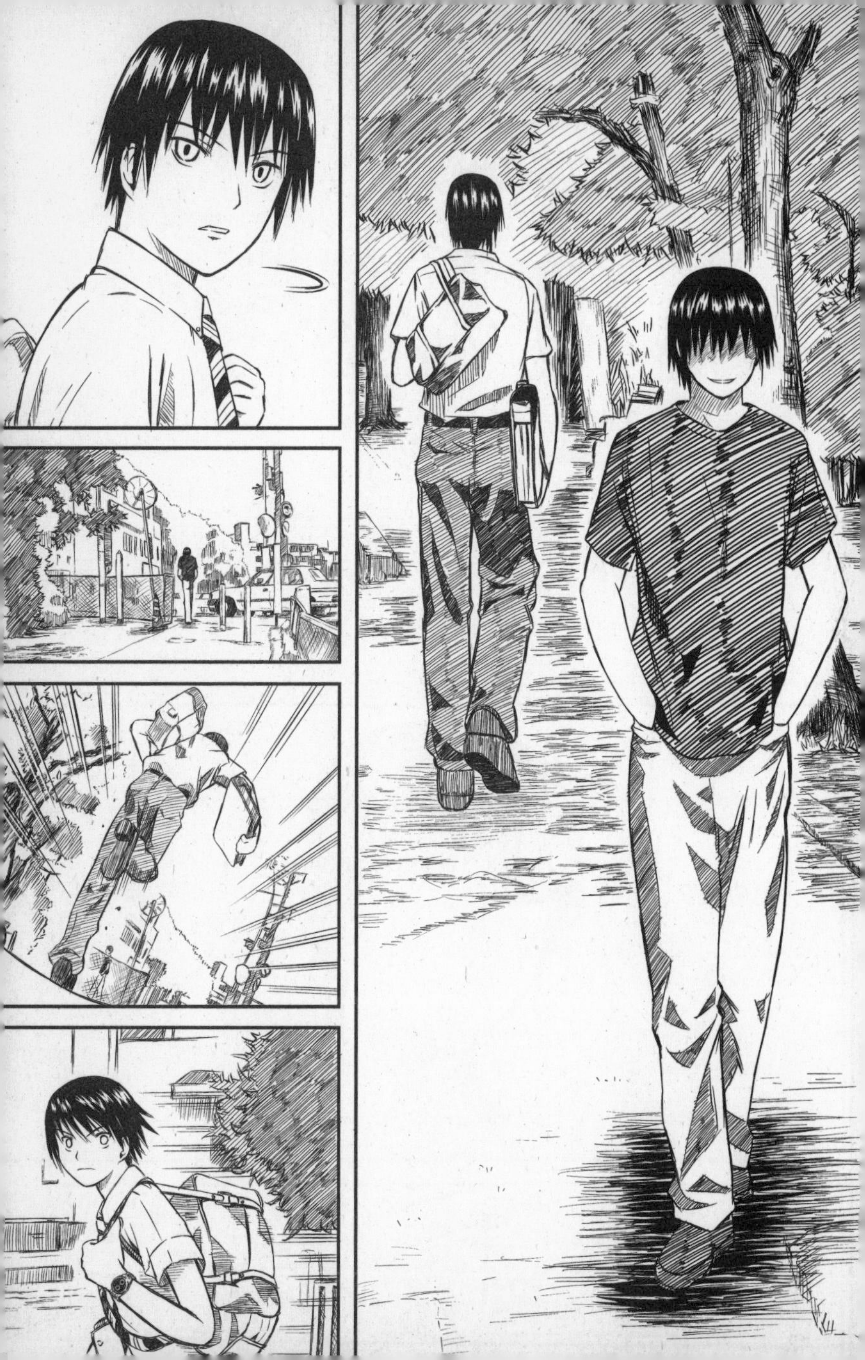

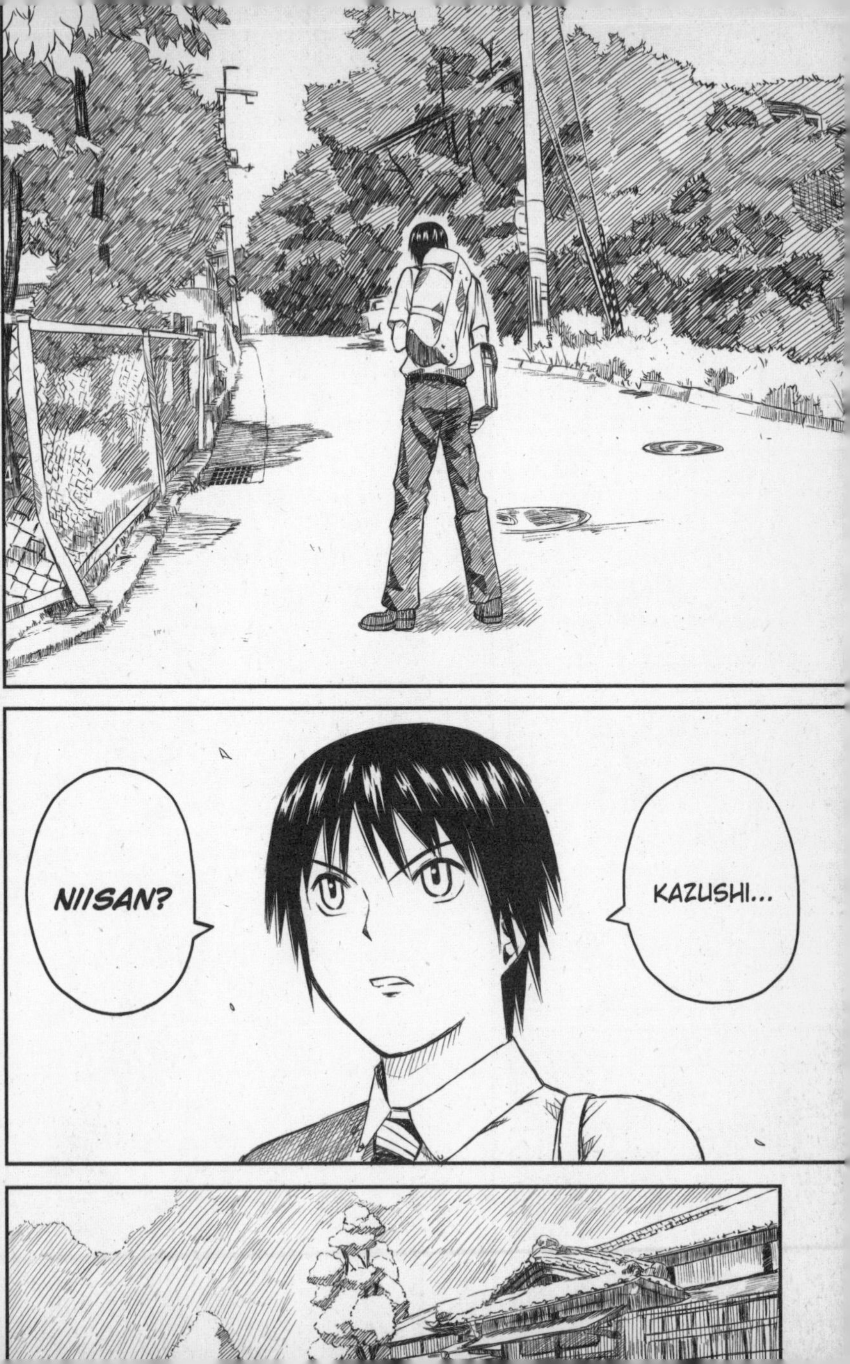
KAZUSHI...
NIISAN?

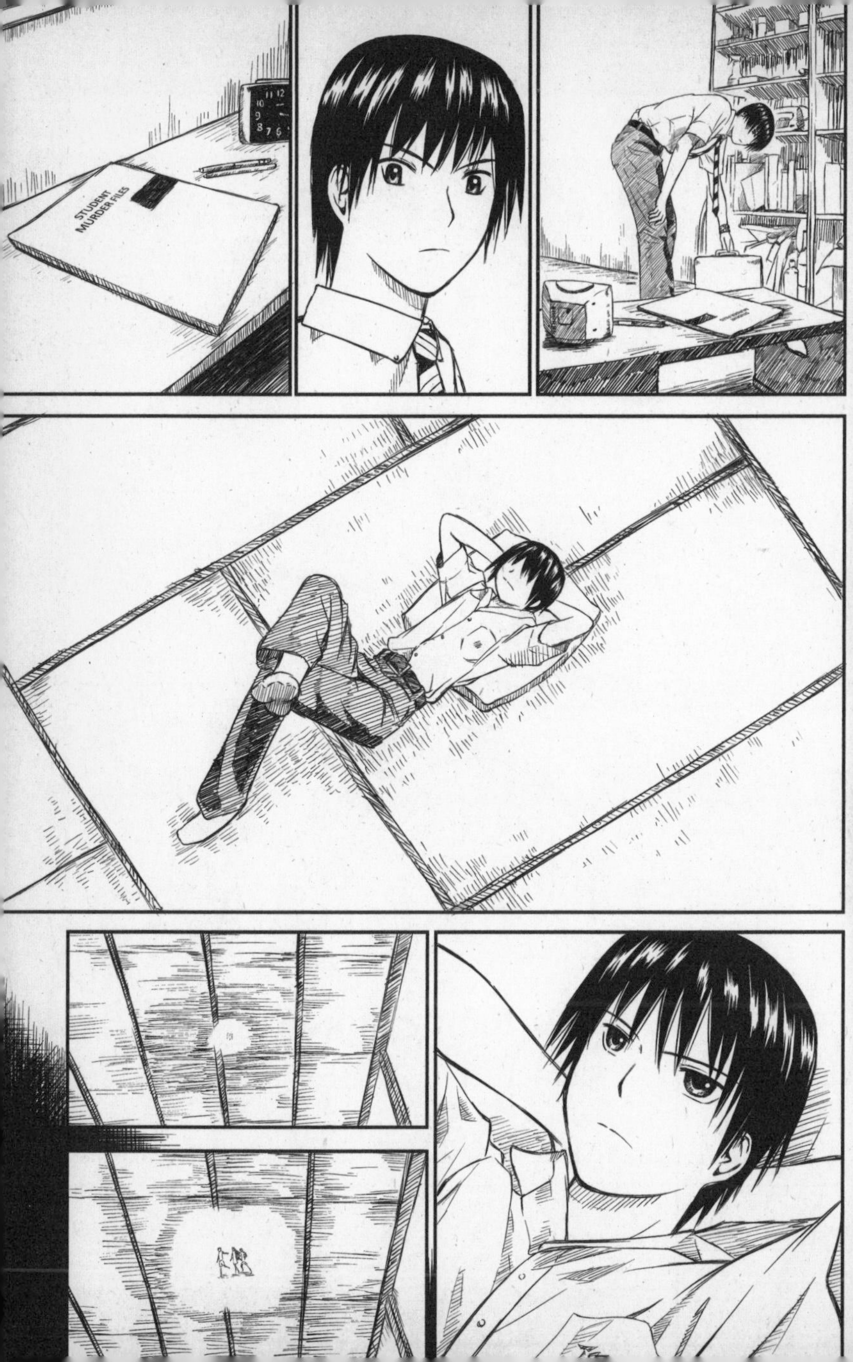
STUDENT
MURDER FILES

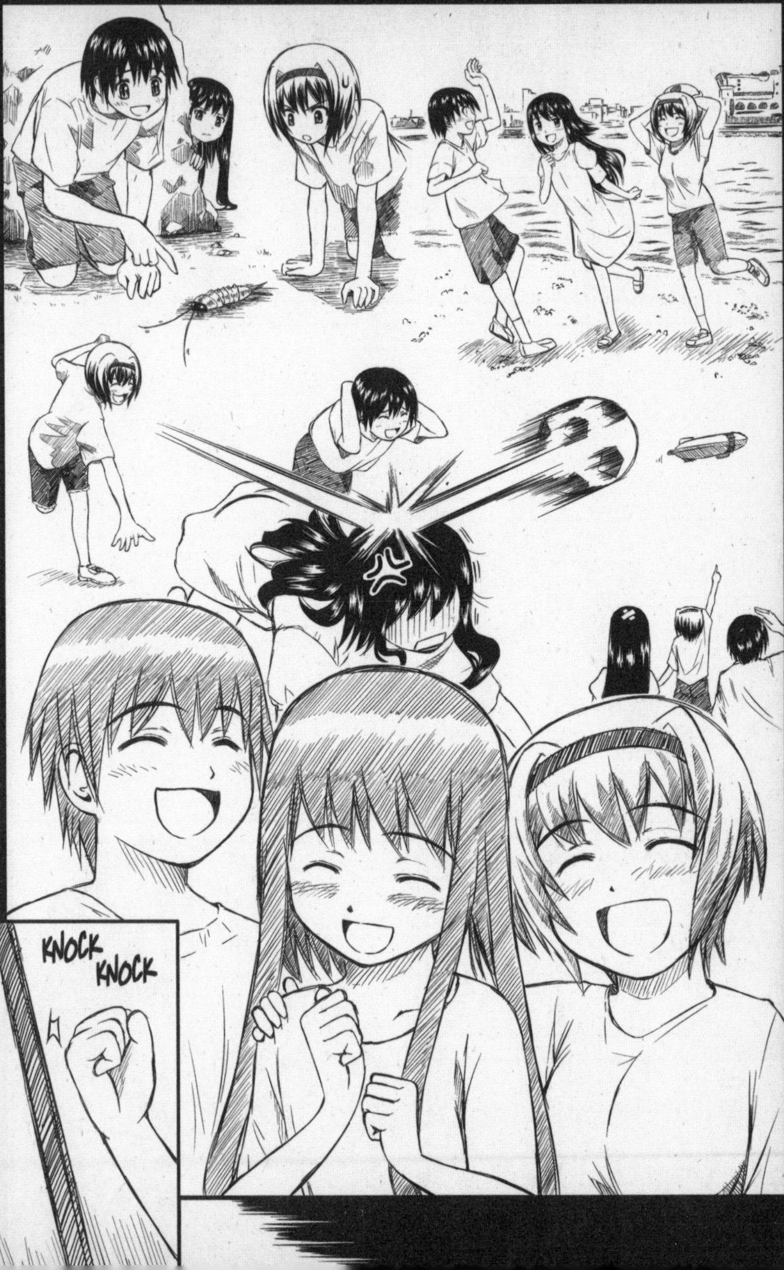
KNOCK
KNOCK

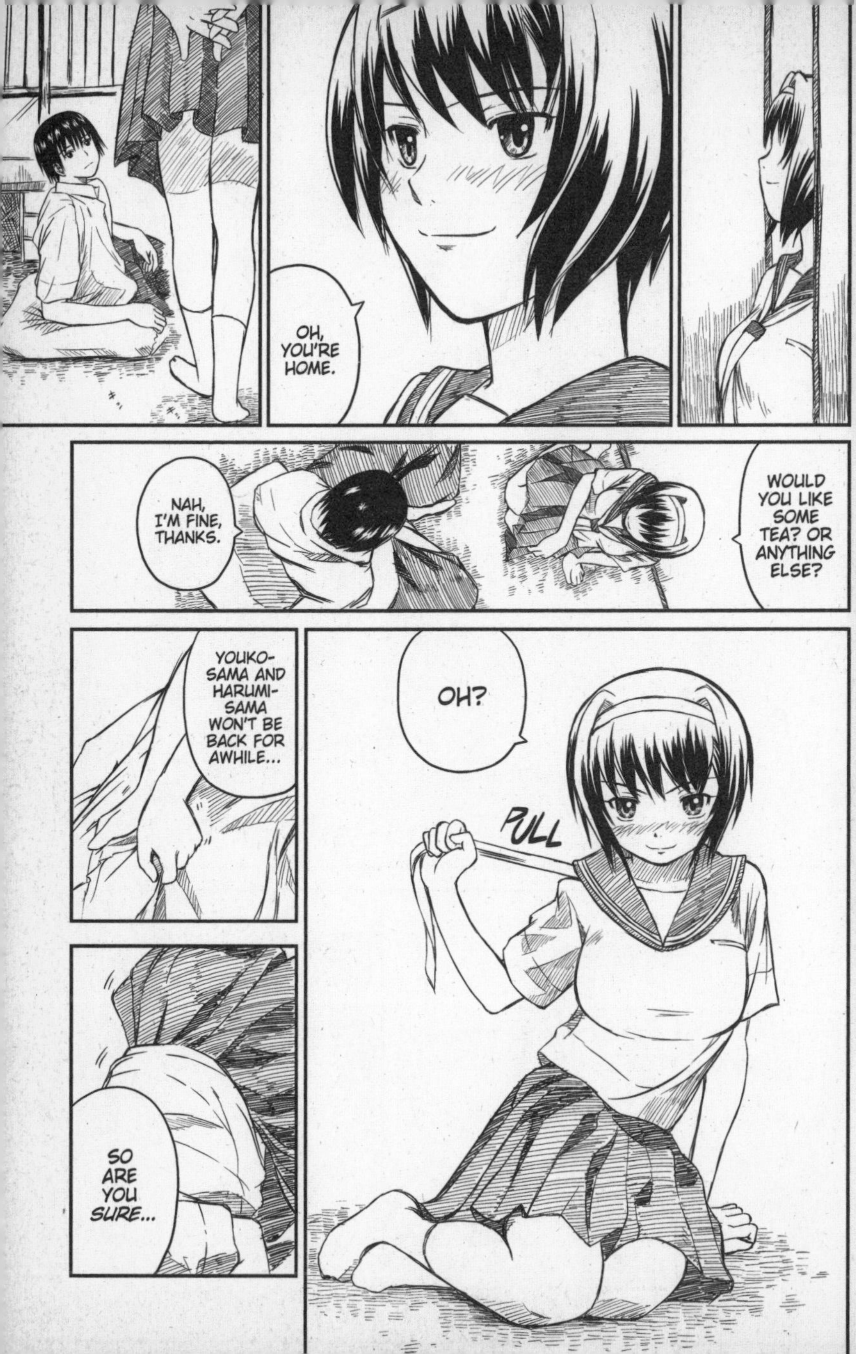
OH, YOU'RE HOME.
WOULD YOU LIKE SOME TEA? OR ANYTHING ELSE?
NAH, I'M FINE, THANKS.
OH?
PULL
YOUKO-SAMA AND HARUMI-SAMA WON'T BE BACK FOR AWHILE...
SO ARE YOU SURE...

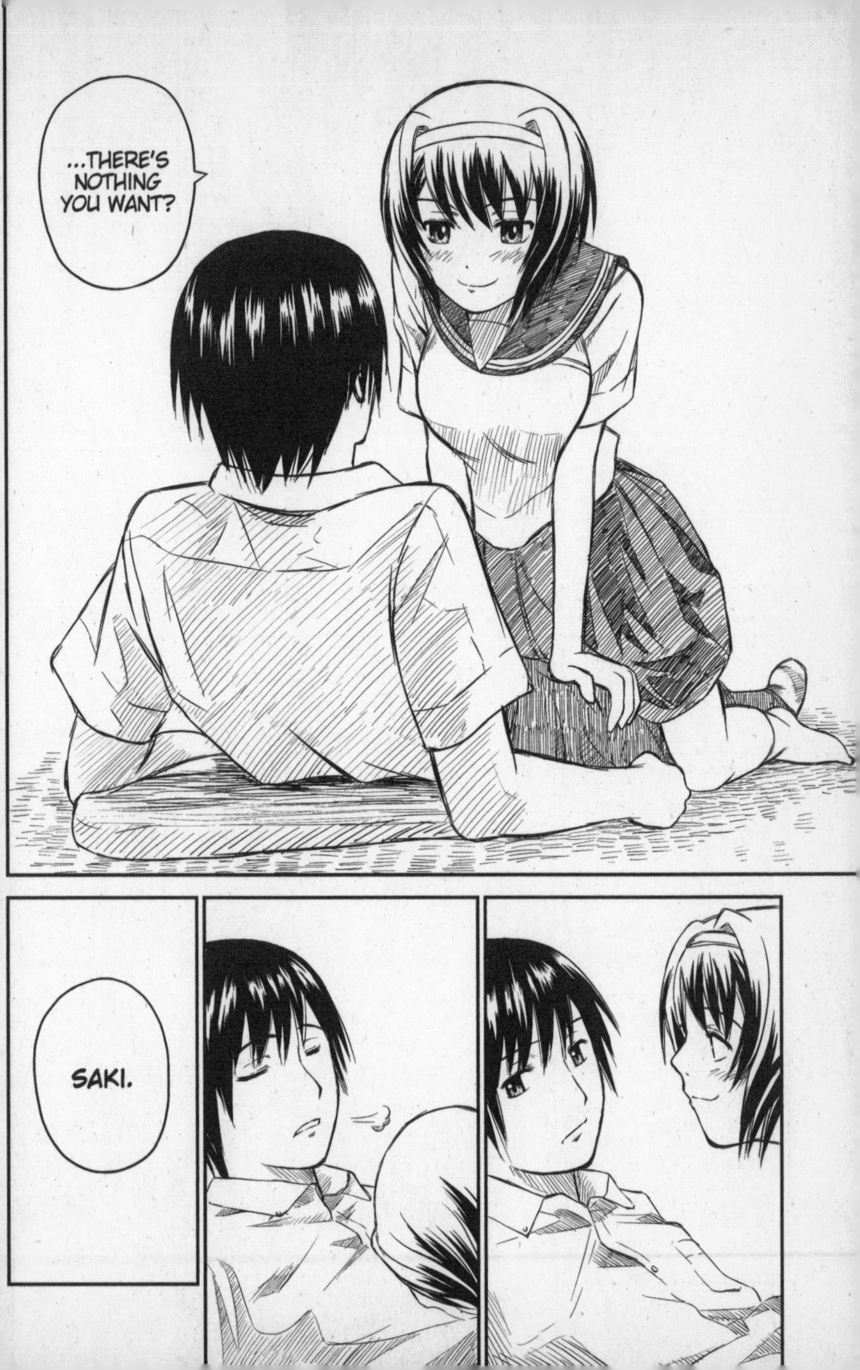
...THERE'S NOTHING YOU WANT?
SAKI.

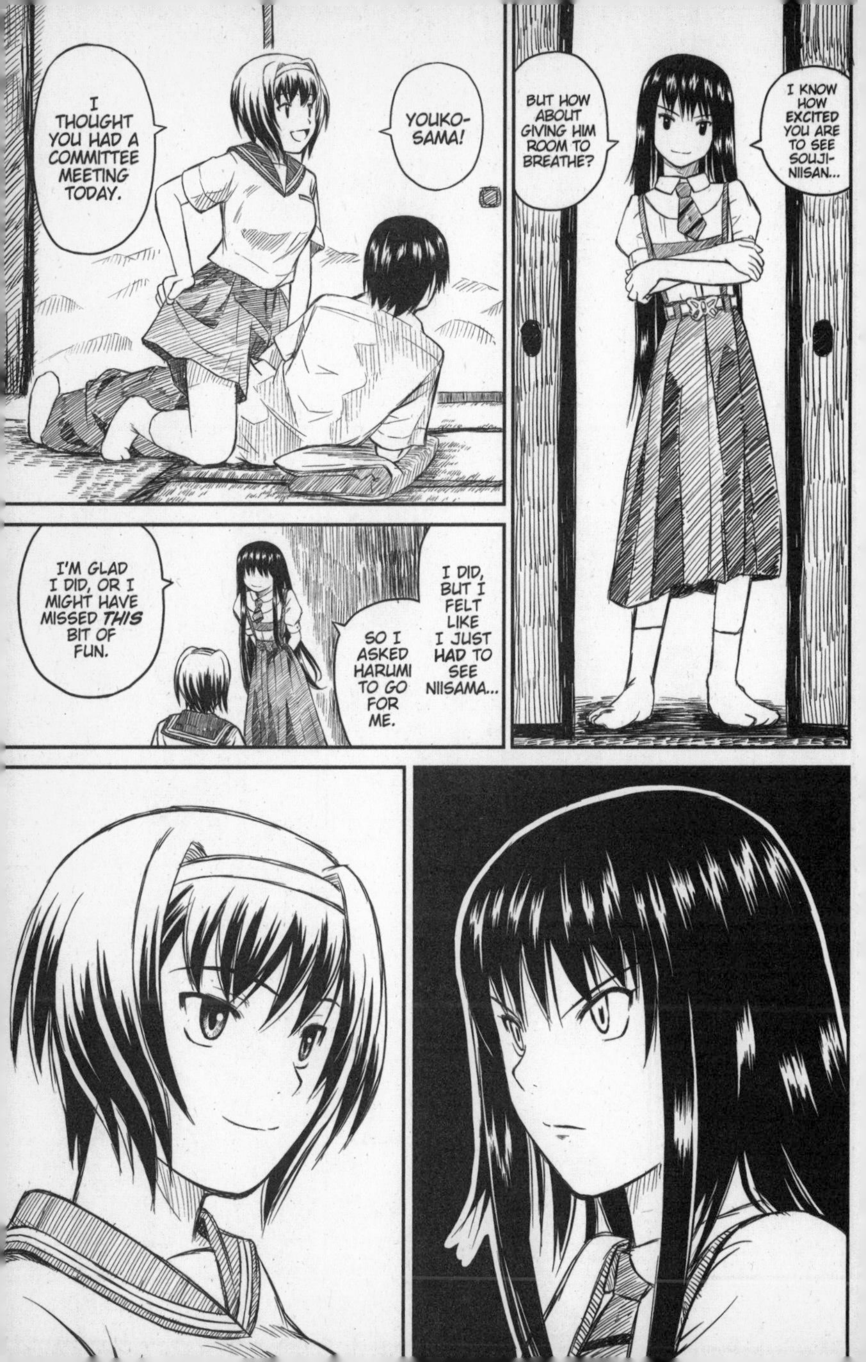
I KNOW HOW EXCITED YOU ARE TO SEE SOUJI-NIISAN...
BUT HOW ABOUT GIVING HIM ROOM TO BREATHE?
YOUKO-SAMA!
I THOUGHT YOU HAD A COMMITTEE MEETING TODAY.
I DID, BUT I FELT LIKE I JUST HAD TO SEE NIISAMA...
SO I ASKED HARUMI TO GO FOR ME.
I'M GLAD I DID, OR I MIGHT HAVE MISSED *THIS* BIT OF FUN.

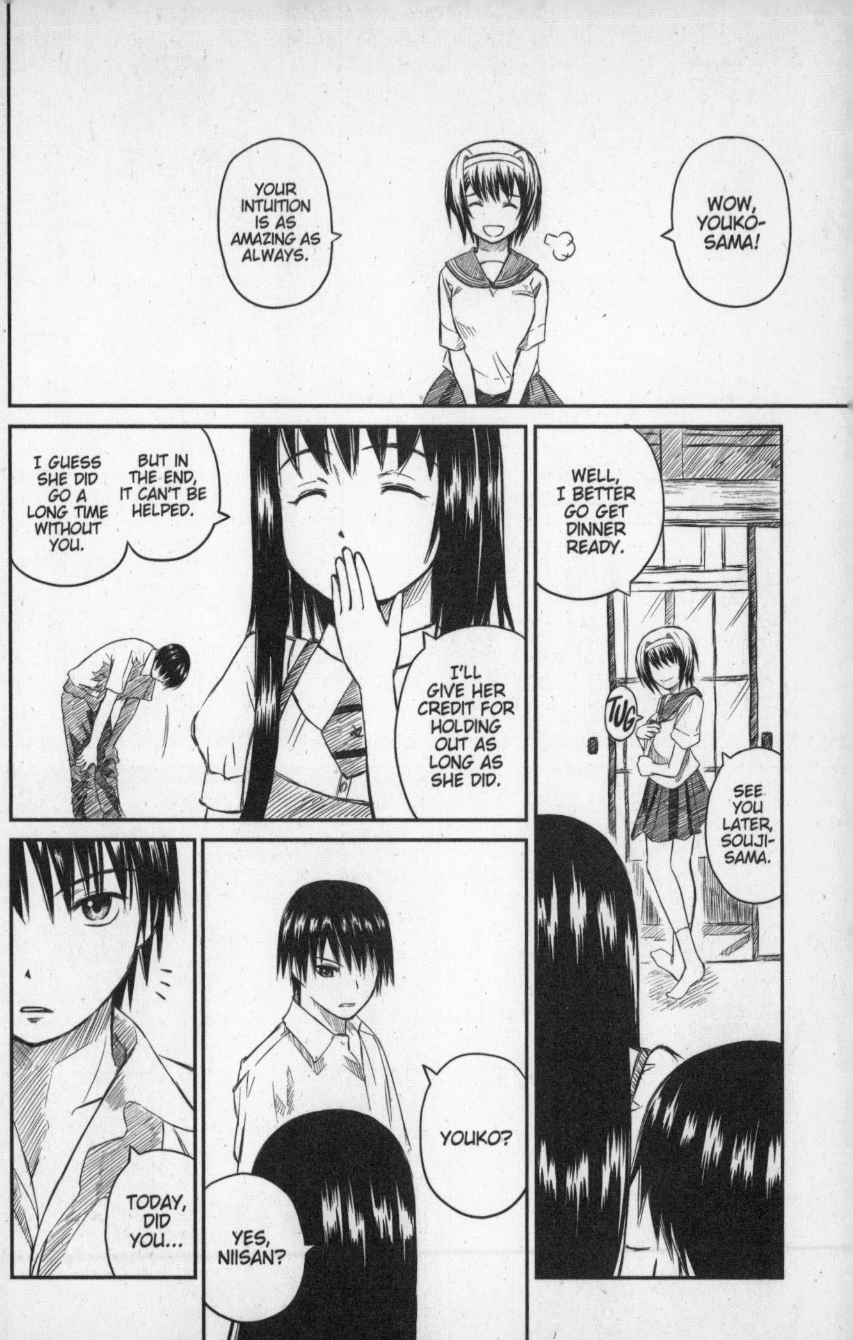
WOW, YOUKO-SAMA!
YOUR INTUITION IS AS AMAZING AS ALWAYS.
WELL, I BETTER GO GET DINNER READY.
TUG
SEE YOU LATER, SOUJI-SAMA.
BUT IN THE END, IT CAN'T BE HELPED.
I GUESS SHE DID GO A LONG TIME WITHOUT YOU.
I'LL GIVE HER CREDIT FOR HOLDING OUT AS LONG AS SHE DID.
YOUKO?
YES, NIISAN?
TODAY, DID YOU...

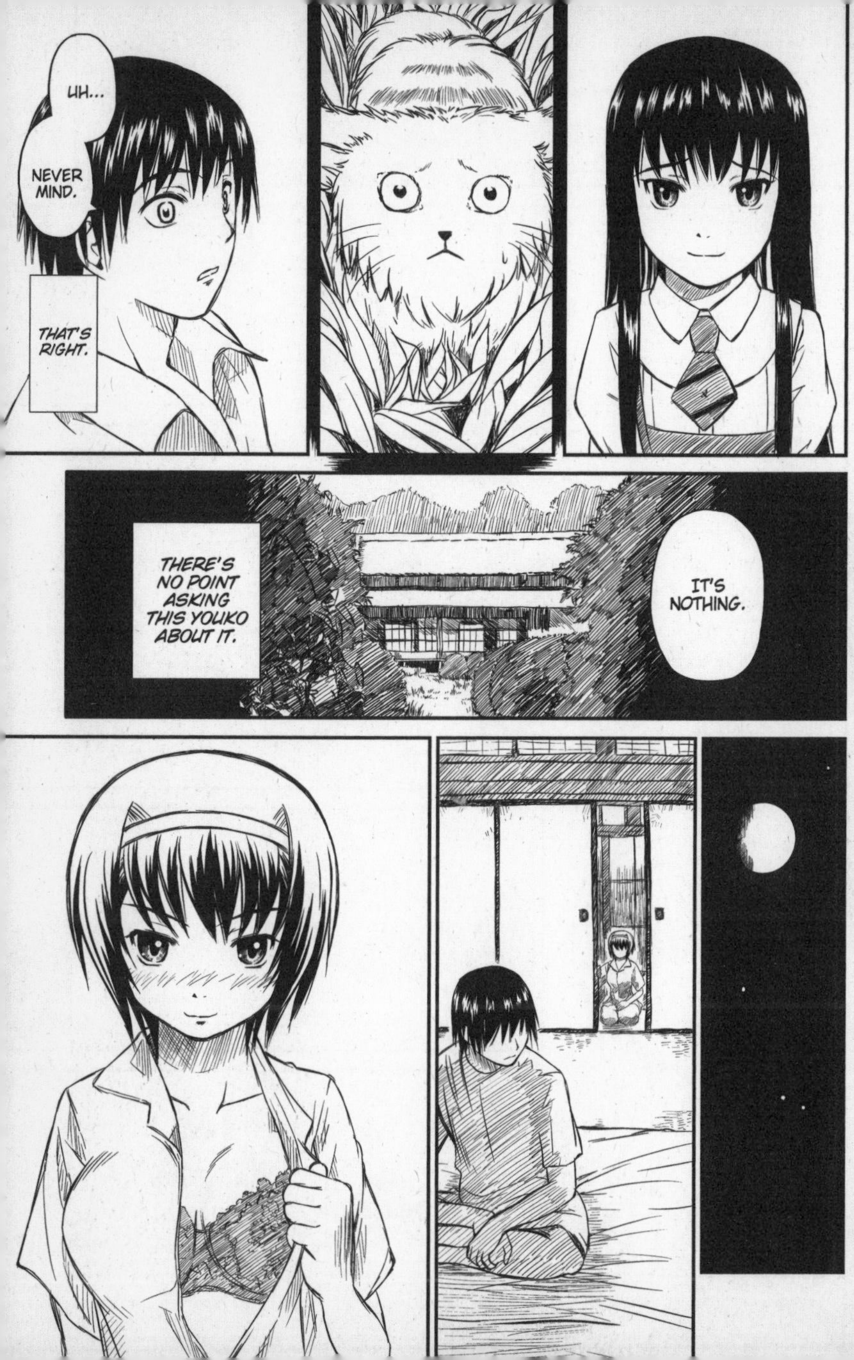
UH...
NEVER MIND.
THAT'S RIGHT.
IT'S NOTHING.
THERE'S NO POINT ASKING THIS YOUKO ABOUT IT.

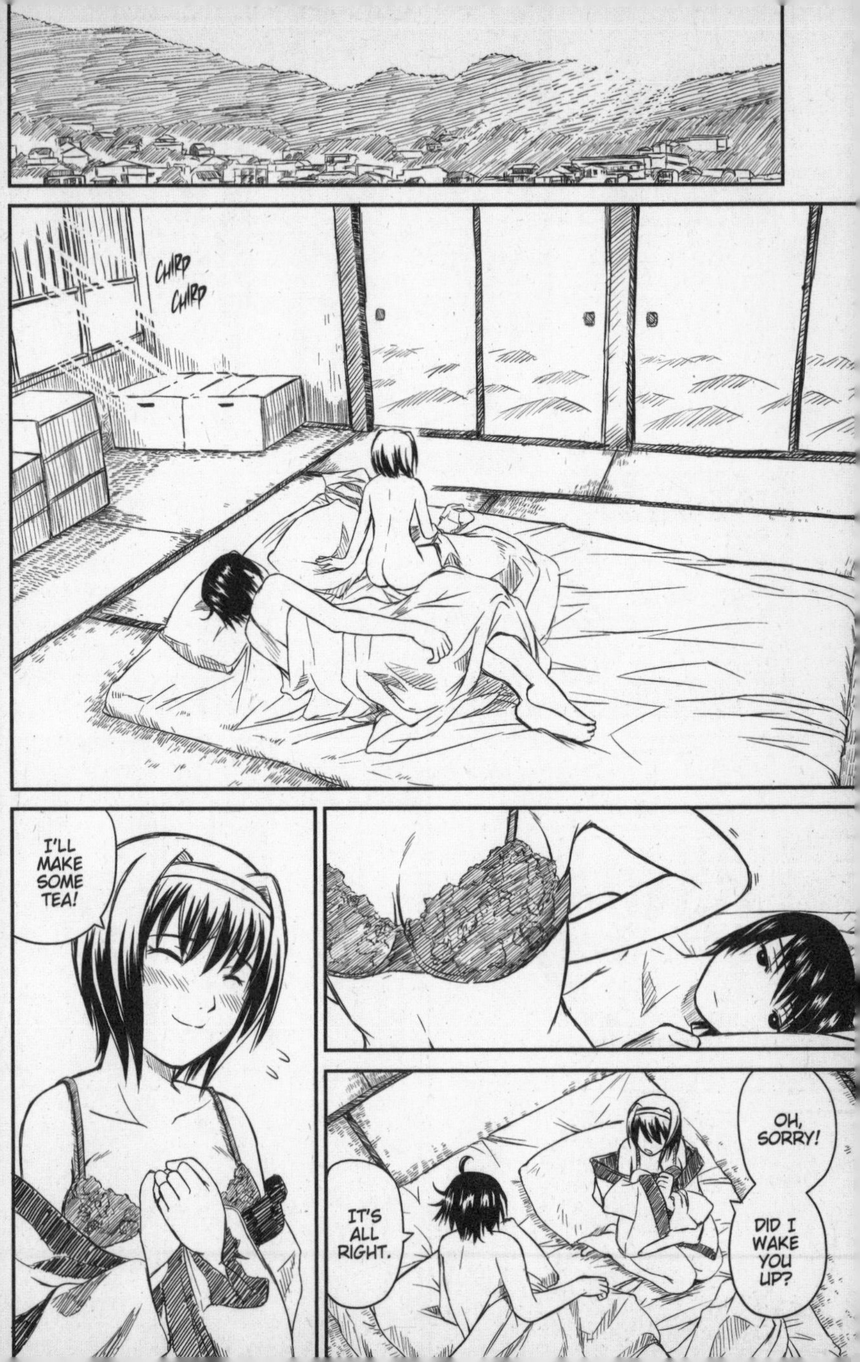
CHIRP
CHIRP
OH, SORRY!
DID I WAKE YOU UP?
IT'S ALL RIGHT.
I'LL MAKE SOME TEA!

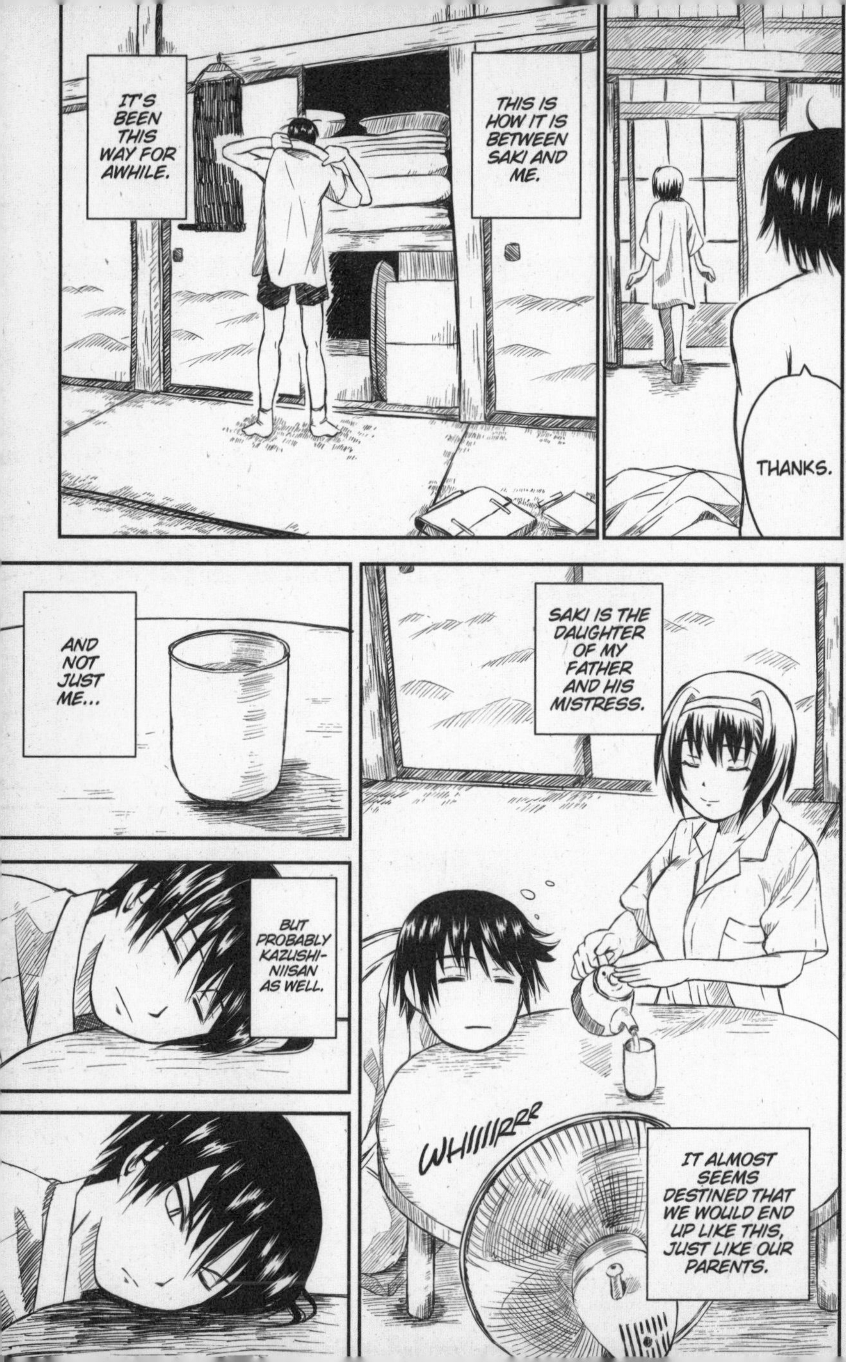
THANKS.
THIS IS HOW IT IS BETWEEN SAKI AND ME.
IT'S BEEN THIS WAY FOR AWHILE.
SAKI IS THE DAUGHTER OF MY FATHER AND HIS MISTRESS.
WHIIIIRRR
IT ALMOST SEEMS DESTINED THAT WE WOULD END UP LIKE THIS, JUST LIKE OUR PARENTS.
AND NOT JUST ME...
BUT PROBABLY KAZUSHI-NIISAN AS WELL.

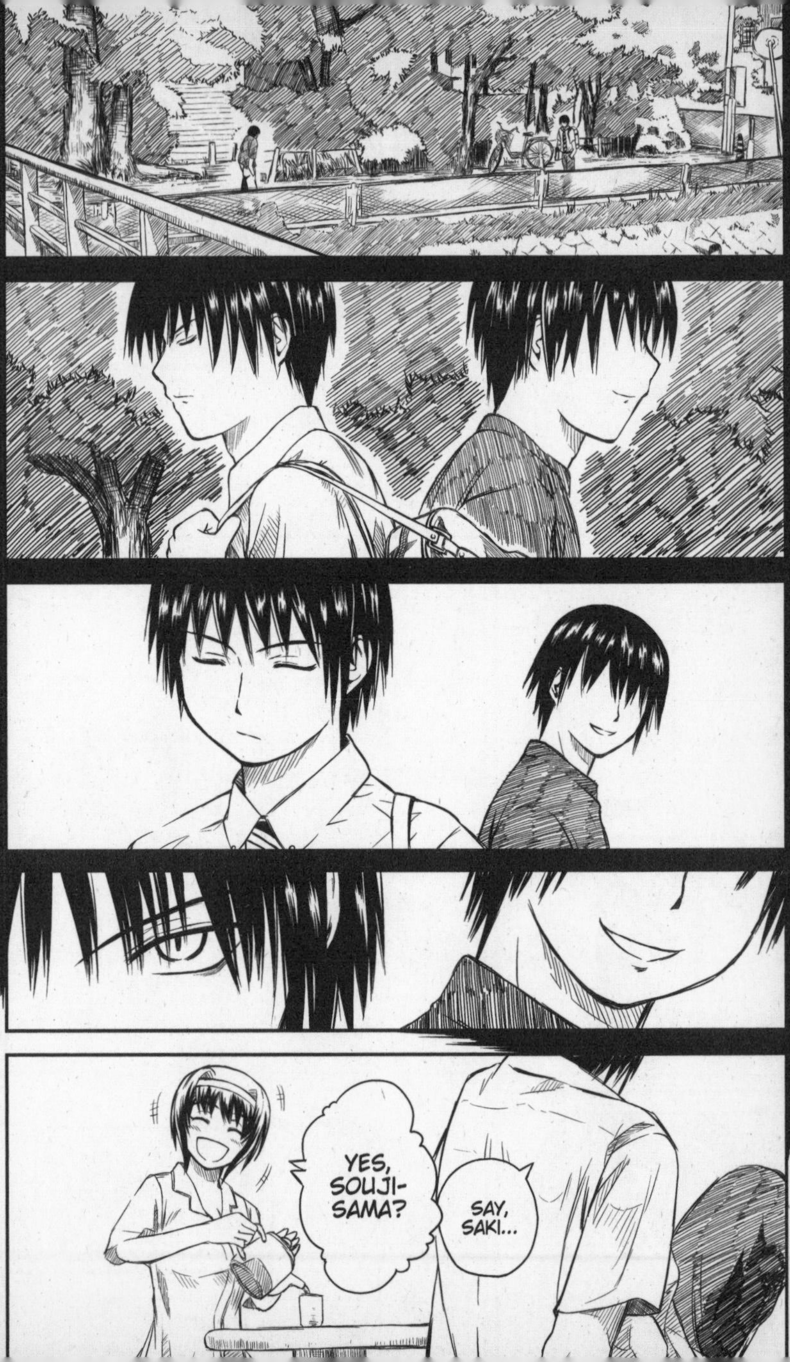
SAY, SAKI...
YES, SOUJI-SAMA?

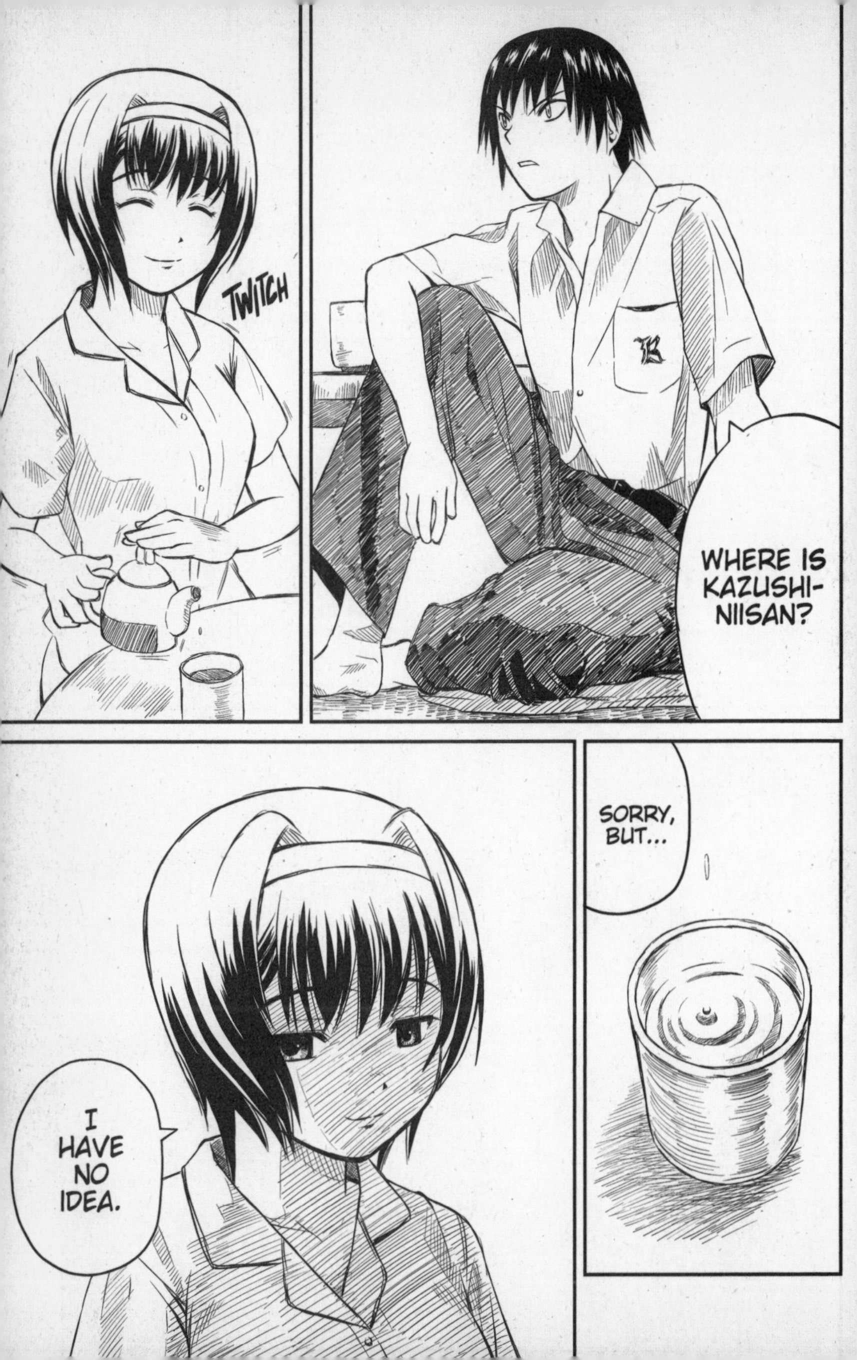
WHERE IS KAZUSHI-NIISAN?
TWITCH
SORRY, BUT...
I HAVE NO IDEA.

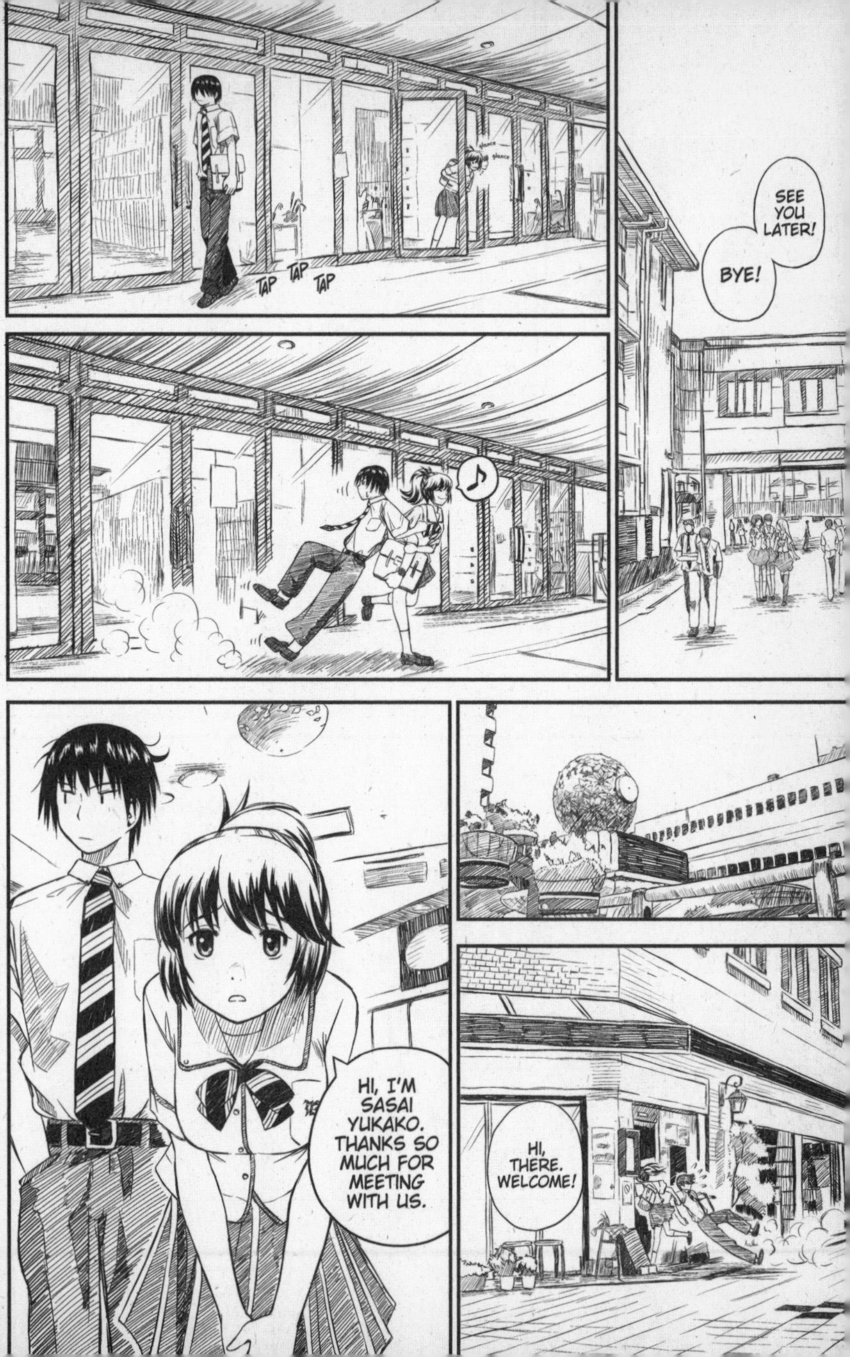
SEE YOU LATER!
BYE!
glance glance
TAP TAP TAP
♪
HI, THERE. WELCOME!
HI, I'M SASAI YUKAKO. THANKS SO MUCH FOR MEETING WITH US.

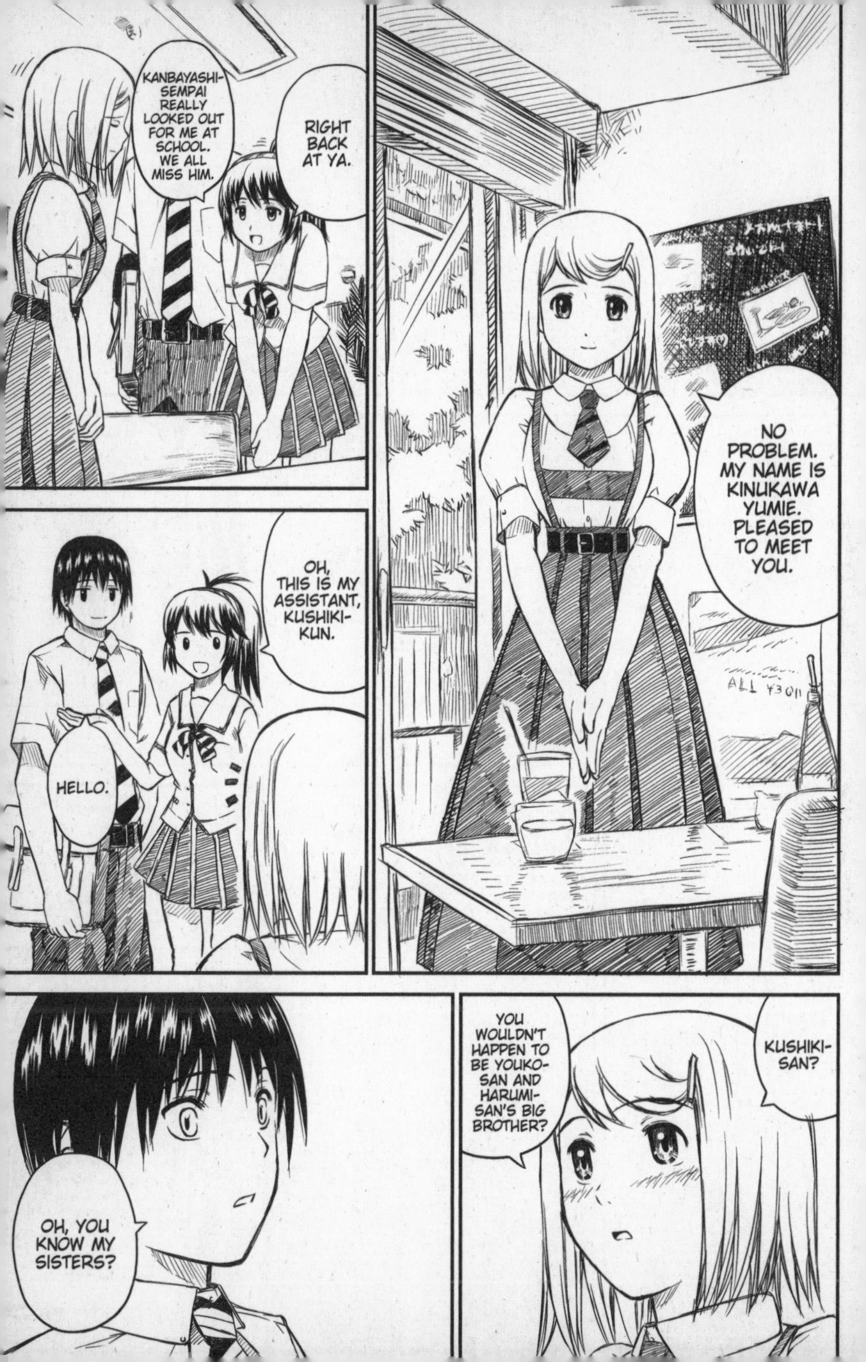
NO PROBLEM. MY NAME IS KINUKAWA YUMIE. PLEASED TO MEET YOU.
ALL ¥300
RIGHT BACK AT YA.
KANBAYASHI-SEMPAI REALLY LOOKED OUT FOR ME AT SCHOOL. WE ALL MISS HIM.
OH, THIS IS MY ASSISTANT, KUSHIKI-KUN.
HELLO.
KUSHIKI-SAN?
YOU WOULDN'T HAPPEN TO BE YOUKO-SAN AND HARUMI-SAN'S BIG BROTHER?
OH, YOU KNOW MY SISTERS?

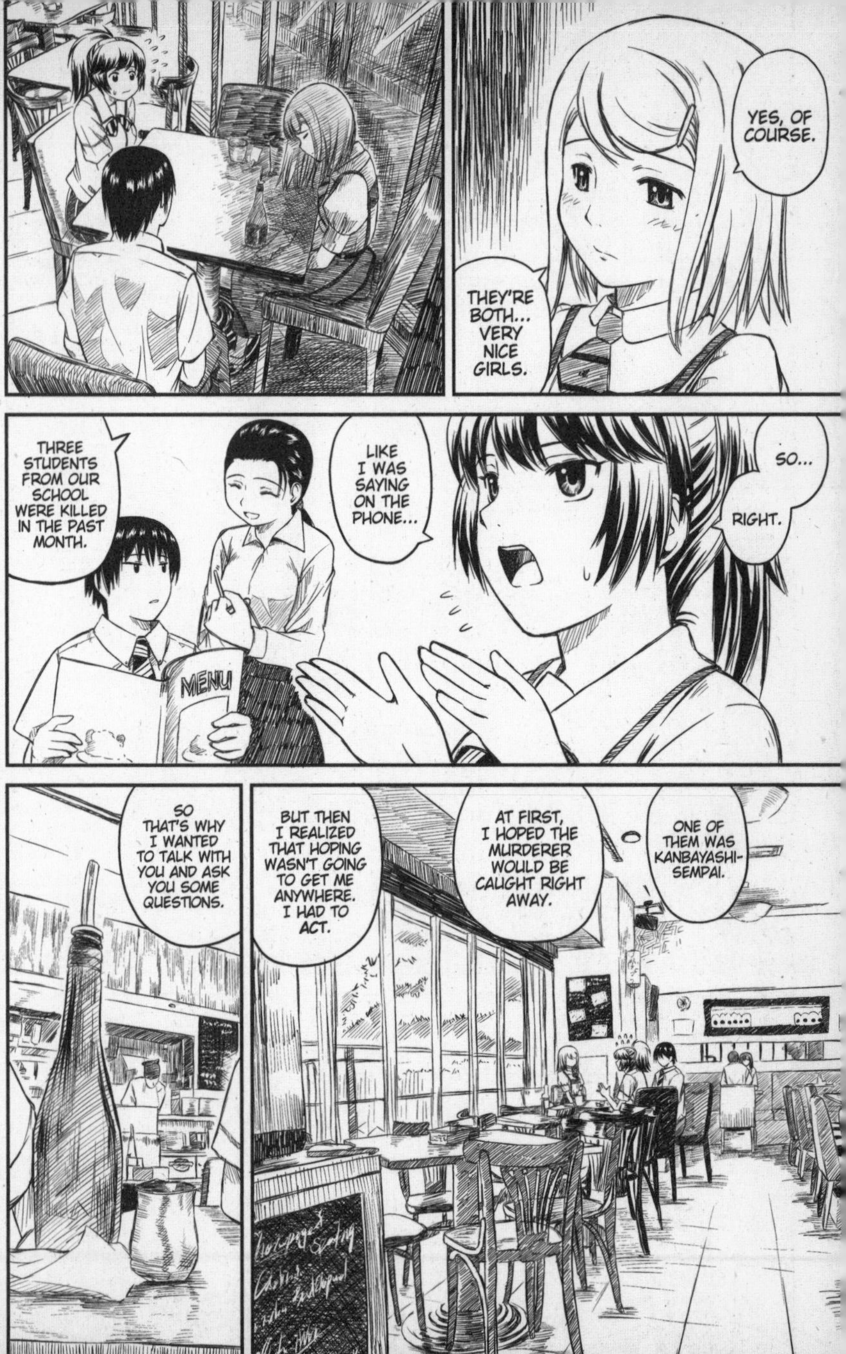
YES, OF COURSE.
THEY'RE BOTH... VERY NICE GIRLS.
SO...
RIGHT.
LIKE I WAS SAYING ON THE PHONE...
THREE STUDENTS FROM OUR SCHOOL WERE KILLED IN THE PAST MONTH.
MENU
ONE OF THEM WAS KANBAYASHI-SEMPAI.
AT FIRST, I HOPED THE MURDERER WOULD BE CAUGHT RIGHT AWAY.
BUT THEN I REALIZED THAT HOPING WASN'T GOING TO GET ME ANYWHERE. I HAD TO ACT.
SO THAT'S WHY I WANTED TO TALK WITH YOU AND ASK YOU SOME QUESTIONS.

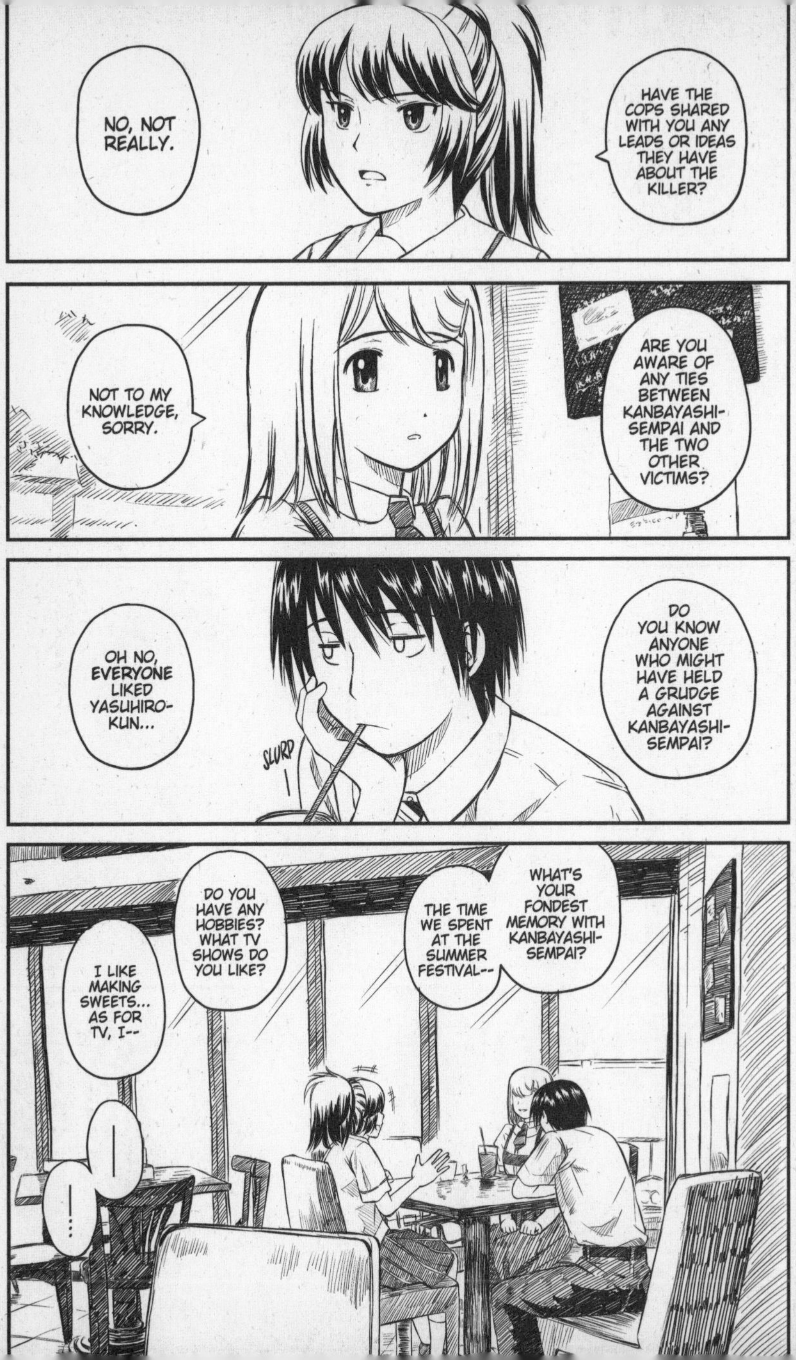
HAVE THE COPS SHARED WITH YOU ANY LEADS OR IDEAS THEY HAVE ABOUT THE KILLER?
NO, NOT REALLY.
ARE YOU AWARE OF ANY TIES BETWEEN KANBAYASHI-SEMPAI AND THE TWO OTHER VICTIMS?
NOT TO MY KNOWLEDGE, SORRY.
DO YOU KNOW ANYONE WHO MIGHT HAVE HELD A GRUDGE AGAINST KANBAYASHI-SEMPAI?
SLURP
OH NO, EVERYONE LIKED YASUHIRO-KUN...
WHAT'S YOUR FONDEST MEMORY WITH KANBAYASHI-SEMPAI?
THE TIME WE SPENT AT THE SUMMER FESTIVAL--
DO YOU HAVE ANY HOBBIES? WHAT TV SHOWS DO YOU LIKE?
I LIKE MAKING SWEETS... AS FOR TV, I--

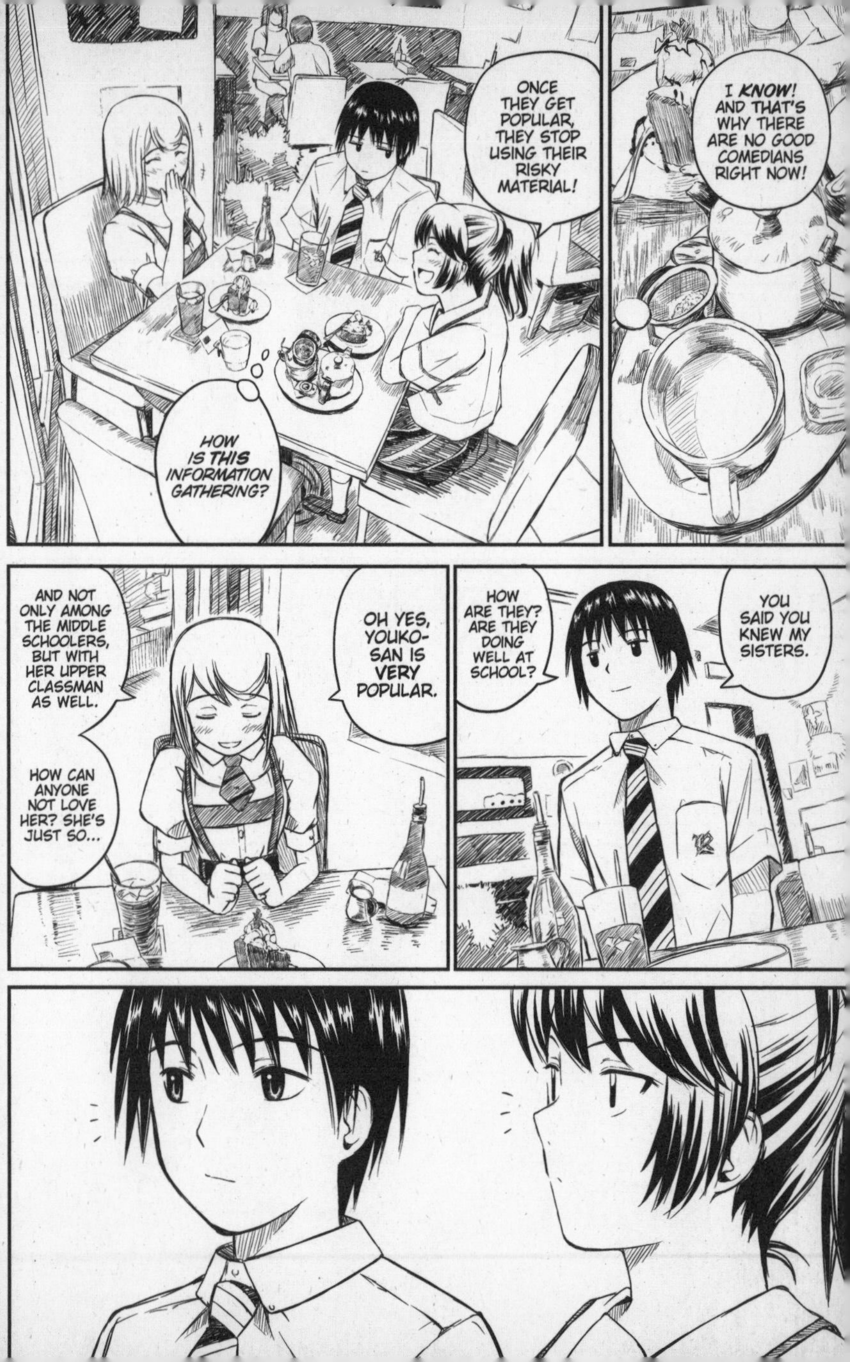
I KNOW! AND THAT'S WHY THERE ARE NO GOOD COMEDIANS RIGHT NOW!
ONCE THEY GET POPULAR, THEY STOP USING THEIR RISKY MATERIAL!
HOW IS THIS INFORMATION GATHERING?
YOU SAID YOU KNEW MY SISTERS.
HOW ARE THEY? ARE THEY DOING WELL AT SCHOOL?
OH YES, YOUKO-SAN IS VERY POPULAR.
AND NOT ONLY AMONG THE MIDDLE SCHOOLERS, BUT WITH HER UPPER CLASSMAN AS WELL.
HOW CAN ANYONE NOT LOVE HER? SHE'S JUST SO...

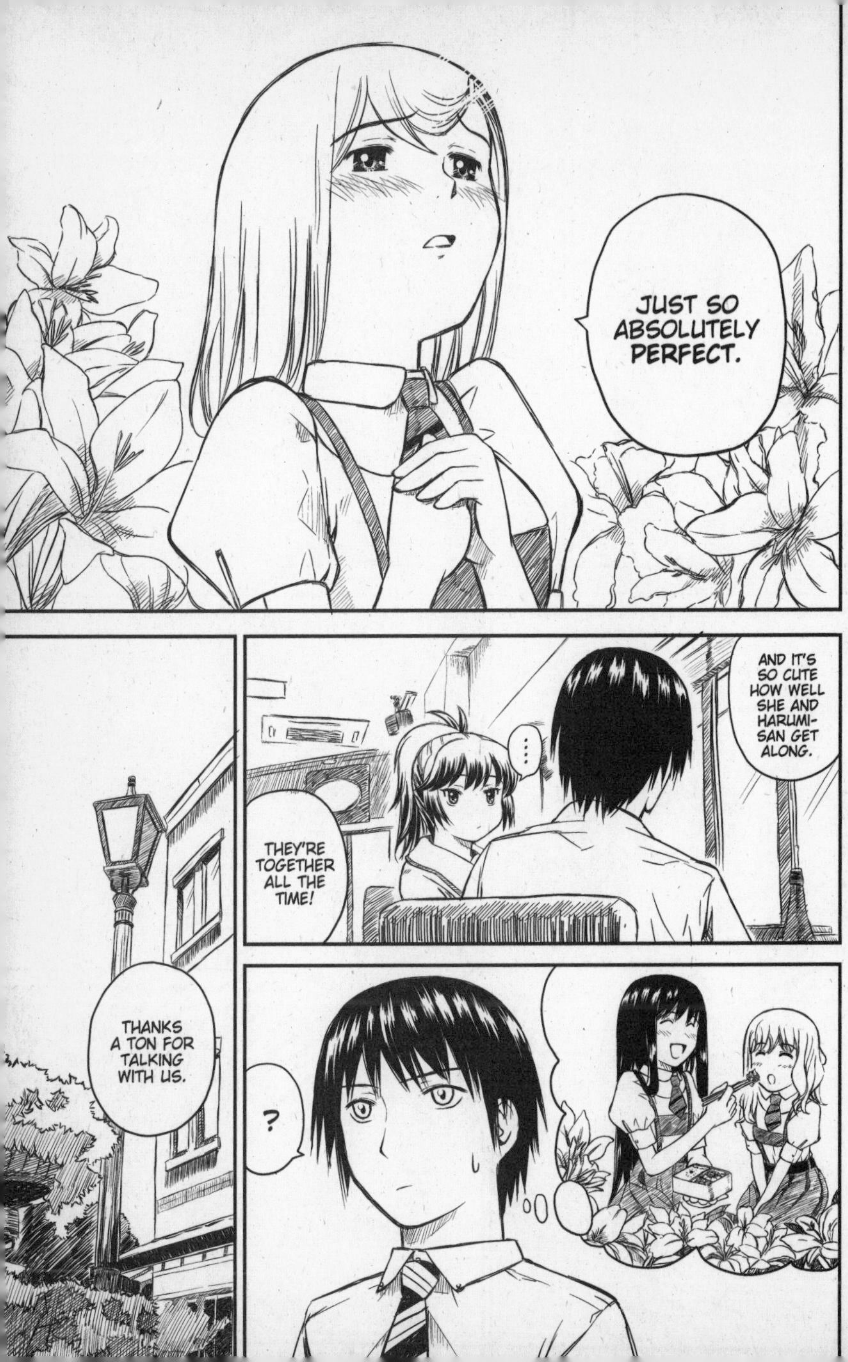
JUST SO ABSOLUTELY PERFECT.
AND IT'S SO CUTE HOW WELL SHE AND HARUMI-SAN GET ALONG.
....
THEY'RE TOGETHER ALL THE TIME!
?
THANKS A TON FOR TALKING WITH US.

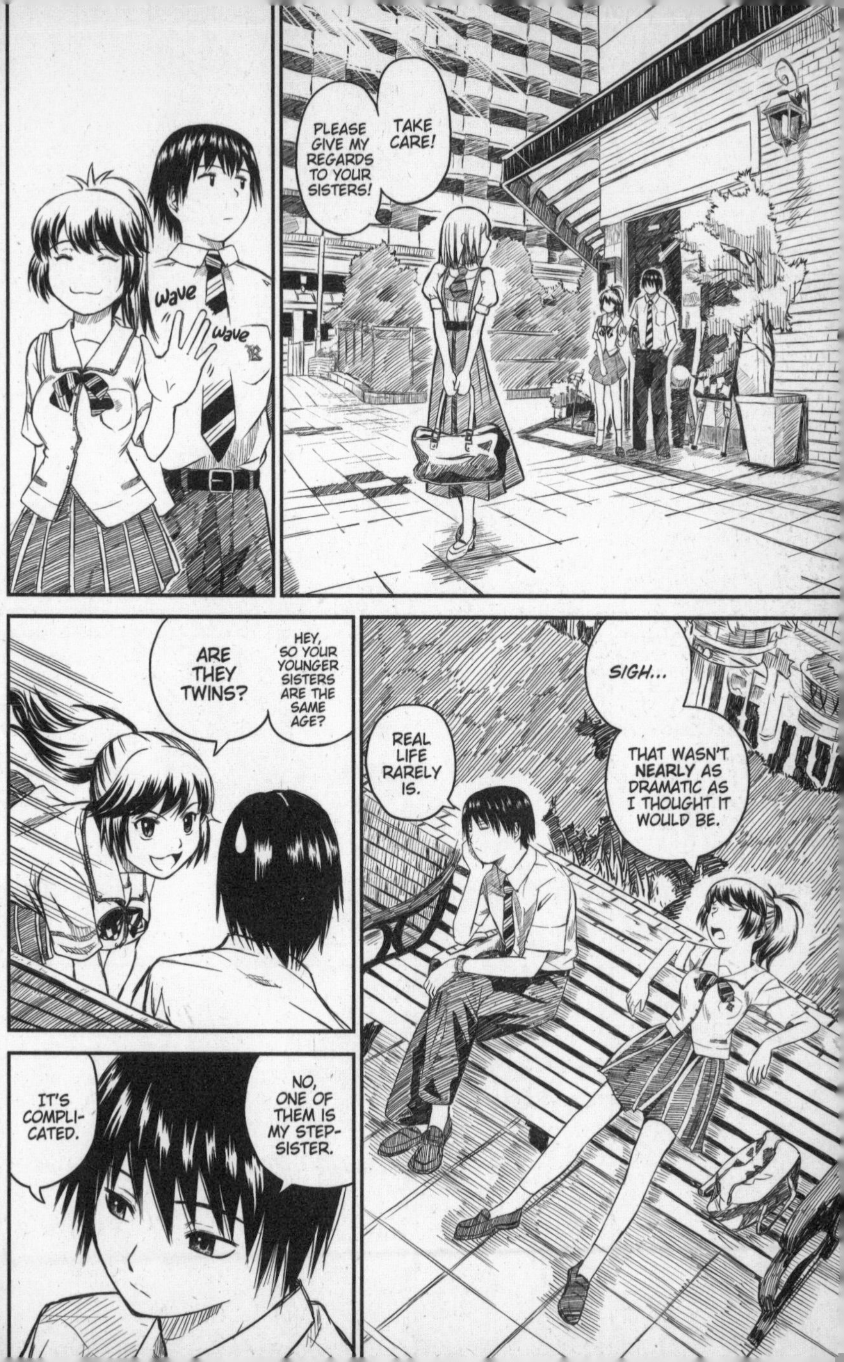
TAKE CARE!
PLEASE GIVE MY REGARDS TO YOUR SISTERS!
wave
wave
SIGH...
THAT WASN'T NEARLY AS DRAMATIC AS I THOUGHT IT WOULD BE.
REAL LIFE RARELY IS.
HEY, SO YOUR YOUNGER SISTERS ARE THE SAME AGE?
ARE THEY TWINS?
NO, ONE OF THEM IS MY STEP-SISTER.
IT'S COMPLI-CATED.

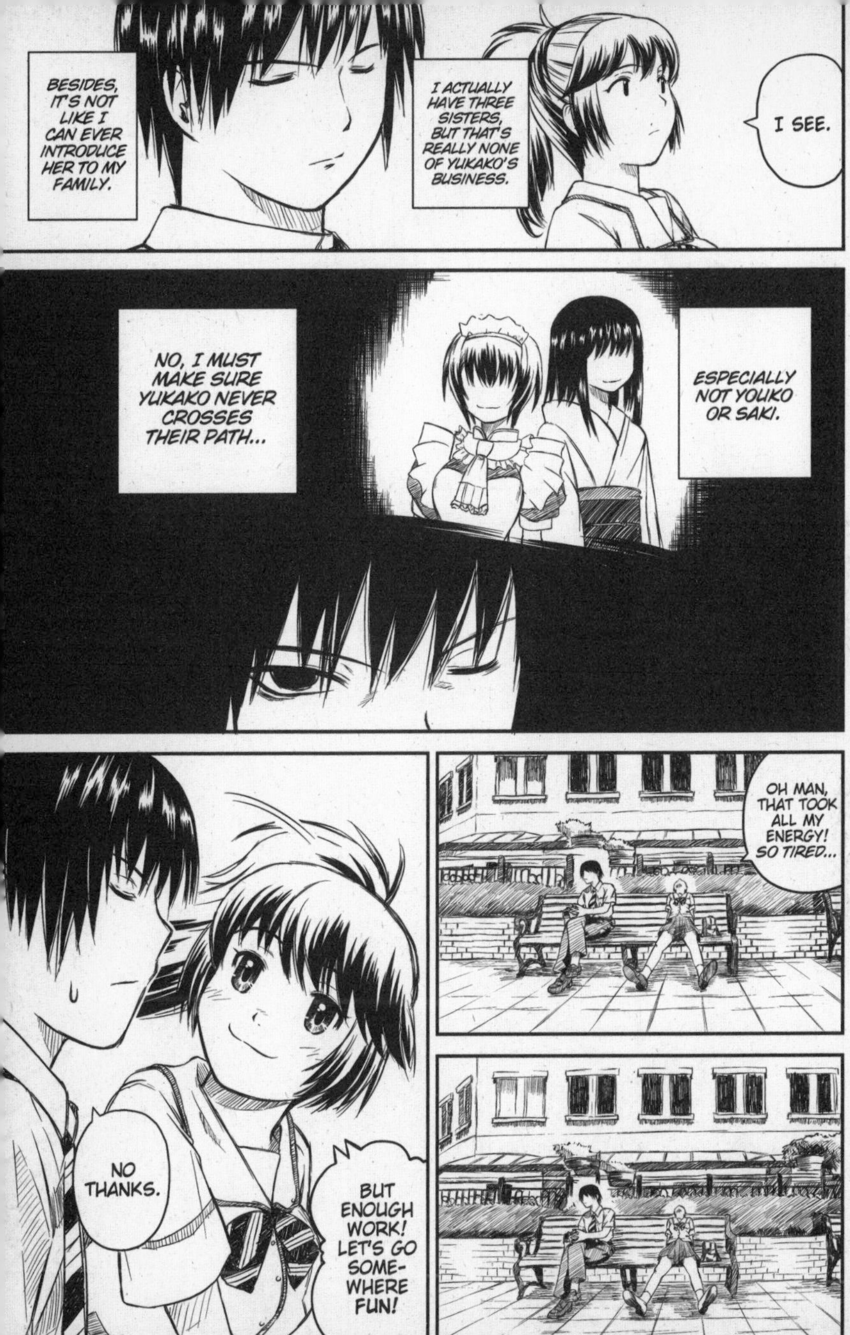
I SEE.
I ACTUALLY HAVE THREE SISTERS, BUT THAT'S REALLY NONE OF YUKAKO'S BUSINESS.
BESIDES, IT'S NOT LIKE I CAN EVER INTRODUCE HER TO MY FAMILY.
ESPECIALLY NOT YOUKO OR SAKI.
NO, I MUST MAKE SURE YUKAKO NEVER CROSSES THEIR PATH...
OH MAN, THAT TOOK ALL MY ENERGY! SO TIRED...
BUT ENOUGH WORK! LET'S GO SOME-WHERE FUN!
NO THANKS.

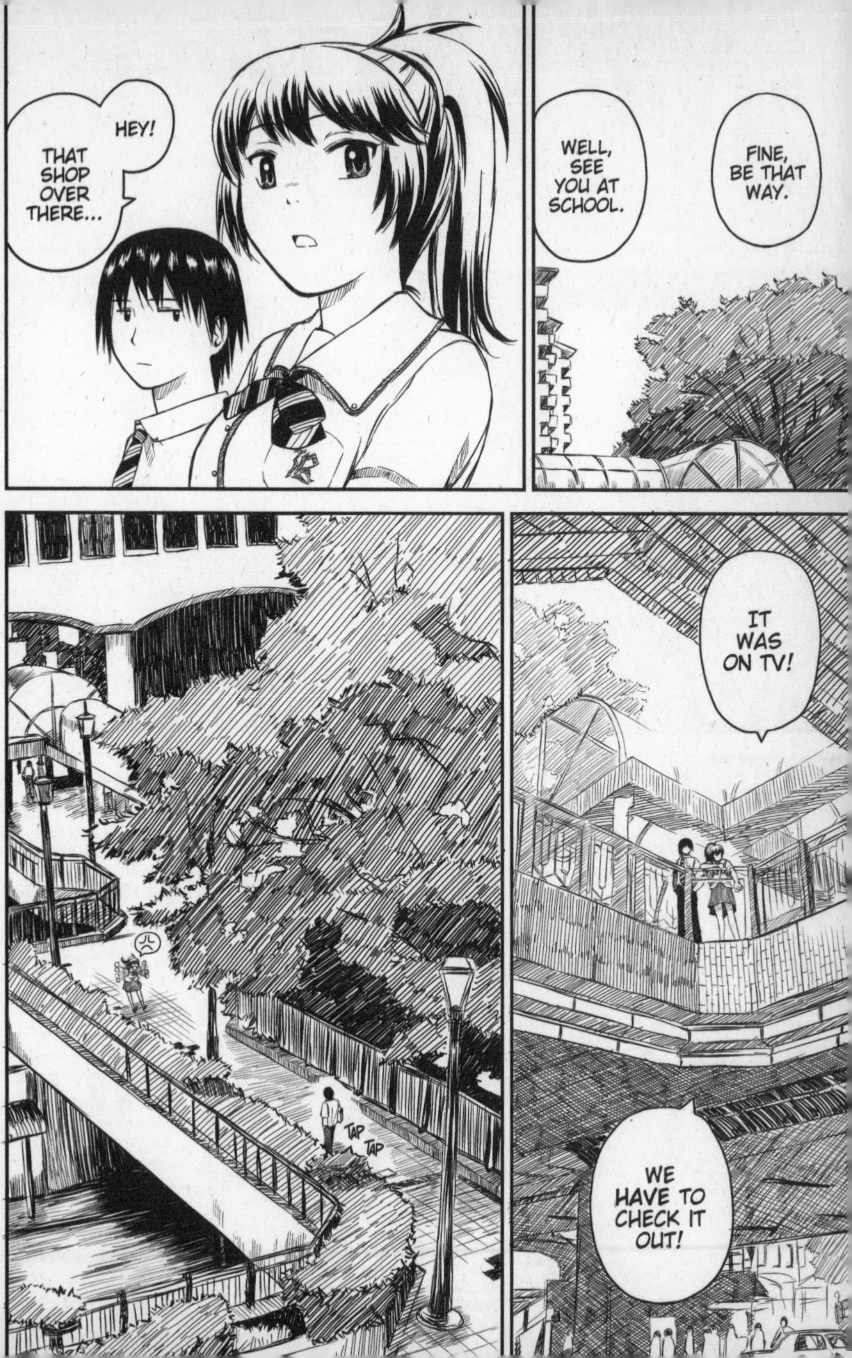
FINE, BE THAT WAY.
WELL, SEE YOU AT SCHOOL.
HEY!
THAT SHOP OVER THERE...
IT WAS ON TV!
WE HAVE TO CHECK IT OUT!
TAP TAP

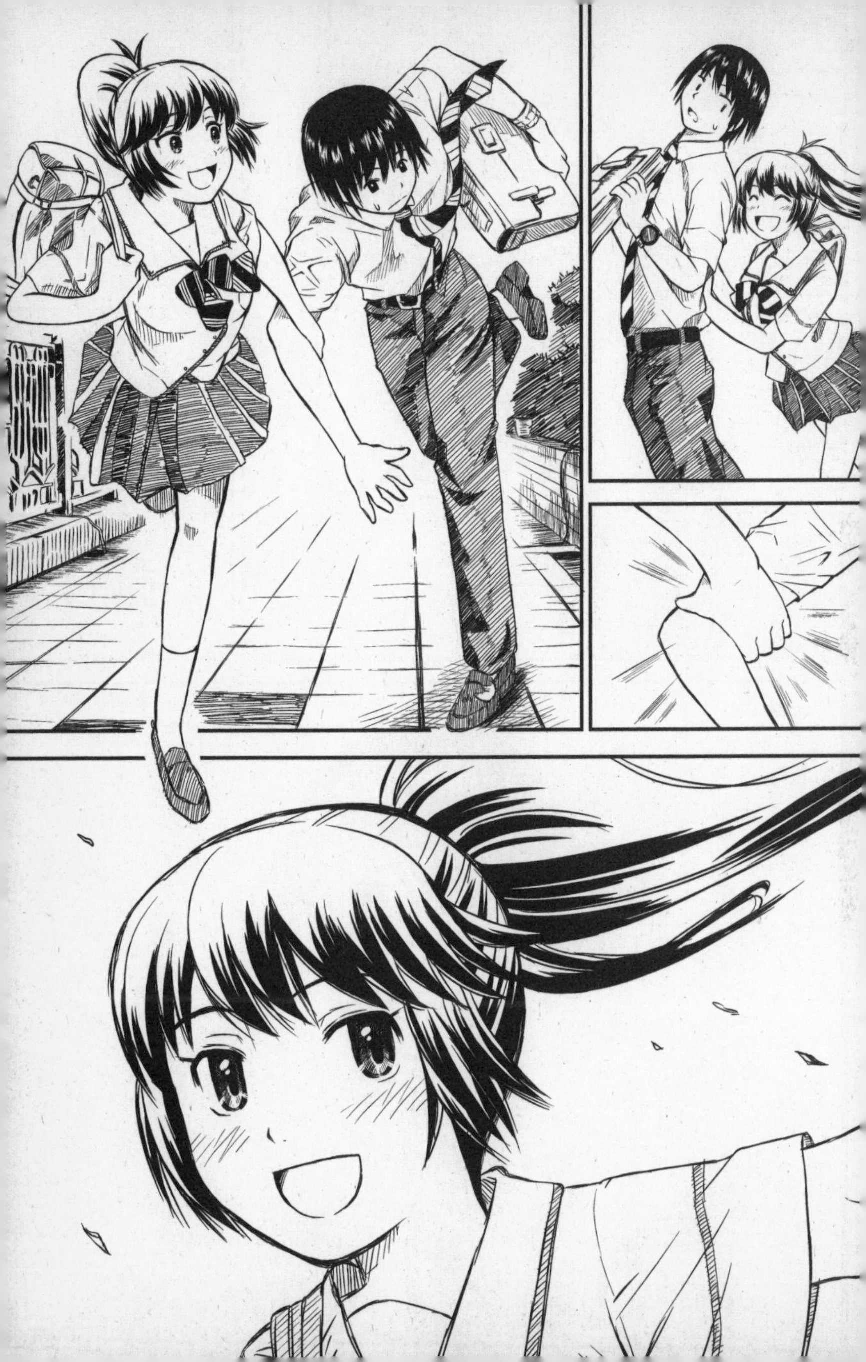

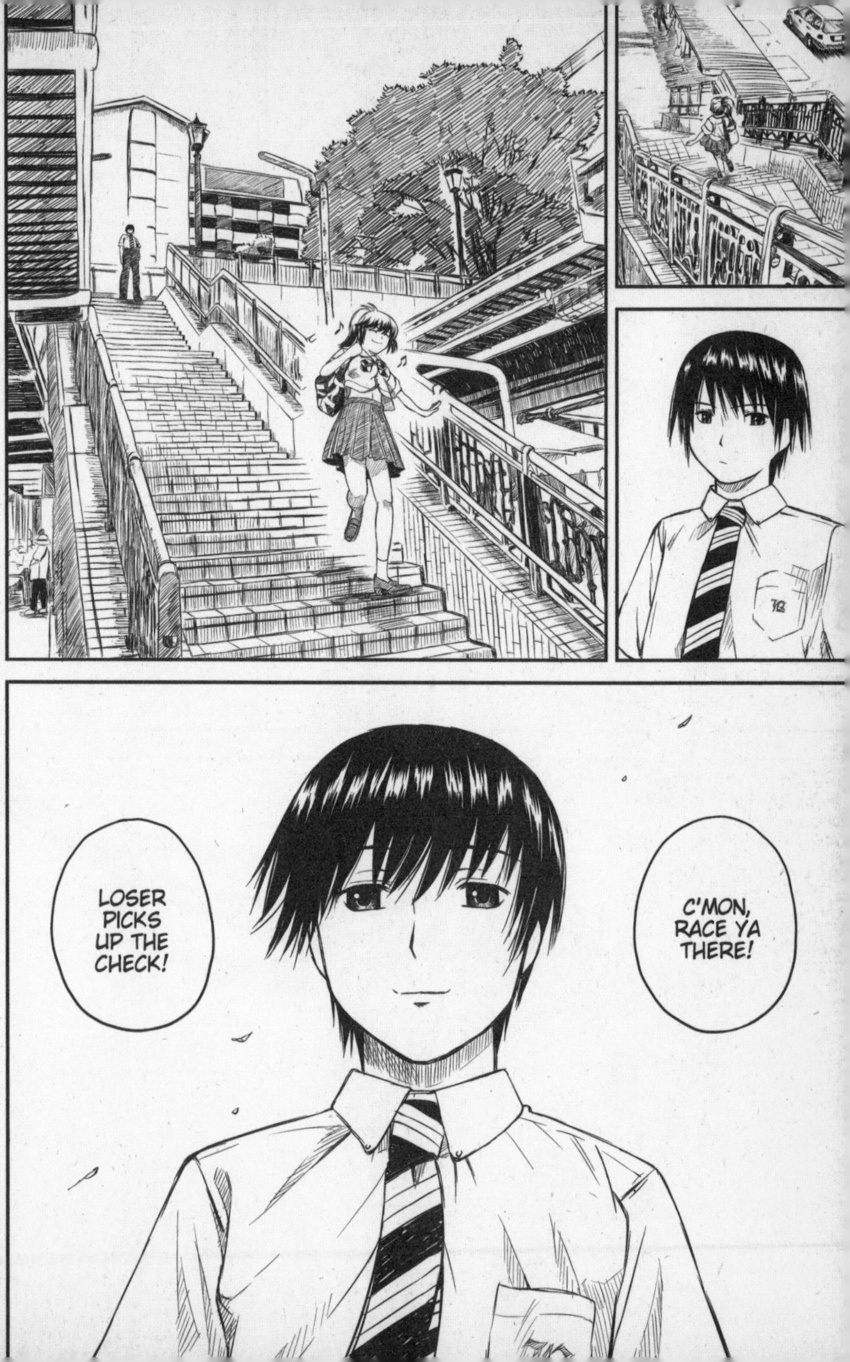
C'MON, RACE YA THERE!
LOSER PICKS UP THE CHECK!

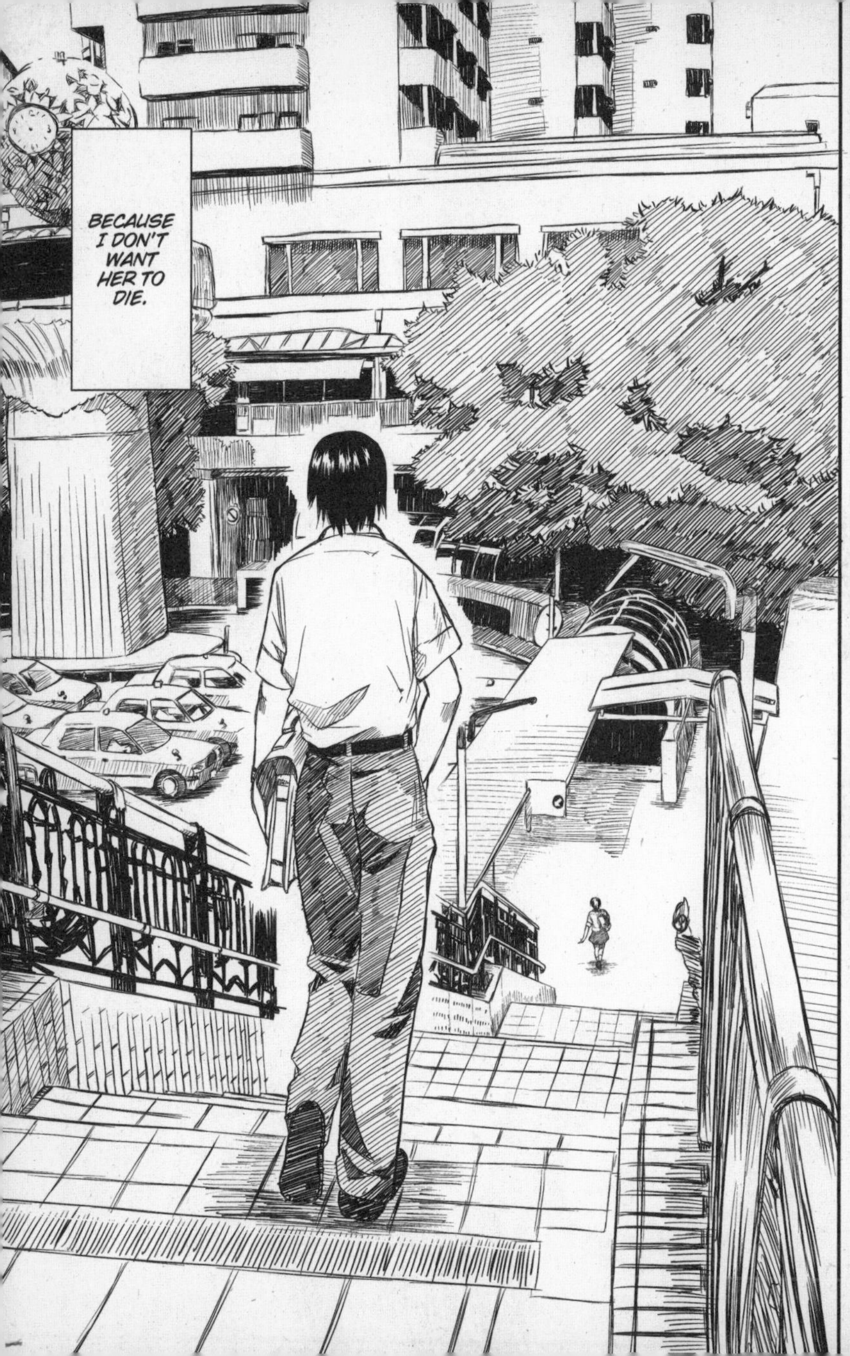
BECAUSE I DON'T WANT HER TO DIE.

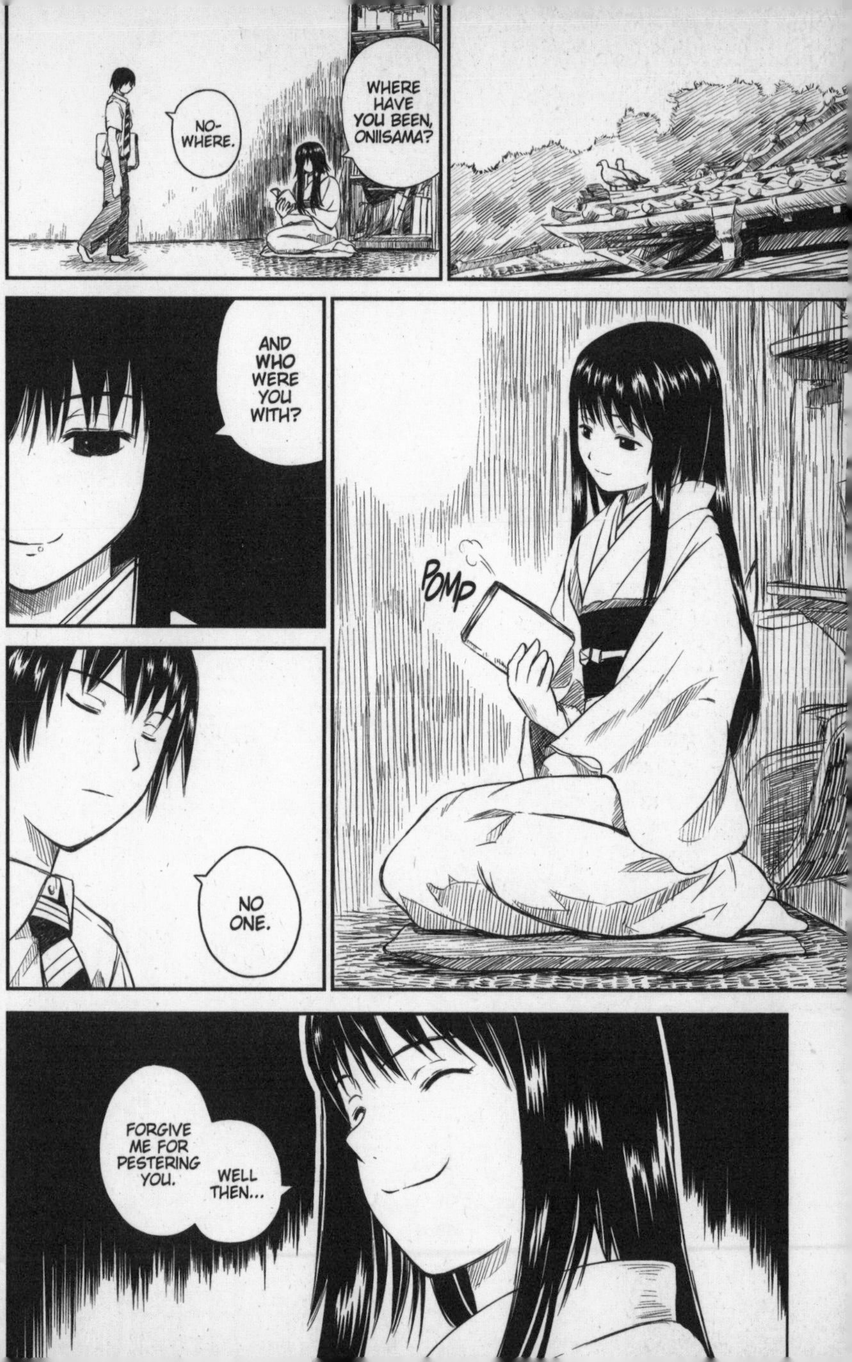
WHERE HAVE YOU BEEN, ONIISAMA?
NO-WHERE.
POMP
AND WHO WERE YOU WITH?
NO ONE.
FORGIVE ME FOR PESTERING YOU.
WELL THEN...

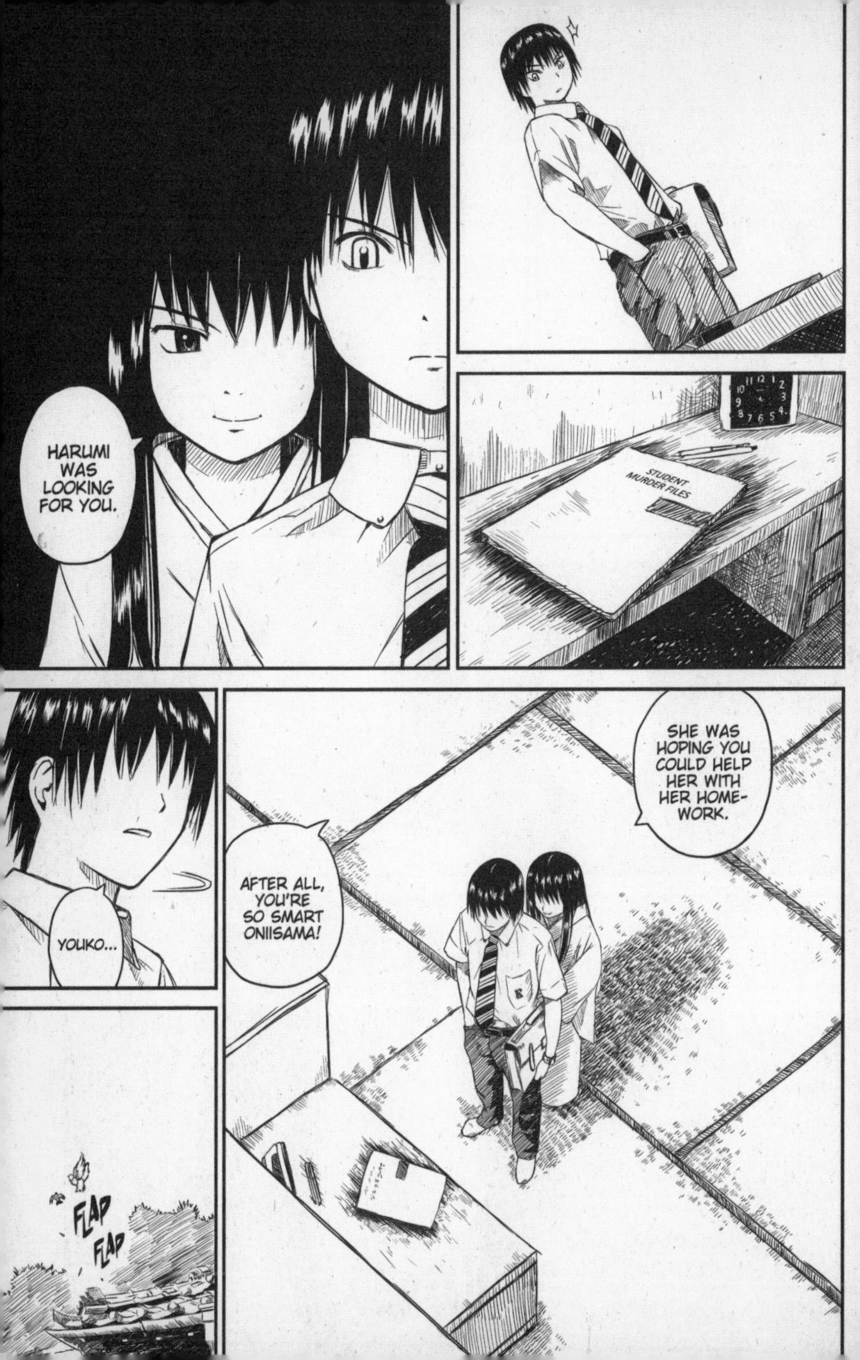
STUDENT MURDER FILES
HARUMI WAS LOOKING FOR YOU.
SHE WAS HOPING YOU COULD HELP HER WITH HER HOME-WORK.
AFTER ALL, YOU'RE SO SMART ONIISAMA!
YOUKO...
FLAP FLAP

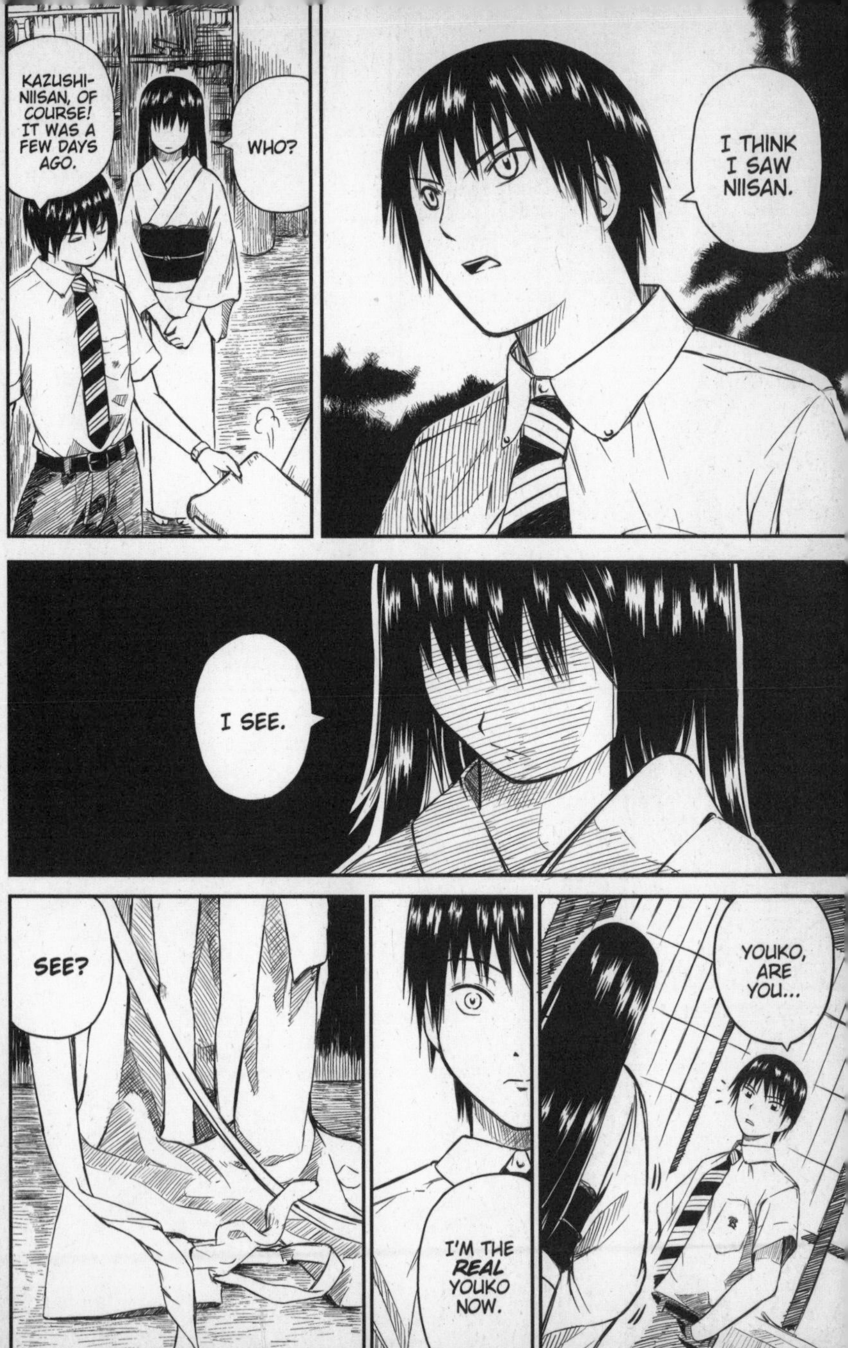
I THINK I SAW NIISAN.
WHO?
KAZUSHI-NIISAN, OF COURSE! IT WAS A FEW DAYS AGO.
I SEE.
YOUKO, ARE YOU...
I'M THE *REAL* YOUKO NOW.
SEE?

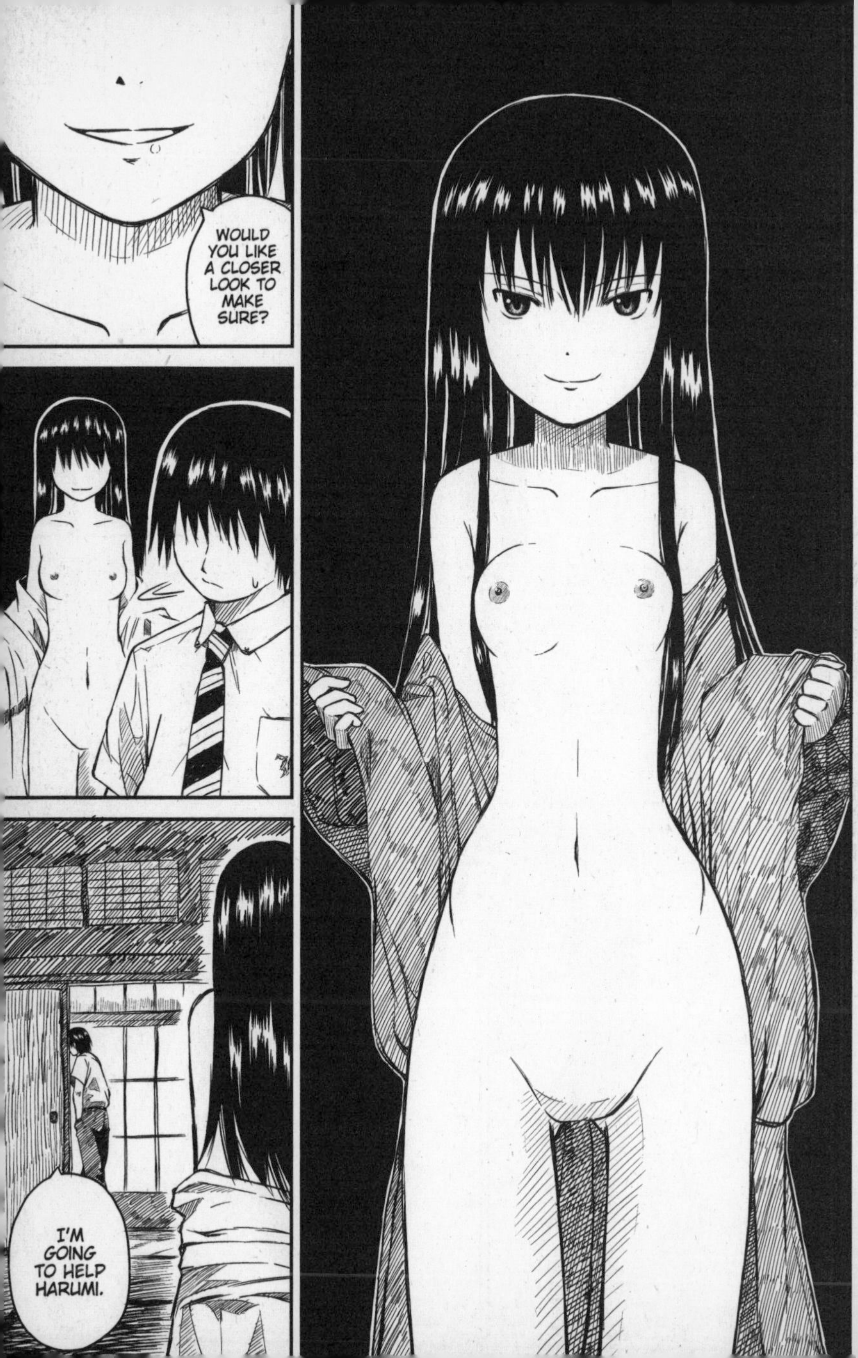
WOULD YOU LIKE A CLOSER LOOK TO MAKE SURE?
I'M GOING TO HELP HARUMI.

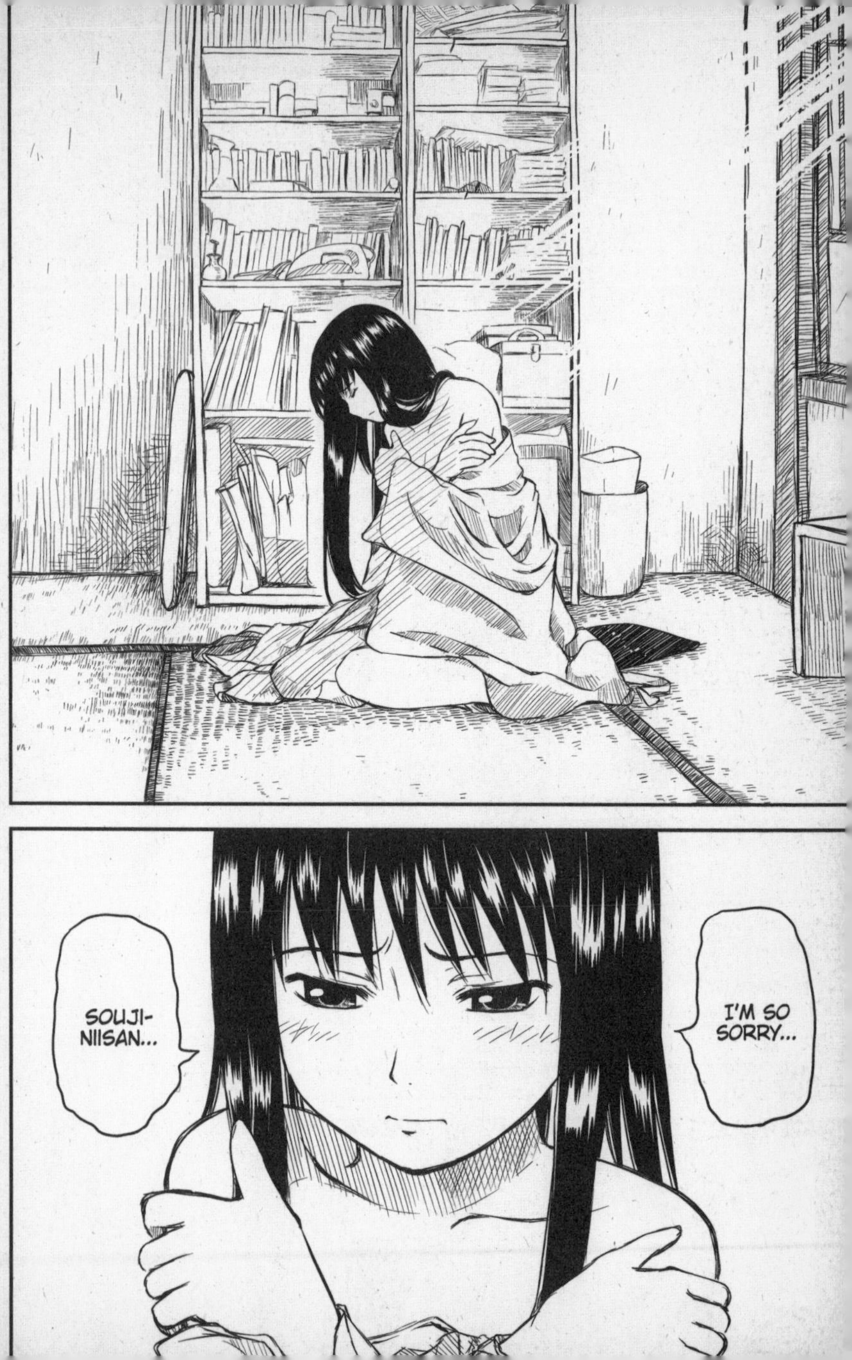
I'M SO SORRY...
SOUJI-NIISAN...

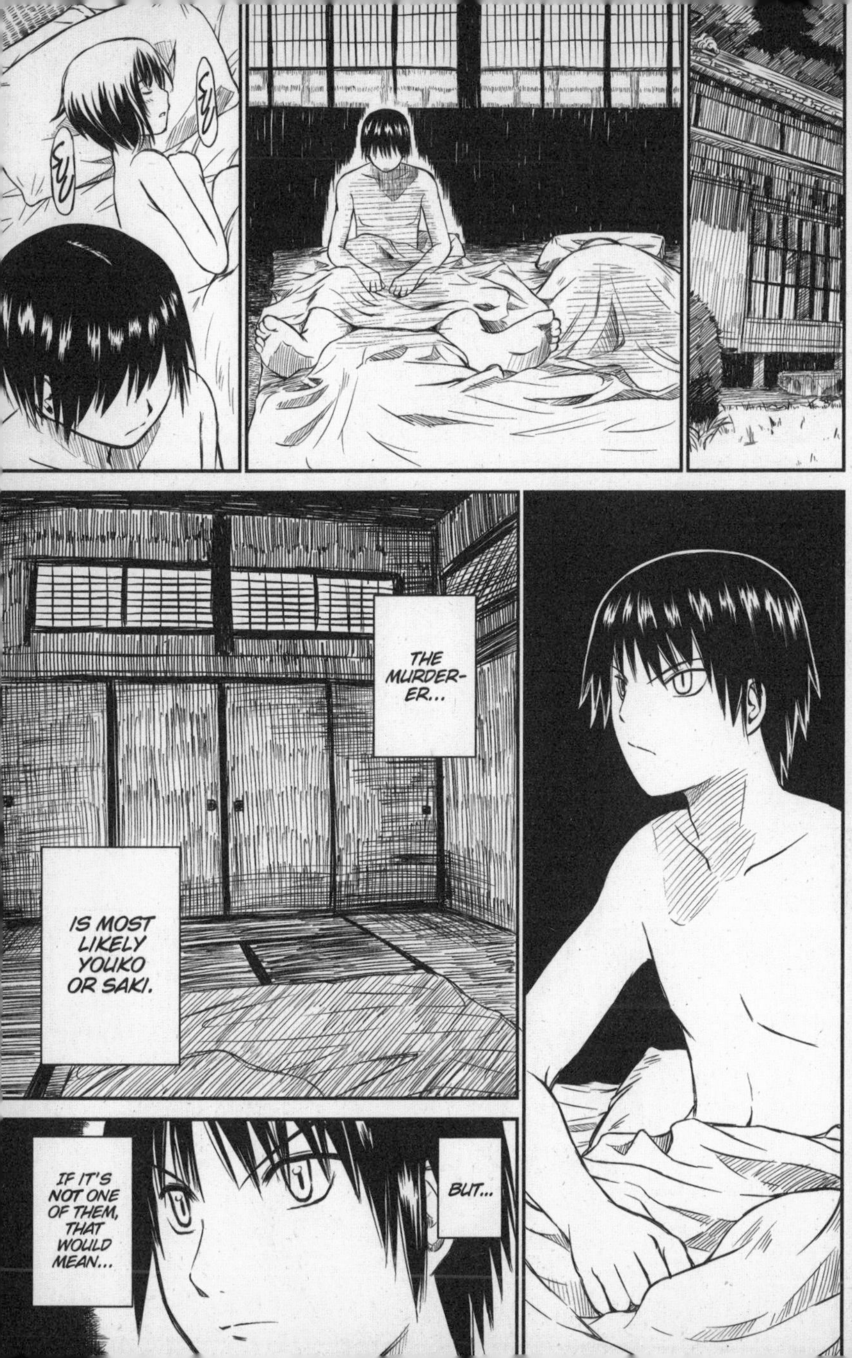
THE MURDERER...
IS MOST LIKELY YOUKO OR SAKI.
BUT...
IF IT'S NOT ONE OF THEM, THAT WOULD MEAN...

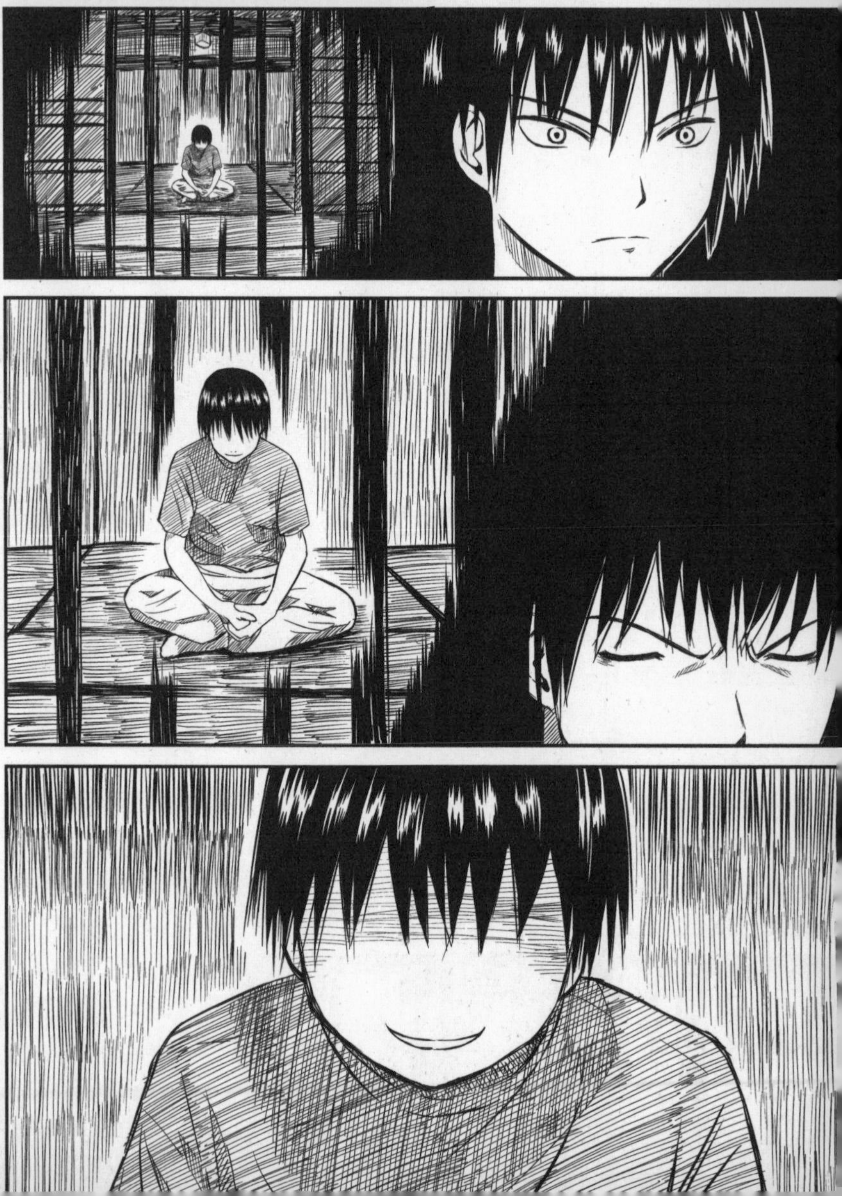

AMNESIA
LABYRINTH

Amnesia Labyrinth CHARACTER FILE 3

KUSHIKI HARUMI

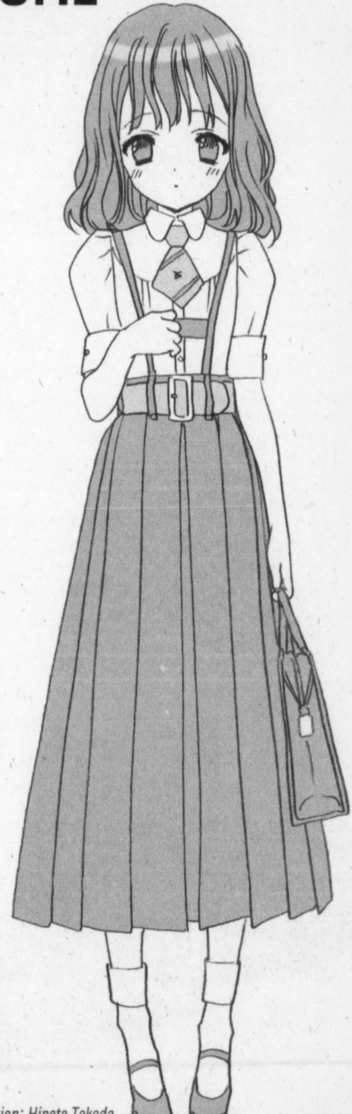

Second daughter of the Kushiki Household, and Souji's younger stepsister (his stepmother's daughter). She tends to stick out amongst the members of the Kushiki Household due to her meek and gentle personality, and is often teased by Youko for it. She adores Souji and their relationship is one of mutual affection.

Illustration: Hinata Takeda

CHAPTER 4

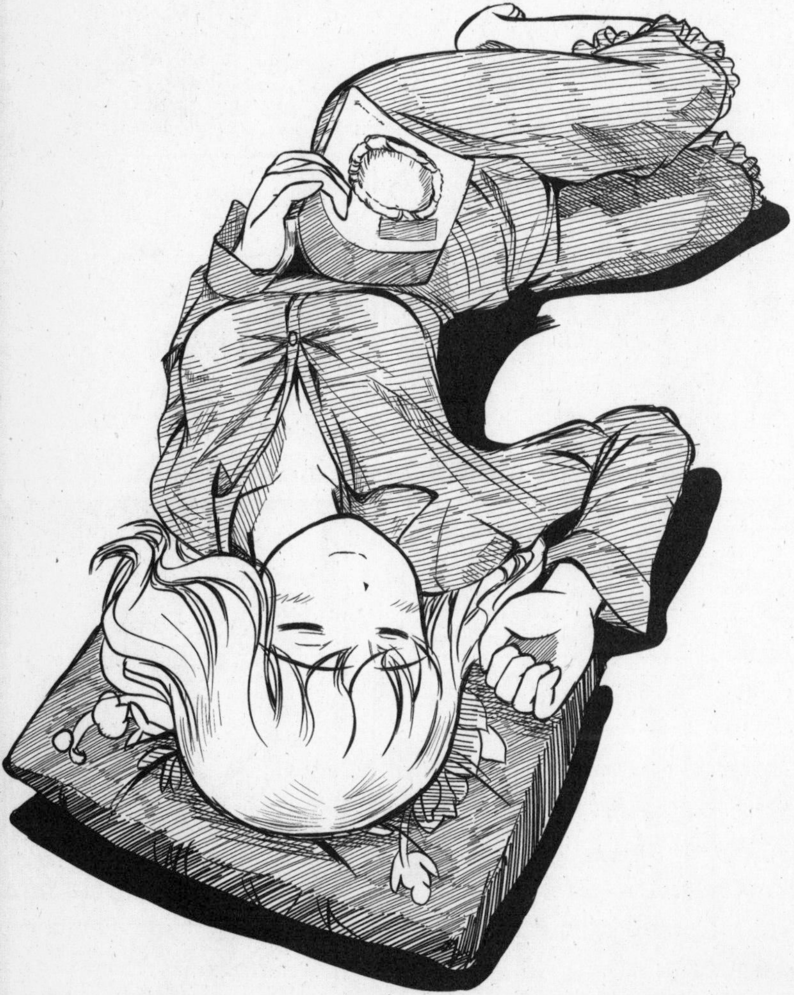

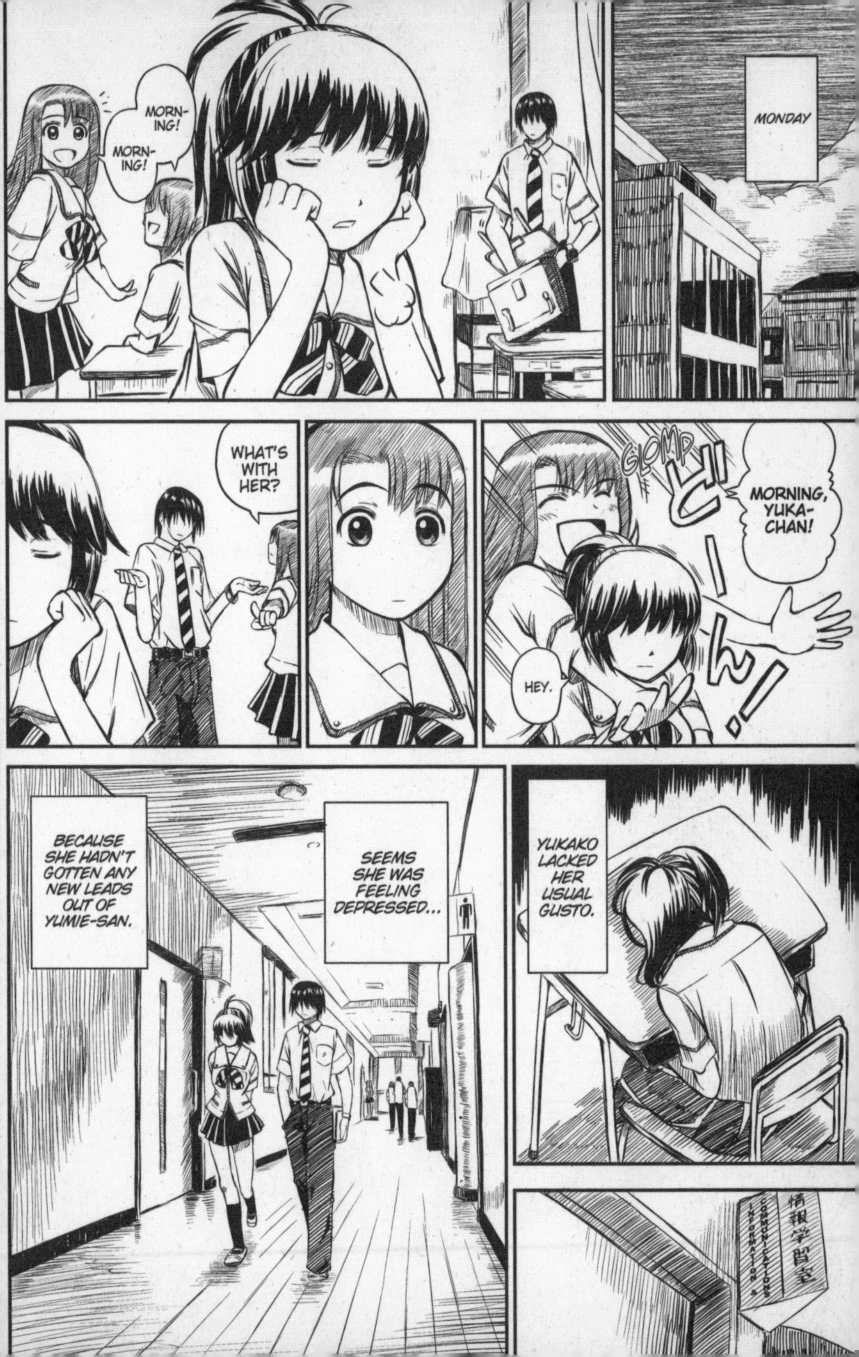
MONDAY
MORNING!
MORNING!
MORNING, YUKA-CHAN!
GLOMP
どーん!
HEY.
WHAT'S WITH HER?
YUKAKO LACKED HER USUAL GUSTO.
情報学習室
INFORMATION & COMMUNICATIONS
SEEMS SHE WAS FEELING DEPRESSED...
BECAUSE SHE HADN'T GOTTEN ANY NEW LEADS OUT OF YUMIE-SAN.

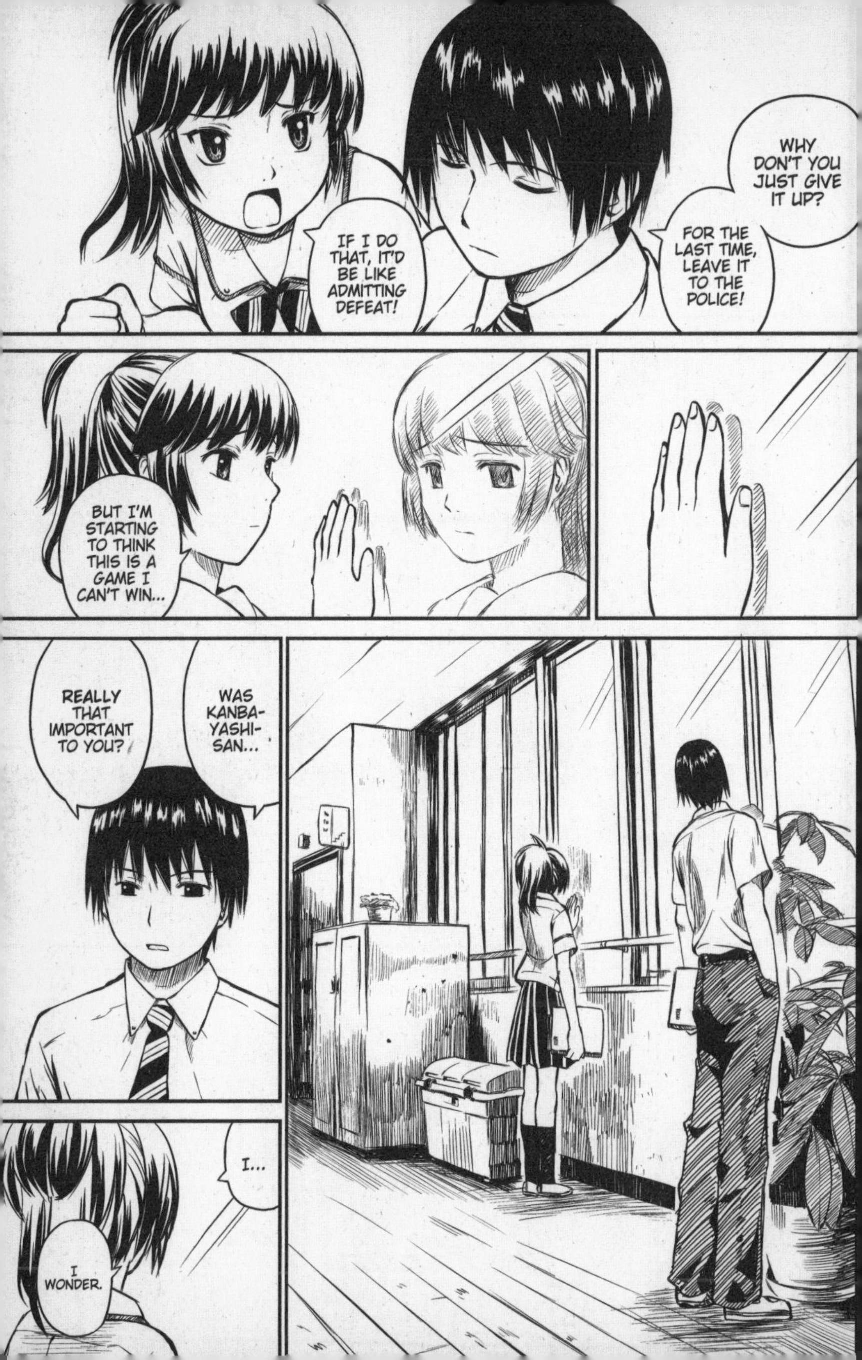
WHY DON'T YOU JUST GIVE IT UP?
FOR THE LAST TIME, LEAVE IT TO THE POLICE!
IF I DO THAT, IT'D BE LIKE ADMITTING DEFEAT!
BUT I'M STARTING TO THINK THIS IS A GAME I CAN'T WIN...
WAS KANBA-YASHI-SAN...
REALLY THAT IMPORTANT TO YOU?
I...
I WONDER.

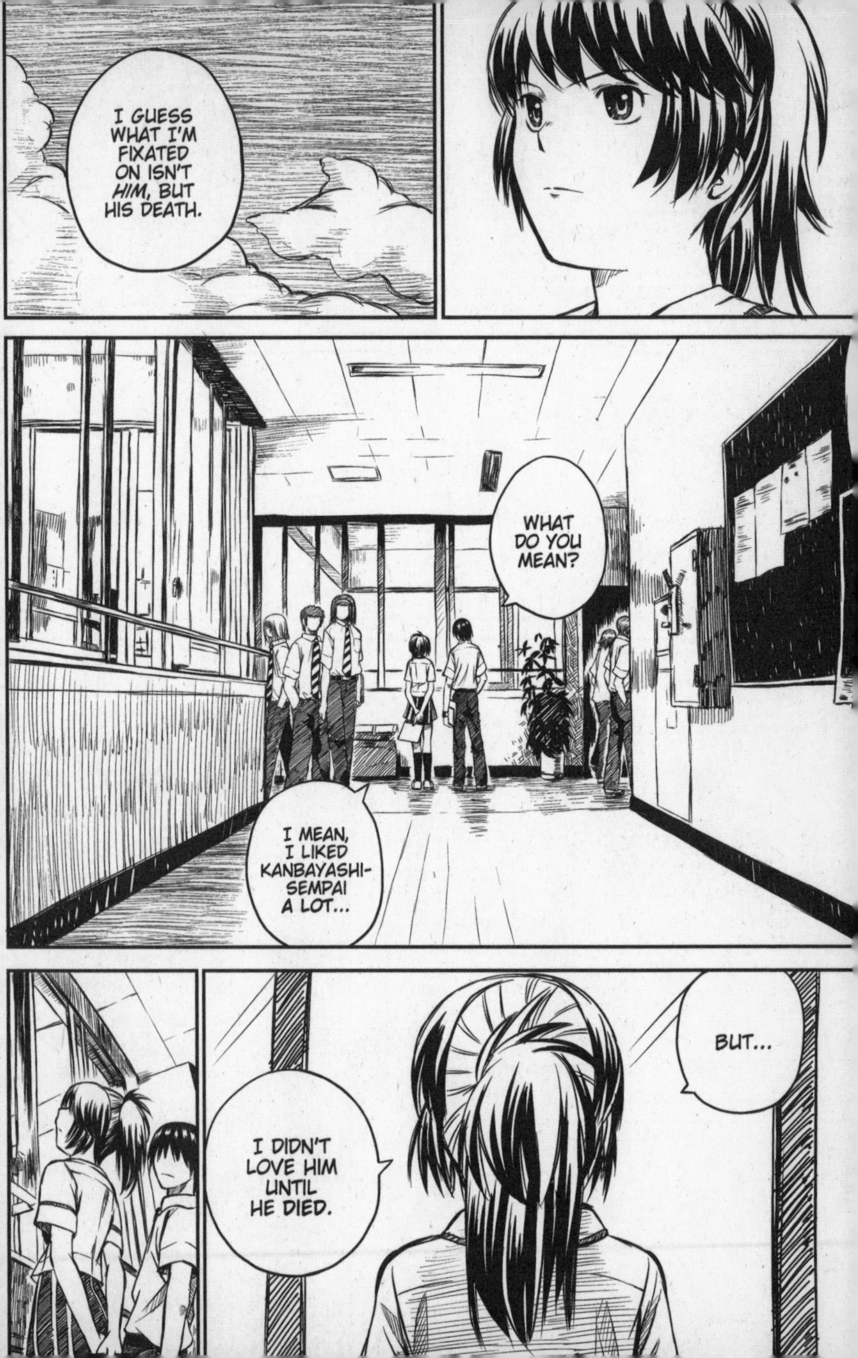
I GUESS WHAT I'M FIXATED ON ISN'T *HIM*, BUT HIS DEATH.
WHAT DO YOU MEAN?
I MEAN, I LIKED KANBAYASHI-SEMPAI A LOT...
BUT...
I DIDN'T LOVE HIM UNTIL HE DIED.

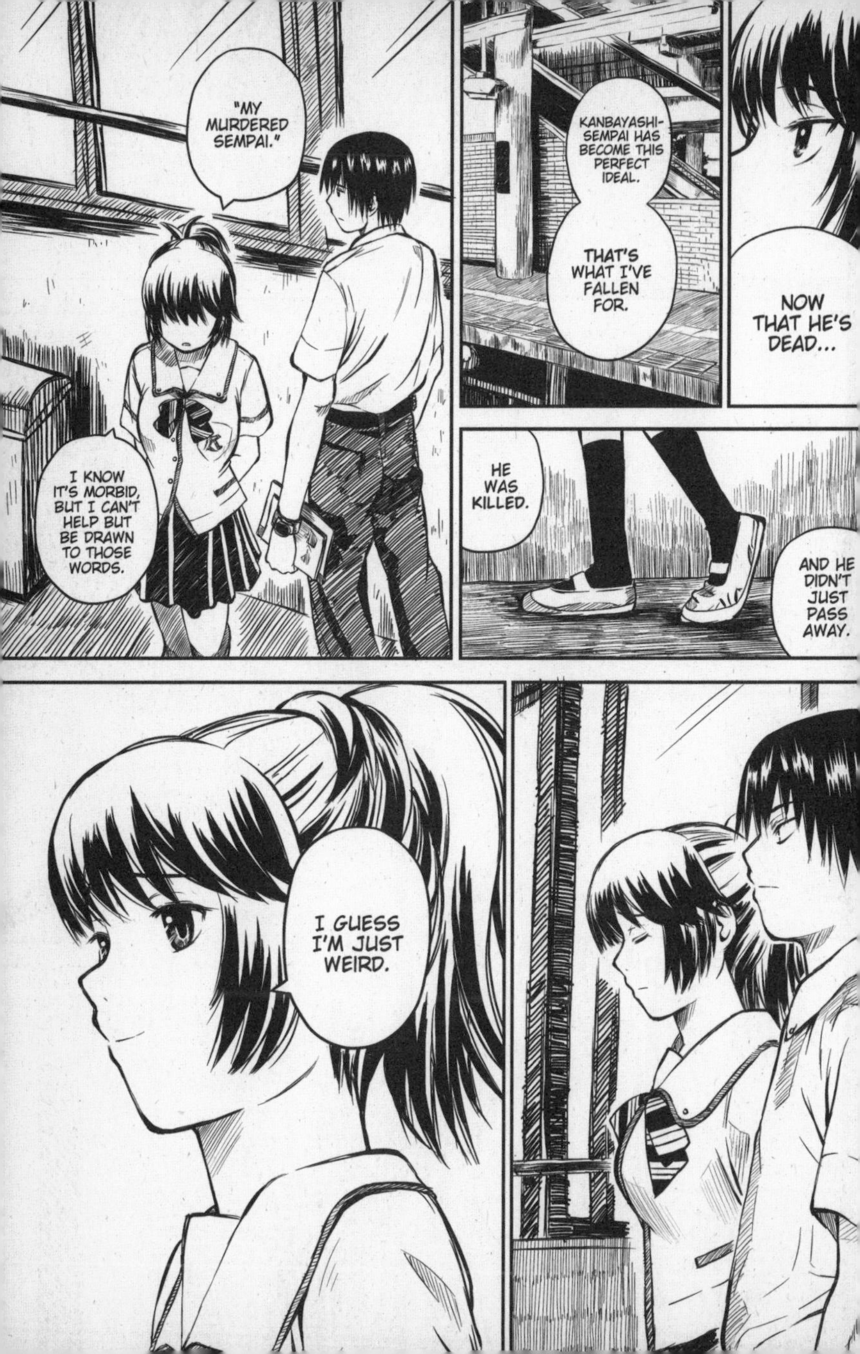
NOW THAT HE'S DEAD...
KANBAYASHI-SEMPAI HAS BECOME THIS PERFECT IDEAL.
THAT'S WHAT I'VE FALLEN FOR.
AND HE DIDN'T JUST PASS AWAY.
HE WAS KILLED.
"MY MURDERED SEMPAI."
I KNOW IT'S MORBID, BUT I CAN'T HELP BUT BE DRAWN TO THOSE WORDS.
I GUESS I'M JUST WEIRD.

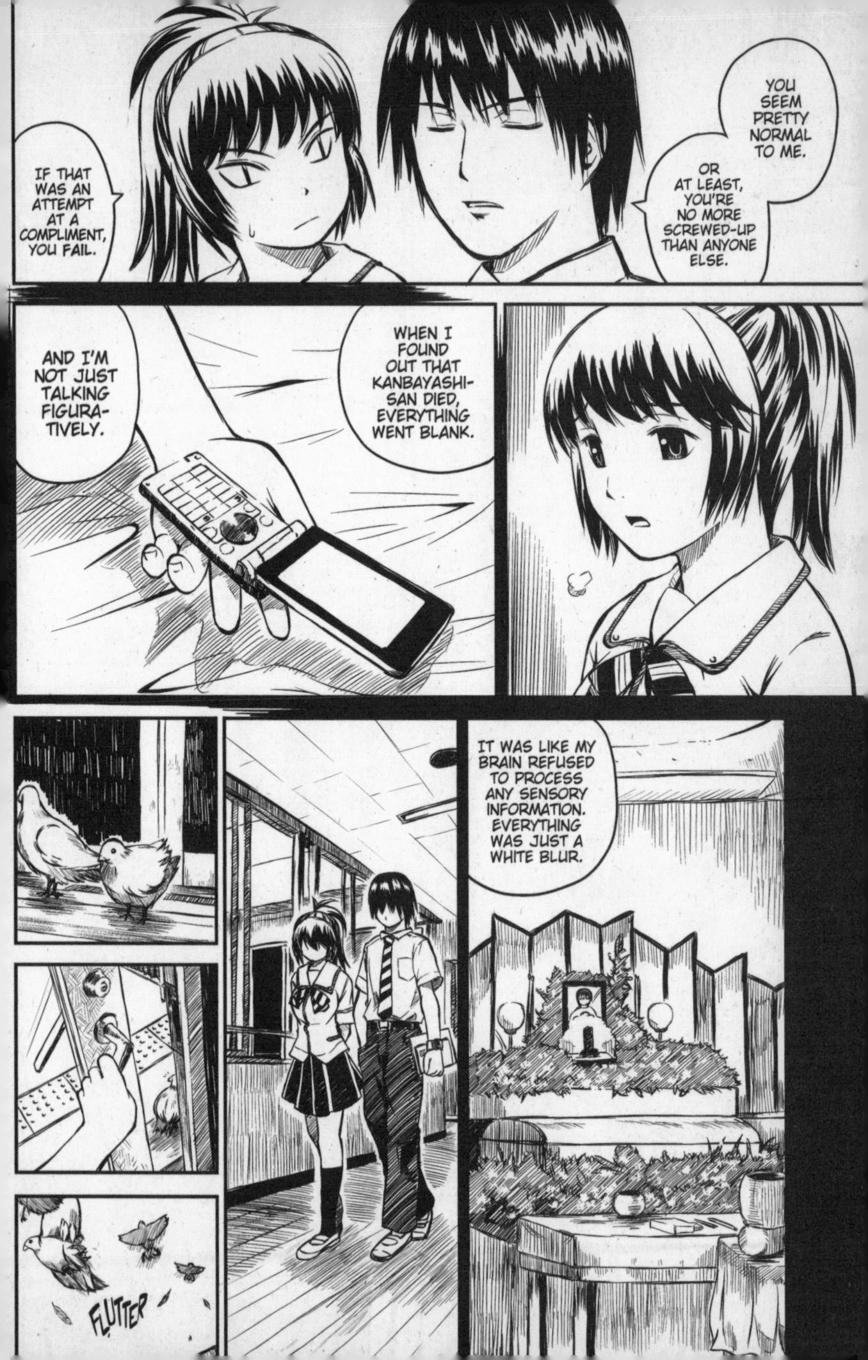
YOU SEEM PRETTY NORMAL TO ME.
OR AT LEAST, YOU'RE NO MORE SCREWED-UP THAN ANYONE ELSE.
IF THAT WAS AN ATTEMPT AT A COMPLIMENT, YOU FAIL.
WHEN I FOUND OUT THAT KANBAYASHI-SAN DIED, EVERYTHING WENT BLANK.
AND I'M NOT JUST TALKING FIGURATIVELY.
IT WAS LIKE MY BRAIN REFUSED TO PROCESS ANY SENSORY INFORMATION. EVERYTHING WAS JUST A WHITE BLUR.
FLUTTER

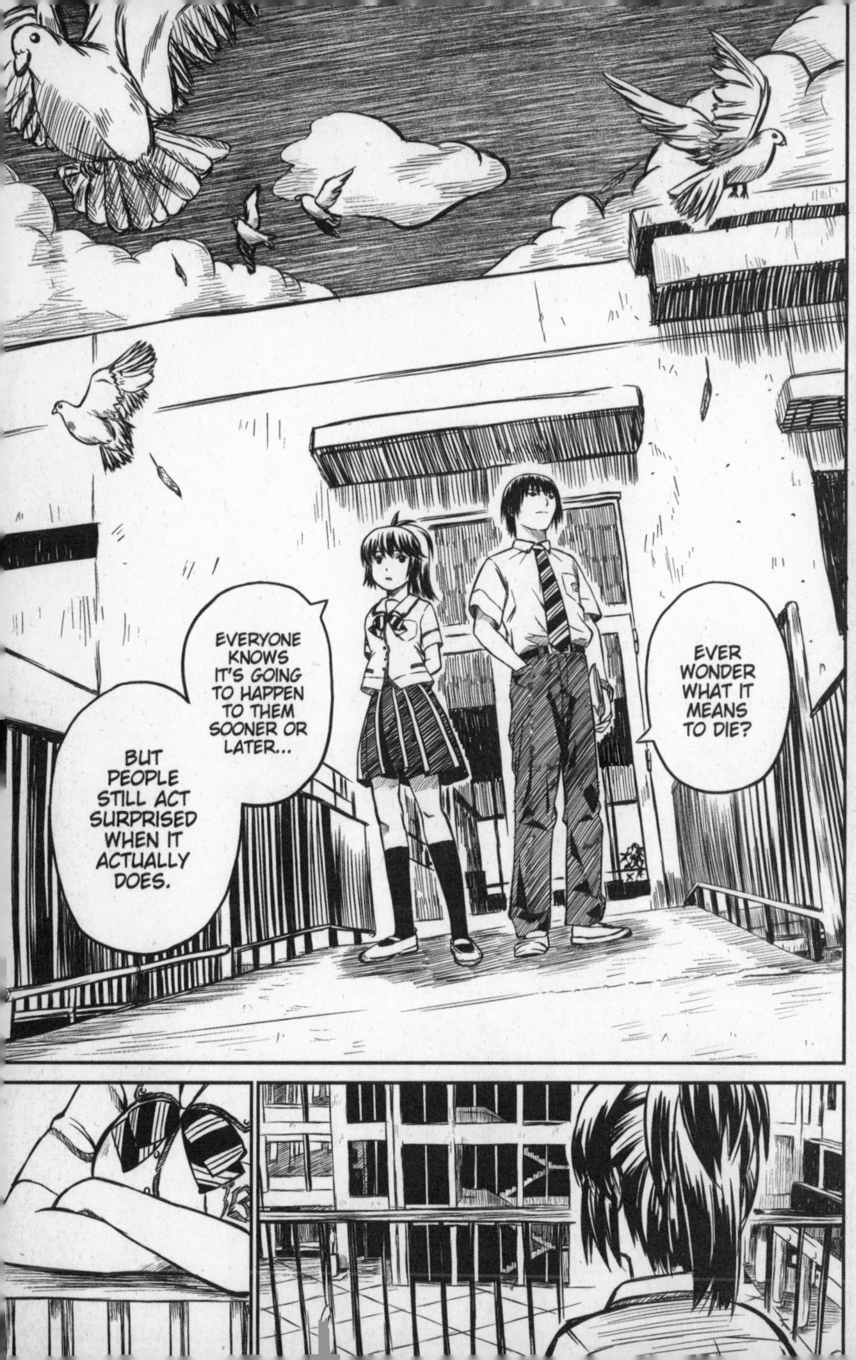
EVER WONDER WHAT IT MEANS TO DIE?
EVERYONE KNOWS IT'S GOING TO HAPPEN TO THEM SOONER OR LATER...
BUT PEOPLE STILL ACT SURPRISED WHEN IT ACTUALLY DOES.

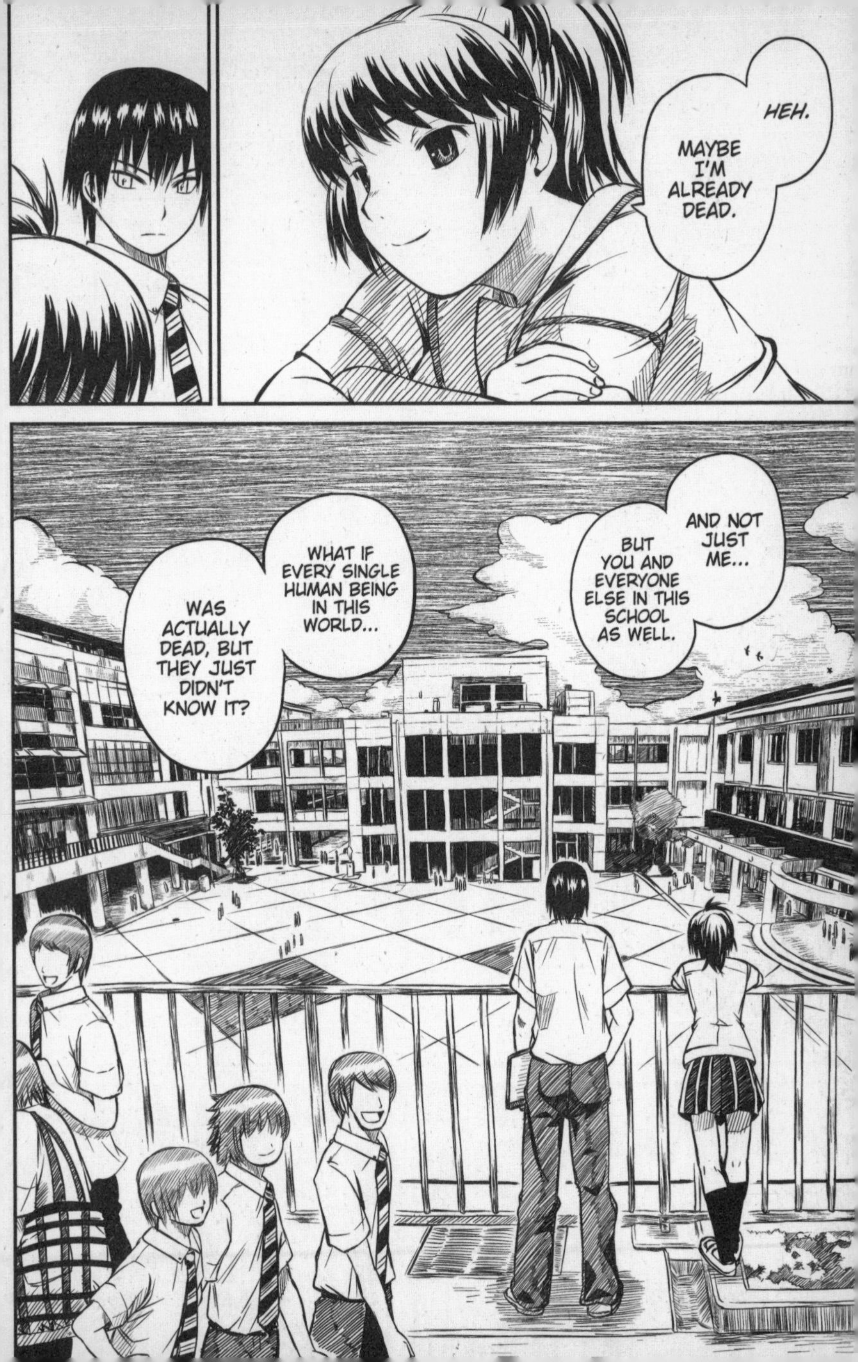
HEH.
MAYBE I'M ALREADY DEAD.
AND NOT JUST ME...
BUT YOU AND EVERYONE ELSE IN THIS SCHOOL AS WELL.
WHAT IF EVERY SINGLE HUMAN BEING IN THIS WORLD...
WAS ACTUALLY DEAD, BUT THEY JUST DIDN'T KNOW IT?

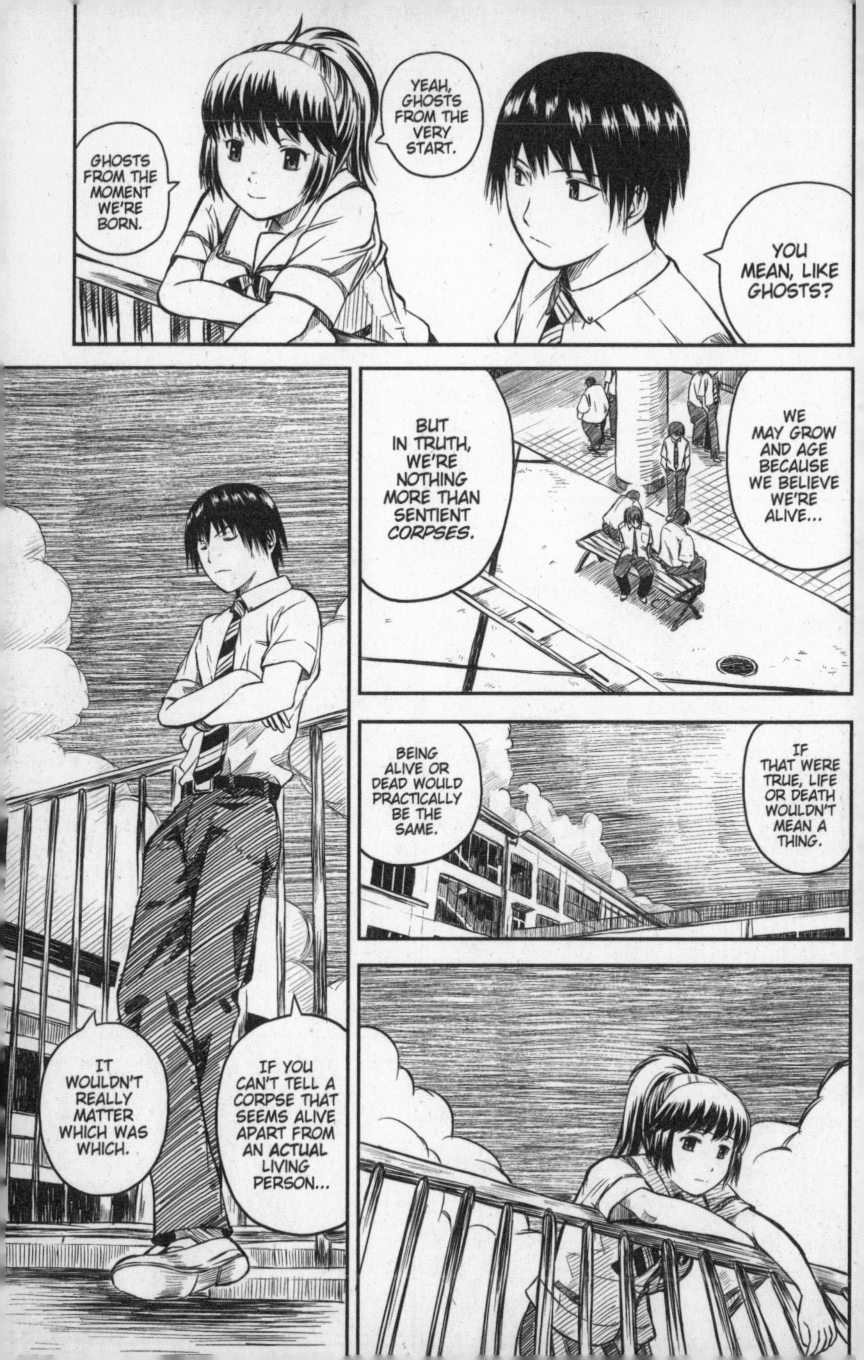
YOU MEAN, LIKE GHOSTS?
YEAH, GHOSTS FROM THE VERY START.
GHOSTS FROM THE MOMENT WE'RE BORN.
WE MAY GROW AND AGE BECAUSE WE BELIEVE WE'RE ALIVE...
BUT IN TRUTH, WE'RE NOTHING MORE THAN SENTIENT *CORPSES*.
IF THAT WERE TRUE, LIFE OR DEATH WOULDN'T MEAN A THING.
BEING ALIVE OR DEAD WOULD PRACTICALLY BE THE SAME.
IF YOU CAN'T TELL A CORPSE THAT SEEMS ALIVE APART FROM AN ACTUAL LIVING PERSON...
IT WOULDN'T REALLY MATTER WHICH WAS WHICH.

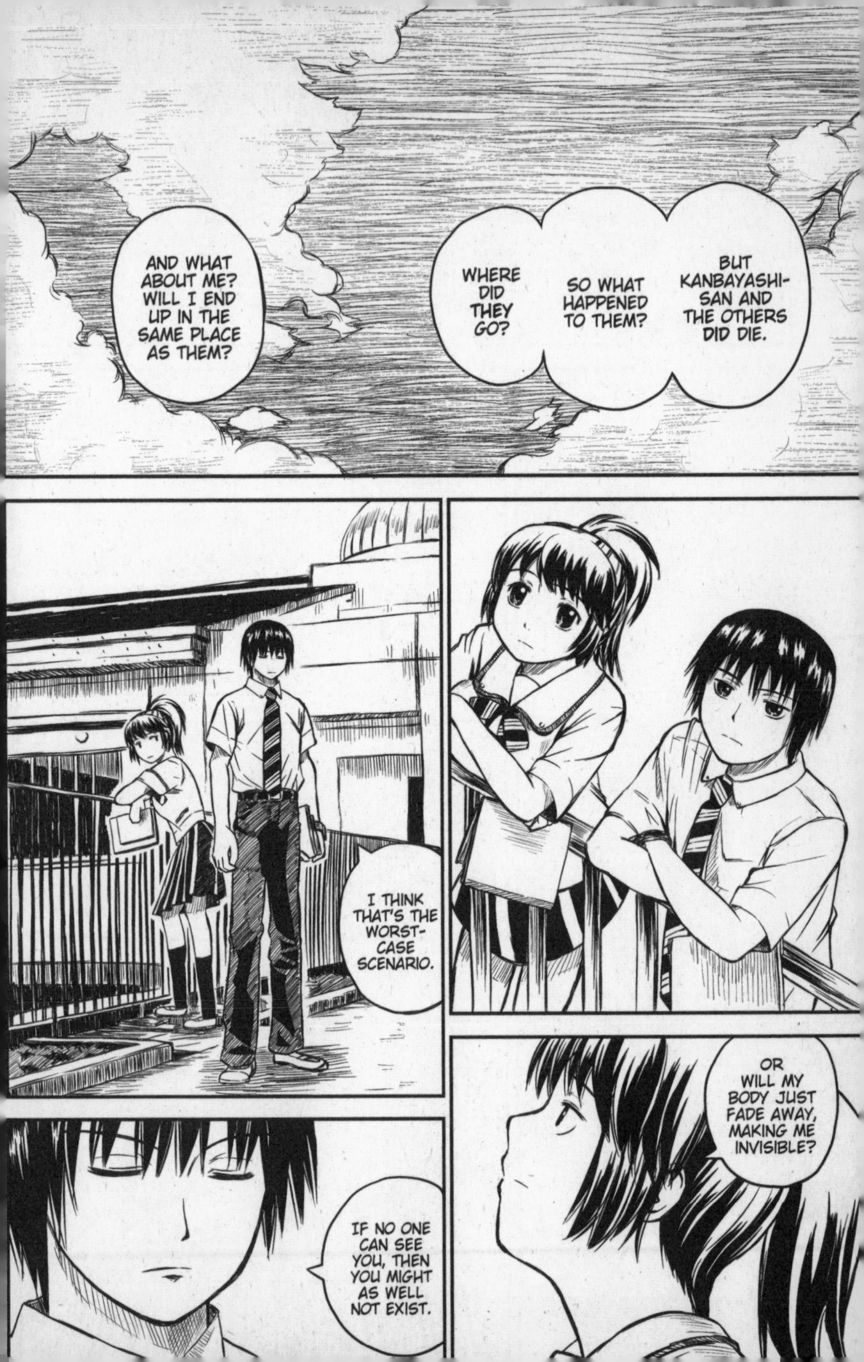
BUT KANBAYASHI-SAN AND THE OTHERS DID DIE.
SO WHAT HAPPENED TO THEM?
WHERE DID THEY GO?
AND WHAT ABOUT ME? WILL I END UP IN THE SAME PLACE AS THEM?
OR WILL MY BODY JUST FADE AWAY, MAKING ME INVISIBLE?
I THINK THAT'S THE WORST-CASE SCENARIO.
IF NO ONE CAN SEE YOU, THEN YOU MIGHT AS WELL NOT EXIST.

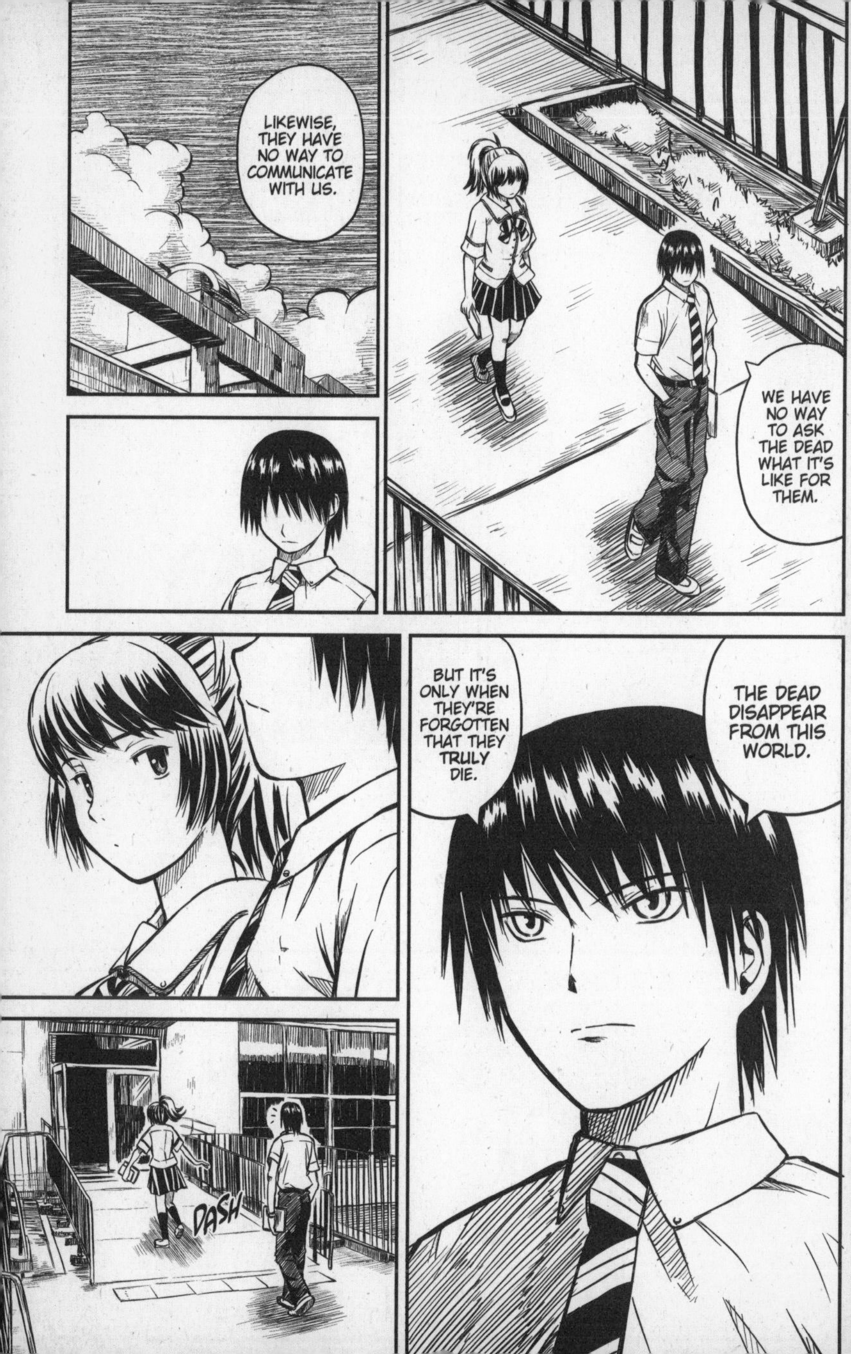
WE HAVE NO WAY TO ASK THE DEAD WHAT IT'S LIKE FOR THEM.
LIKEWISE, THEY HAVE NO WAY TO COMMUNICATE WITH US.
THE DEAD DISAPPEAR FROM THIS WORLD.
BUT IT'S ONLY WHEN THEY'RE FORGOTTEN THAT THEY TRULY DIE.
DASH

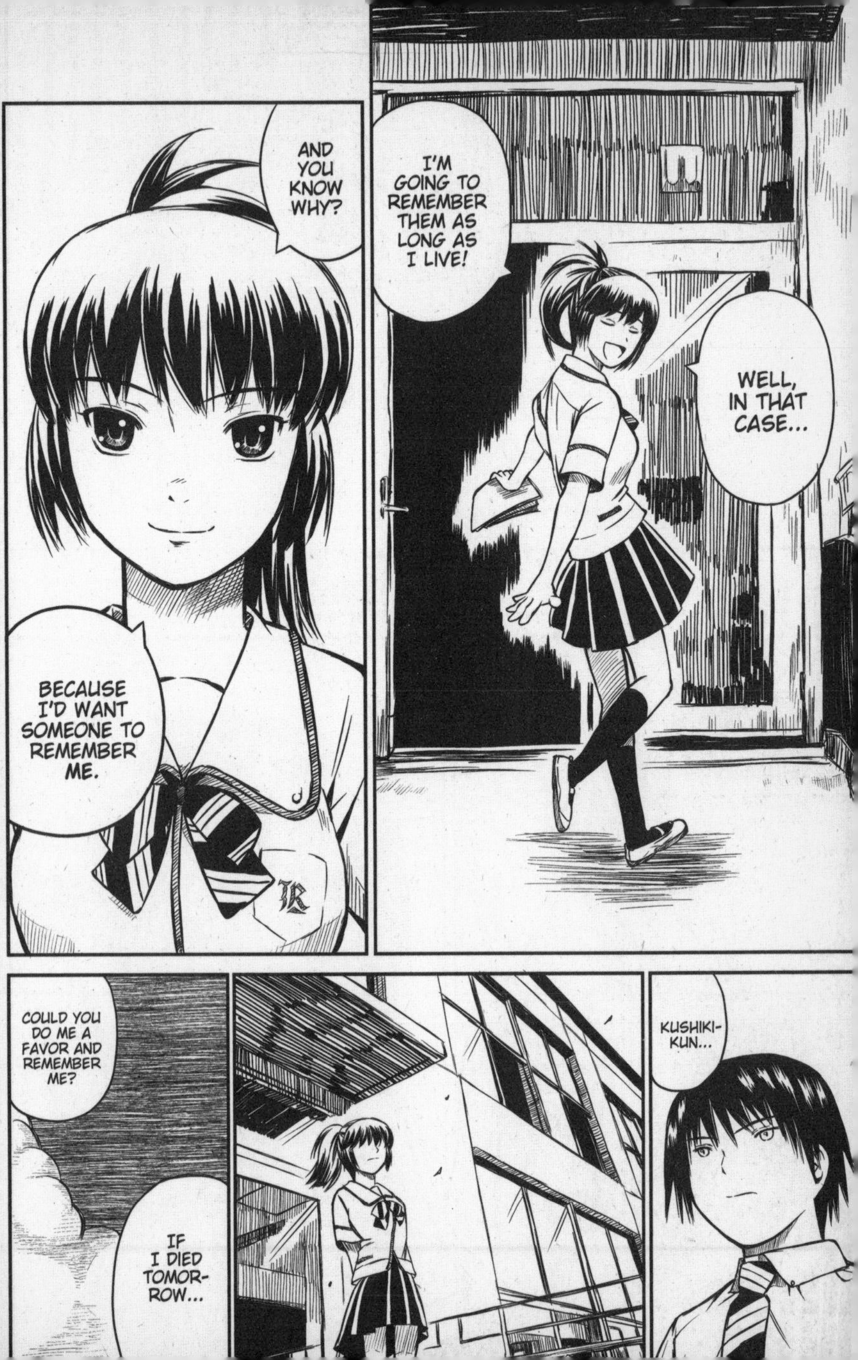
WELL, IN THAT CASE...
I'M GOING TO REMEMBER THEM AS LONG AS I LIVE!
AND YOU KNOW WHY?
BECAUSE I'D WANT SOMEONE TO REMEMBER ME.
KUSHIKI-KUN...
COULD YOU DO ME A FAVOR AND REMEMBER ME?
IF I DIED TOMOR-ROW...

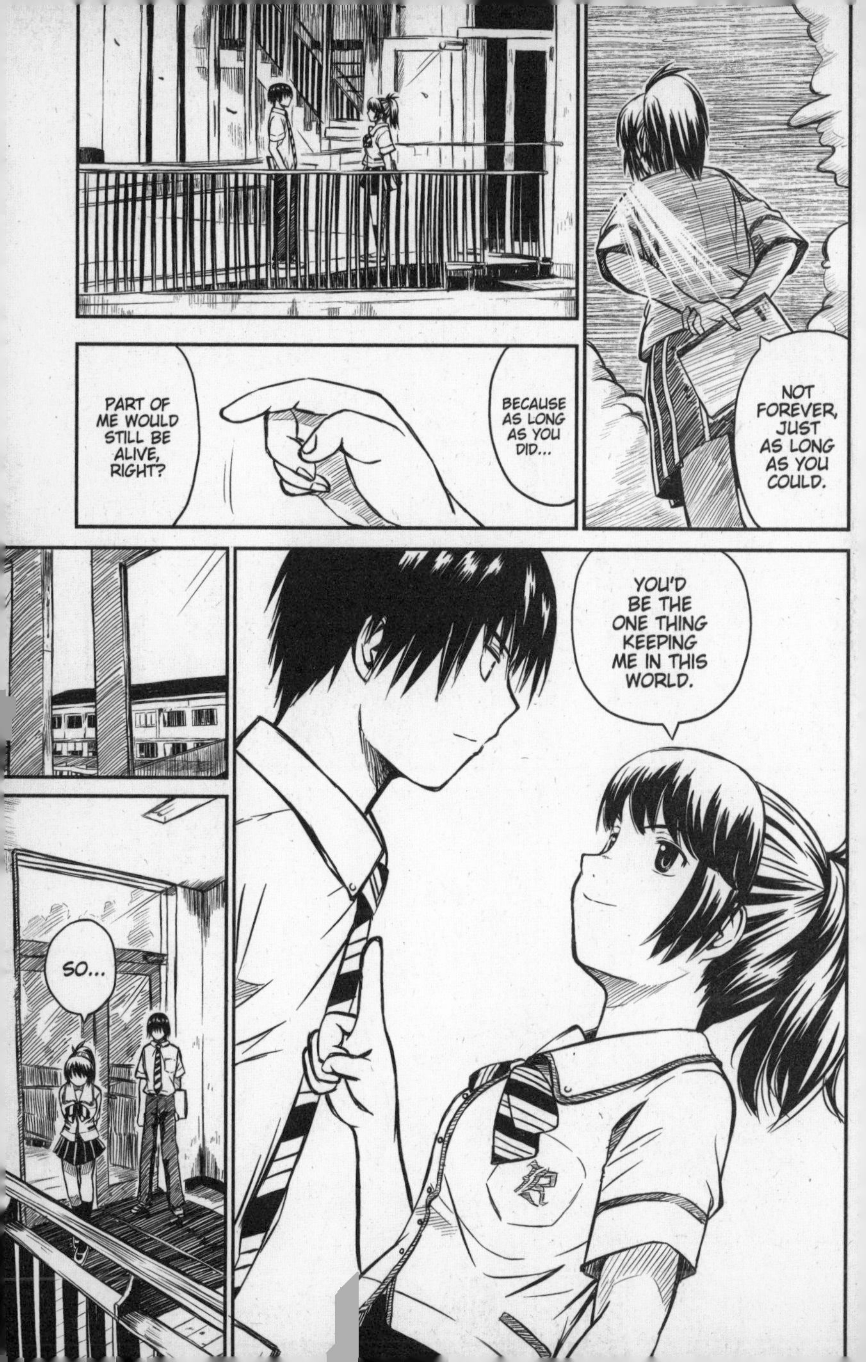
NOT FOREVER, JUST AS LONG AS YOU COULD.
BECAUSE AS LONG AS YOU DID...
PART OF ME WOULD STILL BE ALIVE, RIGHT?
YOU'D BE THE ONE THING KEEPING ME IN THIS WORLD.
SO...

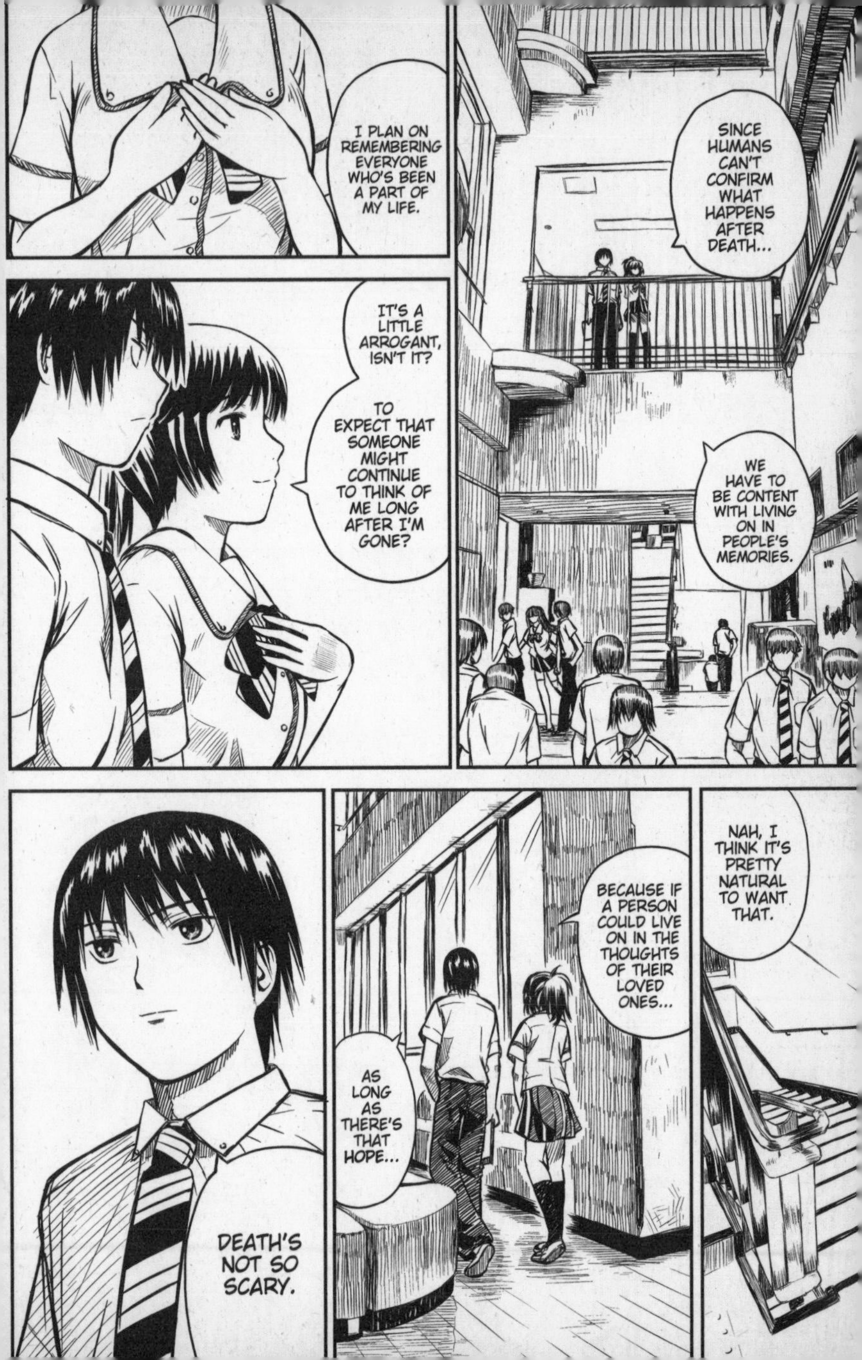
SINCE HUMANS CAN'T CONFIRM WHAT HAPPENS AFTER DEATH...
WE HAVE TO BE CONTENT WITH LIVING ON IN PEOPLE'S MEMORIES.
I PLAN ON REMEMBERING EVERYONE WHO'S BEEN A PART OF MY LIFE.
IT'S A LITTLE ARROGANT, ISN'T IT?
TO EXPECT THAT SOMEONE MIGHT CONTINUE TO THINK OF ME LONG AFTER I'M GONE?
NAH, I THINK IT'S PRETTY NATURAL TO WANT THAT.
BECAUSE IF A PERSON COULD LIVE ON IN THE THOUGHTS OF THEIR LOVED ONES...
AS LONG AS THERE'S THAT HOPE...
DEATH'S NOT SO SCARY.

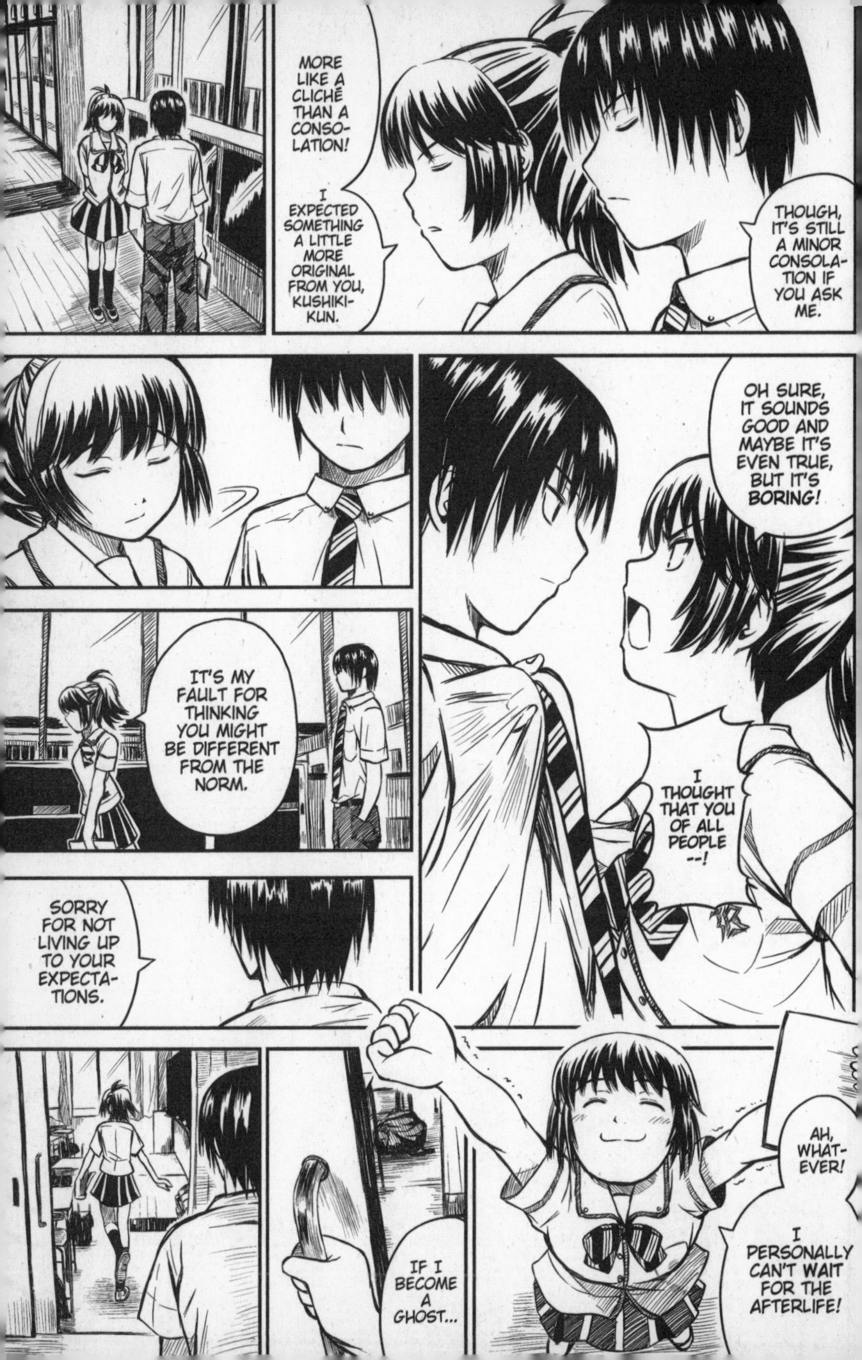
THOUGH, IT'S STILL A MINOR CONSOLA-TION IF YOU ASK ME.
MORE LIKE A CLICHÉ THAN A CONSO-LATION!
I EXPECTED SOMETHING A LITTLE MORE ORIGINAL FROM YOU, KUSHIKI-KUN.
OH SURE, IT SOUNDS GOOD AND MAYBE IT'S EVEN TRUE, BUT IT'S BORING!
I THOUGHT THAT YOU OF ALL PEOPLE --!
IT'S MY FAULT FOR THINKING YOU MIGHT BE DIFFERENT FROM THE NORM.
SORRY FOR NOT LIVING UP TO YOUR EXPECTA-TIONS.
AH, WHAT-EVER!
I PERSONALLY CAN'T WAIT FOR THE AFTERLIFE!
IF I BECOME A GHOST...

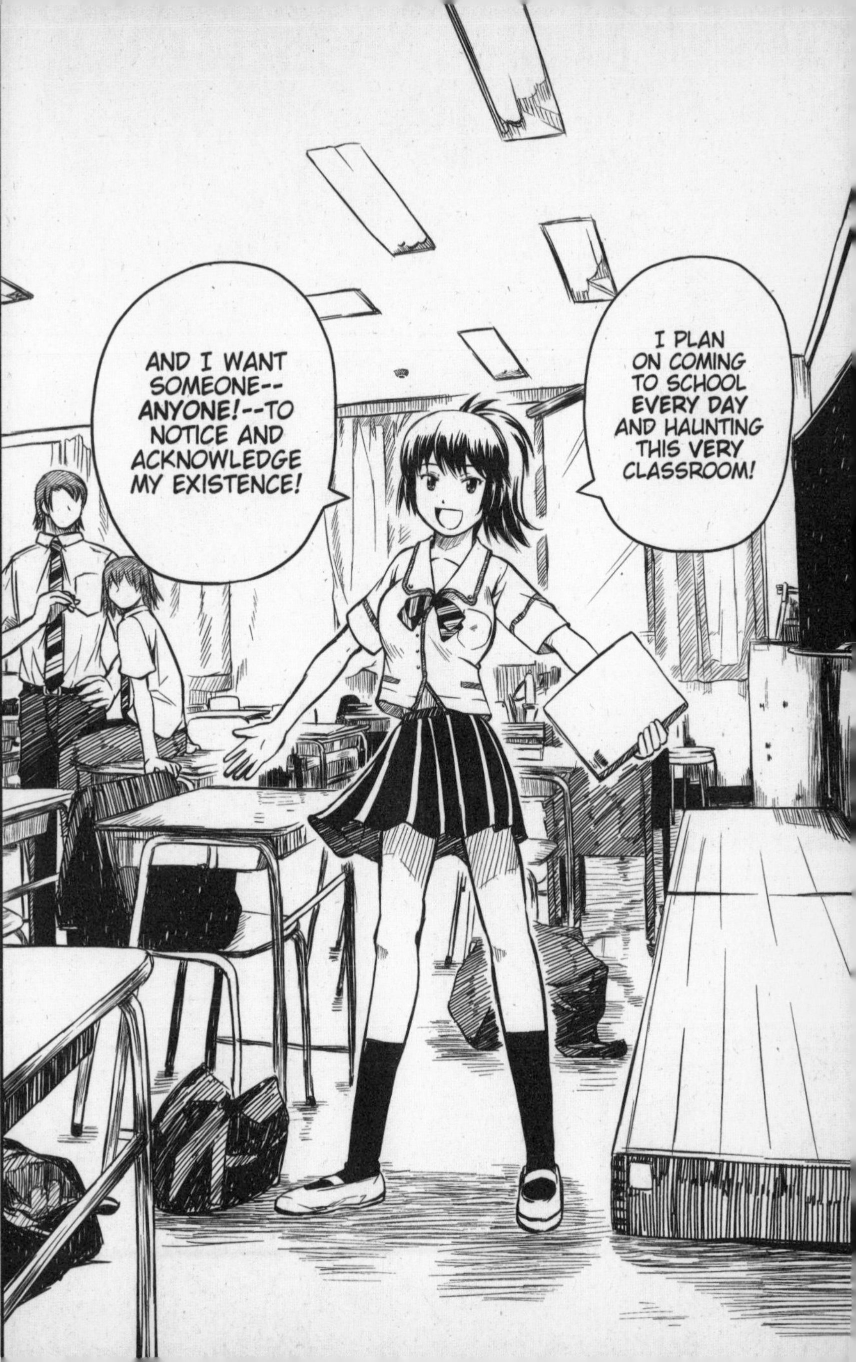
I PLAN ON COMING TO SCHOOL EVERY DAY AND HAUNTING THIS VERY CLASSROOM!
AND I WANT SOMEONE--ANYONE!--TO NOTICE AND ACKNOWLEDGE MY EXISTENCE!

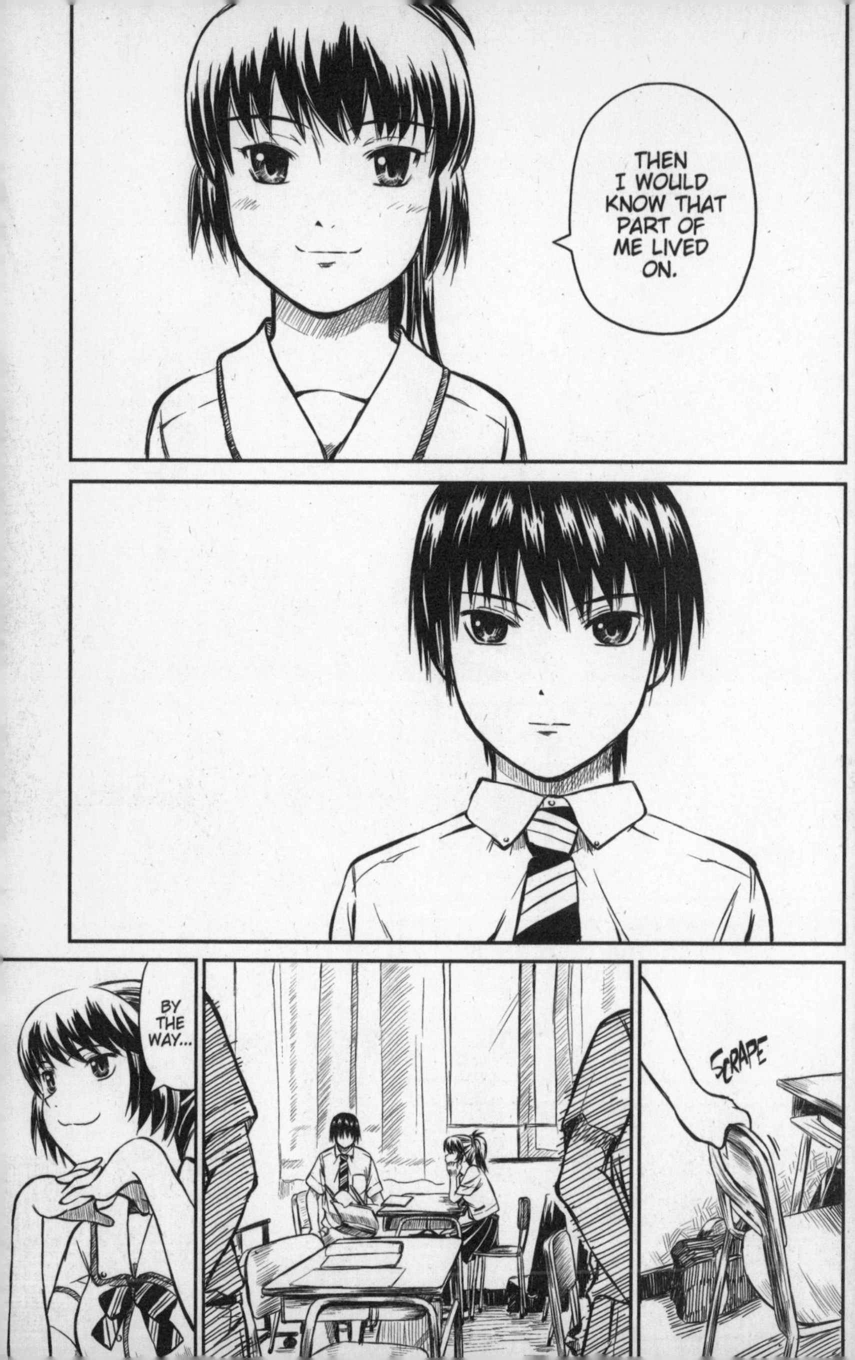
THEN I WOULD KNOW THAT PART OF ME LIVED ON.
SCRAPE
BY THE WAY...

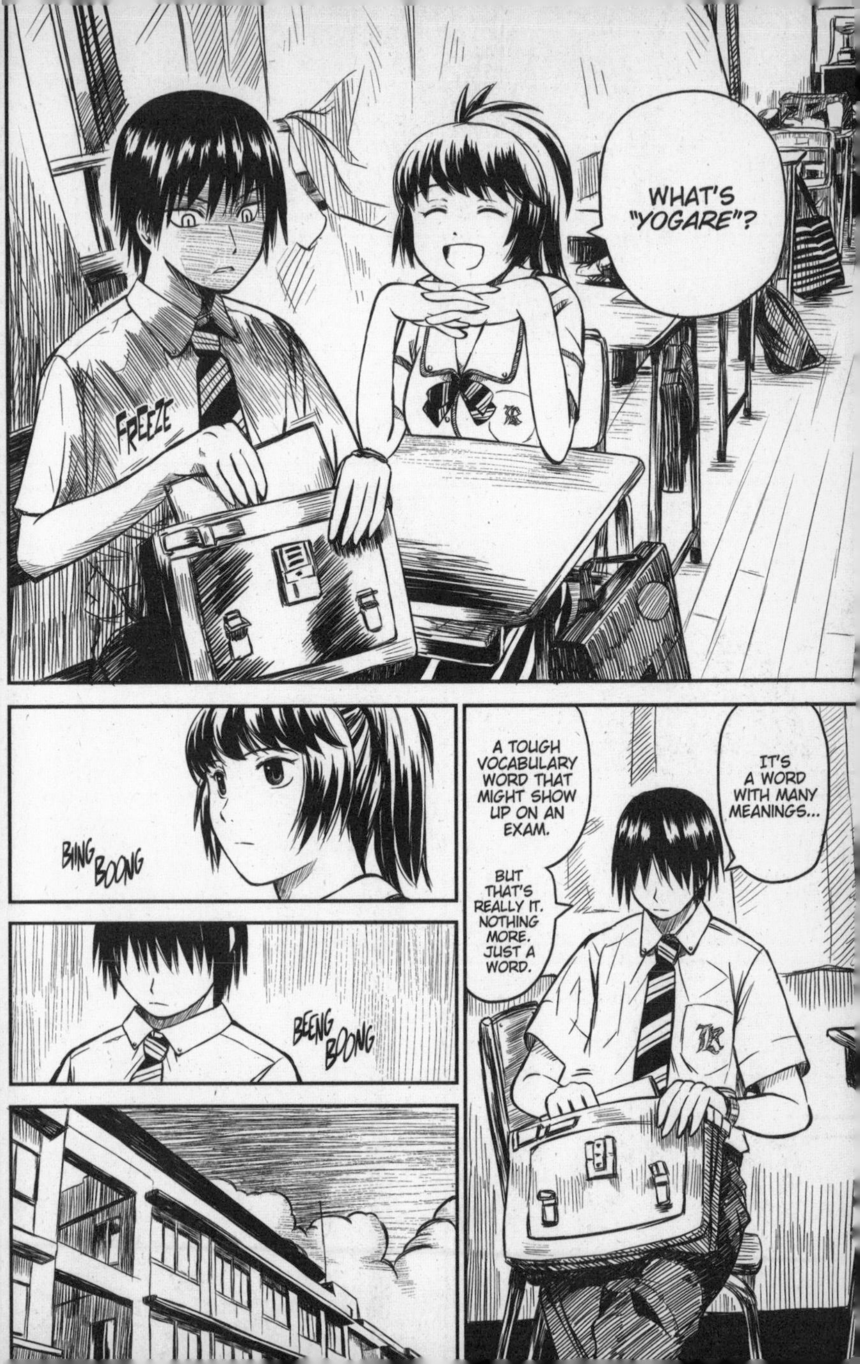

WHAT'S "YOGARE"?
FREEZE
IT'S A WORD WITH MANY MEANINGS...
A TOUGH VOCABULARY WORD THAT MIGHT SHOW UP ON AN EXAM.
BUT THAT'S REALLY IT. NOTHING MORE. JUST A WORD.
BING BOONG
BEENG BOONG

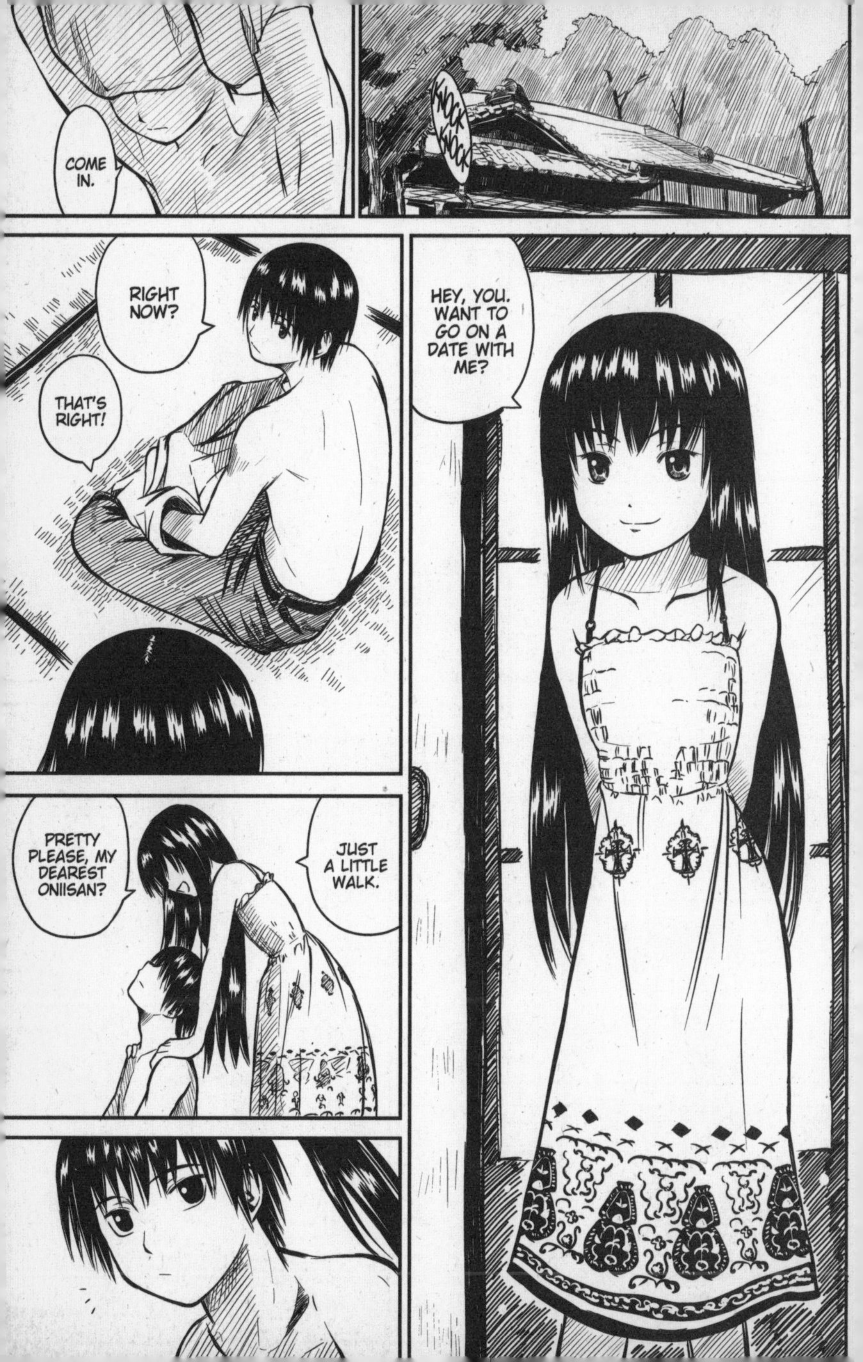
KNOCK KNOCK
COME IN.
HEY, YOU. WANT TO GO ON A DATE WITH ME?
RIGHT NOW?
THAT'S RIGHT!
JUST A LITTLE WALK.
PRETTY PLEASE, MY DEAREST ONIISAN?

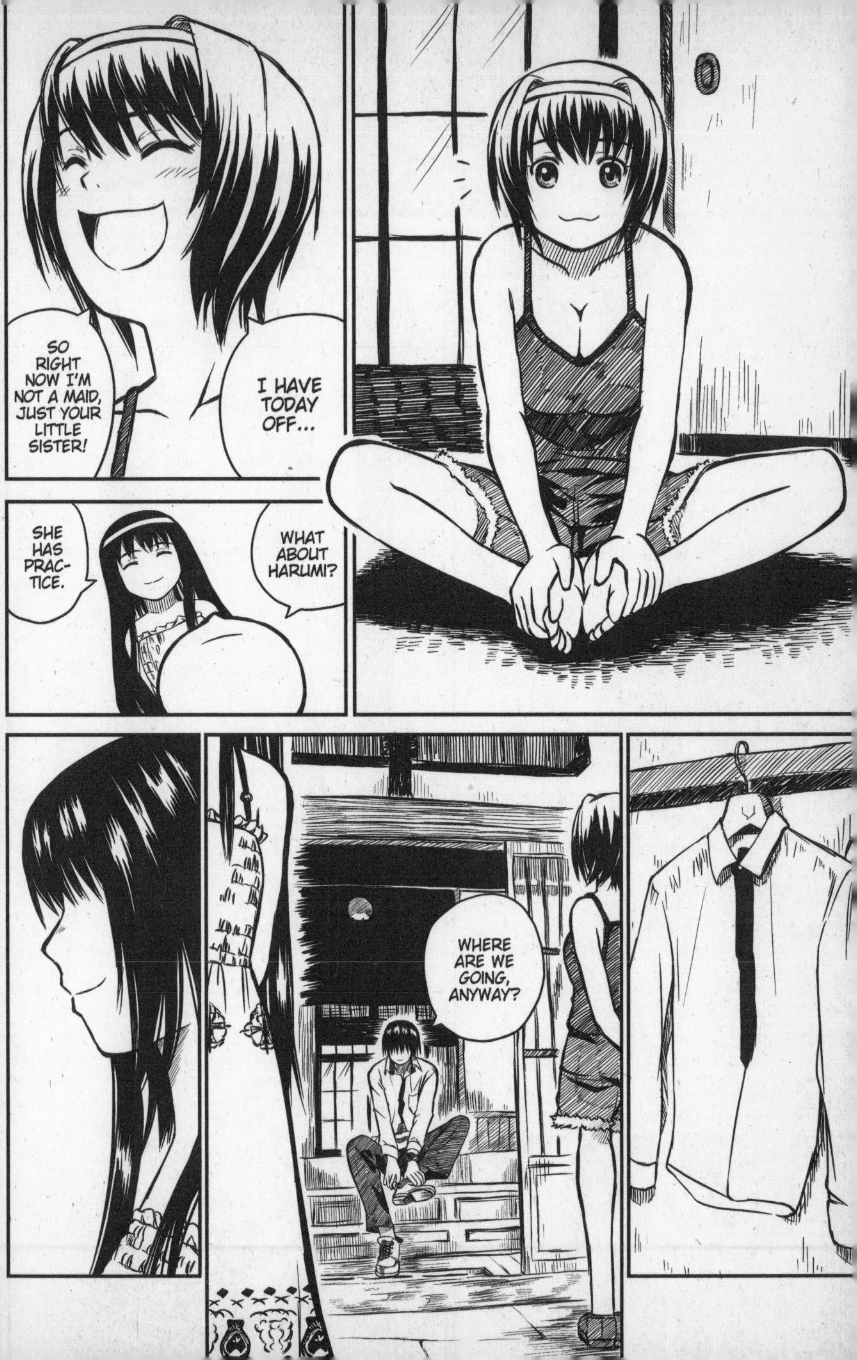
I HAVE TODAY OFF...
SO RIGHT NOW I'M NOT A MAID, JUST YOUR LITTLE SISTER!
WHAT ABOUT HARUMI?
SHE HAS PRAC-TICE.
WHERE ARE WE GOING, ANYWAY?

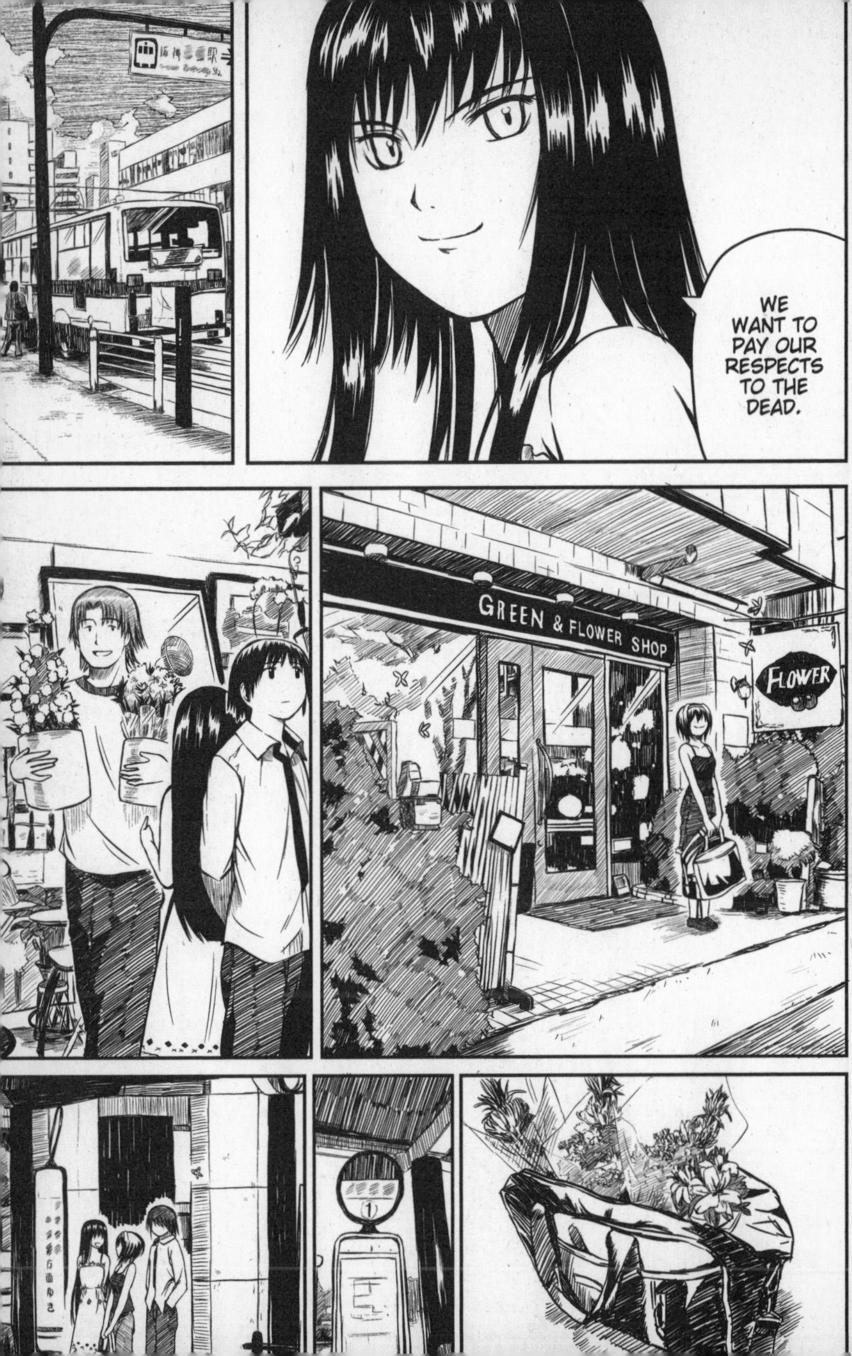
WE WANT TO PAY OUR RESPECTS TO THE DEAD.
GREEN & FLOWER SHOP
FLOWER

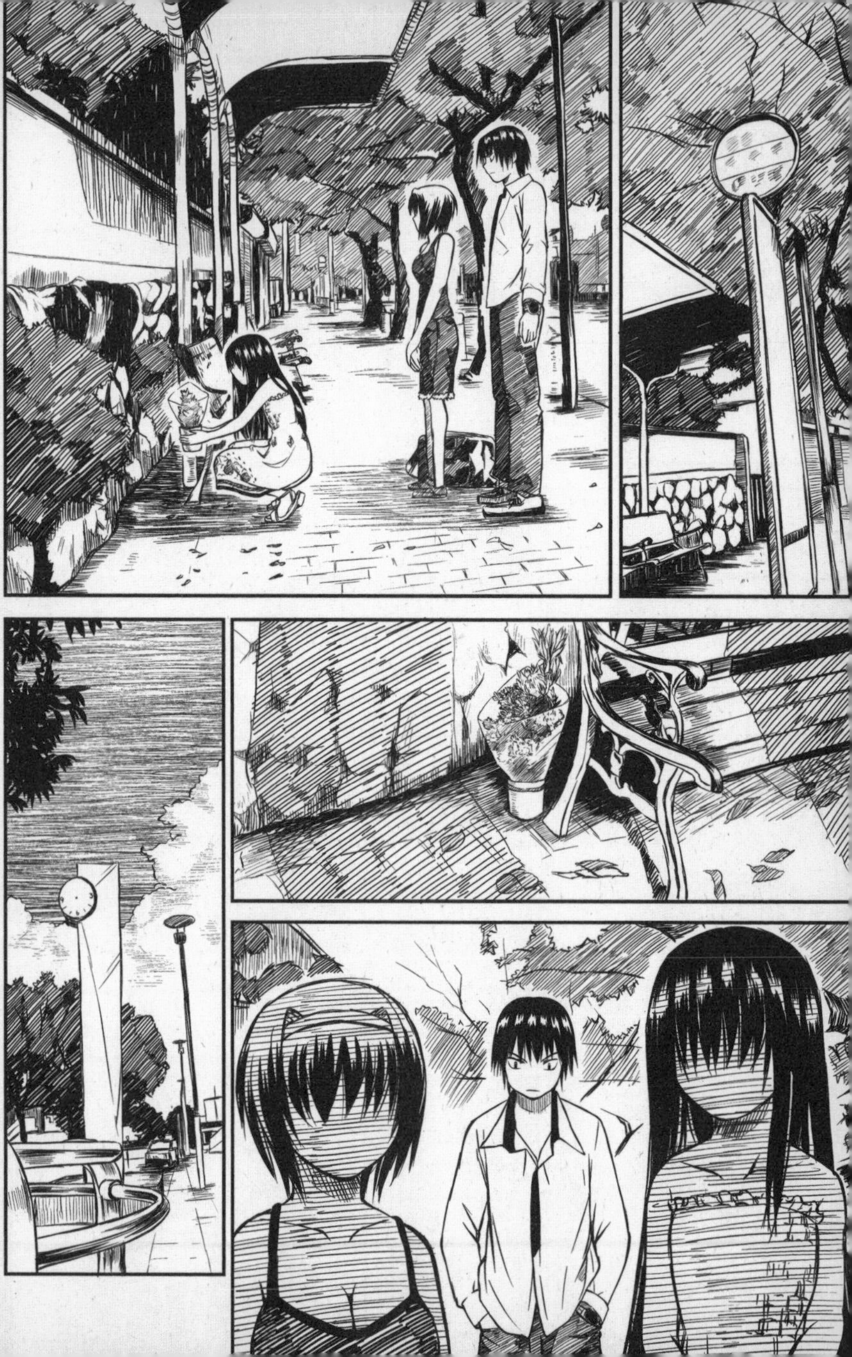

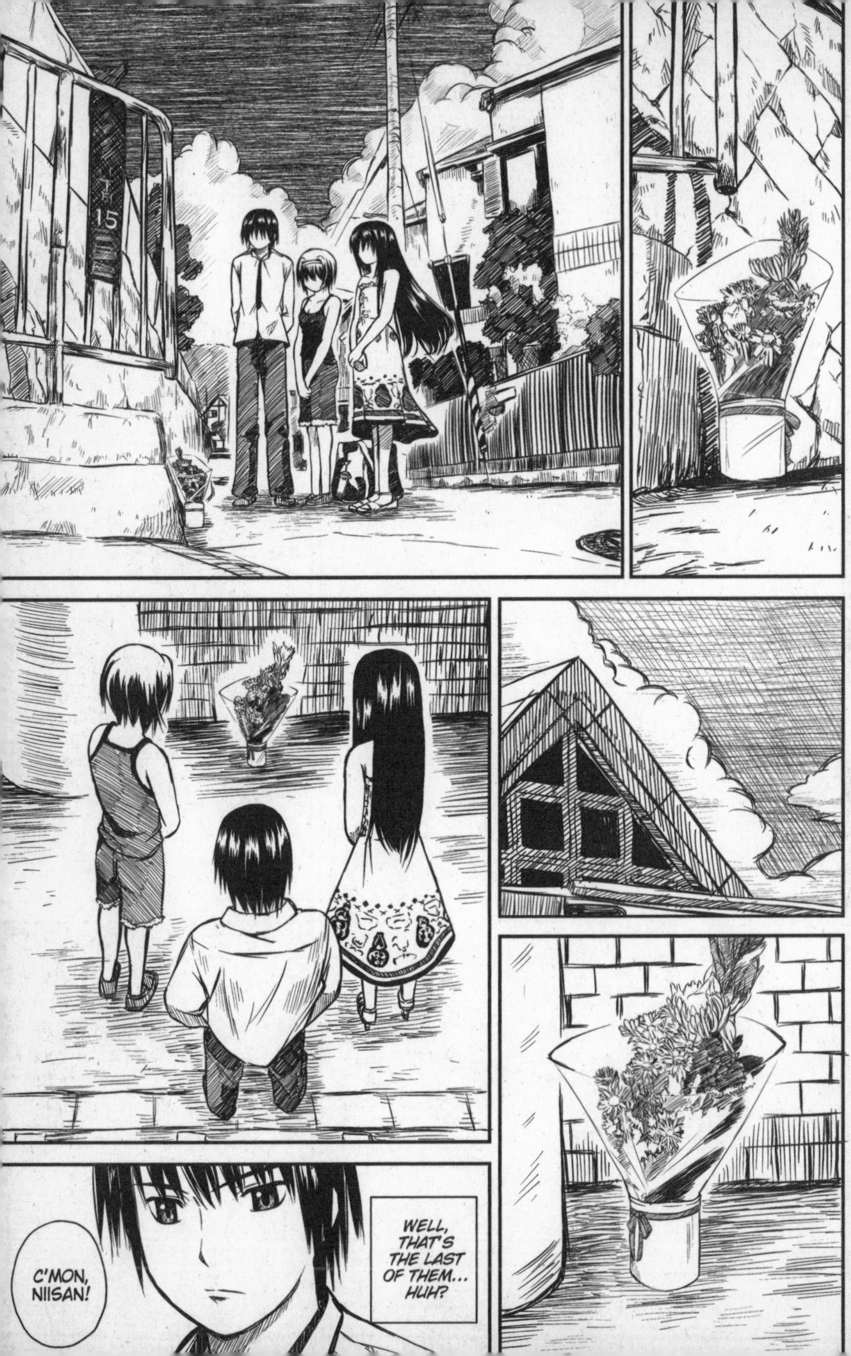
15
WELL, THAT'S THE LAST OF THEM... HUH?
C'MON, NIISAN!

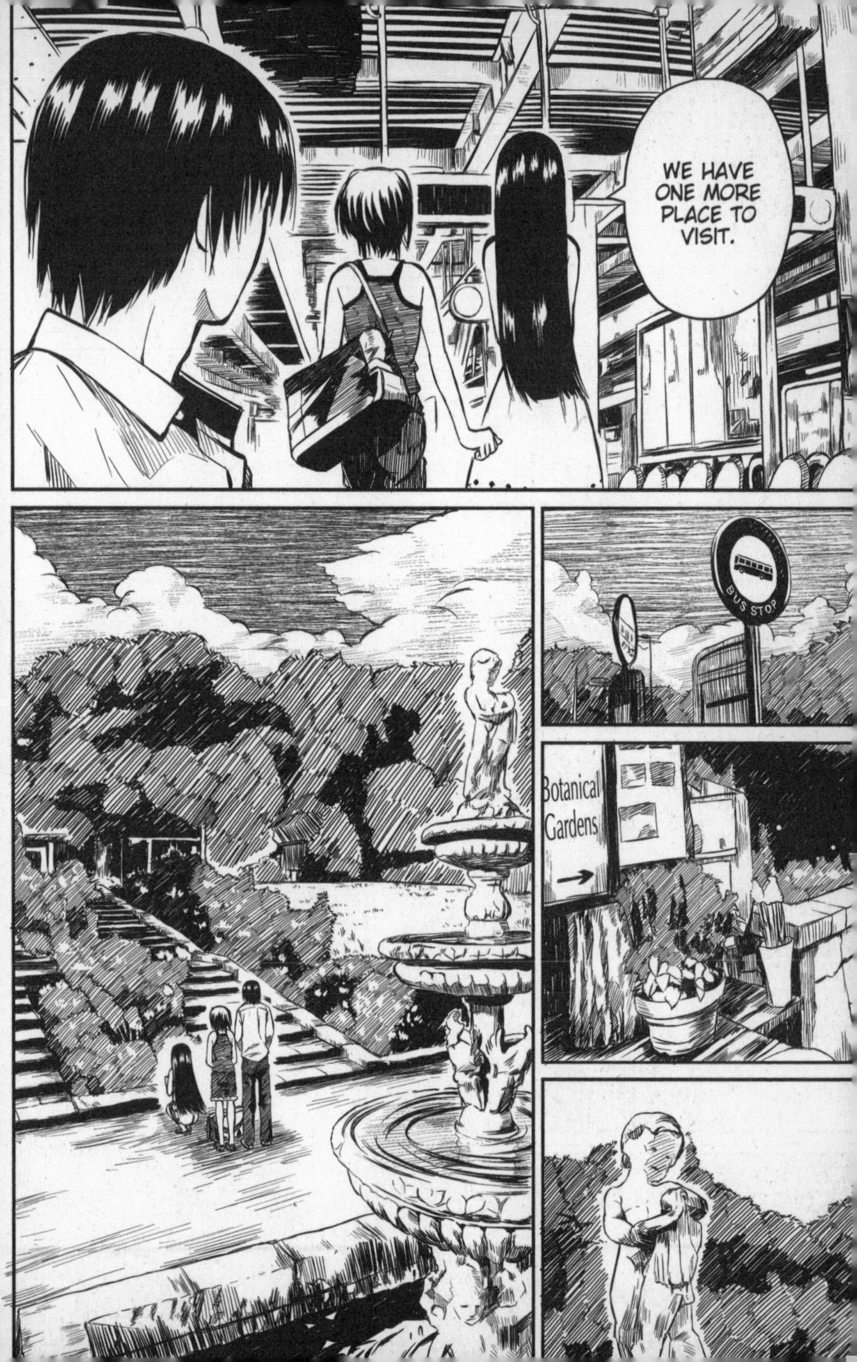
WE HAVE ONE MORE PLACE TO VISIT.
BUS STOP
Botanical Gardens

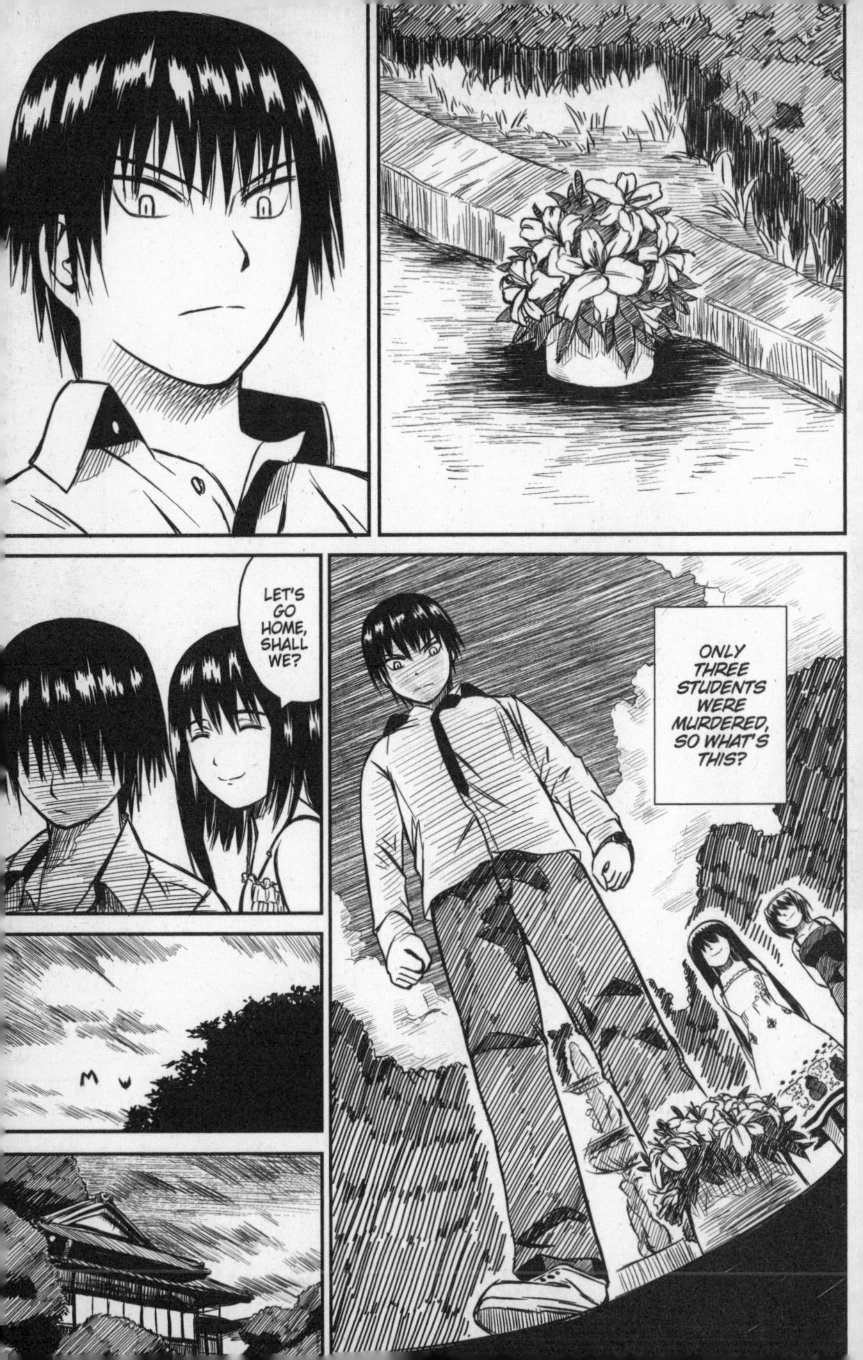
ONLY THREE STUDENTS WERE MURDERED, SO WHAT'S THIS?
LET'S GO HOME, SHALL WE?

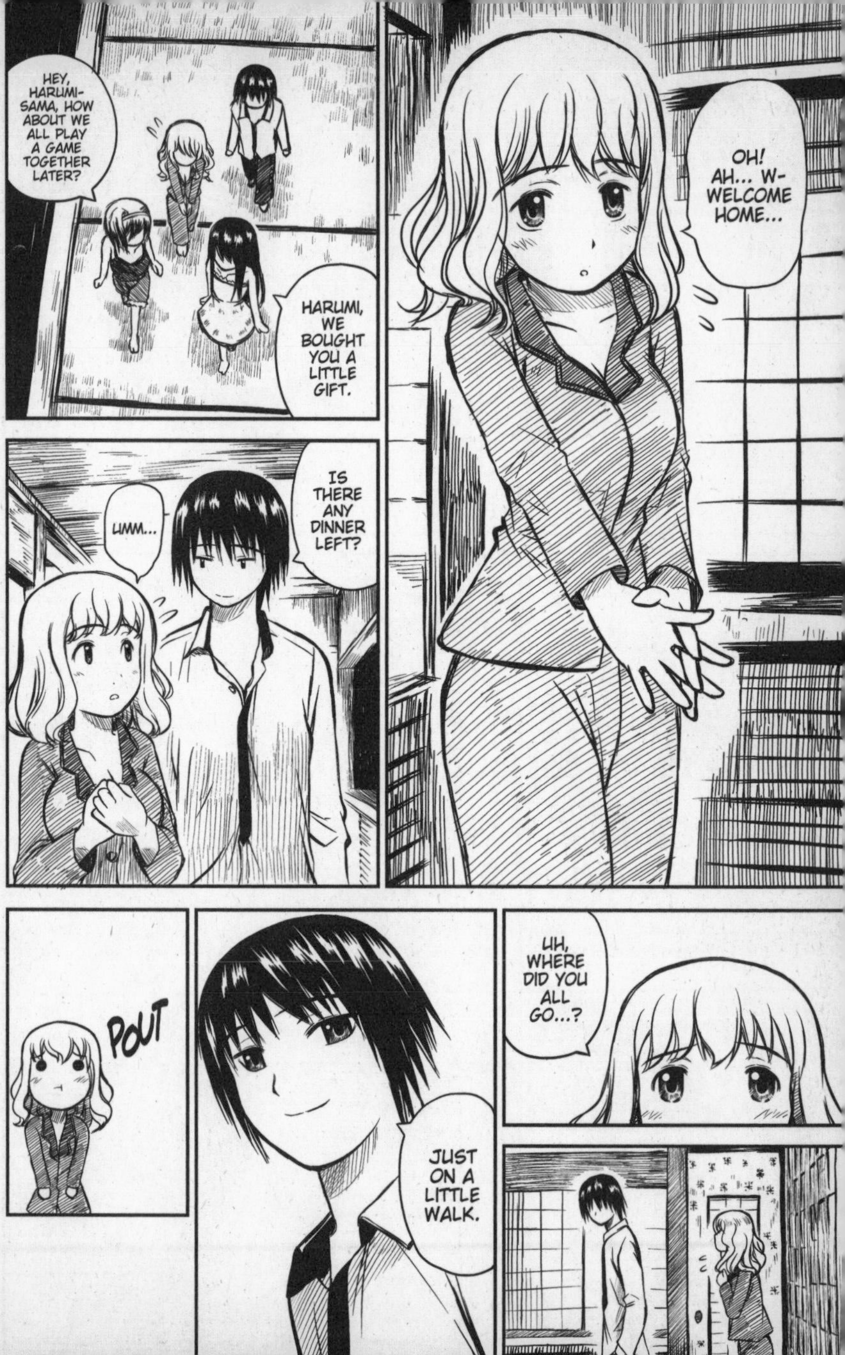
OH! AH... W-WELCOME HOME...
HARUMI, WE BOUGHT YOU A LITTLE GIFT.
HEY, HARUMI-SAMA, HOW ABOUT WE ALL PLAY A GAME TOGETHER LATER?
IS THERE ANY DINNER LEFT?
UMM...
UH, WHERE DID YOU ALL GO...?
JUST ON A LITTLE WALK.
POUT

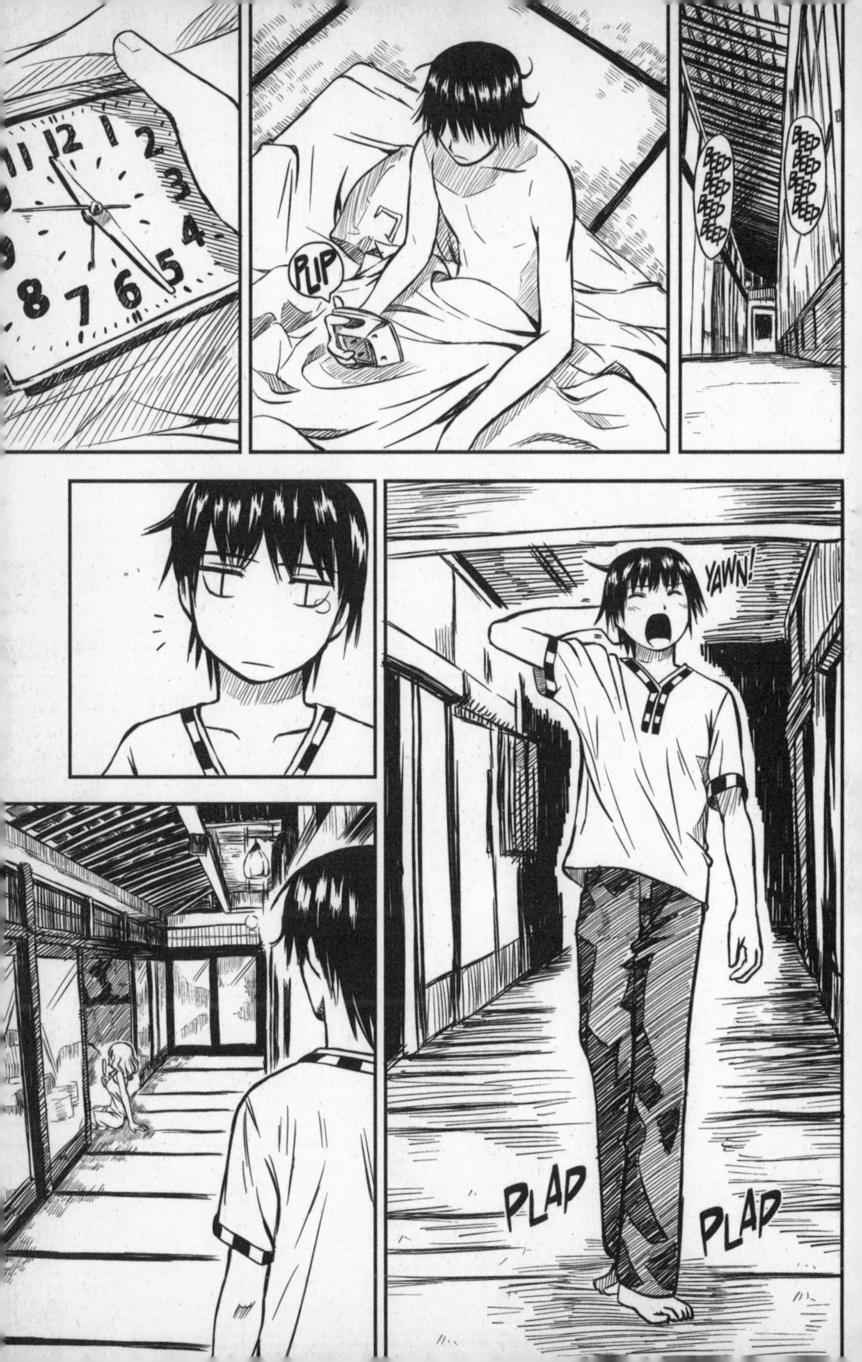
BEEP BEEP BEEP BEEP
BEEP BEEP BEEP BEEP
PLIP
YAWN!
PLAP
PLAP

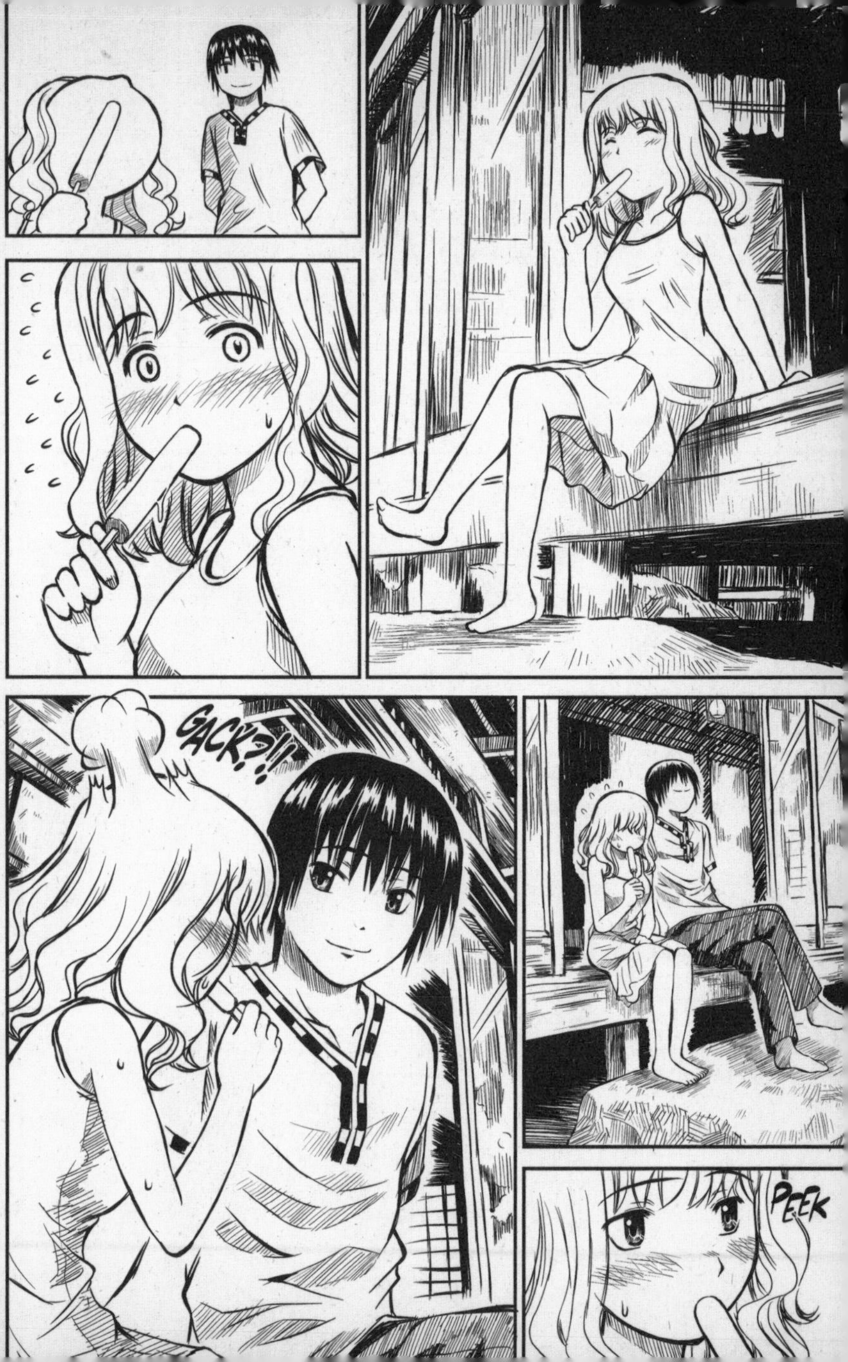
PEEK
GACK?!!

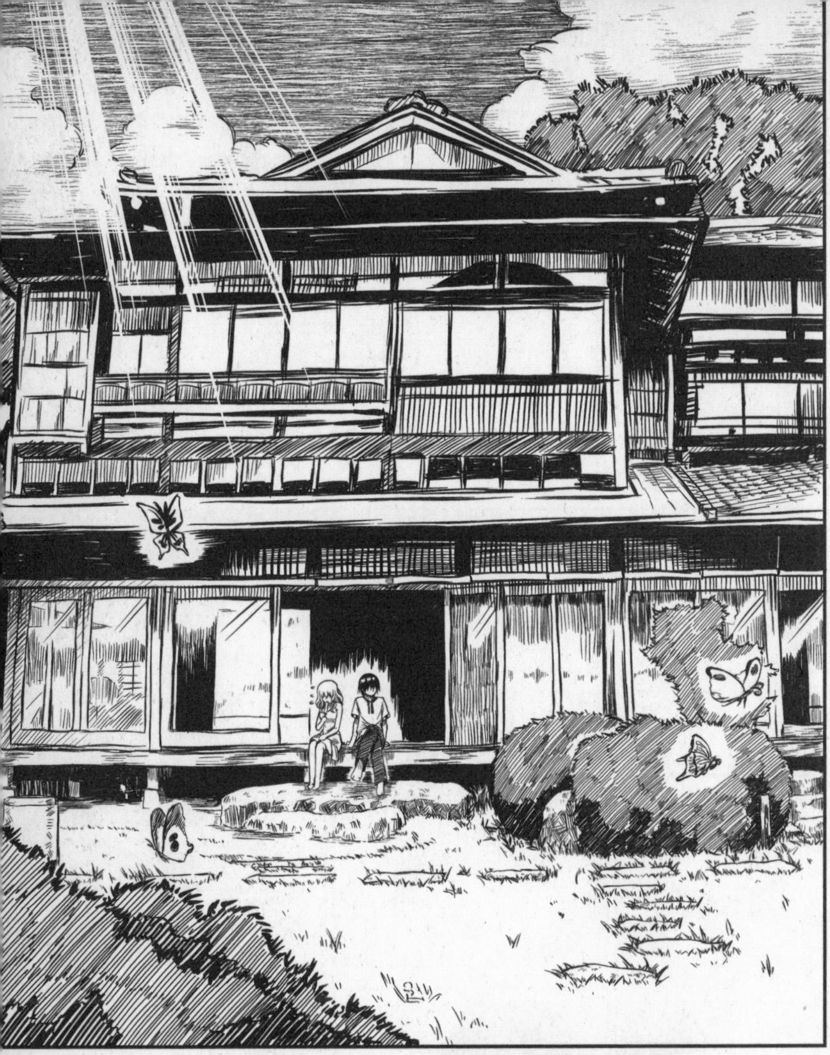

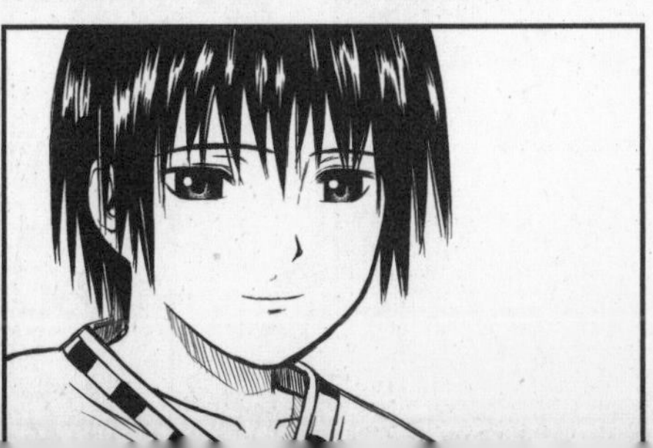

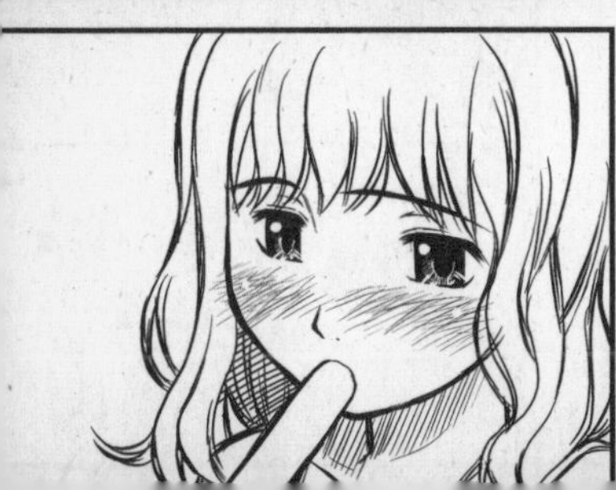

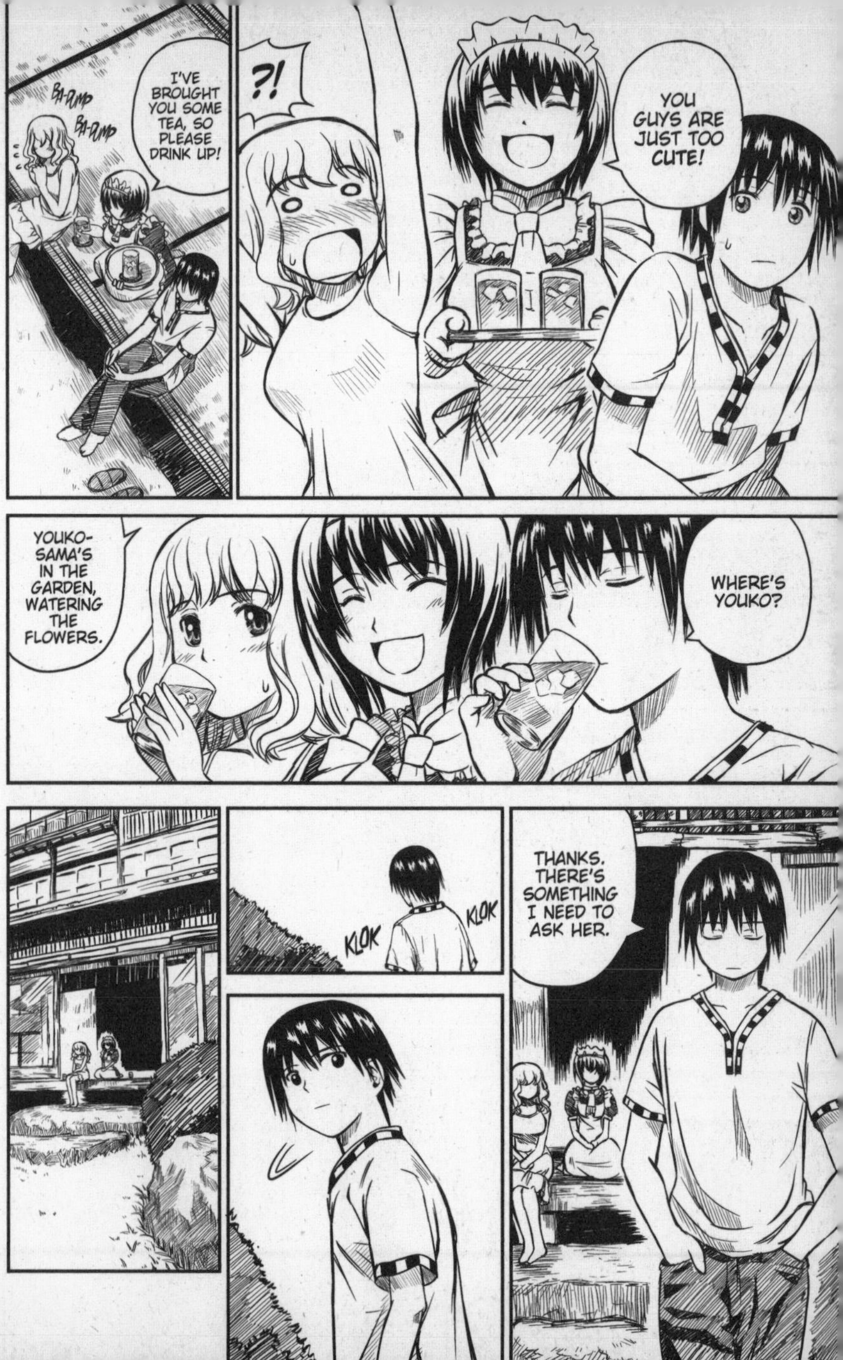
YOU GUYS ARE JUST TOO CUTE!
?!
I'VE BROUGHT YOU SOME TEA, SO PLEASE DRINK UP!
BA-DUMP
BA-DUMP
WHERE'S YOUKO?
YOUKO-SAMA'S IN THE GARDEN, WATERING THE FLOWERS.
THANKS. THERE'S SOMETHING I NEED TO ASK HER.
KLOK
KLOK

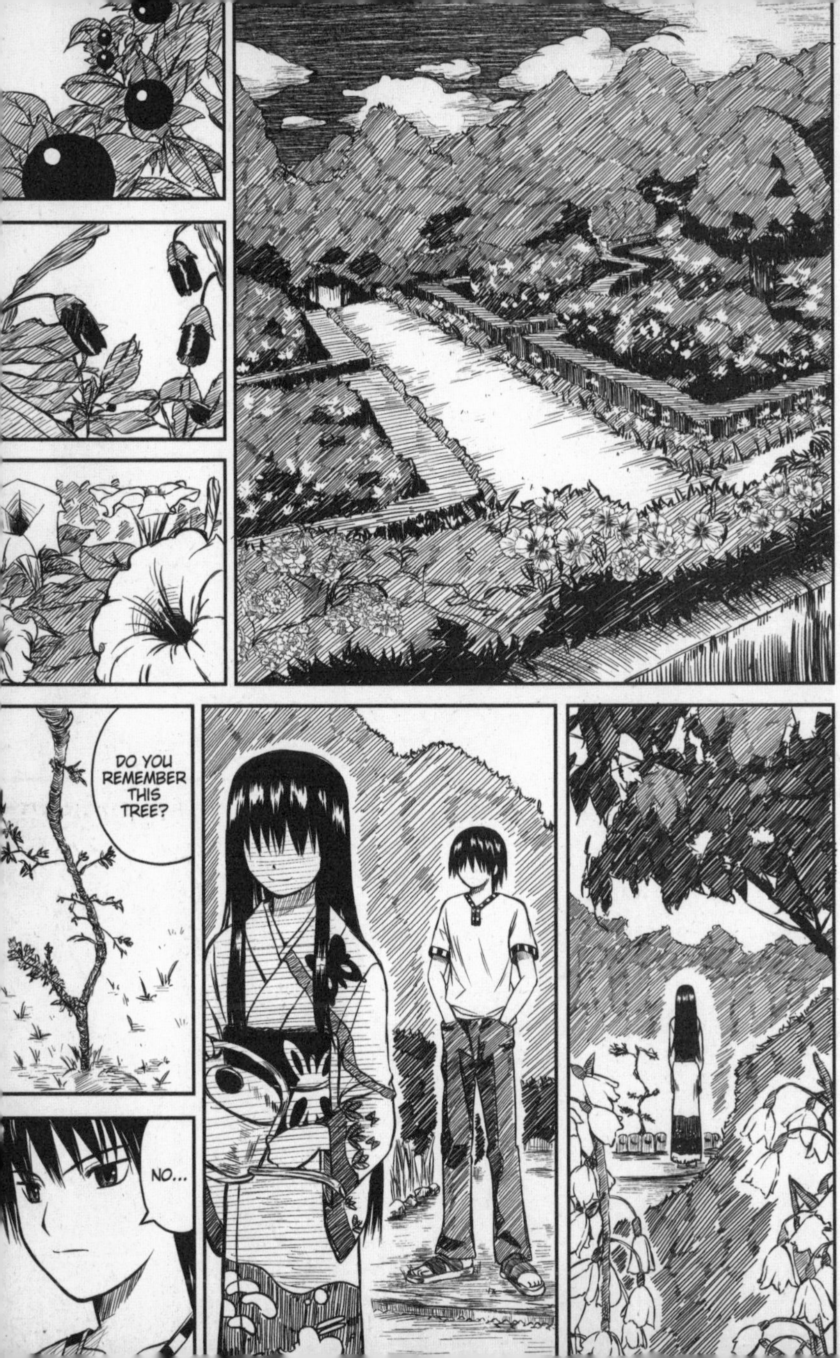
DO YOU REMEMBER THIS TREE?
NO...

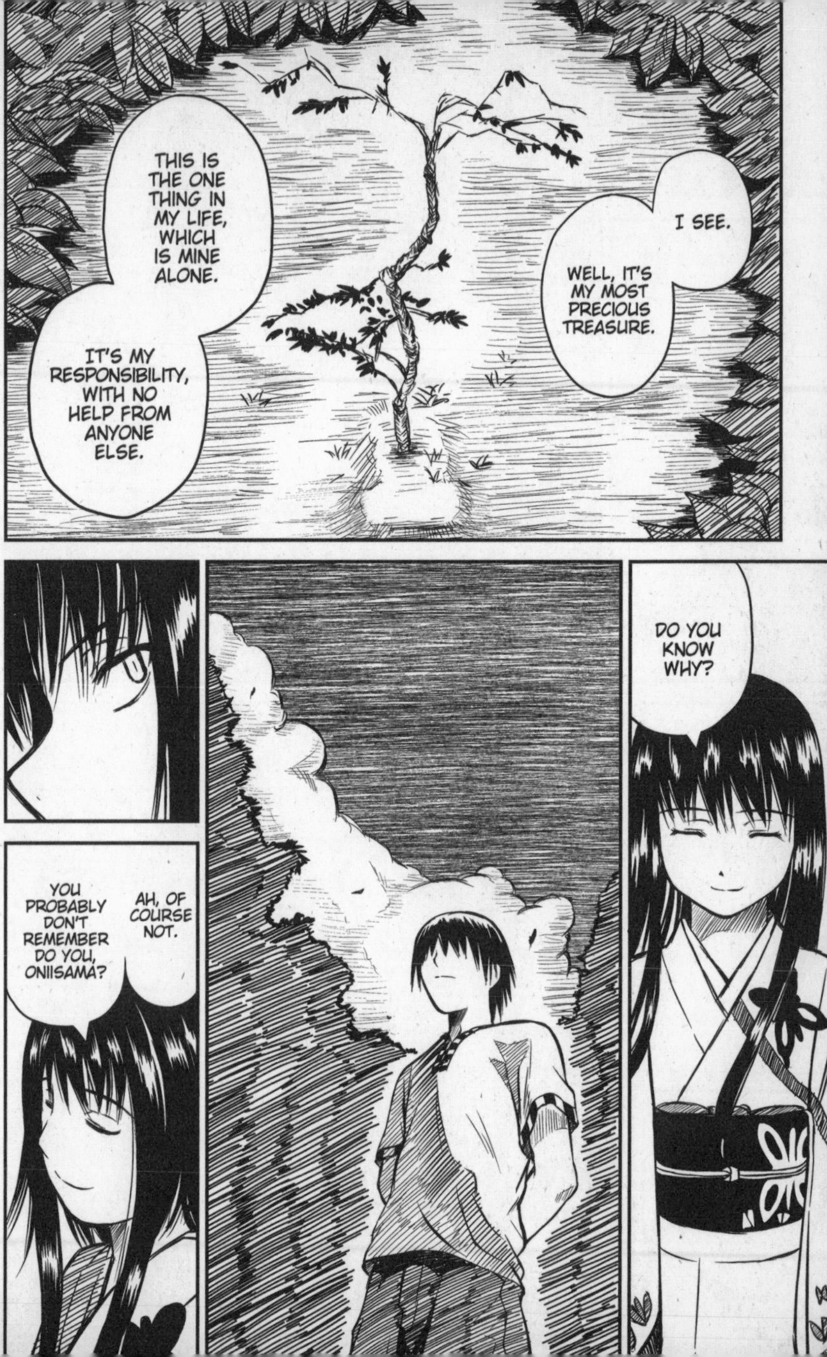
I SEE.
WELL, IT'S MY MOST PRECIOUS TREASURE.
THIS IS THE ONE THING IN MY LIFE, WHICH IS MINE ALONE.
IT'S MY RESPONSIBILITY, WITH NO HELP FROM ANYONE ELSE.
DO YOU KNOW WHY?
AH, OF COURSE NOT.
YOU PROBABLY DON'T REMEMBER DO YOU, ONIISAMA?

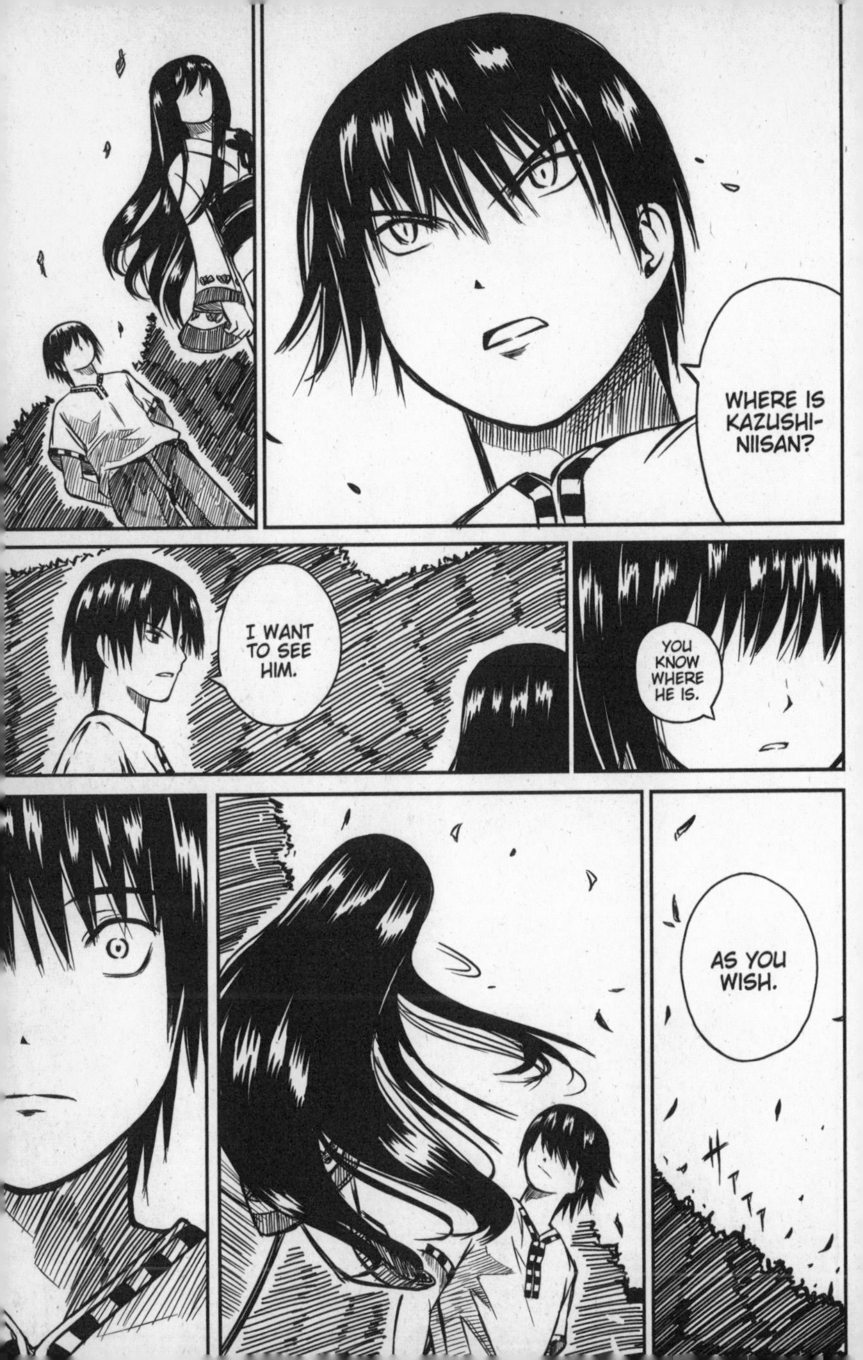
WHERE IS KAZUSHI-NIISAN?
YOU KNOW WHERE HE IS.
I WANT TO SEE HIM.
AS YOU WISH.

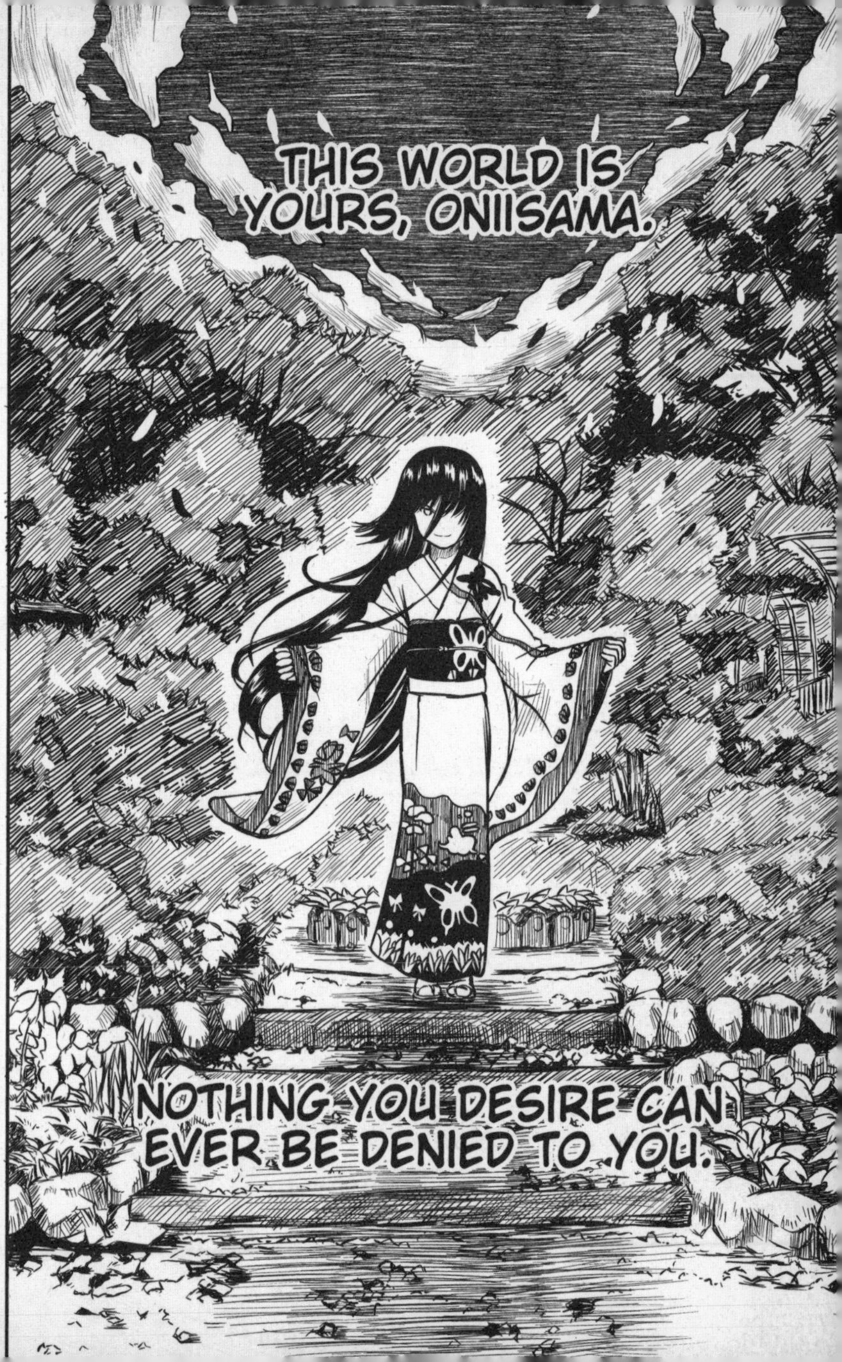
THIS WORLD IS YOURS, ONIISAMA.
NOTHING YOU DESIRE CAN EVER BE DENIED TO YOU.

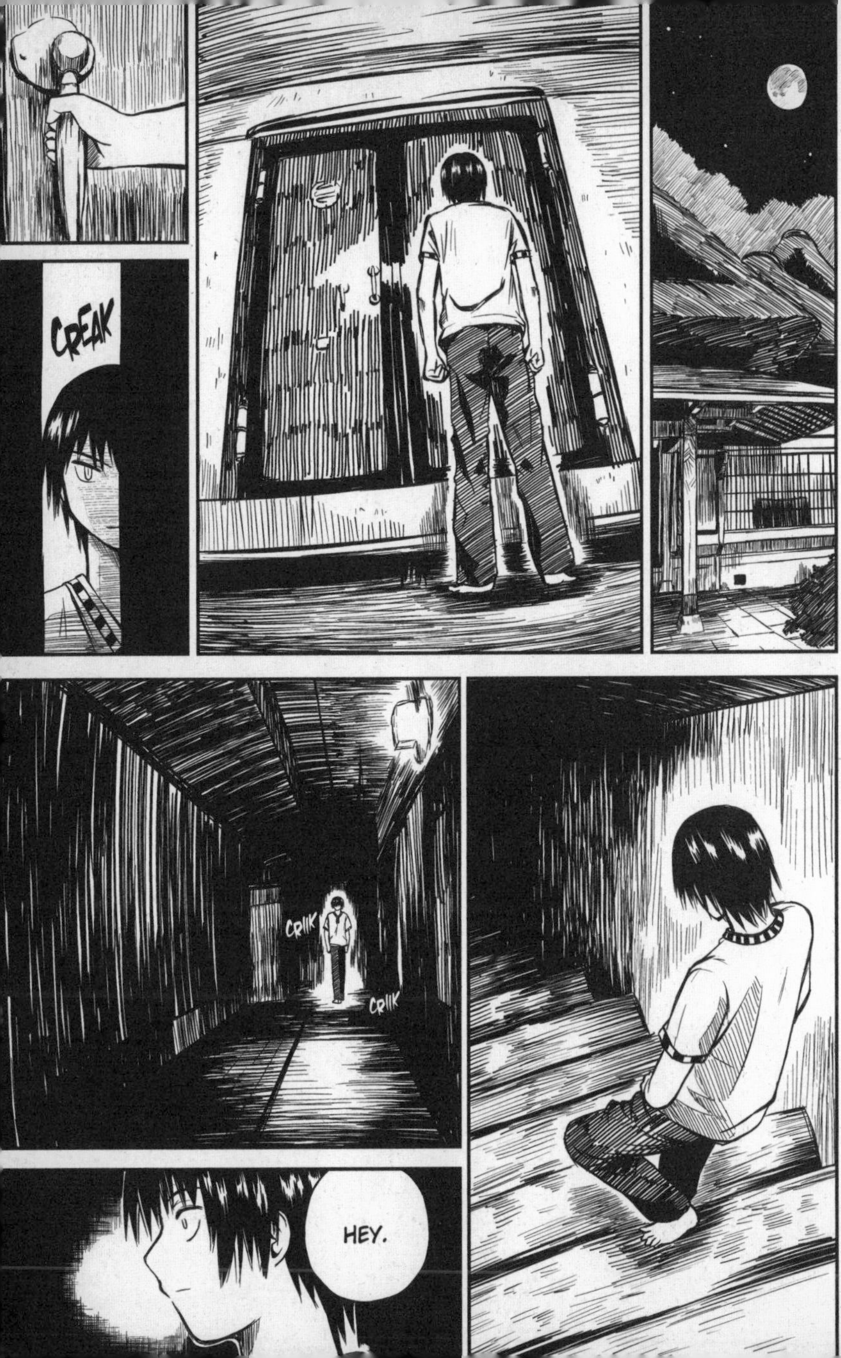
CREAK
CRIIK
CRIIK
HEY.

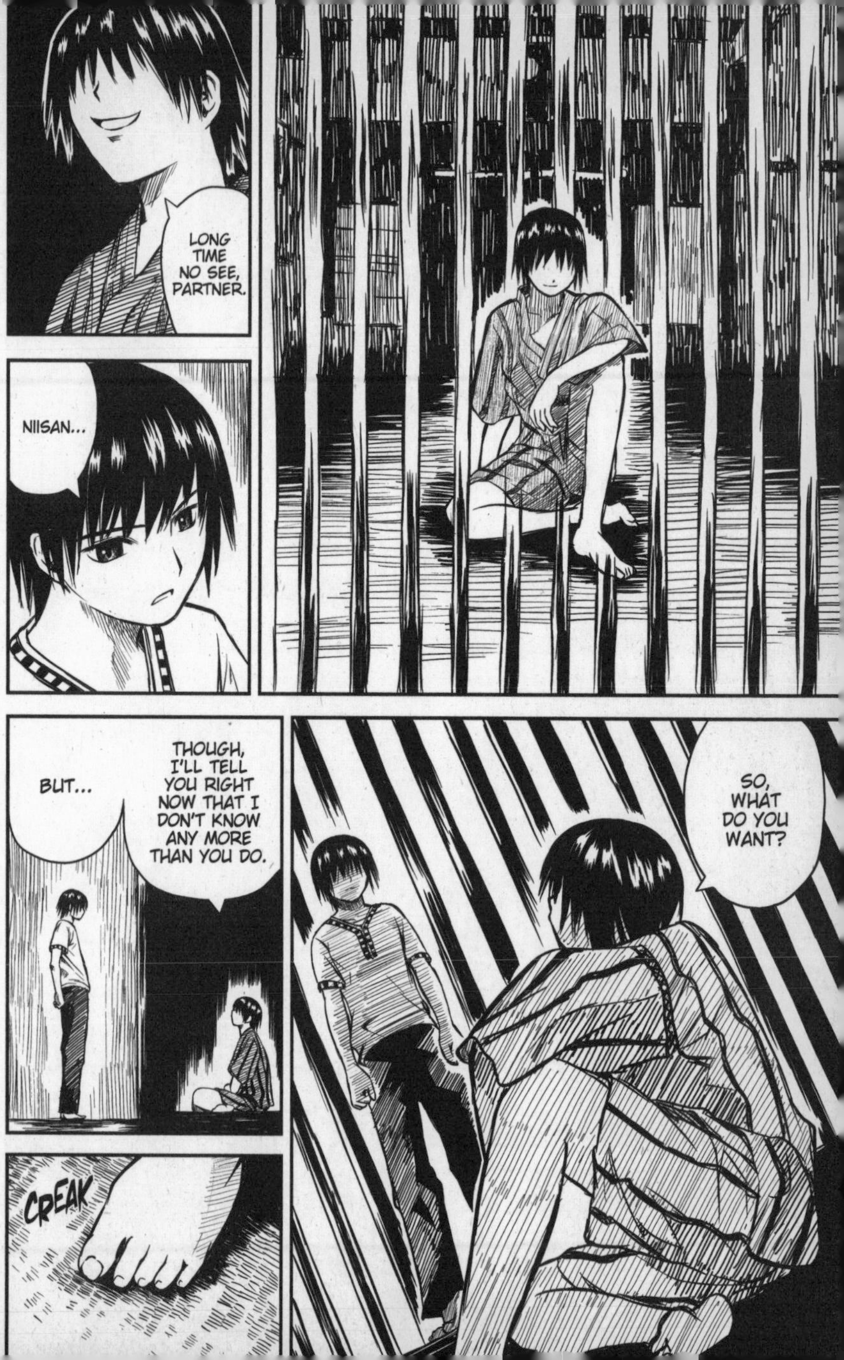
LONG TIME NO SEE, PARTNER.
NIISAN...
SO, WHAT DO YOU WANT?
THOUGH, I'LL TELL YOU RIGHT NOW THAT I DON'T KNOW ANY MORE THAN YOU DO.
BUT...
CREAK

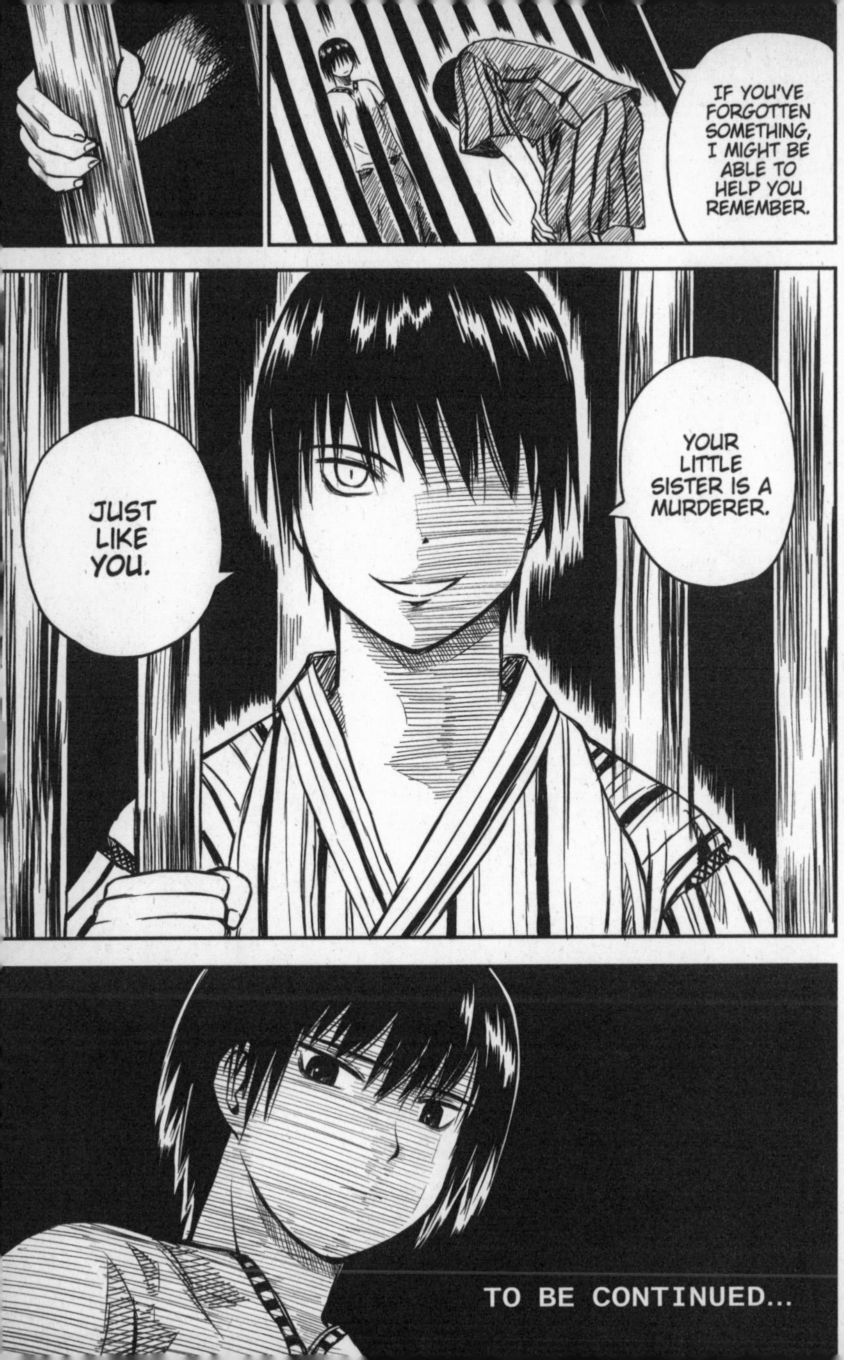
IF YOU'VE FORGOTTEN SOMETHING, I MIGHT BE ABLE TO HELP YOU REMEMBER.
YOUR LITTLE SISTER IS A MURDERER.
JUST LIKE YOU.
TO BE CONTINUED...

Amnesia Labyrinth CHARACTER FILE 4

KUSHIKI SOUJI

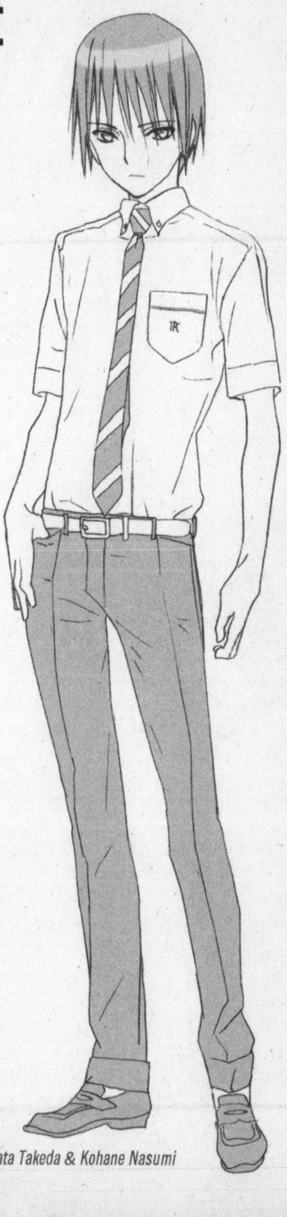

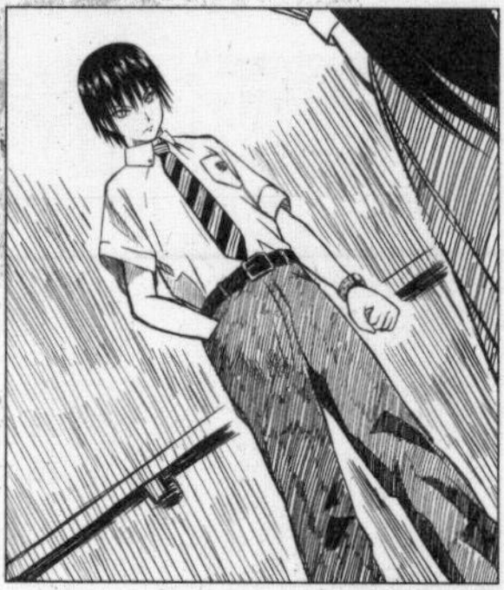

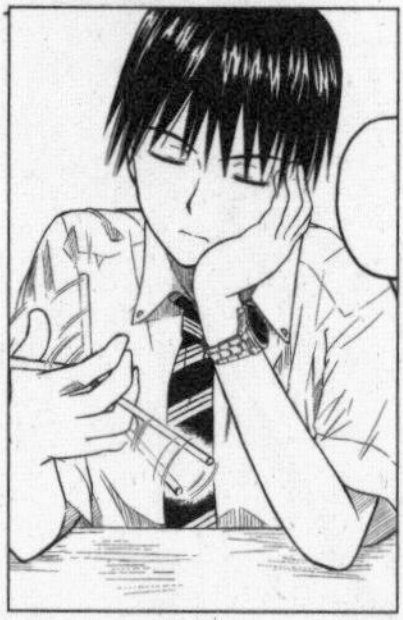

The second son of the Kushiki Household. He had been living a carefree life after getting into an out of prefecture high school, but after the sudden flight of his elder brother, Kazushi, he was called back to his home to become heir of the Kushiki Household. Souji is also a pessimist with an anti-social disposition.

Illustration! Hinata Takeda & Kohane Nasumi

Amnesia Labyrinth CHARACTER FILE 5

SASAI YUKAKO

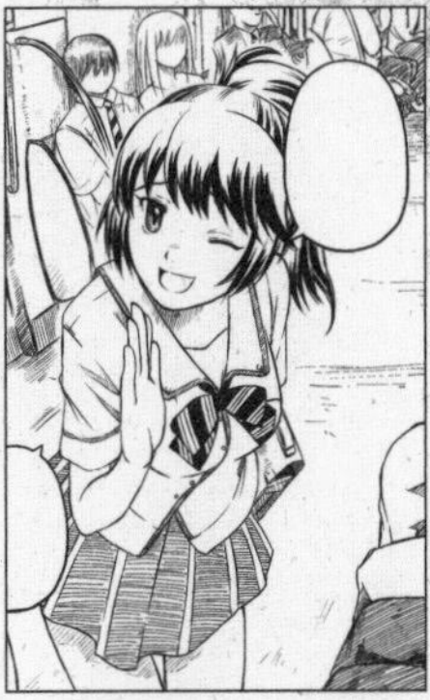

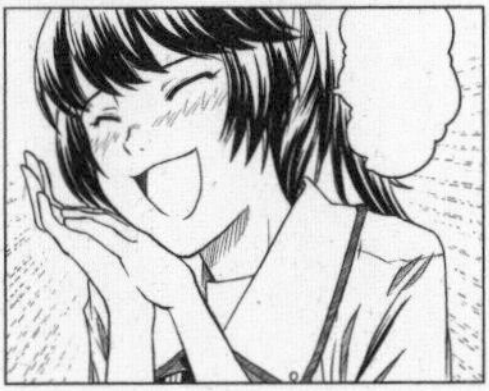

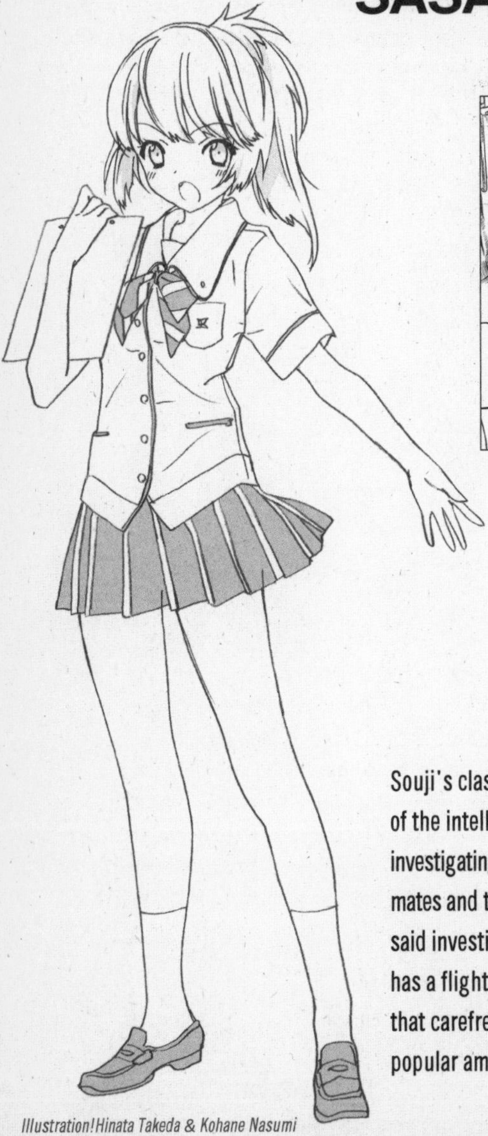

Souji's classmate and the sole member of the intelligence committee. She is investigating the murders of her school-mates and tries to get Souji involved in said investigation. Though at times she has a flighty personality, it's precisely that carefree nature that makes her popular amongst her classmates.

Illustration! Hinata Takeda & Kohane Nasumi

Message From the Writer

Although an overall plot does exist for this story, when everything was said and done, I sort of ran out of things to write, and therefore I admit there are a number of lazy, phantom passages scattered throughout. This work was based on a story that, while it didn't have enough to become a full-fledged novel, had been kicking around my head for years now.

While my editor Miki-san took care of the minor details, I had to dismantle a story that had been set in my mind for so long and reinvent the characters. It was incredibly tough, but very fun at the same time. Nasumi-sama, who was in charge of illustrating this manga, rendered everything faithfully down to a T, even after I said, "You can change anything you want." But at any rate, I am humbled, no, in awe, of how everything turned out. As if drawing a manga were not hard enough, I'm sorry for bothering you so much each and every time. And to Hinata Takeda-sama, who did the character designs, thank you so much for so many things. I'm so sorry the story turned out this way, however. And to my readers, I do apologize for all the various delays this work has suffered. But if you continue to follow this series to the very end, it would make me the most insanely happy person ever.

On that note, see you again in the next volume! Until then...

Nagaru Tanigawa

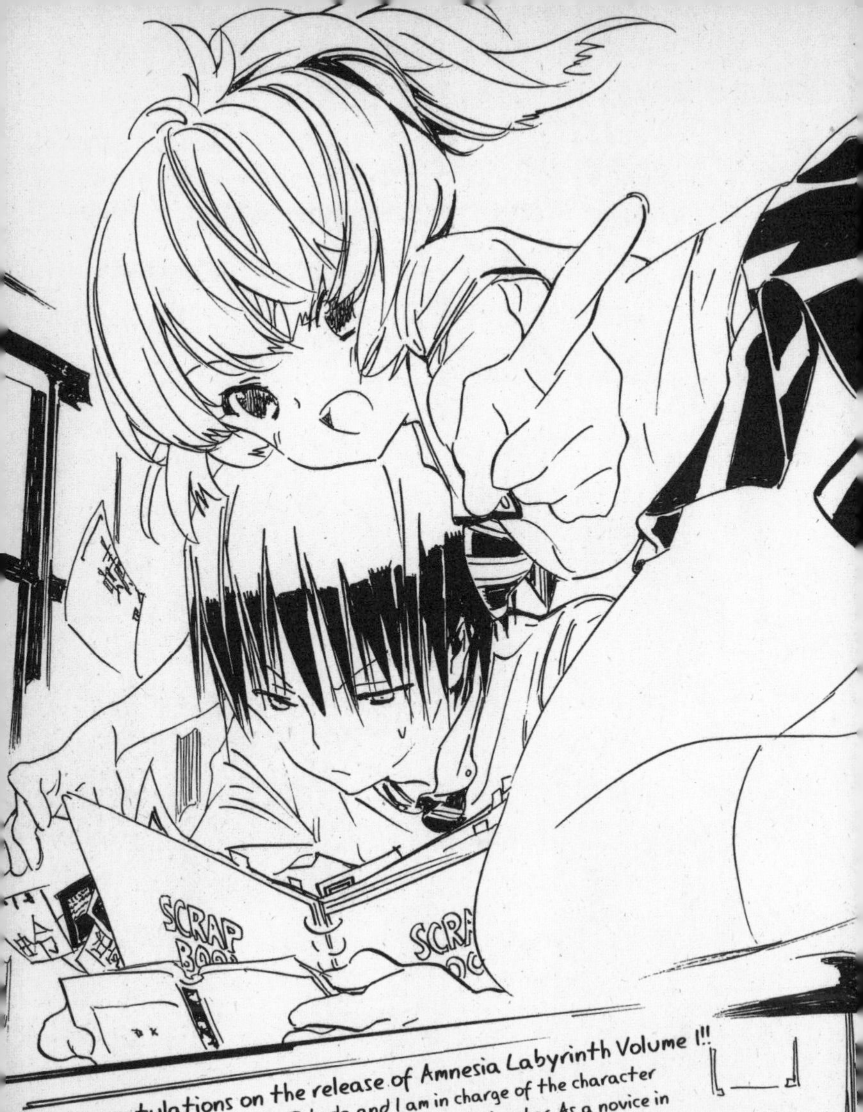
SCRAP
SCRAP

Congratulations on the release of Amnesia Labyrinth Volume 1!!

Hello, everyone. My name is Takeda and I am in charge of the character designs. I must say, I've been entertained by each chapter. As a novice in the industry, I find myself bowing my head down each and every time over how tense and suspenseful the story is, and over the beautiful and detailed the art. I'm so blessed to work with these two immensely talented people in terms of story and artwork. And I'm just so, so, so, so, so thankful to have been given the opportunity to take part in a project like this. Please look forward to Volume 2! Thank you so much!

Hinata Takeda

Harumi's yearning for Souji.
SHE WANTS TO BE PART OF THE FAMILY.
IT WOULD BE BEST IF YOU WERE NO LONGER ASSOCIATED WITH THIS HOUSE-HOLD.
I AM TELLING YOU THIS FOR YOUR OWN GOOD.
Saki's machinations, envious of Yukako.
IF I COULD WISH ANYTHING FOR OUR BLOOD-LINE...
IT WOULD BE TO CORRECT THE WAYS OF THE WORLD.
And a vision of the Heian dancing in a dream—

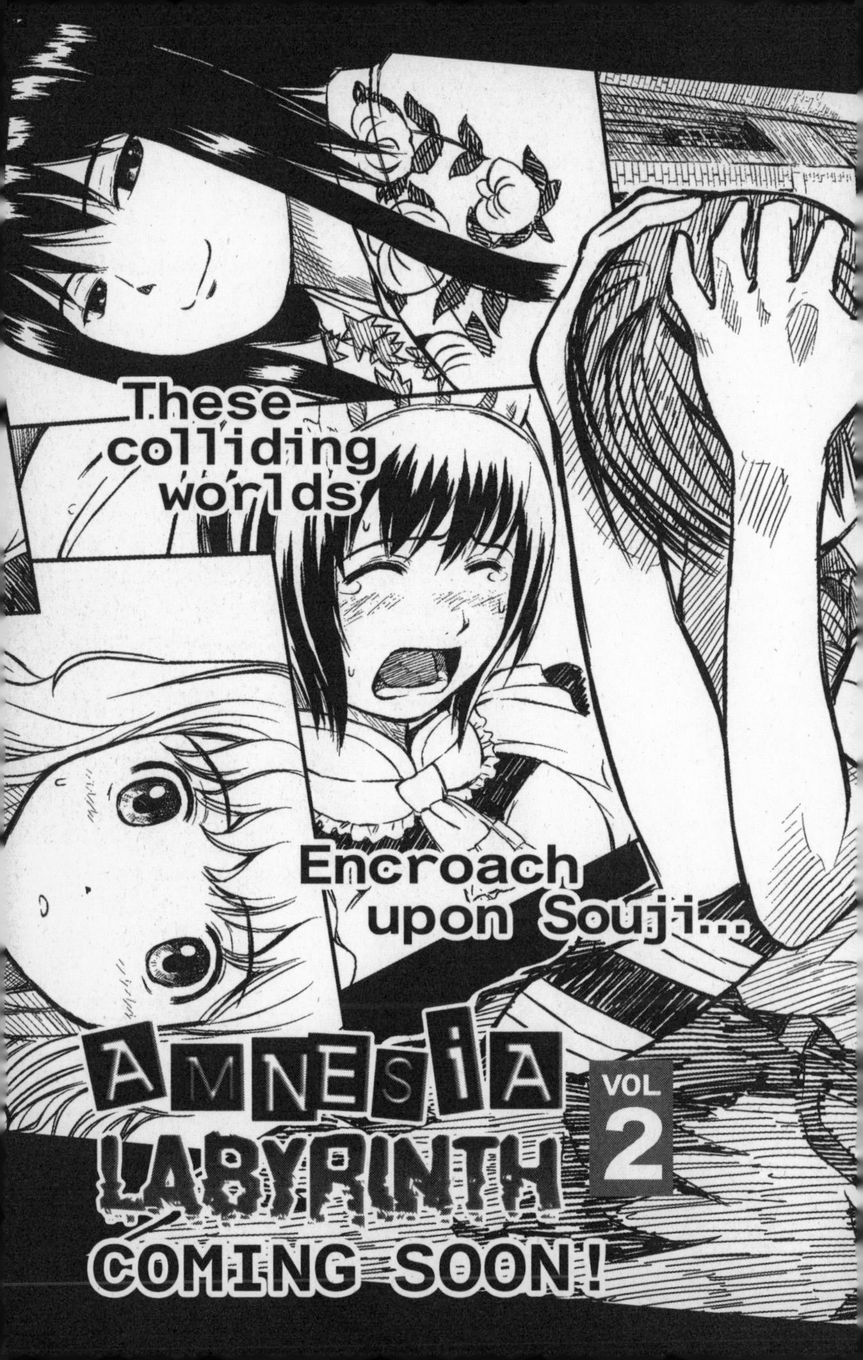
These colliding worlds
Encroach upon Souji...
AMNESIA LABYRINTH
VOL 2
COMING SOON!

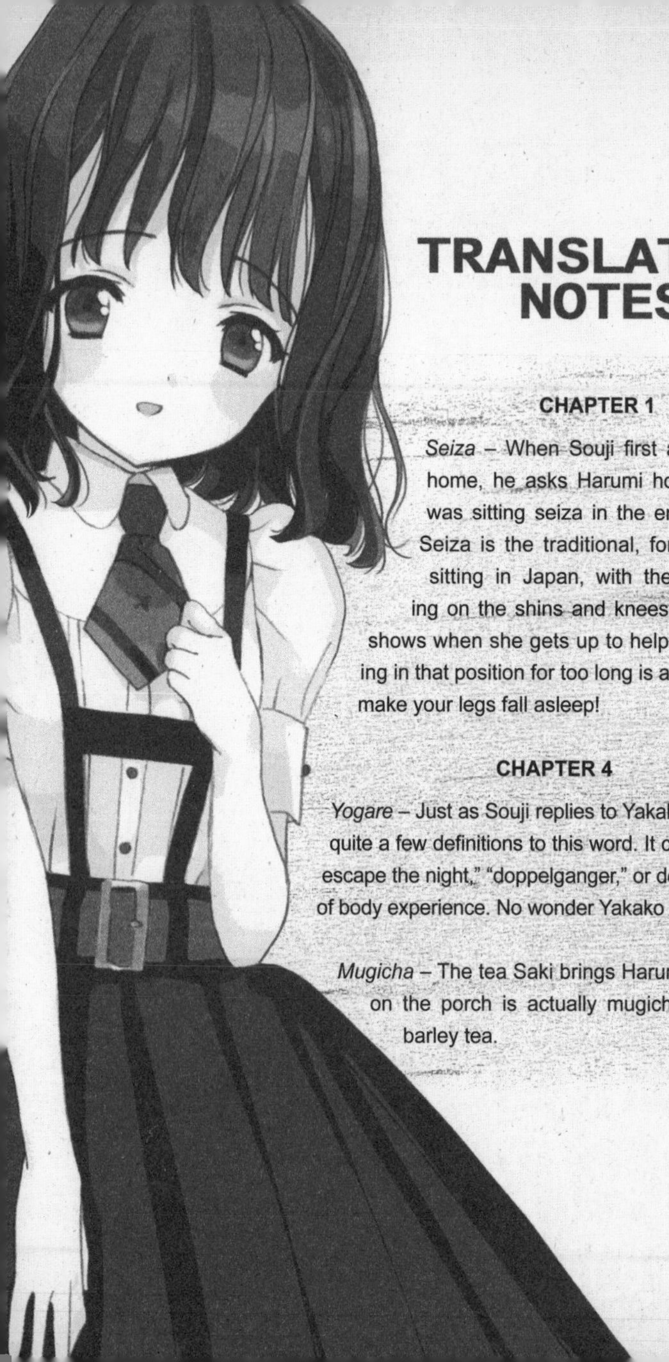

TRANSLATION NOTES

CHAPTER 1

Seiza – When Souji first arrives back home, he asks Harumi how long she was sitting seiza in the entrance hall. Seiza is the traditional, formal way of sitting in Japan, with the body resting on the shins and knees. As Harumi shows when she gets up to help Souji, staying in that position for too long is a sure way to make your legs fall asleep!

CHAPTER 4

Yogare – Just as Souji replies to Yakako, there are quite a few definitions to this word. It can mean "to escape the night," "doppelganger," or denote an out of body experience. No wonder Yakako is puzzled.

Mugicha – The tea Saki brings Harumi and Souji on the porch is actually mugicha, a chilled barley tea.

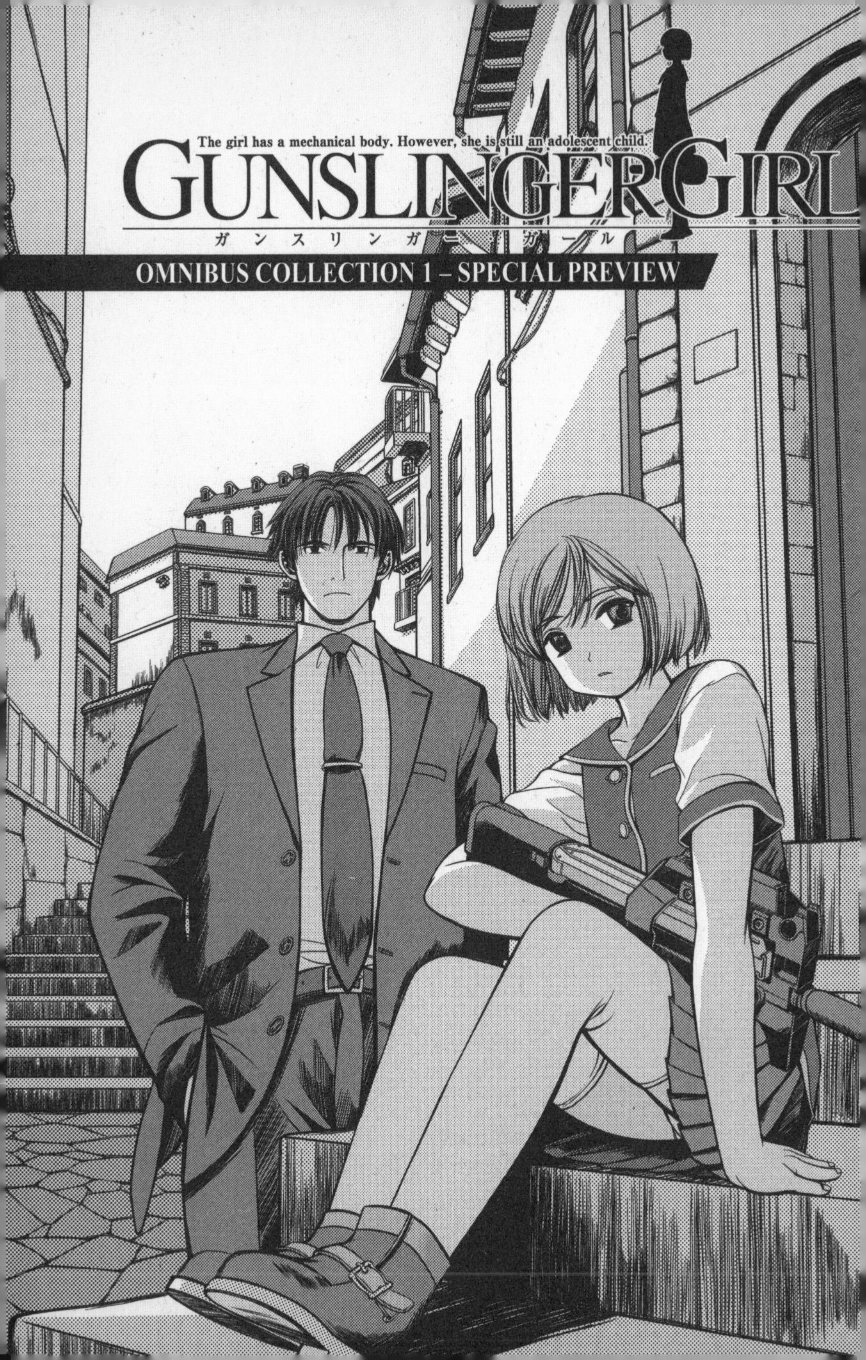
The girl has a mechanical body. However, she is still an adolescent child.
GUNSLINGER GIRL
ガンスリンガー ガール
OMNIBUS COLLECTION 1 – SPECIAL PREVIEW

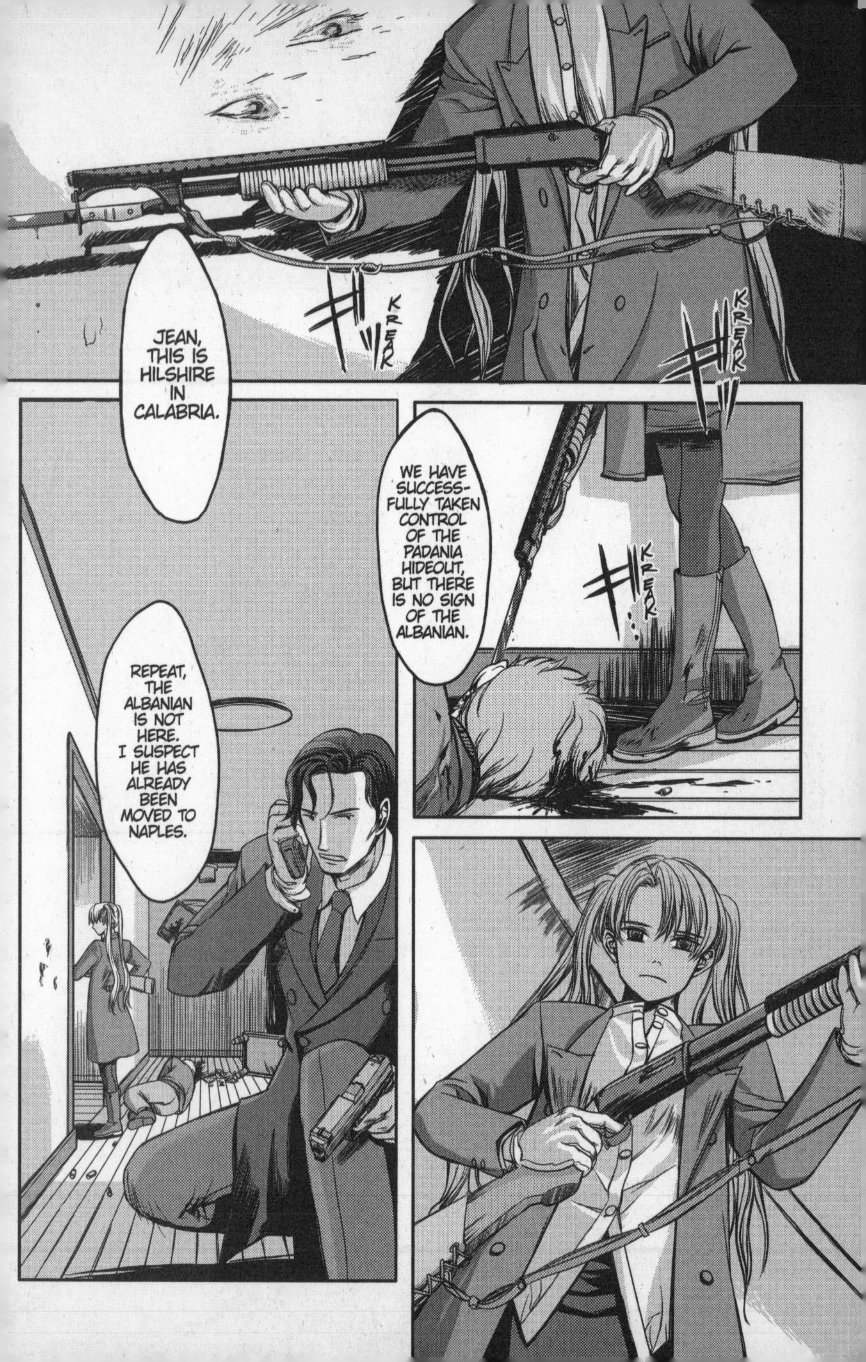
KREAK
KREAK
JEAN, THIS IS HILSHIRE IN CALABRIA.
WE HAVE SUCCESS-FULLY TAKEN CONTROL OF THE PADANIA HIDEOUT, BUT THERE IS NO SIGN OF THE ALBANIAN.
KREAK...
REPEAT, THE ALBANIAN IS NOT HERE. I SUSPECT HE HAS ALREADY BEEN MOVED TO NAPLES.

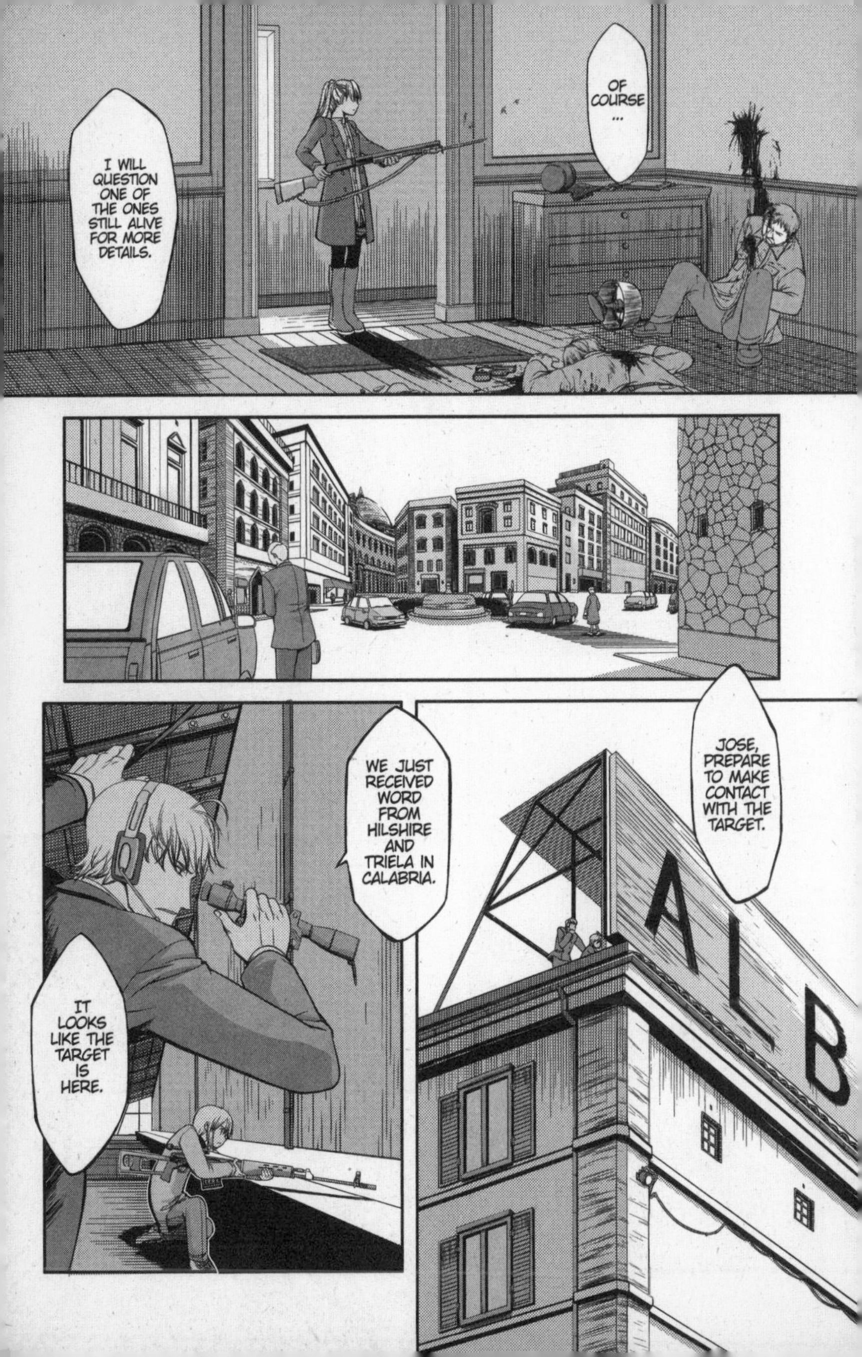
OF COURSE ...
I WILL QUESTION ONE OF THE ONES STILL ALIVE FOR MORE DETAILS.
JOSE, PREPARE TO MAKE CONTACT WITH THE TARGET.
WE JUST RECEIVED WORD FROM HILSHIRE AND TRIELA IN CALABRIA.
IT LOOKS LIKE THE TARGET IS HERE.

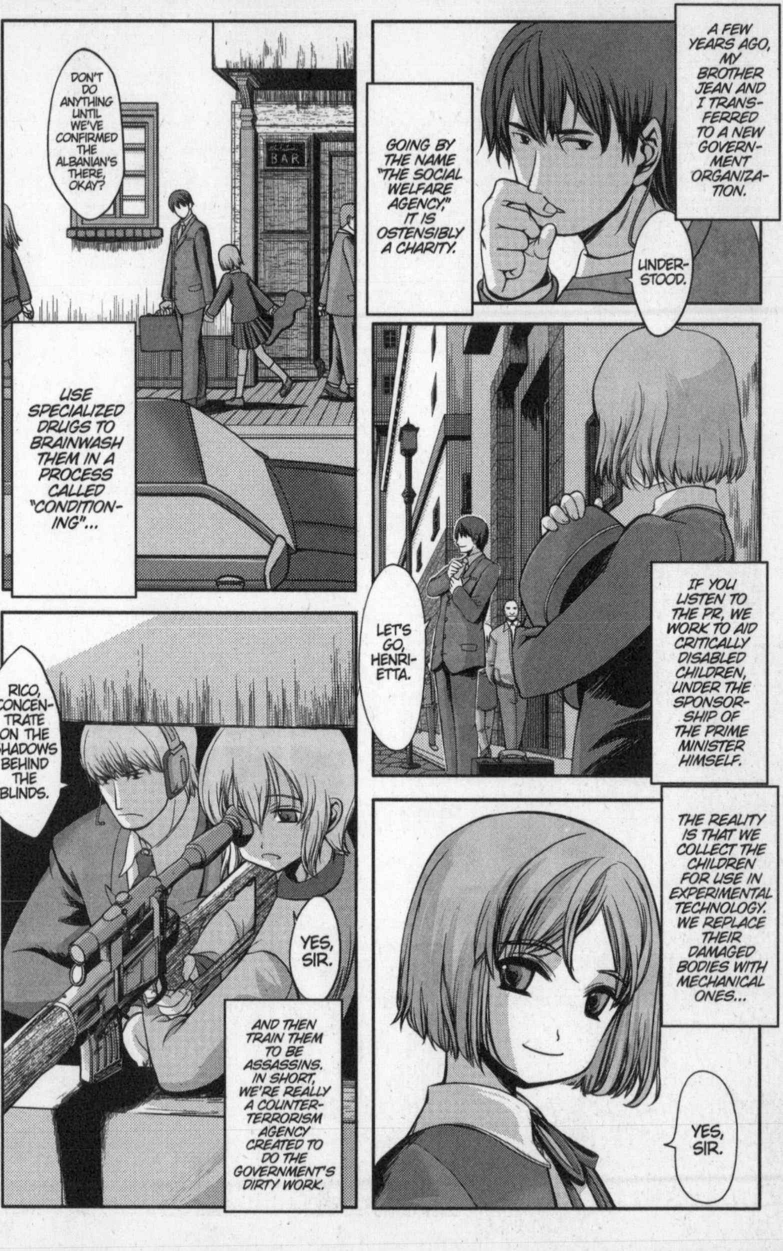
A FEW YEARS AGO, MY BROTHER JEAN AND I TRANSFERRED TO A NEW GOVERNMENT ORGANIZATION.
GOING BY THE NAME "THE SOCIAL WELFARE AGENCY," IT IS OSTENSIBLY A CHARITY.
UNDERSTOOD.
IF YOU LISTEN TO THE PR, WE WORK TO AID CRITICALLY DISABLED CHILDREN, UNDER THE SPONSORSHIP OF THE PRIME MINISTER HIMSELF.
LET'S GO, HENRIETTA.
THE REALITY IS THAT WE COLLECT THE CHILDREN FOR USE IN EXPERIMENTAL TECHNOLOGY. WE REPLACE THEIR DAMAGED BODIES WITH MECHANICAL ONES...
YES, SIR.
DON'T DO ANYTHING UNTIL WE'VE CONFIRMED THE ALBANIAN'S THERE, OKAY?
BAR
USE SPECIALIZED DRUGS TO BRAINWASH THEM IN A PROCESS CALLED "CONDITIONING"...
RICO, CONCENTRATE ON THE SHADOWS BEHIND THE BLINDS.
YES, SIR.
AND THEN TRAIN THEM TO BE ASSASSINS. IN SHORT, WE'RE REALLY A COUNTER-TERRORISM AGENCY CREATED TO DO THE GOVERNMENT'S DIRTY WORK.

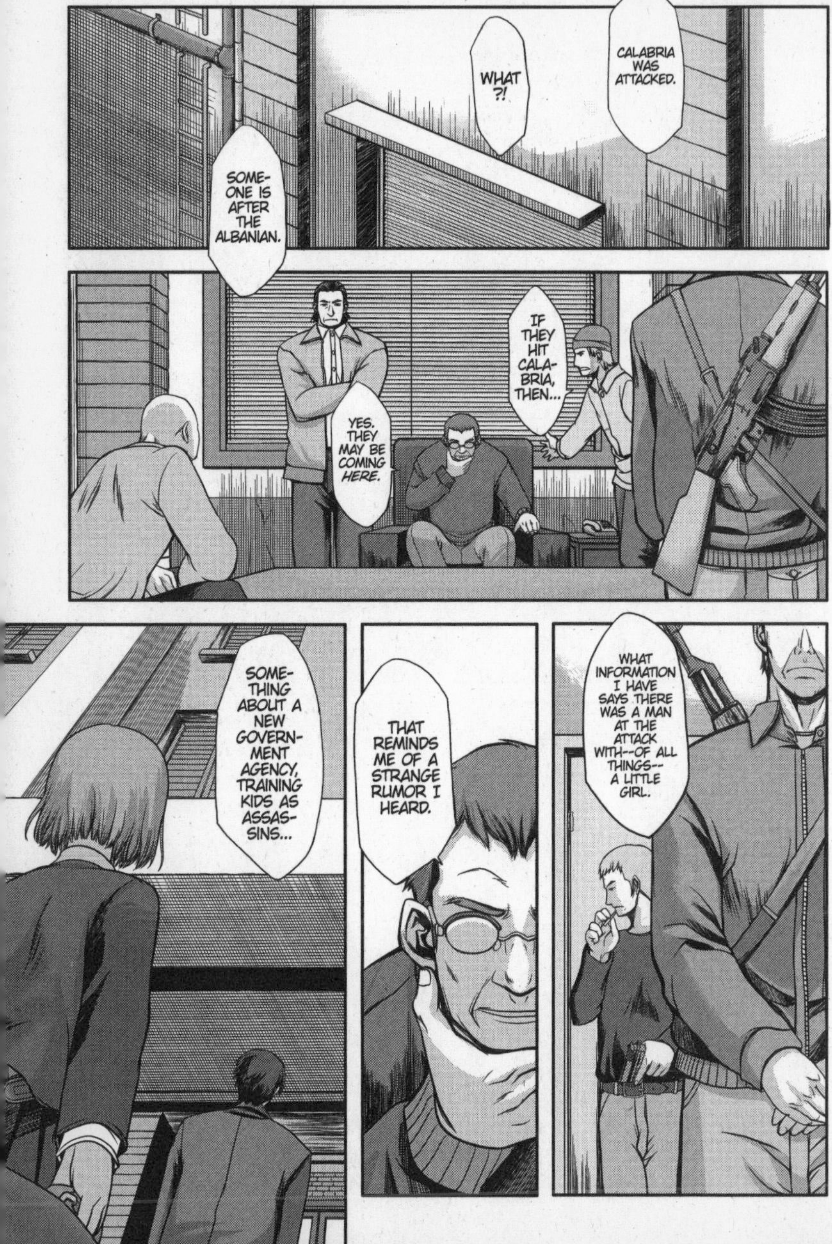
CALABRIA WAS ATTACKED.
WHAT ?!
SOMEONE IS AFTER THE ALBANIAN.
IF THEY HIT CALABRIA, THEN...
YES. THEY MAY BE COMING HERE.
WHAT INFORMATION I HAVE SAYS THERE WAS A MAN AT THE ATTACK WITH--OF ALL THINGS--A LITTLE GIRL.
THAT REMINDS ME OF A STRANGE RUMOR I HEARD.
SOMETHING ABOUT A NEW GOVERNMENT AGENCY, TRAINING KIDS AS ASSASSINS...

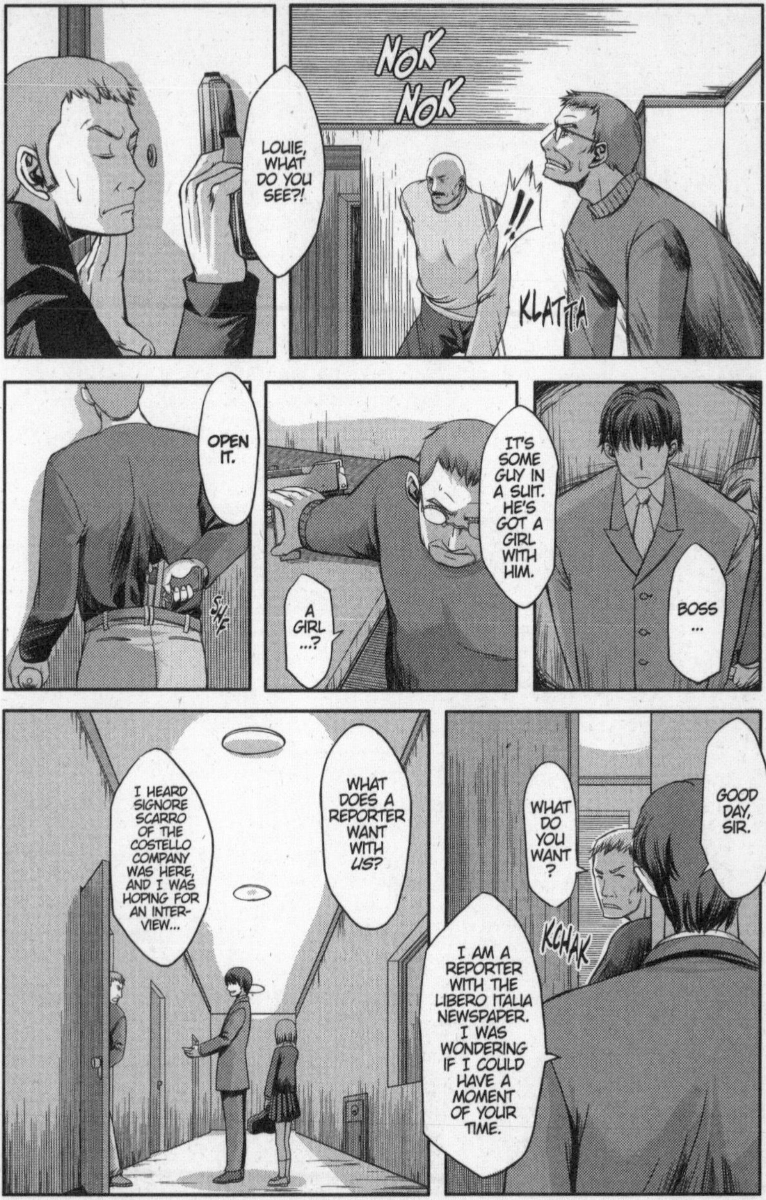
NOK NOK
KLATTA
LOUIE, WHAT DO YOU SEE?!
BOSS...
IT'S SOME GUY IN A SUIT. HE'S GOT A GIRL WITH HIM.
A GIRL...?
OPEN IT.
SHF
GOOD DAY, SIR.
WHAT DO YOU WANT?
KCHAK
I AM A REPORTER WITH THE LIBERO ITALIA NEWSPAPER. I WAS WONDERING IF I COULD HAVE A MOMENT OF YOUR TIME.
WHAT DOES A REPORTER WANT WITH US?
I HEARD SIGNORE SCARRO OF THE COSTELLO COMPANY WAS HERE, AND I WAS HOPING FOR AN INTER-VIEW...

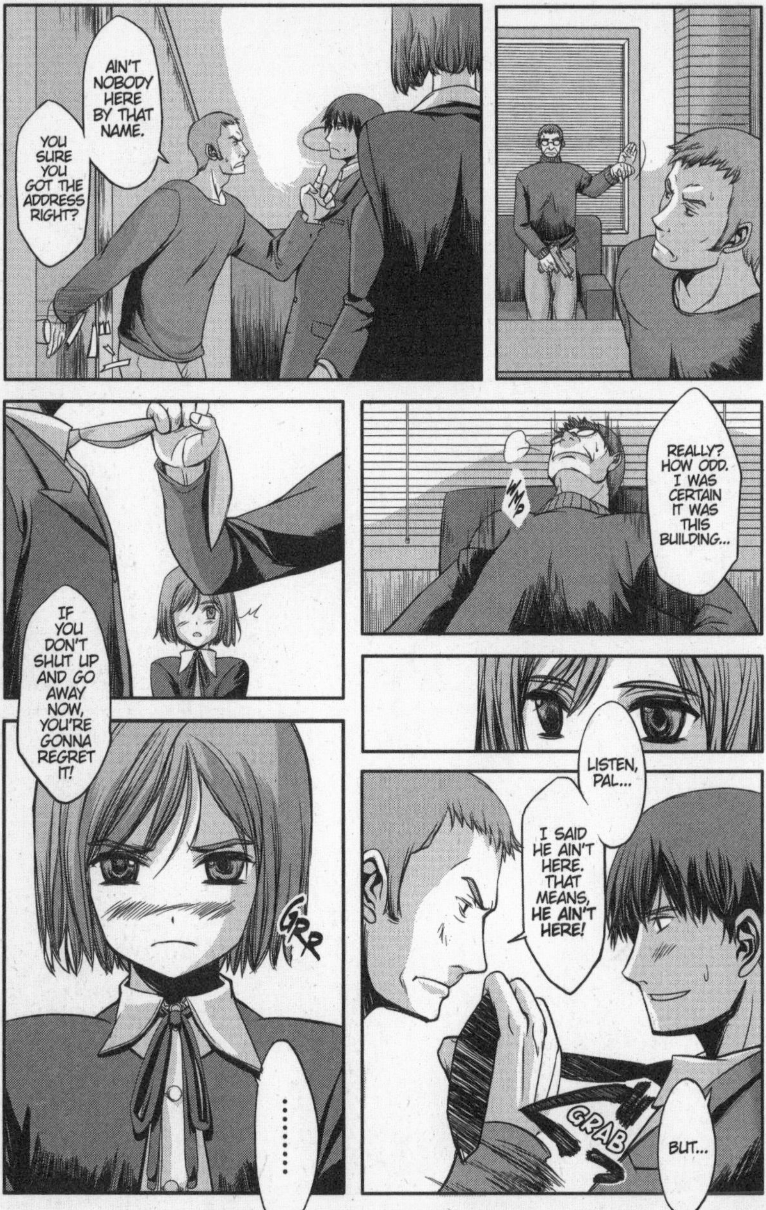
AIN'T NOBODY HERE BY THAT NAME.
YOU SURE YOU GOT THE ADDRESS RIGHT?
REALLY? HOW ODD. I WAS CERTAIN IT WAS THIS BUILDING...
WMP
IF YOU DON'T SHUT UP AND GO AWAY NOW, YOU'RE GONNA REGRET IT!
LISTEN, PAL...
I SAID HE AIN'T HERE. THAT MEANS, HE AIN'T HERE!
GRAB
BUT...
GRR
....

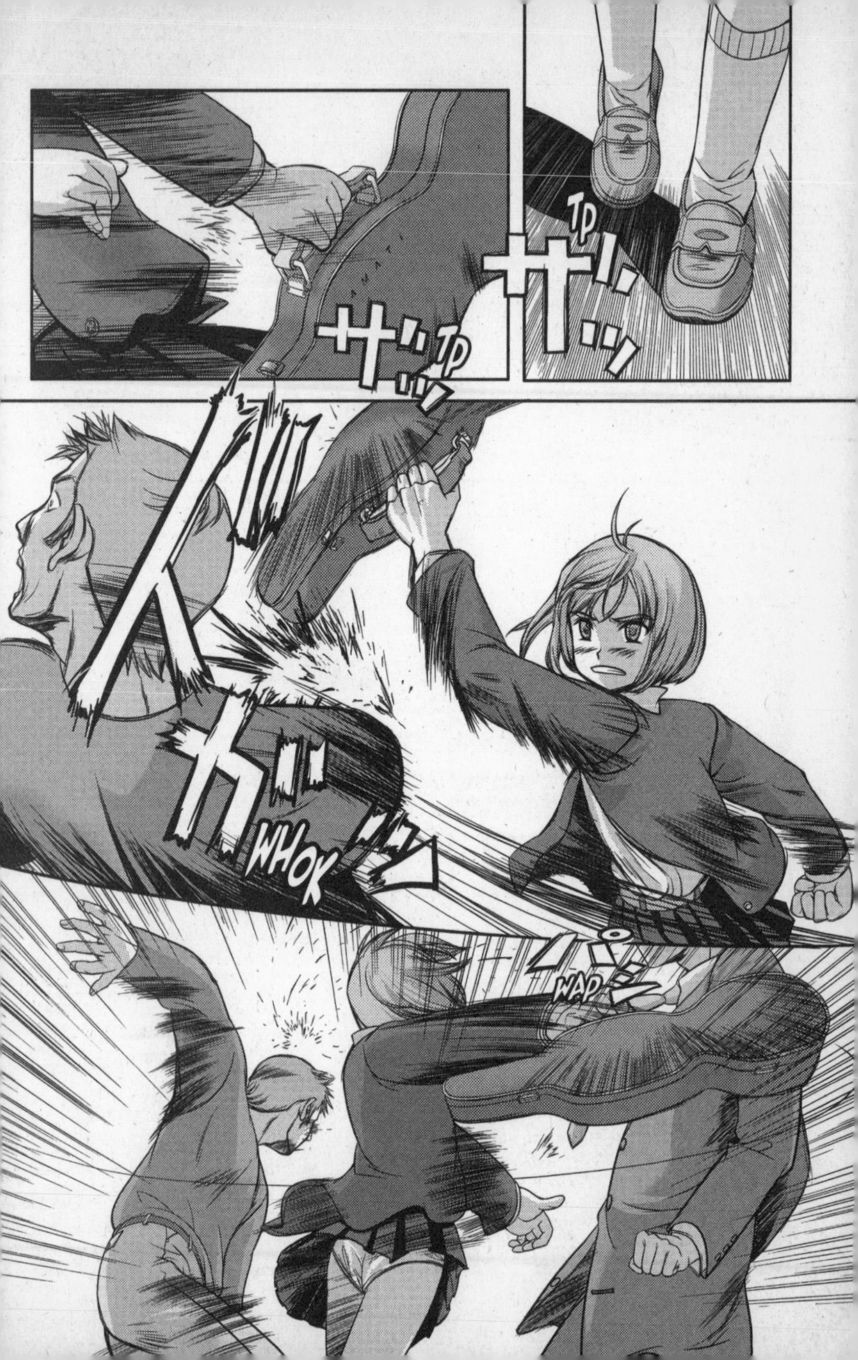
TP
TP
WHOK
WAP

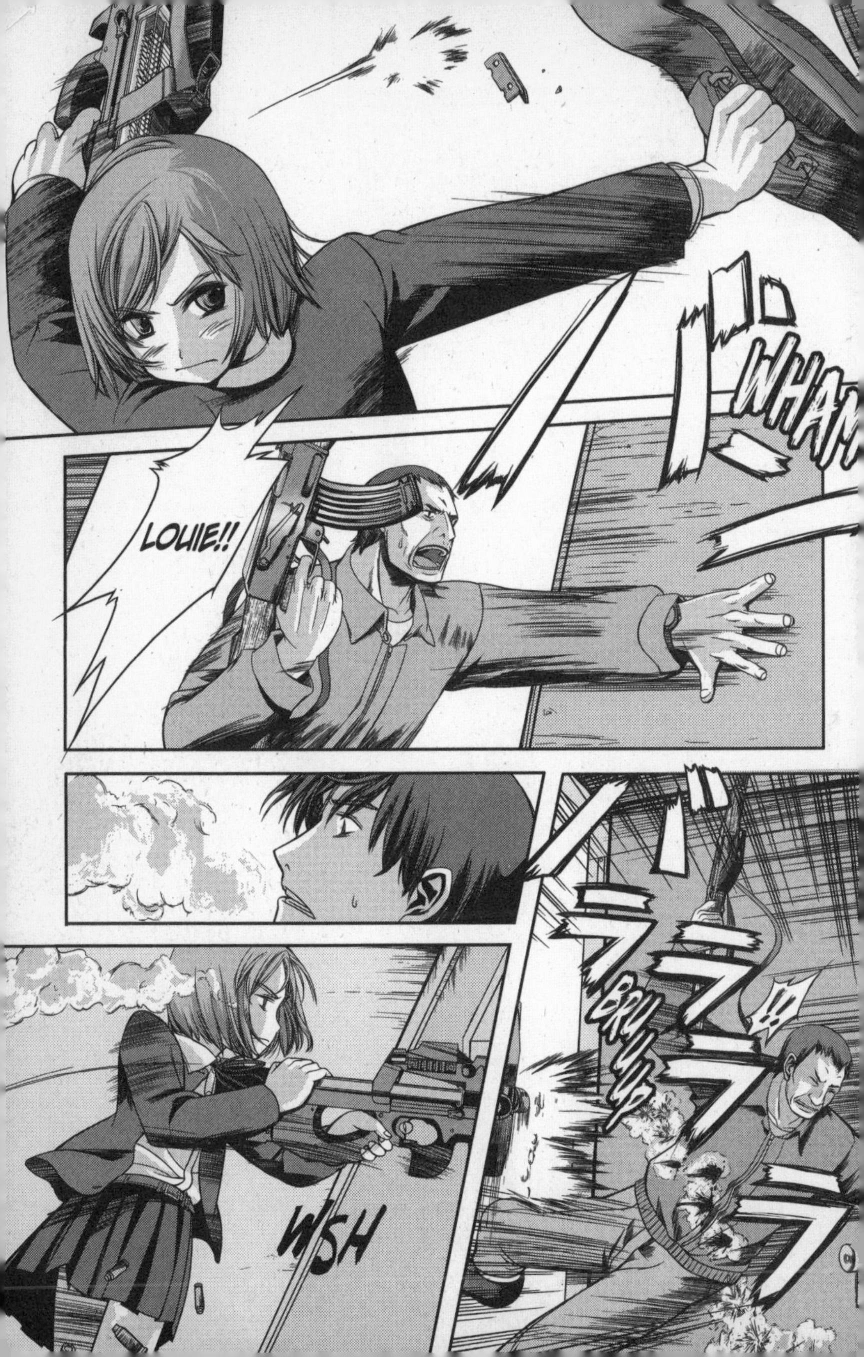
WHAM
LOUIE!!
BRUUUP
!!
WSH

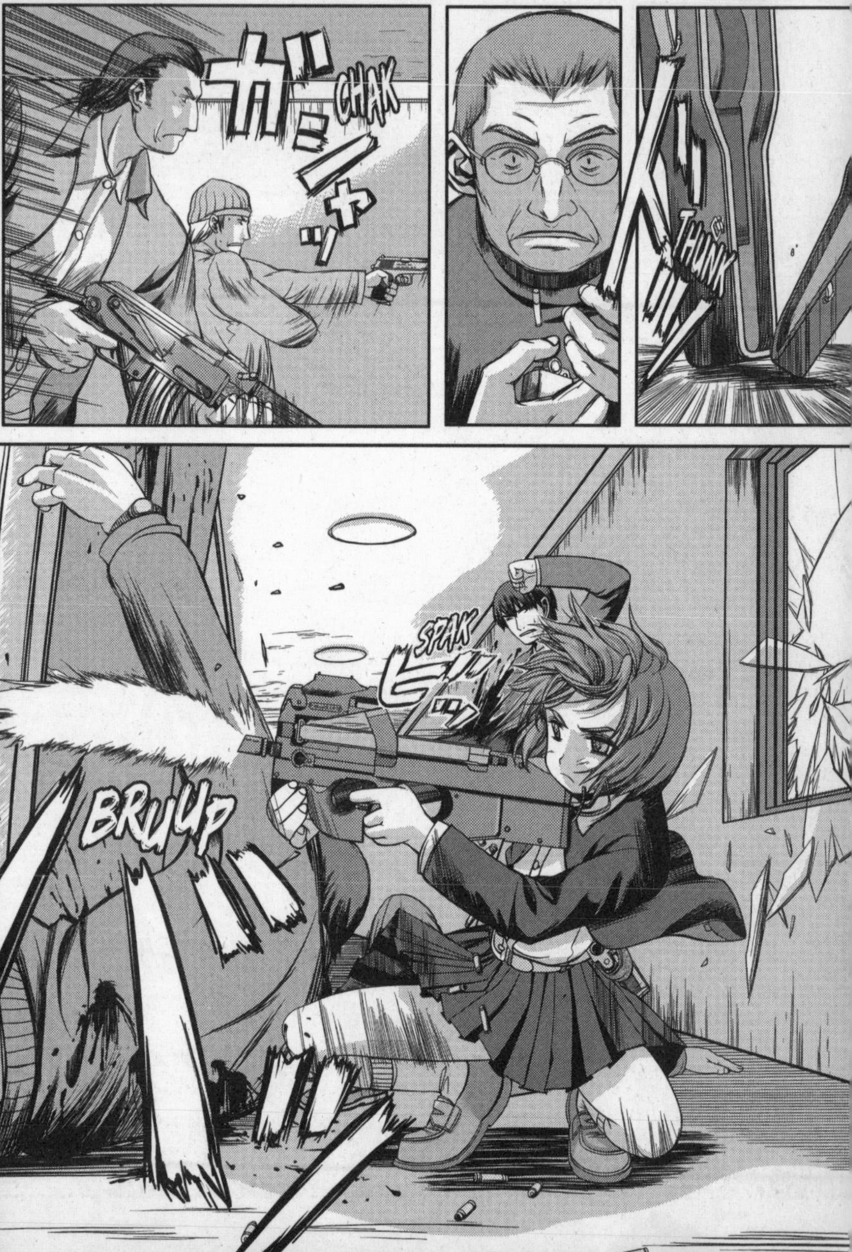
ドッ
THUNK
ガシャッ
CHAK
SPAK
ビシッ
BRUUP

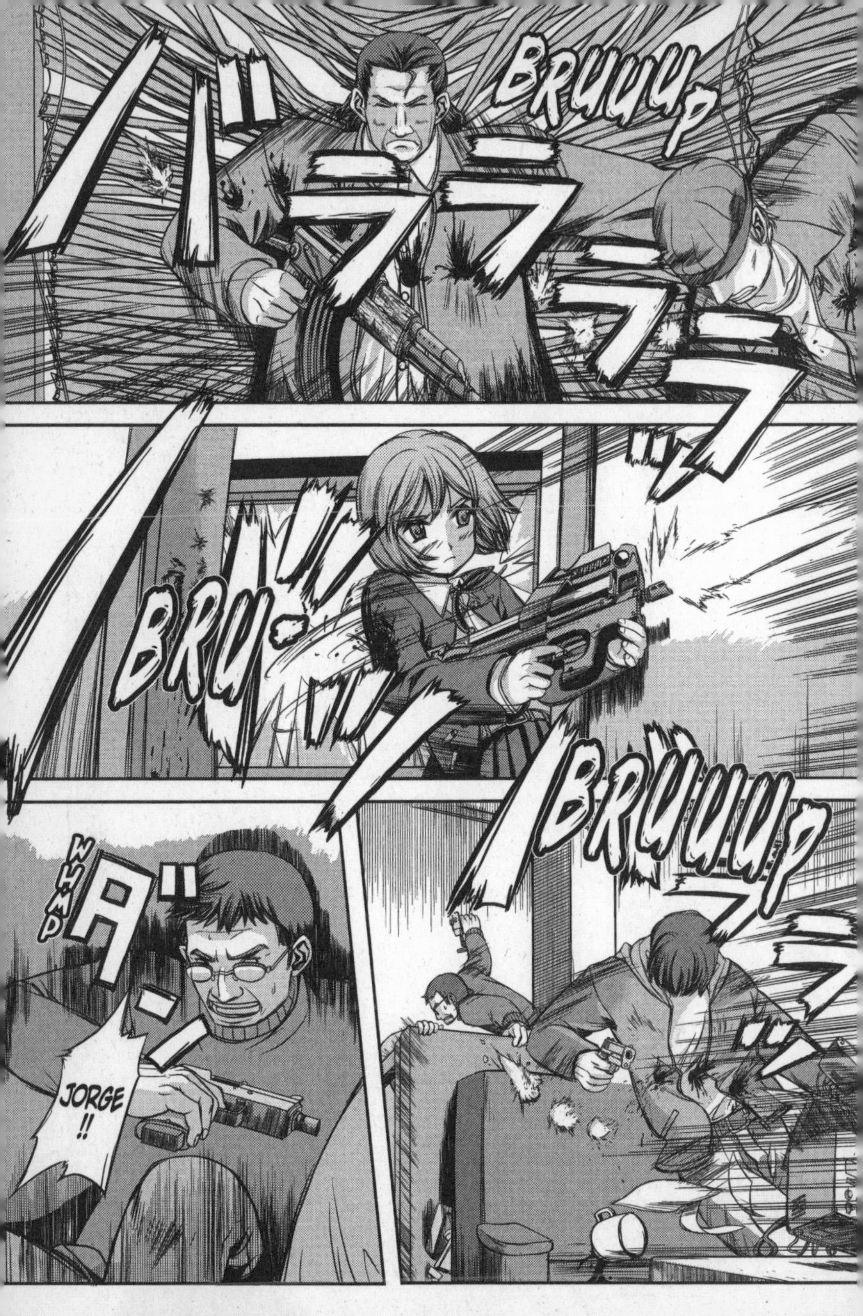
BRUUUP
BRU-
BRUUUP
WHMP
JORGE !!

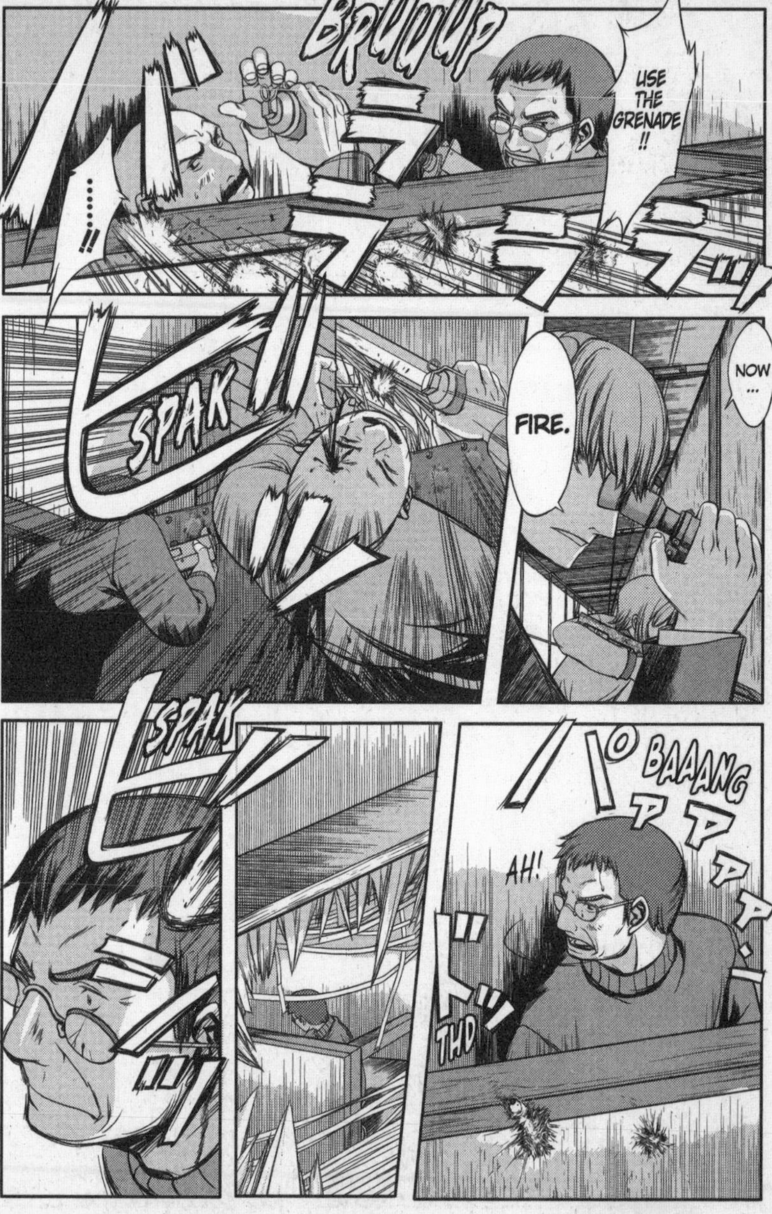
USE THE GRENADE !!
BRUUUP
......!!
NOW ...
FIRE.
SPAK
BAAANG
AH!
THD
SPAK

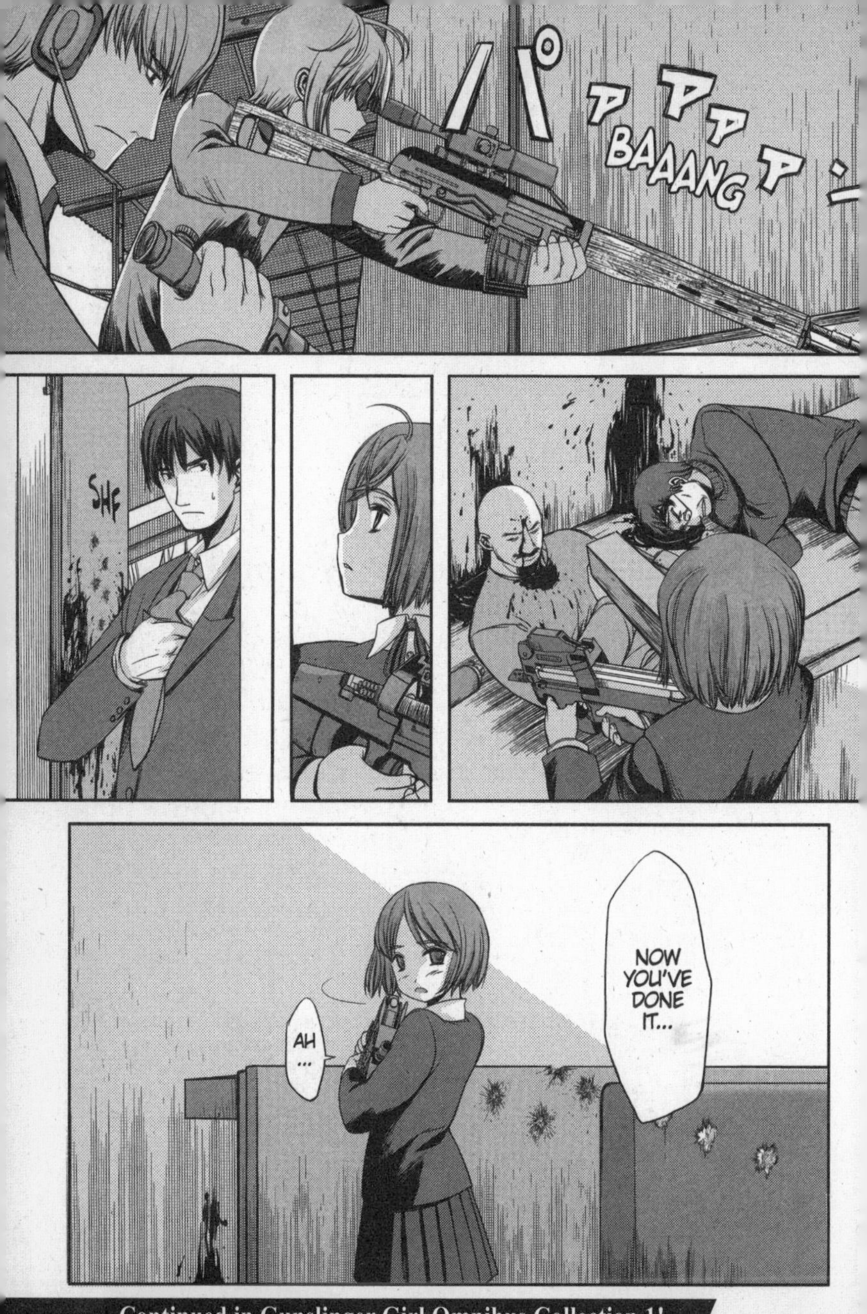
BAAANG
SHF
NOW YOU'VE DONE IT...
AH ...

Continued in Gunslinger Girl Omnibus Collection 1!

THE END

YOU'RE READING THE WRONG WAY

This is the last page of
Amnesia Labyrinth Volume 1

This book reads from right to left, Japanese style. To read from the beginning, flip the book over to the other side, start with the top right panel, and take it from there.

If this is your first time reading manga, just follow the diagram. It may seem backwards at first, but you'll get used to it! Have fun!